Motor Learning and Control for Practitioners

With an array of critical and engaging pedagogical features, the fourth edition of *Motor Learning and Control for Practitioners* offers the best practical introduction to motor learning available. This reader-friendly text approaches motor learning in accessible and simple terms, and lays a theoretical foundation for assessing performance; providing effective instruction; and designing practice, rehabilitation, and training experiences that promote skill acquisition.

Features such as Exploration Activities and Cerebral Challenges involve students at every stage, while a broad range of examples helps readers put theory into practice. The book also provides access to a fully updated companion website, which includes laboratory exercises, an instructors' manual, a test bank, and lecture slides.

As a complete resource for teaching an evidence-based approach to practical motor learning, this is an essential text for practitioners and students who plan to work in physical education, kinesiology, exercise science, coaching, physical therapy, or dance.

Cheryl A. Coker currently teaches in both the Physical Therapy Program and the Department of Health and Human Performance at Plymouth State University, USA. She received her undergraduate degree in Physical Education from Louisiana State University, where she was also an All-American and a member of the NCAA Championship Women's Track and Field Team. Upon completion of her master's and doctorate degrees from the University of Virginia, she joined the faculty at New Mexico State University, where she taught for 14 years.

Coker is a motor learning specialist who draws from her experiences as a teacher, coach, and athlete to assist practitioners in putting theory into practice. In addition to *Motor Learning and Control for Practitioners*, she has authored numerous journal articles and book chapters, and has given more than 80 presentations throughout the United States and internationally. She is a fellow of the Research Consortium in the Society of Health and Physical Educators and of the North American Society of Health, Physical Education, Recreation, Sport and Dance Professionals.

"*Motor Learning and Control for Practitioners* continues to evolve. The new chapter dedicated to Attention, Arousal, and Visual Search in Movement is fantastic! It is THE essential guide for physical education teachers, athletic coaches, and physical therapists."

John Jones, Freelance Coach, Teacher, and Presenter, Virginia, USA

"Without question, the decision to adopt the third edition of this textbook was one of the better ones I have made in my higher education academic career. *Motor Learning and Control for Practitioners* is a great link between the professional literature and the applications that the physical educator/practitioner is encouraged to understand and utilize."

Jay Albrecht, Associate Professor, Health and Physical Education Department, Minnesota State University Moorhead, USA

Motor Learning and Control for Practitioners

Fourth Edition

CHERYL A. COKER

Routledge
Taylor & Francis Group

NEW YORK AND LONDON

Fourth edition published 2018
by Routledge
711 Third Avenue, New York, NY 10017

and by Routledge
2 Park Square, Milton Park, Abingdon, Oxon, OX14 4RN

Routledge is an imprint of the Taylor & Francis Group, an informa business

First edition published by McGraw-Hill 2003

Third edition published by Holcomb Hathaway 2013

British Library Cataloguing-in-Publication Data
A catalogue record for this book is available from the British Library

Library of Congress Cataloging-in-Publication Data
Names: Coker, Cheryl A., author.
Title: Motor learning and control for practitioners / Cheryl Coker.
Description: Fourth edition. | Abingdon, Oxon ; New York, NY :
Routledge, 2018. | Includes bibliographical references and index.
Identifiers: LCCN 2017014531| ISBN 9781138736986 (hardback) |
ISBN 9781138737013 (pbk.) | ISBN 9781315185613 (ebook)
Subjects: LCSH: Motor learning.
Classification: LCC BF295 .C645 2018 | DDC 152.3/34–dc23
LC record available at https://lccn.loc.gov/2017014531

ISBN: 978-1-138-73698-6 (hbk)
ISBN: 978-1-138-73701-3 (pbk)
ISBN: 978-1-315-18561-3 (ebk)

Typeset in Sabon and Helvetica
by Florence Production Ltd, Stoodleigh, Devon, UK

Visit the companion website: www.routledge.com/cw/coker

Every effort has been made to contact copyright-holders. Please advise
the publisher of any errors or omissions, and these will be corrected in
subsequent editions.

Recently the field of motor learning lost two pioneers,
Richard Schmidt and Anne Gentile. In their spirit,
I dedicate this book to all those in our profession who
have dared to ask the question why.

Contents

Preface

Human movement is a complex phenomenon. For practitioners concerned with movement enhancement, that complexity presents a constant challenge. The key to meeting this challenge lies in understanding how people learn. *Motor Learning and Control for Practitioners*, Fourth Edition, introduces practitioners to the processes that underlie human movement learning. Bridging the gap between research and practice, this text provides practitioners with the necessary tools to build a solid foundation for assessing performance, providing effective instruction, and designing practice, rehabilitation, and training experiences that will optimize skill acquisition and performance.

APPROACH

The purpose of this textbook extends beyond simply presenting the concepts and principles of motor learning and control. In each edition, one important goal of *Motor Learning and Control for Practitioners* has been to actively engage readers with its content through an applications-based approach. Before readers can be challenged to apply theoretical constructs, however, they must first understand them. To facilitate this understanding, material is presented in an easy-to-read style that incorporates a wide range of examples from everyday life, teaching, coaching, and rehabilitation. Readers have abundant opportunities to interact with the book's key concepts, principles, and basic terminology and then apply that information to real-life situations.

AUDIENCE

This text is designed for future practitioners in physical education, kinesiology, exercise science, physical and occupational therapy, dance, and coaching. Special care has been taken to accommodate the diverse needs of this multifaceted audience, as reflected in the great variety of examples, scenarios, and activities provided throughout the text. Readers in each specific content area will have numerous opportunities to apply principles and concepts to their area of specialization and to develop a working knowledge of motor learning and control as it applies to their chosen profession.

ORGANIZATION

The focus of Chapters 1 through 5 is on the behavioral and neurological processes that influence performance. The text begins by introducing readers to the foundational concept that human movement is a complex phenomenon that is a function of the interaction of the learner, the task, and the environment in which the task is performed (Chapter 1). Readers' working knowledge of this interaction is further developed in Chapter 2, which introduces the underlying processes that govern movement execution and control. Chapter 3 extends this discussion, examining the role of attention in the decision making process. While Chapters 2 and 3 focus on the factors that influence movement preparation, Chapter 4 explores the theoretical constructs underlying the coordination and control of human movement. Movement is then examined from a neurological perspective in Chapter 5.

Chapters 6 through 12 build on this foundational knowledge of how skilled movements are produced, examining the factors involved in their acquisition and refinement. Chapter 6 begins this discussion, introducing the changing characteristics of learners as they progress from novices to experts, and the role of these characteristics in guiding the practitioner's decision-making throughout the instructional process. Beginning with Chapter 7, the sequence in which concepts are introduced parallels that typically used by practitioners during the instructional process. Chapter 7 discusses pre-instruction considerations to facilitate learning, including learning styles, transfer, and motivation to learn and practice. Methods of presenting skills—through both direct instruction and a hands-off approach—are then examined in Chapter 8. Next, to provide learners with ample opportunities to practice presented skills, Chapter 9 examines a number of practice variables, including sequencing and psychological strategies that a practitioner can manipulate to optimize gains in skill proficiency. This focus on practice design continues in Chapter 10, which highlights practice organization and scheduling. Once the learner begins to practice a skill, the role of the practitioner becomes one of error detection and correction. Chapter 11, unique to this text, investigates the role of motor learning and control in diagnosing errors, while Chapter 12 addresses principles and guidelines regarding the provision of feedback as an intervention strategy and the manipulation of practice and task variables for shaping movement patterns. Finally, an epilogue contains two real-life scenarios to test readers' abilities to apply what they have learned.

NEW TO THIS EDITION

This text continues to provide a balance between conceptual and practical material. Substantive changes have been made to several chapters, including the reorganization of material to create a new chapter examining the role of attention, arousal and visual search in movement preparation as well as the restructuring of Chapter 8 (Skill Presentation) into two categorical approaches—

hands-on and hands-off instruction. Also new to this edition is the introduction of an integrative model for facilitating motor learning and performance to assist practitioners in designing effective learning experiences. A new feature called *Putting it into Practice* can be found at the end of each chapter, which tests readers' ability to synthesize material through two exemplar scenarios and compare their response to an example response provided online at www.routledge. com/cw/coker. Other new and expanded topics include the distinction between slow decision making, slow movement execution or a combination of both in response delays, planned vs. reactive agility, mechanisms of reaching and grasping, neural plasticity and motivation for learning and performance. This edition also offers students 18 online lab experiences at www.rouledge.com/cw/coker, representing a significant link between theory and practice. Every chapter includes at least one lab, and many of the labs include videos demonstrating procedural aspects. New Cerebral Challenges, examples, and Research Notes will aid student understanding and inform them about developments in the field. The marginal website feature includes new examples that will appeal to students and instructors alike, directing readers to online resources, including videos, web-based activities, apps, and additional informational sources. Finally, materials for instructors include key talking points for selected Cerebral Challenges as well as suggestions about Exploration Activities that can be converted to additional/ alternative laboratory experiences.

FEATURES

- **Accessible for all students:** The text's readability and varied applications and examples make it appealing to students pursuing careers as practitioners.
- **Theoretical coverage:** Balanced coverage is provided of movement preparation theories, motor program and dynamic interaction theories, and theoretical models of attention and memory.
- **Broad range of examples:** Examples from sport, physical education, dance, exercise science, athletic training, rehabilitation, and "everyday life" will accommodate the great variety of majors and future professionals in this course.
- **Pretest:** The text opens with a pretest to determine students' current knowledge level with respect to motor learning and control. The test is based on Common Myths that readers will encounter marginally throughout the text, introducing and discussing common misconceptions in the field.
- **Epilogue:** The text concludes with two real-life scenarios, one physical education and one rehabilitation, with associated questions and answers, allowing students to put concepts to work in an applied setting.
- **Error diagnosis and correction:** Chapter 11's unique coverage explores errors based on motor learning and control issues and their diagnosis. The chapter presents critical factors for conducting an observation, offers a categorical model for determining an error and its resolution, and discusses situational factors that should be considered before correcting an error.

PEDAGOGICAL FEATURES

- Online labs use typical classroom and everyday items and enable students to explore key motor learning concepts and translate chapter content into practice.
- Exploration Activities are experiential mini-labs and can serve as an instructor-directed starting point for class discussion, be converted to lab-oratory experiences, or be completed by students outside the classroom.
- Critical thinking exercises, called Cerebral Challenges, interspersed throughout the text, require readers to engage in higher-order problem-solving activities. This feature can further serve as an instructor-directed starting point for class discussions.
- Putting it into Practice offers the opportunity to apply key chapter concepts to a learning situation in both coaching and rehabilitation.
- Web links (in text margins, in Exploration Activities, and in Cerebral Challenges) direct readers to relevant videos, web-based activities, and additional information sources.
- Boxed Research Notes provide examples of research conducted on the topics discussed in the chapter.
- Key terms are bolded in the text and included in a comprehensive book-end Glossary.

END-OF-CHAPTER FEATURES INCLUDE:

- **A Look Ahead,** previewing the coming chapter.
- **Focus Points,** offering concise bulleted summaries of key concepts.
- **Review Questions,** allowing students to test their comprehension of material.

INSTRUCTOR MATERIALS

- An **Instructor's Manual** available to text adopters.
- A **test bank** with multiple choice and true/false questions.
- A **PowerPoint presentation** focusing on key content and art is also available.

Acknowledgements

The undertaking of a project of this magnitude would not be possible without the support of countless individuals. First and foremost, I would like to thank Colette Kelly, Gay Pauley, and the incredible publishing team at Holcomb Hathaway for their guidance and vision over the years. You truly did exceed expectations, one book at a time and I am grateful to have had the opportunity to work with you. Appreciation is also extended to my new publishing team at Routledge. I look forward to a rewarding partnership. Many thanks to my students, colleagues, and adopters who inspire me to raise the bar each edition. A special word of gratitude is also due to my family and friends for their continued support and encouragement and to my partner Kim for, well, everything.

Pretest

As a student of human movement, you bring to this course extensive knowledge from your past experiences. To determine your current level of knowledge with respect to motor learning and control, complete the following pretest.

TRUE OR FALSE?

1. Future success in a specific skill can be easily predicted.
2. The higher the level of arousal, the better the performance.
3. All sensory messages must go to the brain for integration.
4. Unless the learner displays some overt changes in performance, he or she is no longer learning.
5. All learners are motivated to learn the skills presented to them.
6. Experts are always the most effective instructors.
7. In order for an observer to learn a movement, the demonstration must be performed correctly.
8. Practice makes perfect.
9. Long-term retention of a motor skill is best achieved by practicing a skill repeatedly before moving to either a different version of the task or a different task altogether.
10. When teaching a youngster how to catch, you should toss the ball with a high arch in order to give them enough time to follow it and get underneath it for a successful catch.
11. The more frequently a practitioner provides feedback to the learner, the greater the gains in learning.
12. A practitioner should give the learner feedback immediately following a movement/performance attempt.

Answers: The answer to all of the above items is "False." You may have chosen "True" in some cases because these statements represent common myths regarding motor learning and control. Throughout the textbook, each of these statements appears as a "Common Myth" in the margin, indicating where the concept is discussed in detail. Look for them as you begin your journey through the field of motor learning and control.

Introduction to Motor Learning and Control

1

I have come to a frightening conclusion. I am the decisive element in the classroom. It is my personal approach that creates the climate. It is my daily mood that makes the weather. As a teacher, I possess the tremendous power to make a child's life miserable or joyous. I can be the tool of torture or an instrument of inspiration. I can humiliate or humor, hurt or heal. In all situations, it is my response that decides if a crisis will be elevated or de-escalated, and a child humanized or dehumanized.

Haim Ginott, educator

The message of this quotation is clear: the role of instructor—whether in a classroom, playing field, gymnasium, clinic, or other context—is a very powerful one. The climate you create will determine the level of success that your students, patients, clients, or athletes will achieve. Fundamental to creating an effective climate is an understanding of how people learn. *Motor Learning and Control for Practitioners* focuses on the processes that govern movement acquisition and control and provides a foundation for developing effective instructional strategies that facilitate learning and performance.

DESIGNING EFFECTIVE LEARNING EXPERIENCES: AN INTEGRATIVE MODEL

The continuous challenge faced by practitioners is how to best assist learners when introduced to re-learning or refining a motor skill; whether to successfully negotiate a sit to stand transfer, intercept a ball at the correct time and location, or improve landing mechanics to reduce the risk of injury and optimize performance. Paramount to the design and implementation of effective learning experiences is the creation of an informed action plan grounded in an understanding of the learning process, the current learning situation and the potential instructional strategies available from which to draw. An integrative model depicting the components of this action plan is illustrated in Figure 1.1.

The first half of the model draws from Schmidt and Wrisberg's (2008) situation-based learning approach and begins with the determination of the intended outcome. Next, a situation profile must be created that considers three elements—the learner, the task, and the environment or context in which the task is performed—critical interacting determinants of movement at any given time (see Figure 1.2). Once the learning situation has been profiled, practitioners can make informed decisions as to how to design and implement the learning experience, the next step in the process. The second half of the model incorporates Knudson's (2013) comprehensive view of qualitative movement diagnosis (QMD). At this point, the practitioner enters a cyclical process that begins with the observation of the learner's performance attempts. Through observations of both specific aspects of the skill's execution (process assessment) and the outcome of the performance (product assessment), the learner's progress towards goal achievement is evaluated and critical errors identified and prioritized. Intervention strategies for skill refinement are then selected and implemented

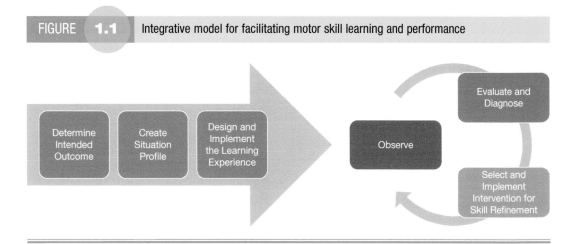

FIGURE **1.1**   Integrative model for facilitating motor skill learning and performance

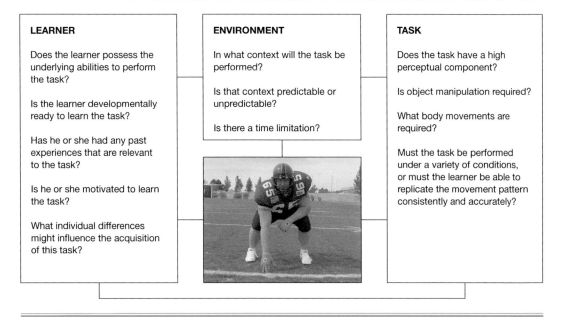

FIGURE **1.2**   The interaction of the learner, the task, and the environment in which the task is performed is fundamental to the understanding and facilitation of motor skill acquisition and performance

LEARNER

Does the learner possess the underlying abilities to perform the task?

Is the learner developmentally ready to learn the task?

Has he or she had any past experiences that are relevant to the task?

Is he or she motivated to learn the task?

What individual differences might influence the acquisition of this task?

ENVIRONMENT

In what context will the task be performed?

Is that context predictable or unpredictable?

Is there a time limitation?

TASK

Does the task have a high perceptual component?

Is object manipulation required?

What body movements are required?

Must the task be performed under a variety of conditions, or must the learner be able to replicate the movement pattern consistently and accurately?

which again consider the learner, task, and environment because each element and its reciprocal interaction with the other two are constantly changing. Performance is further observed and the effectiveness of the intervention evaluated. Accordingly, selected intervention strategies are either continued or modified as the learner strives to achieve the intended outcome.

As you progress through the upcoming chapters, keep this model in mind. Details and considerations for each step will be revealed. Can you connect them to the Integrative Model?

MOTOR LEARNING, CONTROL, AND PERFORMANCE

As indicated in the previous section, an understanding of the learning process provides the human movement practitioner with foundational knowledge that provides the basis for assessing performance; providing effective instruction; and designing optimal practice, rehabilitation, and training experiences. So how, exactly, do people acquire motor skills? What processes allow the musculoskeletal system to produce intended movements? What variables facilitate or hinder skill acquisition? Questions such as these have led to the evolution of a field of study known as motor learning. Motor learning is the study of the processes involved in acquiring and refining motor skills and of variables that promote or inhibit that acquisition. Other questions of interest to motor learning researchers include: How should practice be organized? Where should instruction focus the learner's attention when practicing a new skill? What type and amount of feedback facilitates skill acquisition? A related field of study, motor control, focuses on the neural, physical, and behavioral aspects that underlie human movement. Examples of questions that a motor control researcher might ask are: What factors influence postural stability? How does sensory information contribute to movement production and the accuracy of those movements? How are muscular actions coordinated to produce skilled movement? Understanding both motor learning and motor control is necessary for developing a complete understanding of motor skill acquisition.

What Is Learning?

The first question we should ask when we look at how people learn is *What is learning?* Before continuing, complete Exploration Activity 1.1.

When used in reference to motor learning and control, learning is defined as a relatively permanent change in a person's capability to execute a motor skill as a result of practice or experience. To know whether you have learned how to juggle as a result of participating in Exploration Activity 1.1, you must determine whether a persistent change in your juggling behavior has occurred.

Part of the problem we face when trying to determine whether a motor skill has been learned is that we can't actually *see* learning, because the underlying or internal processes that result in a relatively permanent change cannot be directly observed. What we can see, however, is performance. Performance is the act of executing a skill. Through repeated observations of an individual's performance, we infer whether the individual has learned a skill. These inferences are based on changes that we observe in the individual's performance over time, such as improvements in movement proficiency and consistency. Exercise caution,

exploration ACTIVITY   **1.1**

Learning to Juggle

EQUIPMENT NEEDED

- 2 tennis balls
- Some space to move!

GOAL

The goal of this exercise is to juggle two tennis balls successfully using your non-dominant hand.

PROCEDURE

To start, place both tennis balls in your non-dominant hand. Toss one ball upward. As that ball reaches its peak height, toss the second ball upward, leaving the hand empty to catch the first ball. Continue this pattern, attempting to achieve as many successive catches as possible. Repeat for 10 minutes, recording the number of successful catches you achieve on each trial (from the starting position to the time you drop a ball or miss a catch).

QUESTIONS

1. Assuming that you were eventually able to make two or more catches, could you conclude that you had learned how to juggle two balls with your non-dominant hand? Why or why not?
2. Let's say that in your first nine minutes of juggling, you spent more time chasing balls than catching them. Up until the nine-minute mark, your record number of catches was two. All of a sudden, in the last minute, you catch six! Does this mean you have learned how to juggle?
3. Based on this juggling experience, can you formulate a definition for learning?
4. What learner, task, and environmental factors affected your performance and learning?

however, to ensure that the inferences are accurate. Numerous learner variables, such as fatigue or anxiety, and task variables, such as problems with equipment, may impair performance but do not necessarily indicate a loss of capability. Alternatively, a learner may perform a given skill at a new level of proficiency during one practice, only to return to the original level at the next practice.

THE NATURE OF MOTOR SKILLS

As we begin our exploration of factors that influence skill acquisition and performance, we must define the term *skill*. That definition depends on the context in which the term is used. The term *skill* may be used to describe the quality of a performance. To identify an individual as *skillful* implies that the person has achieved a high degree of proficiency. LeBron James, for example, is considered a highly skilled basketball player.

The term motor skill describes an act or task that satisfies four criteria:

1. It is goal oriented, meaning it is performed in order to achieve some objective.
2. Body and/or limb movements are required to accomplish the goal.
3. Those movements are voluntary. Given this stipulation, reflexive actions, such as the stepping reflex in infants, are not considered skills because they occur involuntarily.
4. Motor skills are developed as a result of practice. In other words, a skill must be learned or relearned.

Crutch walking would be considered a motor skill, as it satisfies these four criteria. It requires voluntary body and or limb movement to achieve a goal (e.g., move across a room), and it must be learned.

Practitioners should note the distinction between a skill and a sport. Volleyball is a sport. It consists of multiple skills, including the serve, the forearm pass, the overhead pass, and the spike, all of which have different characteristics and impose different demands on the performer.

Skill Classifications

The nature of a skill imposes specific demands on the learner, which practitioners must consider when designing learning experiences. To assist practitioners in understanding the nature of motor skills and the demands they impose, several classification systems or taxonomies have been developed that organize motor skills by their common elements. Knowing the relationships among diverse skills can aid the practitioner in planning learning and practice experiences, as well as provide a starting point for performance assessment.

CEREBRALchallenge   1.1

Determine which of the following can be classified as a motor skill. Explain each classification choice.

1. Brushing your teeth
2. Tapping your pencil
3. Solving a word problem
4. Taping a wrist
5. Removing your hand after touching a hot stove
6. Sewing on a button
7. Walking
8. Playing the trumpet
9. Parachute reflex of an infant
10. Performing proprioceptive neuromuscular facilitation (PNF) exercises.

Fine versus Gross Motor Skills

Frequently used in adapted physical education and motor development is the classification system that distinguishes between fine and gross motor skills. This system is based on the precision of movements and corresponding size of the musculature required for their successful performance. Skills involving very precise movements, which are accomplished using smaller musculature, are known as fine motor skills. These skills tend to be manipulative in nature; examples include sewing on a button, tying a fly (fishing), controlling dental or surgical instruments, entering contact information on a smartphone, or pulling the trigger of a biathlon rifle. Larger muscles are used in the performance of gross motor skills, which place less emphasis on precision and are typically the result of multi-limb movements. Examples of these skills, generally known in physical education as fundamental motor skills, include running, hopping, and skipping.

Given that many skills require the combined effort of both large and small muscle groups, a continuum is used for classification. Skills with more large muscle elements are placed closer to the gross end of the continuum, and vice versa. In bowling, for instance, large muscles of the legs propel the body forward in the approach, and the muscles of the shoulder create the arm swing necessary to launch the ball, making these movements predominately gross in nature. At the

FIGURE **1.3**

The precise movements required for sewing make it a fine motor skill

FIGURE **1.4**

Jumping over a puddle requires larger muscle groups and less precision, making it a gross motor skill

CEREBRALchallenge   1.2

Determine whether each of the following skills would be classified as a fine (F) or a gross (G) motor skill or has elements of both (B).

1. Signing a check
2. Dribbling a basketball
3. Throwing a discus
4. Walking with crutches

5. Tackling
6. Making a surgical incision
7. Picking up a paper clip
8. Setting a volleyball

same time, however, the bowler needs a high degree of fine motor control to manipulate the spin of the ball upon release. In fact, fine motor control has a significant impact on the extent to which many skills can be performed proficiently (Payne & Isaacs, 2016). Accordingly, the degree of fine motor control displayed during the performance of a skill may be used to assess skill development.

Children tend to achieve gross motor skill proficiency before they develop control over fine motor skills (Eichstaedt & Kalakian, 1993). Developmental readiness must, therefore, be a consideration when designing teaching progressions in which learning tasks become increasingly more difficult. Skills or skill components should be introduced in a sequence moving from gross to fine.

Discrete versus Serial versus Continuous Skills

A second taxonomy classifies skills into one of three categories based on the nature of their organization. A discrete skill is one whose beginning and end points are clearly defined. Examples are swinging a golf club, moving from sitting to standing, and throwing a horseshoe. When a number of discrete skills are combined into an integrated sequence, such as roping a calf, performing a figure skating routine, or emptying the flatware bin of a dishwasher, it is classified as a serial skill. Finally, continuous skills are those whose beginning and ending points are either arbitrary or determined by some environmental factor (such as a finish line) rather than by the task itself. Typically, continuous skills are repetitive in nature. They include cycling, working out on an elliptical machine, rowing, propelling a manually powered wheelchair, and tracing a picture.

The nature of a task's organization has implications for practice. Because the movements in continuous skills are highly interdependent, they are typically best practiced as a whole. Serial skills, however, can often be simplified when necessary by practicing their components separately. The relationship between task organization and whole versus part practice will be discussed in detail in Chapter 9.

CEREBRALchallenge 1.3

Categorize each of the following skills as discrete (D), continuous (C), or serial (S).

1. Triple jump
2. Crochet shot
3. Punting a football
4. Lunges

5. Gymnastics vault
6. Transfer from wheelchair to bed
7. Walking with assisted walking device
8. Cross-country skiing

Closed versus Open Skills

The predictability of the environment in which a skill is performed determines the third classification system. This system is also based on a continuum, as the degree of predictability can vary between low and high. On one end of the continuum are skills performed in stable, predictable environments; these are closed skills. With closed skills, the performer controls the performance situation because the object being acted on or the context in which the skill is being performed does not change. For example, in bowling, regardless of how busy the bowling alley is, the pins are stationary and the performer chooses when to initiate the movement. Other examples of closed skills include chopping wood, a free throw, picking up a cup of coffee, zipping up a jacket, and taping an athlete's ankle.

Open skills are at the other end of the continuum, as these are performed in an unpredictable, ever-changing environment. In open skills, the performer will not be aware of what movement type is required until moments before making it (Smith, 2011). Fielding a groundball is a good example. Once the ball is hit, an infielder receives direction and trajectory information but does not know the exact location where it will bounce. In addition, upon impact or anytime while traveling across the infield, the ball could curve or take a bad hop, forcing players to be ready to make adjustments up to the last moment. Similarly, in mountain biking riders must continually adapt their responses to conform to the trail. Other examples of open skills include pursuing an opponent in field hockey and walking through a crowd after a concert, movie, or sporting event. Figure 1.5 shows the continuum and guiding questions to assist the practitioner in identifying where along that continuum a skill would fall.

The closed/open distinction is an important one for practitioners, as the instructional goals for each differ significantly. For closed skills, consistency is the objective and technique refinement should be emphasized. However, because they are performed in a variety of contexts, some closed skills are known as *closed skills with inter-trial variability.* For these types of skills, while technique development remains important, learners must also be able to adapt that technique according to the situation. For example, bowlers must adjust their performance based on the placement of the pins during any given trial, so they

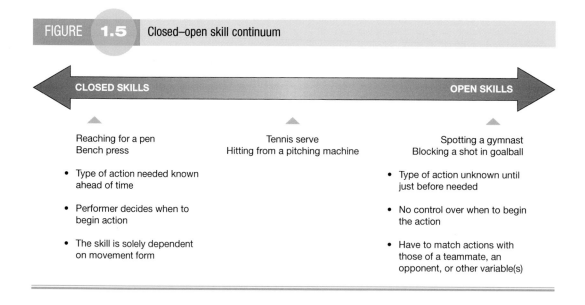

FIGURE 1.5 Closed–open skill continuum

CLOSED SKILLS   **OPEN SKILLS**

Reaching for a pen
Bench press

- Type of action needed known
  ahead of time

- Performer decides when to
  begin action

- The skill is solely dependent
  on movement form

Tennis serve
Hitting from a pitching machine

Spotting a gymnast
Blocking a shot in goalball

- Type of action unknown until
  just before needed

- No control over when to begin
  the action

- Have to match actions with
  those of a teammate, an
  opponent, or other variable(s)

should practice various potential pin combinations. Similarly, putting practice in golf should incorporate a variety of slopes and green conditions, as well as different locations and distances from the hole.

For open skills, where learners must constantly conform their movements to an unstable, unpredictable environment, successful performance depends less on mastering technique and more on the learners' ability to select the appropriate response in a given situation. Consequently, practice should simulate the game or context in which the skill will be performed, with an emphasis on learning to anticipate and adapt to the demands of the ever-changing performance situation.

The closed/open distinction can also assist practitioners in regulating task complexity. For example, throwing a football may be considered either a closed or an open skill, depending on the context. Throwing at a stationary target is considered a closed skill. As other variables are added, such as a moving receiver or a pursuing defense, throwing a football becomes a progressively more open and more complex task. In the early stages of skill acquisition, it is difficult for learners to focus on the execution of the movement while also being aware of aspects of the environment (such as the position of receivers or the movements of defensive players)—traits inherent in open skills. By changing the context of a skill to make it more closed initially, the practitioner can strategically decrease attention demands and simplify the learning process.

Multidimensional Classification System

According to Gentile (2000), one cannot completely understand the demands a task places on a performer by using a single-dimensional system. Instead, Gentile proposed a taxonomy that categorizes skills according to two general charac-

CEREBRAL**challenge**   **1.4**

1. Determine where along the closed–open continuum the following skills fall, by placing the item letters accordingly on the line.

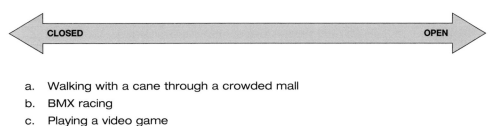

CLOSED   OPEN

   a. Walking with a cane through a crowded mall
   b. BMX racing
   c. Playing a video game
   d. Guiding a patient through proprioceptive neuromuscular facilitation (PNF) stretching exercises
   e. Hitting a ball from a tee
   f. Hitting a pitched ball
   g. Mowing the lawn
   h. Snowboarding
   i. Balancing on a wobble board
   j. Evasion belt drill shown at www.youtube.com/watch?v=J7t8NnWEkS4

2. José has been driving since he was 16. Now, in college, he wants to buy a certain car, but it has a manual transmission. He has never driven a manual stick shift before and has asked if you will teach him. You agree. Rank order the following settings for José's first lesson, with 1 being the best and 3 being the worst. Explain your rankings.

      On a rural road
      In an empty parking lot
      In city traffic

teristics: (1) the context in which they are performed (regulatory conditions) and (2) the action requirements of the skills. Combined, these two dimensions provide insight into the processes involved in skill acquisition.

Regulatory Conditions

Skills are not performed in a vacuum. To perform a jump header in soccer, for example, performers must conform their movement to the height, size, speed, and trajectory of the ball, as well as the location of the intended target. For any given skill, therefore, a number of environmental factors exist that specify the movement characteristics necessary for successful performance. These factors are known as regulatory conditions (Gentile, 2000), and their determination may be used to differentiate skills.

CEREBRALchallenge 1.5

1. Determine whether each of the items listed below would be considered as a regulatory (R) or non-regulatory (N) condition for dart throwing:

    a. Height of the dart board
    b. Crowd noise
    c. Distance from the dart board
    d. Sharpness of the dart tip
    e. Score

2. On a separate sheet, identify regulatory conditions for each of the following:

    a. Performing a bicep curl
    b. Hiking along a forest trail
    c. Diving from a springboard
    d. Cross-country skiing
    e. Stepping onto an escalator
    f. Picking up your change from a counter
    g. Dusting the furniture in your house
    h. Retrieving your suitcase from a baggage carousel

3. An occupational therapist instructs a child to string pasta on a cord to improve fine motor control. Determine whether or not this activity has inter-trial variability. Justify your answer.

When examining the environmental context in which a task is performed, one must first determine whether the regulatory conditions are stationary, as in shooting at a stationary target, or in motion, such as in skeet shooting. Notice that this concept parallels that of the open versus closed skill classification, in that the regulatory conditions for closed skills tend to be stationary, whereas those for open skills tend to be in motion. As indicated earlier, when learners must conform to environmentally imposed constraints, they must engage in more complex processes to assess the situation and select appropriate responses.

The next question is whether there is inter-trial response variability—that is, do the regulatory conditions remain fixed or change with each performance attempt. A free throw, for example, has low inter-trial variability, because the context in which it is performed does not change from one shot to the next. The basket does not change, the distance from which one shoots remains constant, and defenders do not oppose the shooter. Tail backs, on the other hand, experience a great deal of inter-trial variability; they must change their running pattern each time they receive the ball in order to avoid tackles and gain maximum yardage.

Action Requirements

The other dimension that Gentile (2000) proposed pertains to the action requirements of a skill, specifically with respect to body movement and object manipulation. In this context, body movement refers to whether the performer must change locations (move the body from point A to point B) when performing the skill. Cross-country skiing, performing the high jump, and using an assisted walking device are examples of skills that require the performer to change locations from one place to another (body transport). On the other end of the spectrum are skills that require body stability. Performing push-ups, lifting a coffee mug while seated, executing a golf putt, and playing a drum set all fall into this category. Note that although the body changes locations when, for example, an individual is driving a motorcycle, this action would be categorized as body stability. In this case, the individual is not actually moving the body but the body is instead moving with the motorcycle. Other examples would be getting transported to the top of a ski hill by a rope tow, troll fishing, and doing a city tour on a Segway.

A second determinant of action requirements is object manipulation. Some skills require the performer to manipulate objects or opponents. Knitting, washing dishes, pole vaulting, and wrestling fall into this category. Other skills, such as performing pelvic tilt exercises, the hexagon agility test, and the rhythmic step pattern of the tango, do not require object manipulation.

Application of the Multidimensional Classification System

To use this classification system to understand the demands that a task imposes on a learner, practitioners must ask four questions:

1. Are the regulatory conditions stationary or in motion?
2. Do the regulatory conditions remain fixed (no inter-trial variability), or do they change (inter-trial variability) with each performance attempt?
3. Is the performer required to change locations or maintain body position when performing the task?
4. Does the task require the performer to manipulate an object or opponent?

Once the answer to each question is determined, the skill can be classified into one of 16 resulting categories, as shown in Table 1.1.

For example, in the forearm pass in volleyball, the performer must first track a moving ball, move to a position to intercept it, and then control its deflection to propel it in the desired direction. Consequently, the regulatory conditions are moving (open skill) and change from trial to trial, and the performer is required to change locations and manipulate an object. Given this assessment, the forearm pass falls into category 16.

The human movement practitioner may use Gentile's multidimensional classification system in several ways. First, as you move diagonally from the top left cell to the bottom right cell, task complexity increases, with a corresponding increase in the demands placed on the performer. Accordingly, the simplest skill

TABLE 1.1 Gentile's multidimensional classification system, with task examples

		ACTION REQUIREMENTS			
		Neither body transport nor object manipulation	**Object manipulation only**	**Body transport only**	**Both body transport and object manipulation**
REGULATORY CONDITIONS	**Stationary and fixed**	Doing a sit-up 1	Moving a chess piece 2	Climbing a ladder 3	Shot put 4
	Stationary and variable	Writing ABCs with foot for ankle rehabilitation 5	"Round the clock" in darts 6	Following a dance pattern that has been placed on the floor 7	With a partner, following a dance pattern that has been placed on the floor 8
	In motion and fixed	Floating on a river in an inner tube 9	Quality control inspector retrieving a bottle from a moving conveyor belt in a bottling plant 10	Running down a hill 11	Stepping onto a moving sidewalk when using crutches 12
	In motion and variable	Riding in a tube pulled by a speedboat 13	Catching a variety of different sized balls while balancing on one foot 14	Skating on a crowded ice rink 15	A forearm pass in volleyball 16

is one where the environment is stationary, involves no inter-trial variability or body transport, and does not require object manipulation. At the other end of the spectrum, the most complex skill is one performed in an environmental context that is in motion, involving high inter-trial variability and requiring both body transport and object manipulation. To perform such a skill successfully, the performer must be able to scan the environment to identify and process relevant information, decide how to respond, and allocate attentional resources to control body transport and object manipulation concurrently.

Second, by understanding the level of complexity of a skill, the practitioner can better design challenging yet realistic learning experiences. A logical progression that moves from simple to complex ultimately leads to simulation of the actual context in which the skill will be performed. Refer to Figure 1.6 for an example of a simple-to-complex progression for the forearm pass in volleyball.

CEREBRALchallenge 1.6

ASSESSMENT OF REGULATORY CONDITIONS

Using the chart below, assess the regulatory conditions and action requirements of each skill. Based on your assessment, determine into which of the 16 categories in Gentile's multidimensional classification system (Table 1.1) the skill would be classified.

SKILL	Regulatory Conditions (environment)		Regulatory Conditions (inter-trial variability)		Body Transport (changing locations)		Object Manipulation		Category Number
	stationary	in motion	fixed	change	yes	no	yes	no	
Putting a golf ball	X			X		X	X		6
Propelling a wheelchair through a crowd of people at a concert									
Performing a lunge on a BOSU ball									
Texting on your cell phone									
Short track speed skating									
Wii Fit Game shown at www.youtube.com/watch?v=fmHRVjAlt_c									

Designing progressions becomes more challenging, however, when multiple skills or variations of a skill share the same category in the taxonomy. For example, the forearm pass can be used to return the ball over the net, receive a serve or opponent's attacking shot, or to place the ball in the air for an offensive attack. While all of these variations would fall into Category 16, ball placement accuracy differs in each changing the complexity of the task. Similarly, balancing on one leg with your eyes open or closed falls into Category 1 yet the latter is more difficult to perform due to the absence of visual cues. Performing the same

FIGURE **1.6**	Sample simple-to-complex progression for the forearm pass

SKILL: Volleyball Forearm Pass

VARIABLES THAT CAN BE MANIPULATED:

1. Stability of regulatory conditions
2. Inter-trial variability
3. Body transport

Activity	Gentile's Taxonomy
1. Partner tosses the ball at a constant trajectory and location.	1. Regulatory conditions are relatively stable 2. No inter-trial variability 3. No body transport 4. Object manipulation
2. Partner tosses the ball at a constant location but changes the trajectory each time.	1. Regulatory conditions are moving 2. Inter-trial variability 3. No body transport 4. Object manipulation
3. Partner tosses the ball to different locations and with different trajectories but indicates where the ball will go prior to tossing it.	1. Regulatory conditions are relatively stable 2. Inter-trial variability 3. Body transport 4. Object manipulation
4. Partner randomly tosses the ball to different locations and with different trajectories without giving prior notification as to where it is going.	1. Regulatory conditions are moving 2. Inter-trial variability 3. Body transport 4. Object manipulation

task with your hands raised above your head versus out at your side also changes the complexity of the skill due to a shift in the location of the center of gravity, but the skill remains in Category 1. In such cases, practitioners must consider what other task attributes influence the demands the skill places on a performer when sequencing practice activities.

Finally, practitioners may also use Gentile's model to systematically evaluate a learner's movement capabilities and limitations. This evaluation affords a better understanding of the degree of complexity that a learner is able to handle and insight into what performance demands (e.g., scanning the environment, processing information, allocating attention) are problematic. For example, if a learner is no longer able to successfully complete the forearm pass when required to change locations to intercept the ball (Activity #3 in Figure 1.6; Category 8 classification), the processing demands of body transport and object manipulation combined may be too high. A potential solution might be to have the learner practice changing locations and positioning themselves for a forearm pass

CEREBRALchallenge   1.7

Design a simple-to-complex progression that might be used to teach dribbling (basketball) using Gentile's taxonomy.

without involving the ball. Movement could initially be self-paced and in the same direction each trial (Category 3), progressing to quickly changing locations forward, backwards, and side to side where directional information is given in advance (Category 7) and finally to having to move into position without prior notification of direction (Category 15). Once the learner is comfortable with the footwork, Activity #3 in Figure 1.6 would be reintroduced, progressing eventually to Activity #4 where the direction and trajectory of the toss are no longer predictable, simulating game conditions.

INDIVIDUAL DIFFERENCES

One challenge facing practitioners is the fact that all learners are unique. Each person's uniqueness is a function of relatively stable and enduring characteristics known as individual differences. Factors such as height, body type, sleep deprivation, physiological makeup (e.g., number of fast vs. slow twitch fibers), learning styles, type and amount of previous movement experience, motivation, developmental level, cultural background, psychological makeup, attitude, and confidence all affect the rate of and potential for developing skill proficiency. Because of individual differences, teaching strategies will not be equally effective for all learners and practitioners must identify the best strategies to employ based on diverse learner needs and qualities.

Motor Abilities

Of interest to human movement practitioners are individual differences in motor abilities. Abilities are genetic traits that are prerequisite for skilled performance. Accordingly, the degree to which learners could potentially develop proficiency in a particular motor skill depends on whether they possess the necessary underlying abilities.

Although many different abilities have been identified to date, researchers initially hypothesized that there existed a single general motor ability (Brace, 1927; McCloy, 1934). Behind this notion was the observation that accomplished athletes often picked up new skills quickly and excelled at numerous other skills without much practice. Therefore, it seemed reasonable to surmise that there existed a high correlation between one's level of general ability and one's potential for skill proficiency at a variety of tasks. In other words, if you had inherited a high level of general motor ability, you should be able to achieve a high level of proficiency in all motor skills, from golf to bobsledding to kayaking.

Challenging the existence of a general motor ability, the specificity hypothesis proposed that, while individuals may inherit a large number of motor abilities, those abilities are independent of one another (Henry, 1968). In addition, each skill requires a particular set of abilities for successful performance. Consequently, an individual who obtains a high degree of proficiency in archery will not necessarily achieve that same degree of proficiency in wrestling, as these two skills have different underlying ability requirements.

Research examining the strength of interrelationships between motor abilities silenced the debate between proponents of general motor ability and the specificity hypothesis. In general, researchers have found low correlations between an individual's performances of two different tasks (including those that appeared to be closely related), which supported the specificity hypothesis (e.g., Drowatzky & Zucatto, 1967; Henry, 1968; Robertson et al., 1999; Zelaznik, Spencer, & Doffin, 2000). However, because low correlations were found, rather than no correlation at all, it remained possible that some of the same underlying abilities were required by different tasks. Having recognized this earlier, Fleishman (1962) set out not only to identify underlying motor abilities that were predictive of high skill proficiency levels, but also to create a taxonomy by which skills could be classified.

CEREBRALchallenge   1.8

Determine which abilities would be important to become highly proficient in the following:

1. Performing orthopedic surgery
2. Wiring a house (for electricity)
3. Firefighting
4. Decorating a cake

CEREBRALchallenge   1.9

1. Which of the following statements is/are true? Justify your answers.

   a. An individual can have abilities but not be skilled.
   b. An individual can be skilled without ability.

2. Khalilah is strong in control precision, rate control, and finger dexterity but weak in arm–hand steadiness and response orientation. What is her potential for fulfilling her dream of becoming a famous tattoo artist? Fully explain your response.

TABLE 1.2	Fleishman's taxonomy of motor abilities

ABILITIES	DEFINITION	ILLUSTRATION
PERCEPTUAL MOTOR ABILITIES		
Control precision	Ability for highly controlled movement adjustments, especially those involving larger muscle groups	Dribbling a soccer ball
Multi-limb coordination	Ability to coordinate numerous limb movements simultaneously	Volleyball spike
Response orientation	Ability to select a response rapidly from a number of alternatives, as in choice reaction time situations	Tail back trying to find an opening
Reaction time	Ability to initiate a rapid response to an unexpected stimulus	Sprint start in swimming
Speed of limb movement	Ability to make gross rapid limb movement without regard for reaction time	Hockey slap shot
Rate control	Ability to make continuous speed and direction adjustments with precision when tracking	Mountain biking
Manual dexterity	Ability to control manipulations of large objects using arms and hands	Water polo
Finger dexterity	Ability to control manipulations of small objects primarily through use of fingers	Texting on a cell phone
Arm–hand steadiness	Ability to make precise arm–hand positioning movements where involvement of strength and speed are minimal	Dentistry
Wrist–finger speed	Ability to move the wrist and fingers rapidly	Blackjack dealing
Aiming	Ability to direct hand movements quickly and accurately at a small object in space	Marksmanship
PHYSICAL PROFICIENCY ABILITIES		
Static strength	Ability to generate maximum force against a weighty external object	Pushing car out of snowbank
Dynamic strength	Muscular endurance or ability to exert force repeatedly	Rock climbing
Explosive strength	Muscular power or ability to create maximum effort by combining force and velocity	Throwing javelin
Trunk strength	Dynamic strength of trunk muscles	Pole vault
Extent flexibility	Ability to move trunk and back muscles through large range of motion	Circus contortionist
Dynamic flexibility	Ability to make repeated, rapid flexing movements	Diving, aerial ski jumping
Gross body coordination	Ability to coordinate numerous movements simultaneously while the body is in motion	Slalom skiing, synchronized swimming
Gross body equilibrium	Ability to maintain balance without visual cues	Tightrope walking while blindfolded
Stamina	Cardiovascular endurance or ability to sustain effort	Climbing Mt. Everest

Fleishman's taxonomy of motor abilities, as summarized in the attached table, from The description and prediction of perceptual motor learning. In R. Glaser (Ed.), *Training research and education* (pp. 137–175), University of Pittsburgh Press. Used with permission.

Categorizing Motor Abilities

Fleishman's taxonomy groups motor abilities in two categories: (1) perceptual motor abilities and (2) physical proficiency abilities, which are identified in Table 1.2, along with an example of a skill for which the ability is elemental. It should be noted that this list is not all-inclusive, nor is it likely that all abilities have yet been identified.

Practical Implications

We all have different abilities that enhance or limit our capacity to become skilled at a particular task. But even if we possess the prerequisite abilities for accomplishing a task, there is no guarantee that we will become skillful. We only have the *potential* to become skillful. Practice and experience play a role in realizing that potential. Consequently, children should be provided with as many varied movement experiences as possible. Those experiences should be developmentally appropriate. Learners will modify skills according to their current level of ability.

FIGURE **1.7**

Can future success in a skill be predicted?

For example, successful performance of a regulation free throw requires a prerequisite level of strength. A young learner who has not yet developed sufficient strength will modify his or her performance accordingly in an attempt to make a basket. Rather than employing correct technique, the learner may instead execute the free throw using more of a "shot put" type movement in order to generate enough force to project the ball high and far enough. Practitioners should lower the basket to a more suitable height and encourage the learner to employ the correct technique with the nearer target. As learners' physical maturity advances, change the height of the basket accordingly. Note that learners will not progress at the same rate, and that there exists a genetic ceiling for each learner's level of skill regardless of the amount of practice.

The concept of abilities is also useful for skill classification. Through a method known as task analysis, we can determine the underlying abilities important to the successful performance of a specific skill. Skills can then be grouped accordingly. To perform a task analysis, a skill is first broken down into its key elements or component parts. Once the key components have been

| FIGURE | 1.8 | Task analysis of a volleyball spike |

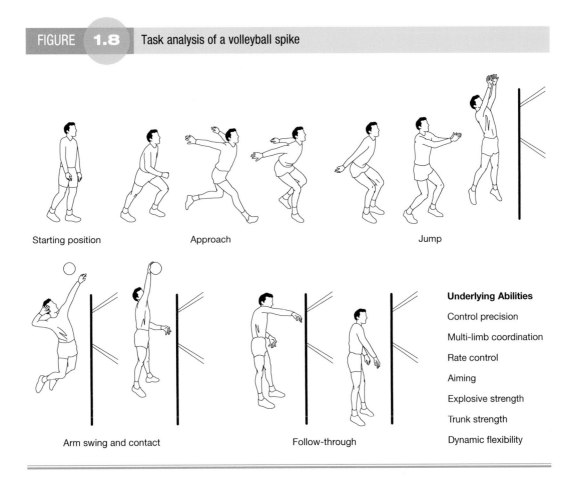

Starting position   Approach   Jump

Arm swing and contact   Follow-through

Underlying Abilities

Control precision

Multi-limb coordination

Rate control

Aiming

Explosive strength

Trunk strength

Dynamic flexibility

identified, the abilities that are necessary to meet their requirements can be more readily determined. By conducting a task analysis, the practitioner can develop a greater understanding of the skill's requirements. Figure 1.8 illustrates a task analysis and subsequent examples of ability prerequisites for a volleyball spike.

If underlying abilities are important to the successful performance of a specific skill, it would stand to reason that an individual who possesses those abilities would be predisposed to achieve a high level of proficiency. Imagine the impact this would have on sports programs, as we could predict future performance simply by screening individuals for certain abilities. In fact, talent identification programs have existed for decades. They screen children and adolescents using a battery of tests constructed to determine the extent to which they possess certain abilities. The test results are then used to select those individuals who appear to have the potential to succeed in a given sport. Other tests screen candidates for professions such as firefighting. Visit the websites provided in the margin to view and hear additional examples of agility and talent identification programs.

> **COMMON MYTH**
>
> Future success in a specific skill can be easily predicted

www

TALENT IDENTIFICATION

Video example of a police physical agility test:
ww.youtube.com/watch?v=8d5e3Enny98

UK Sport talent identification and development program:
www.uksport.gov.uk/our-work/talent-id

Canoe slalom talent identification promotion video from Australia:
www.youtube.com/watch?v=o6V8fe8R-TE

Listen as Dr. Rob Gray discusses talent identification in his podcast at http://perceptionaction.com/26c/

Read the International Society of Sport Psychology's Position Stand: *To Test or Not to Test? The Use of Physical Skill Tests in Talent Detection and in Early Phases of Sport Development* at www.issponline.org/documents/positionstand2009-2.pdf

How successful have these programs been in predicting a person's potential for success in a specific skill? And what can we learn from them to help identify future stars in, for example, T-ball? Results of talent identification programs have been mixed. To understand why, we must consider three limitations of these programs. First, as was indicated earlier, it is likely that not all of the abilities that contribute to skilled performance have been identified. Second, a high level of performance in the early stages of learning does not always correlate to advanced performance later, owing to changes in the requirements of the skill. For example, a child may be an outstanding hitter in T-ball when the ball remains stationary, but the results may be different when he or she moves to the next level, when the ball is pitched. Third, abilities alone cannot predict performance; other individual differences must be considered. Because of differences in reaching physical maturity, for example, players who possess the underlying abilities to excel in a sport but have not yet sufficiently matured may get cut from a team. A great example is Michael Jordan, who did not make the varsity high school basketball team when he was a sophomore, yet went on to become one of the greatest basketball players ever to play the game!

While it is apparent that individual differences must be taken into account for the development of a successful talent identification program, the impact of these differences on learning should be the practitioner's primary concern. Practitioners must remember that all learners are unique in what they bring to the learning environment. Consequently, a particular teaching strategy will not work for everyone. Practitioners should develop a large repertoire of instructional strategies so they can accommodate the needs of all learners. Furthermore, practitioners should take the time to get to know each learner. What types of past experiences do the learners have? What motivates them? What situations lead to increased anxiety? Because of the influence of individual differences, this will be time well spent.

CEREBRALchallenge 1.10

1. For a skill of your choice, perform a task analysis to determine its component parts and the underlying abilities required to achieve a high degree of proficiency.

2. Think about activities that you tend to participate in versus activities you tend to avoid. Speculate as to why you make these choices by comparing the underlying abilities needed to accomplish these activities.

RESEARCH NOTES

Hoare and Warr (2000) conducted a study to examine the effectiveness of applying an Australian talent identification model, traditionally used with individual sports, to the team sport of women's soccer. Subjects (ages 15–19) with a background in team sports or track and field were recruited to participate in the program. After two days of testing—which included the assessment of physiological (vertical jump, acceleration, speed, agility, and aerobic power), anthropometric (height, mass), and skill (juggling, dribbling, ball control, passing, and receiving) attributes—17 of the original 71 athletes were chosen, based on their abilities, to take part in a 12-month training program. At the conclusion of the program, which included 25 competitions, 10 players (59 percent) were selected for regional teams, and two were selected for the state team within six months. Based on their results, the authors recommended that speed and acceleration should be weighed more heavily in the future and suggested that selection procedures would benefit from the development of an objective test of "game sense" (technical and tactical competence).

PUTTING IT INTO PRACTICE

Learning Situation: Rehabilitation of an Ankle Sprain

Darren is a 31-year-old man who works for the forest service as a forestry technician. He spends the majority of his time in the outdoors and his job is physically demanding. On any given day he could be doing trail maintenance, installing drainage systems, cutting trees, stacking wood, preparing an area for revegetation, or a variety of other duties. One of the ways he stays physically active is by playing basketball in the local rec. league. Recently, he went up for a rebound and upon landing, stepped on an opponent's foot and rolled his right ankle. He was diagnosed with a grade 2 ankle sprain that has sidelined him not only from basketball but also any field work at his job. He hates working at a desk so wants to get back to the field as soon as possible.

Darren has been working on regaining his range of motion and restoring muscle strength and has progressed from non-weight bearing to partial and now to full weight bearing. His balance and proprioception have been adversely affected by the sprain and need to be retrained.

Test Your Knowledge

Below are examples of balance tasks from which the therapist can draw. Place them in the appropriate cell of Gentile's taxonomy. Compare your answer with the sample response provided at www.routledge.com/cw/coker.

1. Single leg stance
2. Single leg squat with dumbbell curl
3. Walking a straight line heel to toe
4. Step up to balance position with leg lift and dumbbell press
5. Single leg ball wall toss and catch
6. Squat on Bosu ball
7. Lunge onto Bosu ball with front foot
8. Single leg stance and forward reach to variable illuminated targets (e.g., therapist will turn laser off and on in various locations on the wall)
9. Step up onto Bosu ball with leg lift
10. Walking lunge and weighted ball diagonal chop (alternating sides)
11. Single leg stance reaching forward, to the side and backwards to targets with non-support leg
12. Sharpened or tandem Romberg stance
13. Single leg stance exchanging a ball from hand to hand above the head
14. Single leg hop and hold.

CEREBRALchallenge   1.11

Refer back to the integrative model for facilitating motor skill learning and performance. List the elements introduced in this chapter that should be taken into consideration as you develop a situation profile.

A LOOK AHEAD

Human movement is a complex phenomenon that is a function of the interaction of three elements: the learner, the task, and the environment in which the task is performed. Because this concept is foundational to the development of optimal learning experiences, practitioners must develop a working knowledge of this interaction in order to help learners realize their potential. Further development of this working knowledge requires an understanding of the underlying processes that govern movement execution and control. The following chapter begins this discussion, focusing on the factors that influence movement preparation.

FOCUS POINTS

After reading this chapter, you should know:

- The interaction of the learner, the task, and the environment in which the task is performed is fundamental to understanding and facilitating motor skill acquisition and performance.
- The field of motor learning examines the processes and variables that influence the acquisition and refinement of motor skills, while the field of motor control focuses on the neural, physical, and behavioral aspects that underlie movement.
- Learning and performance are not synonymous. Learning is a relatively permanent change in the capability to execute a motor skill as a result of practice or experience, while performance is simply the act of executing a skill.
- Motor skills are categorized by several classification systems:
  — The gross–fine motor skills classification is based on the precision of the movement.
  — Skills may be classified as discrete, serial, or continuous according to the nature of their movement organization.
  — The open–closed motor skills continuum is based on the predictability of the environment.
  — Gentile's multidimensional classification system categorizes skills according to the context in which they are performed and the action requirements of the skill.
- All teaching strategies will not be equally effective for all learners, owing to individual differences.
- Each of us possesses different levels of abilities, which are genetically determined traits that enhance or limit our potential to become skilled at a particular task.
- By conducting a task analysis, one can identify the underlying abilities important to the successful performance of a specific skill.
- Talent identification programs have shown mixed results when individuals are screened, using a battery of tests, to predict future success based on their possession of a high level of certain abilities.

lab

To complete the lab for this chapter, visit www.routledge.com/cw/coker and select **Lab 1, Abilities**.

REVIEW QUESTIONS

1. Compare and contrast motor learning and motor control.
2. Define learning. What is the relationship between learning and performance?
3. What four criteria must a task meet if it is to be classified as a skill?
4. How are skills and abilities different?
5. Explain why most of the classification systems discussed here involve a continuum.
6. Briefly summarize each classification system.
7. Explain how Gentile's taxonomy differs from the other classification types. Why is this significant?
8. Explain the controversy over general versus specific motor abilities.
9. Explain why predictions of future performance success are not always accurate.
10. What is the relevance of the interaction of the learner, the task, and the environment in human movement?

REFERENCES

Brace, D. K. (1927). *Measuring motor ability*. New York: A. S. Barnes.

Drowatzky, J. N. & Zucatto, F. C. (1967). Interrelationships between selected measures of static and dynamic balance. *Research Quarterly, 38,* 509–510.

Eichstaedt, C. B. & Kalakian, L. H. (1993). *Developmental/adapted physical education: Making ability count* (3rd ed.). New York: Macmillan.

Fleishman, E. A. (1962). The description and prediction of perceptual motor skill learning. In R. Glasser (Ed.), *Training research and education* (pp. 137–175). Pittsburgh: University of Pittsburgh.

Gentile, A. M. (2000). Skill acquisition: Action, movement, and the neuromotor processes. In J. H. Carr & R. B. Shepard (Eds.), *Movement science: Foundations for physical therapy in rehabilitation* (pp. 111–180). Rockville, MD: Aspen.

Henry, F. M. (1968). Specificity vs. generality in learning motor skills. In R. C. Brown & G. S. Kenyon (Eds.), *Classical studies on physical activity* (pp. 331–340). Englewood Cliffs, NJ: Prentice-Hall.

Hoare, D. G. & Warr, C. R. (2000). Talent identification and women's soccer: An Australian experience. *Journal of Sports Sciences, 18,* 751–758.

Knudson, D. V. (2013). *Qualitative diagnosis of human movement: Improving performance in sport and exercise*. Champaign, IL: Human Kinetics.

McCloy, C. H. (1934). The measurement of general motor capacity and general motor ability. *Research Quarterly, 5* (Suppl. 5), 45–61.

Payne, V. G. & Isaacs, L. D. (2016). *Human motor development: A lifespan approach* (9th ed.). Scottsdale, AZ: Holcomb Hathaway.

Robertson, S. D., Zelaznik, H. N., Lantero, D. A., Bojczyk, K. G., Spencer, R. M., Doffin, J. G. & Schneidt, T. (1999). Correlations for timing consistency among tapping and drawing tasks: Evidence against a single timing process for motor control. *Journal of Experimental Psychology: Human Perception and Performance, 25*(5), 1316–1330.

Schmidt, R. A. & Wrisberg, C. A. (2008). *Motor learning and performance: A situation based learning approach*. Champaign, IL: Human Kinetics.

Smith, A. (2011). Classification of motor skills. Retrieved February 7, 2012, from www.livestrong.com/article/246814-classification-of-motor-skills/

Zelaznik, H. N., Spencer, R. M. & Doffin, J. G. (2000). Temporal precision in tapping and circle movements at preferred rates is not correlated: Further evidence against timing as a general-purpose ability. *Journal of Motor Behavior, 32,* 193a–199.

Understanding Movement Preparation

2

After 90 grueling minutes of regulation and two sudden-victory overtime periods of 10 minutes, the score remained tied. The conference championship would be decided by penalty kicks. Jennifer was fourth in the order. She watched anxiously as the opposing team's first shooter easily found the back of the net. Fortunately, her teammate promptly tied the score again, answering back by placing the ball in the lower right corner. Both goalkeepers then made successive saves leaving the game still tied after three rounds. When the fourth shooter on the opposing team kicked a straight shot towards the left corner, Jennifer held her breath. No good! The goalie got her hand on it! Now it was up to her. She approached the ball, waited until the last possible moment to reveal her intention, then drilled it off her left foot. The goalie responded, but she was too late!

Penalty kicks present a critical time of decision making for the goalkeeper and penalty kick taker alike. Faced with the task of blocking a penalty kick, for example, the goalkeeper must assess the situation to determine both where the ball will go and what movement will intercept it. The task is further complicated by a time constraint, as she has a fraction of a second to make these decisions and then organize and execute the motor response before the ball reaches the goal line. In fact, a goalkeeper needs to decide which direction she will dive before the kicker's foot even makes contact with the ball, and it could be argued that this decision is merely a guess. So what differentiates a game-winning save from a failed attempt? Simply guessing correctly? Or are there strategies a goalkeeper can use to increase their odds of making the save? Understanding movement preparation will help answer these questions.

THEORETICAL APPROACHES TO MOVEMENT PREPARATION

Our senses are constantly bombarded with information from both internal and external sources (sensory information or input). Before any of that information can potentially be used to assist a learner in selecting an appropriate response for a given situation, it must first be actively processed. The recognition and interpretation of sensory stimuli—or, said another way, the process by which meaning is attached to sensory information—is known as perception. Two approaches explaining the nature of perception are prevalent today.

Information Processing Model

The first explanation, a product of cognitive psychology, maintains that perceptual processes lead to the creation of some form of symbolic representation of environmental and task information. This information traverses a series of mental processes, including a comparison with existing memory stores, and results in a decision as to which action, if any, is needed in response to the situation. Because there is a "need for sensory input to be processed or elaborated to provide the perceiver a meaningful description of the world," perception in this paradigm is considered to be indirect (Burton, 1987, p. 258).

This view of perception has generally been associated with a model for movement preparation known as information processing, shown in Figure 2.1. In this model, a performer, such as a goalkeeper, will receive a wealth of information or input. In the instance of a goalkeeper, this input includes the opponent's foot as she kicks the ball; characteristics of the ball itself, including velocity, trajectory, spin, and direction; the score; the feel of sweat on the goal-keeper's skin; the sight and sound of the crowd; the sound of a plane flying overhead; the smell and color of the grass; memories of prior successes or failures in similar situations; and an assessment of the area of the net to be covered. When assessing the demands of the task, the goalkeeper will find some of this information relevant or useful; for example, the velocity, trajectory, and direction of the ball. Other information, such as the plane flying overhead, is not relevant and should be ignored. By focusing on pertinent stimuli, the goalkeeper will receive information that is crucial to producing a response that will intercept the shot. Once the information has been gathered, it is transformed into afferent or sensory nerve signals and conducted to the brain; there, during the decision-making process, it is integrated or compared to similar past experiences that are stored in long-term memory. Based on this comparison, a decision is made and a response is selected (dive right, catch, jump), organized, and executed through efferent (motor nerve) commands. This paradigm further suggests that as the movement is initiated, information regarding its progress is fed back to the performer. This information, referred to as intrinsic feedback, may be used to make adjustments to the movement, if there is a discrepancy in what was intended and what is actually occurring (time permitting). It also enables the performer to evaluate the outcome of the response.

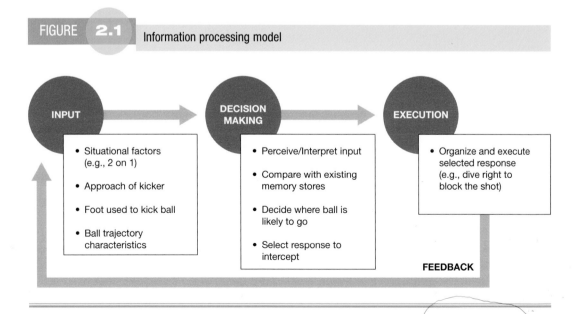

FIGURE 2.1 Information processing model

1. Generate a list of stimuli, both relevant and irrelevant, that may be available to a soccer goalkeeper when facing a one-on-one situation with an attacker who has beat all of the defenders (break away).
2. In addition to deciding what response to make, the performer must determine details regarding that response, such as when to initiate it. Generate a list of possible responses and response details for the above situation.
3. For a skill and situation of your choice, repeat items 1 and 2.
4. Speculate as to the differences in processing demands for open versus closed skills. Give examples to support your response.

Ecological Approach

The second prevailing approach regarding perception suggests that the environment and task are perceived or interpreted directly in terms of affordances. Affordances are the action possibilities of the environment and task in relation to the perceiver's own capabilities (Gibson, 1977, 1979; Burton, 1987). In other words, the environment or task is perceived in terms of the actions the perceiver can potentially exert on it (Burton, 1987). Because of individual differences, several learners could be faced with the same situation and perceive entirely different affordances. For example, while walking through a store, the affordances perceived by an adult will be very different from those of a small child because of their differences in height. The actions afforded by a cell phone in the hands of a college student differ from the actions a toddler might perceive. Typically, college students use a cell phone to talk with or text their friends, whereas toddlers might use it for hitting, banging, or chewing. Since affordances are directly perceived, this perspective, known as the ecological approach to perception, argues against the need to refer to stored representations; it views the relationship between perception and action as circular, as illustrated in Figure 2.2 (Summers, 1988).

Under this paradigm, the goalkeeper needs to decide whether she will catch the ball or dive to block the shot. Rather than making her decision based on a consideration of the ball's characteristics and her memory stores of similar experiences, as suggested by the indirect approach to perception, the goalkeeper directly perceives the ball in terms of its "catchableness" in relation to her own body scaling and capabilities (Burton, 1987). If the goalkeeper believes she is quick enough to jump in front of the ball and make the catch, this action will be selected. If she doesn't think she can make it, or she doubts her catching ability, she may choose to block it instead. It should be noted that affordances, or opportunities for action, can fluctuate "as a result of gradual changes in the player's action capabilities or changes in playing conditions. A ball that was catchable at the beginning of the game may be uncatchable at some later point due to

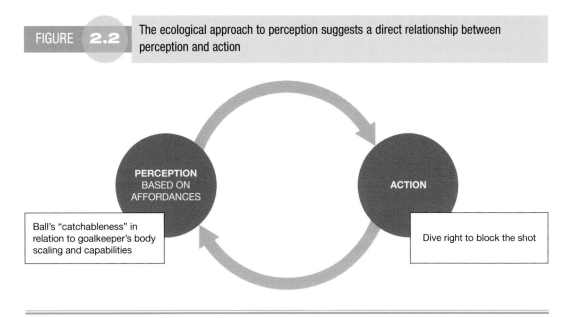

FIGURE **2.2** The ecological approach to perception suggests a direct relationship between perception and action

fatigue" (Fajen, Riley, & Turvey, 2009, p. 80). In addition, opportunities for action can materialize and then vanish in an instant. A gap that affords passing in an 800 m race can open up in one moment and disappear the next, preventing a racer's advances (Fajen et al., 2009).

To gain a better understanding of affordances and how they influence movement decisions, watch the videos about affordances—see the websites listed in the margin—and then try Exploration Activity 2.1.

PREPARING A RESPONSE

Scientists continue to debate and explore the merits of these theoretical approaches regarding movement preparation, in addition to the possible integration of the two. But regardless of the paradigm used to explain the internal processes that occur, research has clearly shown that a brief time lag occurs between the moment when a stimulus is presented and the initiation of a response. This time interval, known as reaction time (RT), is a measure of the time needed to prepare a response. To test your reaction time, try Exploration Activity 2.2.

Reaction time is not constant; it depends on the processing demands imposed by a given situation. As those demands increase, reaction time also increases, indicating the need for more time to prepare a response. The result is a delay that can be detrimental, for example, for avoiding a collision, catching an item that has fallen from the kitchen counter, or defending an opponent from driving

VIDEOS ABOUT AFFORDANCES

General explanation: www.youtube. com/watch?v=81MgPOIq-Uw

Application to Coaching: www.you tube.com/watch?v=qejaHPi9UfE

Check out https://rethinking childhood.com/2012/01/30/ affordance/ to learn more about affordances and play space design

exploration ACTIVITY   2.1

Affordances

EQUIPMENT NEEDED

- Sliding glass door
- Backpack stuffed with clothes
- 3 friends

PROCEDURE

Task A. Fully open the sliding glass door. Ask each of your friends to walk through it. (Participants may choose the manner in which they go through the door—e.g., they may turn to the side—provided they do not change the width of the opening.) Reduce the opening by 4 inches and repeat the procedure. Continue reducing the opening and repeating the procedure until all three friends have indicated that they cannot go through the door. Record your observations for each friend on each trial.

Task B. Repeat Task A, but have each friend wear the backpack on each trial. Record your observations.

QUESTION

Explain your observations in terms of affordances.

exploration ACTIVITY   2.2

Simple Reaction Time

Test your simple reaction time at the following websites:

- www.exploratorium.edu/baseball/reactiontime.html
- http://cognitivelabs.com/mydna_speedtestno.htm

Or download a reaction time app to your smartphone or tablet. Examples:

- Android: Reaction Time (The Commuter Coder)
- iPhone/iPad: Reaction Test Pro

or cutting to the hoop in basketball. Understanding the variables that cause such delays is, therefore, paramount for developing strategies to reduce them and, in some cases, eliminate them during the performance of open skills. Of equal interest to coaches and athletes is how to cause delays in an opponent's response time in order to gain an advantage.

RESEARCH NOTES

Oudejans, Michaels, Bakker, and Dolné (1996) examined the relevance of action in perceiving affordances. The purpose of their study was to determine whether perceptual information about the perceiver's own actions has to be available in order to determine the catchableness of a fly ball. Because catchableness depends on both spatial (distance to be covered) and temporal (time available to cover that distance) aspects, the researchers speculated that judgments regarding catchableness would be more accurate when information about the catcher's action was available. Six non-experts and six expert outfielders were tested in two conditions. The first condition, the perceiving-only condition, required subjects, who remained stationary, to determine as quickly as possible whether a ball could be caught if they were permitted to make an attempt at catching it. The second condition was an actual catching condition. The results revealed that when compared to actual catching, perceivers who are stationary, regardless of experience, make poor judgments as to the catchableness of a ball. These results suggest that stationary perceivers, who were prevented from receiving current information about their running capabilities, did not rely on other information, such as information stored in memory, to determine the catchableness of a ball. A follow-up study was conducted to determine whether judgments of catchableness improved when observers were moving. Twelve non-experts were tested in three conditions. In the first two conditions, participants were to indicate verbally whether the projected ball would have been catchable. Condition 1 required that participants remain stationary, and vision of the projected ball occurred 1 second after its release. Condition 2 differed in that participants started to run in an attempt to catch the ball. Vision was also occluded for this condition for 1 second after the ball was projected. The task of participants in the third condition was actually to catch the projected ball. The results indicated that judgments made when moving were superior to ones made when stationary. The authors concluded that when running is permitted, information that is available regarding the performer's actions makes more accurate judgments of catchableness possible.

Factors Influencing Reaction Time

As indicated, a number of variables influences the length of time needed for information processing and the preparation of a corresponding response. The following section introduces those factors and provides practical suggestions for manipulating them.

Number of Response Choices

A sprint start has one stimulus—the firing of the gun—and one response choice—exploding out of the blocks. Because a sprinter has only one choice in this situation, uncertainty as to how to respond is essentially eliminated. In contrast, a shortstop faces a number of response choices, as he or she may have to catch a fly ball or a line drive or field a ground ball that's been hit directly at, to the right, or to the left of the fielding position. Similarly, in a penalty kick, a number of possible shots can be taken, leading to a corresponding increase in the number of the response choices available to the goalkeeper. Because of the uncertainty of the impending hit or kick, the shortstop or goalie needs additional processing time to prepare a response. This increase in processing demands is reflected by an increase in RT. Complete Exploration Activity 2.3.

The relationship between the number of choices and the time to prepare a response was found to be so stable that it has become known as Hick's Law (Hick, 1952), named for its discoverer. Hick's Law states that choice RT, the reaction time resulting from a situation that involves a choice as to how to respond, is logarithmically related to the number of response choice alternatives. This relationship is illustrated in Figure 2.3.

Notice that in a situation requiring one definitive response, such as the sprint start discussed earlier, RT is approximately 190 ms; in the situation faced by the shortstop, however, RT may be two to three times that long. This increase

FIGURE **2.3** Predicted relationship between number of stimulus–response choices and reaction time (Hick's Law)

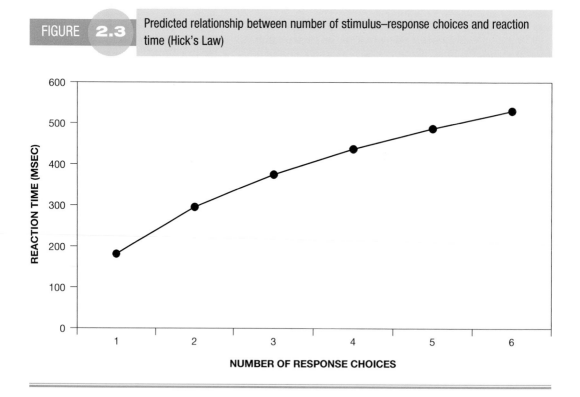

exploration ACTIVITY 2.3

Choice Reaction Time

To examine the influence of the number of response choices on reaction time, try the experiment at www.psytoolkit.org/lessons/simple_choice_rts.html

FIGURE **2.4**	Components of response time

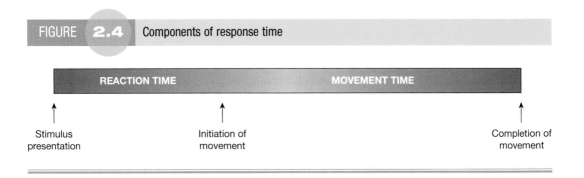

in RT has important implications when the movement situation demands a quick and accurate response.

Response time is measured from the moment when a stimulus is presented to when a response is completed, and it includes both reaction and movement time, as shown in Figure 2.4. Movement time (MT) is the interval between the initiation of the movement and its completion. Both RT and MT must be considered when analyzing a goalkeeper's task of intercepting the ball. For example, suppose that, because of ball placement and speed, a goalkeeper has approximately 360 ms—from the time the ball leaves the kicker's foot until the time the ball crosses the plane of the goal—to decide how to respond and execute that movement (RT + MT). Assuming that she has only two response choices, according to Hick's Law RT will be approximately 300 ms. This leaves only 60 ms to execute the response. When examined from this perspective, it is not surprising that blocking a shot on goal in soccer is such a difficult task. Watch the ESPN's Sport Science video on penalty kicks at www.dailymotion.com/video/x2obk7b to learn more.

Controlling Levels of Uncertainty

Since, according to Hick's Law, increased uncertainty leads to delayed or even inaccurate responses, practitioners should be aware of strategies that can increase or reduce this uncertainty to facilitate learning and performance. The goal of many competitive situations is to gain an advantage over an opponent. By having a large repertoire of proficient serves, plays, moves, pitches, and the like, the player can increase an opponent's uncertainty of which response will be required and diminish that opponent's ability to respond quickly and accurately. In other competitive tasks, such as those involving open skills, successful performance depends on quick decision making. When a quarterback is executing an option play, trying to read all of the stimuli in order to choose the best option can be overwhelming and, as illustrated by Hick's Law, time consuming. As a result, coaches teach their quarterbacks to look systematically for key defensive characteristics in order to reduce the number of choice alternatives. In play, the quarterback assesses the potential success of the first option. If that option looks good, he takes it; if not, he looks for the second option, and so on. Emergency medical personnel employ this same strategy when they arrive at the scene of an accident. Using the ABC mnemonic (airway, breathing, and circulation), they systematically assess the situation, reducing their response preparation time.

The technique of reducing uncertainty by systematically reducing the number of possible response alternatives may be used to facilitate skill learning. When teaching the forearm pass in volleyball, instructors often organize practice so that learners work in pairs. In each pair, one person tosses the ball and the other passes it back. At first, the balls are tossed directly to the learner to eliminate the need to make a choice. Once the learner has developed some proficiency, the tosses may be directed to the right, the left, in front of, or behind the learner, forcing her to move into the correct position and perform the skill. The first step of a normal progression for this drill is for the tosser to tell the passer the direction in which the toss will be made. Because the learner knows in advance where the ball will go, the number of response alternatives is reduced, which

CEREBRAL challenge   2.2

Explain why a racquetball player who can perform five different serves proficiently has an advantage over an opponent who has only two.

CEREBRAL challenge   2.3

1. The goal of some "shooting" video games is to shoot the bad characters but not the good characters. The challenge is that the characters literally jump out of nowhere and the player must quickly decide whether they are "good" or "bad." If you were playing such a video game, what strategies might you use to decrease uncertainty and response time and increase accuracy?

2. What might you suggest to police officers who face this same situation?

3. According to Passos, Araujo, Davids, and Shuttleworth (2008), "Most team-game coaches will agree that a competitive game is a source of unpredictability and uncertainty for all players. A major question faced by all coaches is: How can we reduce the uncertainty inevitably faced by players in all performance contexts" (p. 126). For a skill of your choice, develop strategies that might be used to either increase or decrease uncertainty, depending on your objective.

reduces the processing demands of the task. The next step is to eliminate the pre-toss information, forcing the passer to be prepared for any of the four possible response alternatives.

Anticipation

When the performer is given advance information about what event will occur as well as when it will occur, movement preparation is optimized and response delays are reduced. Although situations exist in which performers are told in advance what to expect (for drivers, for example, a car's turn signals communicate intent, and highway signs communicate driving and road conditions), this is obviously not always the case. Performers typically must learn how to reduce temporal and event uncertainty through anticipation.

Anticipation involves predicting what event will occur (event anticipation) and/or when an event will occur (temporal anticipation). The more predictable a stimulus, the more quickly and accurately a learner can respond. This concept is closely related to the technique of reducing the number of response choices, as the learner essentially narrows down the possible options through anticipation.

Prediction depends on the performer's ability to detect clues, or precues, that are often present in the environment. Therapists, for example, may watch for subtle changes in a patient's posture to anticipate when they should intervene. Similarly, parents use precues to anticipate when to catch a toddler who is learning to walk. In athletic contests, players scrutinize their opponents to

TABLE 2.1 Reading an opponent's precues in tennis

PLAYER'S PRECUES	CLUES TO THE OPPOSING PLAYER
Low to high swing	Expect a topspin shot
High to low swing	Expect an under spin shot (perhaps a drop shot)
Angle of racket face	Indicates height of ball's trajectory
Deceleration of swing	Shorter or slow moving shot
Acceleration of swing	Fast moving return
Controlled swing	Well placed shot
Fast on feet	Will get to most balls
Tendency to go cross court	Expect cross court shots in pressure situations

From: Overdorf, V. & Coker, C. A. (2011, February). Five Tips for Improving Anticipatory Skills. Paper presented at EDAAHPERD. Long Branch, NJ. (Adapted from: www.squashgame.info/squashlibrary/10/26#8.)

identify tendencies that can serve as precues. For example, players may notice that an offense always uses the same play in a given situation, or a pitcher tends to throw a certain pitch depending on the count. Perhaps right before making a pass, a basketball player always looks at the player to whom he is going to pass the ball. A racquetball player might change her back swing depending on the serve she is about to perform. Table 2.1 presents a tennis player's typical precues and the corresponding clues they provide to an opposing player.

RESEARCH NOTES

Compared with their lesser-skilled counterparts, studies have shown that expert performers are both faster and more accurate at anticipating an opponent's impending actions. A critical source of information that experts use to make these anticipatory judgments comes from the opponent's preparatory movements (kinematic cues). Advanced performers also likely use contextual cues or non-movement-related information to make anticipatory decisions, such as opponent's on-court position. To examine this, Loffing and Hagemann (2014) asked skilled ($n = 26$) and novice ($n = 26$) tennis players to anticipate the direction of forehand baseline shots as they watched point light display video clips of tennis strokes (the player and the racket were represented by white dots in front of a dark background). The on-court position of the video model was manipulated and stroke kinematics were held constant. Actions were also occluded (blocked out) at three different time points to vary the amount of stroke information available to the viewer, as it was speculated "that players' expectations as to action outcome should predominantly rely on contextual information at early stages of decision making and then become updated (i.e., modified or amplified) on the basis of sensory input about an unfolding action's kinematics" (Loffing & Hagemann, 2014, p. 17). Findings confirmed that unlike novices, skilled players used context information in the form of an opponent's on-court position to make anticipatory decisions about shot direction. The results further suggest that these position-based judgments occurred earlier in the action sequence, when kinematic information was limited supporting the notion that skilled players' reliance on contextual and kinematic cues varies as the action unfolds.

Research has shown that, as the probability of a particular response increases (at a level of approximately 80 percent), the performer will likely bias his or her response preparation in that direction (Larish & Stelmach, 1982). The result is that the action can be prepared in advance, decreasing RT. In racquetball, if a player anticipates that the shot will go to the right, based on the opponent's positioning and swing motion, she may start moving in that direction before the opponent has made contact with the ball.

Anticipation is not without risks. If the required response is anything other than that which the performer had prepared, the consequence will be a RT that is even slower than if the response had not been biased at all (Larish & Stelmach, 1982). Two tactics that can be employed to take advantage of this (although not always as effective for highly skilled athletes) are deception (Jackson, Warren, & Abernethy, 2006; Wright & Jackson, 2014) and disguise (Rowe, Horswill, Kronvall-Parkinson, Poulter, & McKenna, 2009). Deception is the deliberate presentation of false precues in order to prompt an incorrect response. A lacrosse player faking a movement to the right and then actually moving to the left, a volleyball player feigning a spike and then tipping or dinking the ball, or a soccer player executing a *step-over* maneuver in order to evade a defender are examples. Disguise, on the other hand, is an attempt by a player to hide or delay the onset of precues about the intended action in order to prolong an opponent's decision making. This was the strategy employed by Jennifer, in the opening scenario, who disguised her kicking action until the last possible moment in order to make it more difficult for the goalkeeper to anticipate the direction of her shot.

Practical Implications for Anticipation

Skilled athletes are better able to detect perceptual cues and make anticipatory judgments than their less skilled counterparts (see Mann, Williams, Ward, & Janelle, 2007, and Müller & Abernethy, 2012 for reviews). Consequently, through practice, learners' capability to recognize opponents' cues, idiosyncrasies, and tendencies can be improved, resulting in better anticipation of predictable events and the capacity to prepare required actions in advance. By identifying potential precues, focusing learners' attention to where in the environment they might find precues, and designing drills in which precues are incorporated, practitioners can facilitate this development. Learners must also be taught to avoid presenting the same precues or making the same responses in a competition, which could help the opponent anticipate the impending action.

Scouting is another practical application for anticipation; this strategy is used to assist players in "reading" their opponents to better predict their actions. By purposely watching opponents to analyze their techniques and game play in advance of an upcoming contest, patterns and precues can be identified and a tactical plan devised. Just ask Jens Lehmann, who, with the help of a note about Argentina's penalty kick tendencies that was stuffed in his sock, was able to make the saves needed to advance Germany to the semi-finals of the 2006 World Cup (to see the footage go to www.youtube.com/watch?v=MqjNFjSvHV4).

Today, technology is making scouting even easier. In 2016, Major League Baseball lifted its ban of smartphones, tablets, and laptops in the dugout and announced a multi-year deal giving teams access to iPad Pros along with a new customizable scouting, analytics, and video app called MLB Dugout (go to http://m.mlb.com/video/topic/8879974/v568826983/mlb-tonight-on-ipads-coming-to-all-30-dugouts to learn more). For examples of scouting apps check out Digital Scout and iProScout Baseball.

CEREBRAL challenge   2.4

List examples of both event and temporal anticipation from a movement situation or sport of your choice.

Example: A libero player (a player specialized in defensive skills) performing a
   serve–receive pass in volleyball.

Event anticipation: What type of serve to intercept (topspin, floater)?

Temporal anticipation: Where should I move in order to intercept the ball?

CEREBRAL challenge   2.5

One of the heroines of the 1999 United States World Cup victory over China (5–4) was goalkeeper Briana Scurry. The following is an account of the moment when she made a save that put the United States ahead:

> Briana Scurry looked at the Chinese midfielder, Liu Ying, as she walked to the penalty spot. Liu's head was down and her shoulders drooped, and it seemed to Scurry that Liu did not want the burden of the kick. "This is the one," Scurry said to herself. Liu set the ball down, backed up at a sharp angle, and began her approach with a tentative jog. Her intention became obvious, and her hips rotated in a way that gave the shot away. Scurry lunged with an explosive step, then planted her feet wide and dived to her left.
>
> Longman, 2000, p. 72

Liu's hips served as a precue that allowed Scurry to anticipate what response she would have to make to block the shot. Research supports this notion. Savelsbergh and colleagues (2002) demonstrated that expert soccer goalkeepers do indeed rely on the penalty taker's precues to determine ball direction in a penalty kick. Similar findings have been reported for tennis; highly skilled players were found to use anticipatory cues based on an opponent's movement pattern information to determine shot selection and respond more quickly (Shim, Carlton, Chow, & Chae, 2005). For a skill of your choice, list precues that increase the predictability of a certain response.

Foreperiod Consistency

The extent to which a learner is prepared to respond in a given situation can also influence response preparation time. The provision of a warning signal, for example, leads to significantly faster reaction times, as it alerts the performer to the approach of a stimulus (Brebner & Welford, 1980). The "set" command issued prior to the firing of the starting gun, the toss of the ball in the tennis serve, and the turn signal on a car all serve as warning signals. However, the mere presence of a warning signal is not enough for a performer to achieve and maintain optimal preparedness. Ideally, the interval of time that transpires between the presentation of the warning signal and the stimulus, called the foreperiod, should range from 1 to 4 seconds. Foreperiod durations that fall short of this range do not permit adequate time to prepare, while expectancy levels fall when foreperiod durations are too long.

The consistency of the foreperiod influences the performer's ability to capitalize on anticipation. When foreperiod lengths are constant or predictable, temporal anticipation becomes possible (Queseda & Schmidt, 1970). Provided that the response to the signal is predetermined, such as in a sprint or swimming start, reaction time will be significantly reduced. Good starters prevent this effect by continually varying the foreperiod length prior to firing the starting gun. Considerations of foreperiod consistency are not restricted solely to racing events. To avoid anticipation and quick responses from the defense, for example, a quarterback varies the snap count. Randomizing foreperiod length is, therefore, essential for preventing an opponent from gaining an advantage. Situations do exist where a constant foreperiod is desirable. Successful performance in music and the performing arts, for example, is highly dependent on temporal anticipation, as performers must be able to initiate their movements at a precise moment.

Psychological Refractory Period

If you have ever been faked out, you have experienced what happens when two stimuli, each of which requires a different response, are presented in succession within a short period of time. Those who haven't directly experienced this phenomenon have probably seen it occur. When a performer buys into a head fake to the right, for example, he will prepare and initiate the corresponding

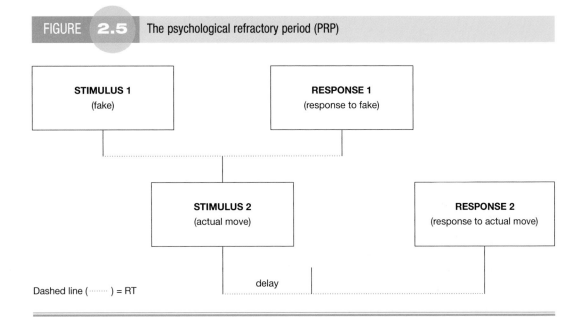

FIGURE 2.5 The psychological refractory period (PRP)

response; if his opponent then quickly moves in the other direction, there is a momentary delay in response to this second stimulus. This delay, known as the psychological refractory period (PRP), is reflected in an RT that is slower than the RT for the first stimulus (the head fake). Figure 2.5 illustrates the PRP.

A successful fake depends on two performance factors. First, it must be realistic. For example, when volleyball players want to draw a block in order to tip the ball around it, they have to execute a convincing spike approach, or the defense will read their actual intentions. Second, timing is critical. If the fake and the actual move are executed too closely in time, the opponent will not have enough time to buy into the fake and will ignore it. On the other hand, if the faker allows too much time to elapse between the fake and the actual move, the opponent will have enough time to respond effectively to both. This timing comes with practice.

Through practice, performers can learn how to read a fake, and they will be fooled less often. Focusing on an opponent's center of gravity, for example, provides clues as to the impending motion, because the center of gravity must be shifted in the desired direction of movement prior to a change in course.

Fakes clearly illustrate the psychological refractory period, but a performer who anticipates incorrectly also experiences a PRP. An excellent example is the batter who, having anticipated a fastball (because the pitcher was behind in

 FIGURE 2.6 Goalies experience delays due to the psychological refractory period when the ball or puck is deflected in front of the net

the count), suddenly realizes that the pitch is a change-up (Shea, Shebilske, & Worchel, 1993). Similarly, goalies often fall victim to PRP delays when a puck or ball is deflected in front of the net, as do players of tennis, table tennis, badminton, and volleyball when a ball's direction suddenly changes after clipping the net on the way over.

Stimulus–Response Compatibility

When a number of stimulus–response (S–R) choices are available, another factor that can affect movement preparation time is stimulus–response compatibility; this refers to the extent to which a stimulus and its required response are naturally related. When stimulus–response compatibility is low, additional time is needed to prepare a response, which is reflected in increased reaction times. A classic example involves the arrangement of stovetop burners and their controls. Traditionally, the burners are arranged in a rectangular pattern and the controls are positioned horizontally. The spatial discrepancy in arrangement creates confusion and results in response delays. A more compatible organization would be to arrange the knobs in the same pattern as their corresponding burners.

Novice sailors will typically experience a short incompatibility delay as they learn that, unlike a car where the steering wheel is turned in the direction of intended travel, the tiller must be moved in the opposite direction. Similarly, delays are common when first learning to back up a trailer; the steering wheel must be turned clockwise to make the trailer go counterclockwise. Fortunately, with practice, responses become more compatible and reaction times improve.

Aerobics instructors pay attention to S–R compatibility when conducting classes. Because of the imitative nature of an aerobics class, the instructor must remember to mirror each move. This means that, when facing the group, an instructor who wants participants to raise their right hands must raise her own left hand. Mirroring increases the compatibility of the stimulus–response choice and reduces response delays and incorrect movements, facilitating participants' ability to perform the routine.

Finally, equipment manufacturers in the therapeutic modality and fitness industries have paid attention to the issue of compatibility. Start and stop buttons on ultrasound machines and treadmills appear in the green and red colors that we are accustomed to. In addition, the buttons and switches used to manipulate intensity levels are often accompanied by + and – signs, to indicate *increase* and *decrease*, respectively.

CEREBRALchallenge   2.6

Suppose the federal government has issued a new law mandating that all brake lights will now be white in color. Explain the likely outcome (1) when the law first goes into effect and (2) one year later.

exploration ACTIVITY 2.4

Stroop Effect

To examine the interference that occurs in a reaction time task when the performer is given two conflicting signals, visit http://faculty.washington.edu/chudler/java/ready.html

Response Time Delays: Decision Making versus Movement Execution

Recall that response time is the combination of both reaction time and movement time (refer back to Figure 2.4). This is important because response delays may be the result of slow decision making, slow movement execution, or a combination of both. For example, in baseball, poor performance in hitting could be the result of slow bat speed or a delay in the performer's assessment of the situation and decision as to how to best respond. Consequently, practitioners need to be able to differentiate between moving slowly and initiating movement slowly in order to determine what course of action to take to improve performance. Slow movement initiation is symptomatic of poor movement preparation, indicating the need for more decision-making drills. If the hitter's bat speed is slow, on the other hand, improving swing mechanics and/or conditioning would be the goal. In other instances, response delays attributed to movement time can be decreased by reducing the length of the movement. This technique is used frequently in self-defense classes, where learners are taught not to cock back their arm fully prior to striking. In hockey, players use little or no backswing for shots in front of the net, in order to get the shot off as quickly as possible. Finally, increasing the distance between a player and his or her opponent can also improve response time. Tennis provides an excellent example of this strategy: the player will stand behind the baseline to receive the serve, allowing more time for both decision making and movement execution.

A performance variable that has recently received attention related to the decision making vs. movement execution distinction is agility. As we saw in Chapter 1, movements can be planned or reactive. Planned movements are characteristic of closed skills since the individual knows when and where they are going to move before doing so. Reactive movements, on the other hand, are associated with open skills, as they are dependent on processing situational information in order to decide how to respond. This is an important distinction as it influences player assessment and training prescription for athletes in many team sports. Bruce, Farrow, and Young (2004) noted that "despite the prevalence of reactive situations in team sport, a review of the typical tests of agility (e.g., the 505 test) reveals that they primarily involve planned situations where a player knows the required movement in advance" (p. 34). Ellis, Gastin, Lawrence, et al. (2000) and Sheppard and Young (2006) concurred, indicating that the majority of agility tests actually test change of direction speed. In response,

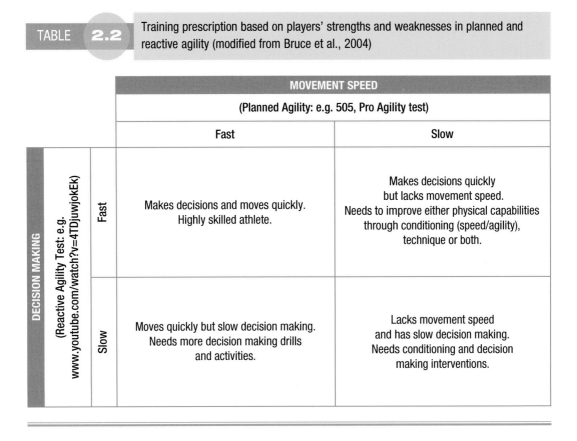

| TABLE 2.2 | Training prescription based on players' strengths and weaknesses in planned and reactive agility (modified from Bruce et al., 2004) |

			MOVEMENT SPEED	
			(Planned Agility: e.g. 505, Pro Agility test)	
			Fast	Slow
DECISION MAKING (Reactive Agility Test: e.g. www.youtube.com/watch?v=4TDjuwjokEk)		Fast	Makes decisions and moves quickly. Highly skilled athlete.	Makes decisions quickly but lacks movement speed. Needs to improve either physical capabilities through conditioning (speed/agility), technique or both.
		Slow	Moves quickly but slow decision making. Needs more decision making drills and activities.	Lacks movement speed and has slow decision making. Needs conditioning and decision making interventions.

Farrow, Young, and Bruce (2005) added a visual-perceptual component to a planned netball agility test and compared the performance of skilled and lesser-skilled players on both it and the original version. They found that the reactive agility test, which included a decision time component, better differentiated between highly skilled players and their lesser skilled counterparts, a finding that has since been replicated (see Young, Dawson, & Henry, 2015 for a review).

What does this mean for the practitioner? Planned (change of direction speed) and reactive tests assess different qualities of performance. Consequently, the development of an accurate situational profile (see Chapter 1) is important in order to select assessments that reflect the nature of the task and its information processing requirements. In addition, if the skill in question requires reactive decision making, Bruce et al. (2004) suggest that assessing both change of direction speed (planned agility) and reactive agility offers coaches valuable information for training prescription (see Table 2.2). Note that the diagnosis and corresponding prescriptions illustrated in Table 2.2 can be generalized to other interceptive and tactical skills, such as the hitting example provided earlier.

RESEARCH NOTES

Agility is a fundamental component of many team sports. More specifically, situations often arise that require quick maneuvers to evade opponents. Wheeler and Sayers (2010) were interested in how, if at all, skill execution is modified during reactive versus preplanned agility maneuvers. Eight elite male rugby players were divided into three speed categories based on their mean agility performance times. Video recordings were then obtained of each player running at maximal effort while carrying a ball through an agility course. Two conditions were examined. In the preplanned condition, before starting each trial players indicated which direction, right or left, they were going to run the course (after an approach). The second condition involved a decision-making element. In this condition, participants had to react to the movements of a defender who was introduced during the pre–change of direction phase of the movement and then run to the left or right accordingly to complete the course. Participants completed 12 trials for each condition, six to the left and six to the right. Condition and direction were randomized. Video analysis revealed that less lateral-movement speed toward the intended-direction change occurred during the reactive as compared to the preplanned condition. This was found to be associated with greater lateral foot displacement at the change-of-direction step. In addition, the side-step of faster performers was executed with greater lateral-movement speed at the change-in-direction step than their moderate- and slow-speed counterparts. These data highlight the need to incorporate sport-specific decision making in rugby agility training programs.

PUTTING IT INTO PRACTICE

Learning Situation: Learning the Indirect Pass in Hockey

Jennifer is a volunteer coach for a youth skill development hockey program. The program focuses on individual skill development that is designed to complement each player's team game and covers skating, stick-handling, shooting, puck protection, and many other dynamic hockey skills.

She is currently working with a group of Peewee players (ages 11–12) on the indirect pass, a skill introduced when they were Squirts (ages 9–10). The indirect pass is a pass made off the boards to an area where the receiver will be. When observing the players in a scrimmage, she noticed a poor success rate for indirect passes. She further assessed the players in both the receiving and passing role in an isolated drill and noted that performance was much better.

Test Your Knowledge

Before Jennifer can design activities to improve indirect pass performance, she needs to determine the underlying cause of the problem. Given what you have learned in this chapter, what variables should be considered that might be responsible for the poor indirect pass performance observed in a game situation? Compare your answer with the sample response provided at www.routledge.com/cw/coker.

A LOOK AHEAD

In this chapter, we have examined many variables that influence the time it takes to gather information and make a decision about what to do and how to do it before organizing and making an overt response. This discussion will continue in the next chapter, where we will examine how attention and visual search influence the decision-making process.

FOCUS POINTS

After reading this chapter, you should know:

- The process by which meaning is attached to sensory information is known as perception.
- Two prevailing theoretical approaches to perception are: the direct approach, in which the environment and task are perceived in terms of affordances, and the indirect approach, which is generally associated with information processing.
- A time lag occurs between the moment when a stimulus is presented and when a response is initiated. This interval of time is known as reaction time and is indicative of the time needed to prepare a response before it can be executed.
- Reaction time is not constant; it depends on the processing demands imposed by a given situation.
- Numerous variables influence the time needed to prepare a response, including the number of response choices available, temporal and/or event anticipation, the psychological refractory period, stimulus–response compatibility, and amount of practice.
- When response time delays are noted, practitioners must make a distinction between moving slowly and initiating movement slowly in order to determine which course of action to take for their correction.

lab

To complete the lab for this chapter, visit www.routledge.com/cw/coker and select **Lab 2, Hick's Law**.

REVIEW QUESTIONS

1.   Compare and contrast direct and indirect perception.

2.   What are affordances?

3.   What is the relationship between reaction time and movement preparation?

4.   Give an example of a situation where your goal would be to reduce response delays.

5.   Compare and contrast deception and disguise.

6.   In World War II, pilots were given a deck of cards that showed pictures of different enemy aircraft on each card. What might have been the purpose of these cards? Support your answer.

7.   Explain the cost–benefit trade-off associated with anticipation.

8.   You are driving along a road when a deer-crossing sign catches your eye. When you look back to the road, you notice the illuminated brake lights of the vehicle in front of you. A car is approaching in the opposite lane, and there is a ditch on your right.

     a.   What objects in this scenario served as warning signals?

     b.   List the relevant and irrelevant stimuli that might be available in this situation.

     c.   How is Hick's Law a factor in this situation?

     d.   Identify an example of stimulus–response compatibility in this situation.

     e.   The car in front of you swerves to the right. As you begin your response, it suddenly changes direction back to the left. What impact will this sudden change in direction have on your performance? Fully explain your answer.

     f.   Explain the 2-second safe-following-distance driving rule, based on what you have learned in this chapter.

REFERENCES

Brebner, J. T. & Welford, A. T. (1980). Introduction: An historical background sketch. In A. T. Welford (Ed.), *Reaction times* (pp. 1–23). New York: Academic Press.

Bruce, L., Farrow, D., & Young, W. (2004). Reactive agility—the forgotten aspect of testing and training agility in team sports. *Sports Coach*, 27(3), 34–35.

Burton, A. W. (1987). Confronting the interaction between perception and movement in adapted physical education. *Adapted Physical Education Quarterly*, 4, 257–267.

Ellis, L., Gastin, P., Lawrence, S., Savage, B., Buckeridge, A., Stapff, A., Tumilty, D., Quinn, A., Woolford, S., & Young, W. (2000). Protocols for the physiological assessment of team sports players. In C. J. Gore (Ed.), *Physiological tests for elite athletes* (pp. 128–144). Champaign, IL: Human Kinetics.

Fajen, B. R., Riley, M. A., & Turvey, M. T. (2009). Information, affordances, and the control of action in sport. *International Journal of Sport Psychology*, 40, 79–107.

Farrow, D., Young, W., & Bruce, L. (2005). The development of a test of reactive agility for netball: a new methodology. *Journal of Science & Medicine in Sport*, 8(1), 52–60.

Gibson, J. J. (1977). The theory of affordances. In R. Shaw & J. Bransford (Eds.), *Perceiving, acting and knowing: Toward an ecological psychology.* Hillsdale, NJ: Erlbaum.

Gibson, J. J. (1979). *The ecological approach to visual perception.* Boston, MA: Houghton Mifflin.

Hick, W. E. (1952). On the rate of gain of information. *Quarterly Journal of Experimental Psychology*, 4, 11–26.

Jackson, R. C., Warren, S., & Abernethy, B. (2006). Anticipation skill and susceptibility to deceptive movement. *Acta Psychologica*, 123(3), 355–371.

Larish, D. D. & Stelmach, G. E. (1982). Preprogramming, programming and reprogramming of aimed hand movements as a function of age. *Journal of Motor Behavior*, 14, 322–340.

Loffing, F. & Hagemann, N. (2014). On-court position influences skilled tennis players' anticipation of shot outcome. *Journal of Sport & Exercise Psychology*, 36(1), 14–26.

Longman, J. (2000). The Girls of Summer. *Women's Sports and Fitness*, July/August.

Mann, D. Y., Williams, A. M., Ward, P., & Janelle, C. M. (2007). Perceptual-cognitive expertise in sport: A meta-analysis. *Journal of Sport & Exercise Psychology*, 29(4), 457–478.

Müller, S. & Abernethy, B. (2012). Expert anticipatory skill in striking sports: A review and a model. *Research Quarterly For Exercise & Sport*, 83(2), 175–187.

Oudejans, R. D., Michaels, C. F., Bakker, F. C., & Dolné, M. A. (1996). The relevance of action in perceiving affordances: Perception of catchableness of fly balls. *Journal of Experimental Psychology: Human Perception and Performance*, 22(4), 879–891.

Overdorf, V. & Coker, C. A. (2011, February). Five Tips for Improving Anticipatory Skills. Paper presented at EDAAHPERD. Long Branch, NJ.

Passos, P., Araujo, D., Davids, K. W., & Shuttleworth, R. (2008). Manipulating constraints to train decision making in rugby union. *International Journal of Sports Science and Coaching*, 3(1), 125–140.

Queseda, D. C. & Schmidt, R. A. (1970). A test of Adam-Creamer decay hypothesis for the timing of motor responses. *Journal of Motor Behavior*, 2, 273–283.

Rowe, R., Horswill, M. S., Kronvall-Parkinson, M., Poulter, D. R., & McKenna, F. P. (2009). The effect of disguise on novice and expert tennis players' anticipation ability. *Journal of Applied Sport Psychology*, 21(2), 178–185.

Savelsbergh, G. J. P., Williams, A. M., van der Kamp, J., & Ward, P. (2002). Visual search, anticipation and expertise in soccer goalkeepers. *Journal of Sports Sciences*, 20, 279–287.

Shea, C. H., Shebilske, W. L., & Worchel, S. (1993). *Motor learning and control.* Englewood Cliffs, NJ: Prentice-Hall.

Sheppard, J. & Young, W. (2006). Agility literature review: Classifications, training and testing. *Journal of Sports Sciences*, 24(9), 919–932.

Shim, J., Carlton, L. G., Chow, J. W., & Chae, W. S. (2005). The use of anticipatory visual cues by highly skilled tennis players. *Journal of Motor Behavior*, 37, 164–175.

Southard, D. (2011). Attentional focus and control parameter: Effect on throwing pattern and performance. *Research Quarterly for Exercise and Sport*, 82, 652–666.

Summers, J. J. (1988). Has ecological psychology delivered what it promised? In J. P. Piek (Ed.), *Motor behavior and human skill: A multi-*

disciplinary approach (pp. 385–402). Champaign, IL: Human Kinetics.

Totsika, V. & Wulf, G. (2003). The influence of external and internal foci of attention on transfer to novel situations and skills. *Research Quarterly for Exercise and Sport, 74*, 220–225.

Wheeler, K. W. & Sayers, M. G. L. (2010). Modification of agility running technique in reaction to a defender in rugby union. *Journal of Sports Science and Medicine, 9*, 445–451.

Wright, M. J. & Jackson, R. C. (2014). Deceptive body movements reverse spatial cueing in soccer. *PLoS ONE, 9*(8), e104290. http://doi.org/10.1371/journal.pone.0104290

Young, W. B., Dawson, B., & Henry, G. J. (2015). Agility and change-of-direction speed are independent skills: Implications for training for agility in invasion sports. *International Journal of Sports Science & Coaching, 10*(1), 159–169.

The Role of Attention, Arousal, and Visual Search in Movement Preparation

3

Aaron is getting frustrated. He has been going to rehab to improve hand function following an accident. To help restore fine motor control, his occupational therapist has tasked him with reproducing the pattern on a card by fitting plastic pegs into holes on a pegboard. She has given him two cues to focus on while executing the movement, but he is having a hard time concentrating because of the background noise in the clinic and the effort needed to move the peg into position.

ATTENTIONAL CAPACITY

As was illustrated in the opening scenario, an individual can only pay attention to or process a limited number of activities at any given time. When this limit is exceeded, a competition for attentional resources occurs, the consequences of which may include a reduction in the speed or quality of the performance of one or more activities or even a complete disregard for one of the activities. In other words, according to this notion of limited attentional capacity, multiple tasks can be successfully performed simultaneously provided that, when combined, they do not exceed the attentional resources available (Kahneman, 1973; Wickens, 1984). For example, if walking on a treadmill requires 25 percent of the total available attentional space and reading a magazine requires 50 percent, the combined total of 75 percent falls within the amount available, and the performer can successfully execute both tasks (Figure 3.1a). Suppose that another task is introduced, such as watching a news report on the TV across from the treadmill; this, combined with walking on the treadmill and reading a magazine, could require more attentional space than is available. In this situation, interference occurs; either the level of performance on one or more tasks declines, or one task may be totally ignored (Figure 3.1b). For an example of what can happen when attentional capacity is exceeded, watch the video at the adjoining link.

FIGURE 3.1   Representation of attentional demands on available attentional resources

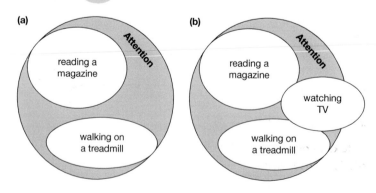

(a)

(b)

In (a), the two tasks can be performed simultaneously, as they do not exceed the attentional capacity.

In (b), the combination of these three tasks requires more attentional space than is available. The level of performance on one or more tasks will decline, or a task may be ignored.

Factors Influencing Attentional Demands

Complicating the issue of limited attentional capacity is the fact that the attentional demands of a given task and their effects on performers are not constant. Practitioners should be aware that environmental, task, and learner characteristics all influence the attentional demands placed on performers. These characteristics have important implications with regard to designing instructional experiences.

EXCEEDING ATTENTIONAL CAPACITY

www.youtube.com/watch?v=wl0Joj
WH1rQ

RESEARCH NOTES

On any given day, as you make your way to work or school, you probably notice drivers engaging in activities that can divert their attention from driving. One such activity is cell phone use. Wanting to gain a clearer understanding of the effects of talking on a cell phone while driving, Strayer, Drews, and Crouch (2006) conducted a study to compare the driving performance of a cell phone–using driver to that of a drunk driver. The study was conducted in a controlled laboratory setting using a driving simulator. Using a car-following paradigm in which participants drove on a multi-lane freeway following a pace car that would randomly brake, the experiment looked at variables such as driving speed, following distance, time to collision, and braking time. The results indicated that drivers using cell phones, regardless of whether they were talking on a handheld or hands-free phone, exhibited delayed braking reactions and were involved in more traffic accidents than when they were not on the phone. The drivers who were intoxicated, on the other hand, were more aggressive in their driving, followed the vehicle in front of them more closely, and applied more force when braking. The authors of the study concluded that the impairments resulting from cell phone use while driving are as profound as those associated with drunk driving.

Another study, conducted by Drews, Yazdani, Godfrey, Cooper, and Strayer (2009), examined the impact of text messaging on simulated driving performance. Forty young adults (ages 19–23) performed two tasks: driving only (single task) and driving and text messaging (dual task). Similar to the methodology employed in the previous study, participants were instructed to follow a pace car that would randomly brake. Results of driving performance revealed that participants in the driving and texting condition were significantly slower to respond to the sudden illumination of the pace car's brake lights, substantially increased their lead-car following distance, had a higher frequency of inadvertent lane departures and lateral lane movements, and were involved in more collisions than those in the driving-only condition. These findings indicate a substantial crash risk when texting and driving; according to the authors, this risk exceeds that of talking on one's cell phone while driving.

To experience the influence of texting on your reaction time, try the activity at www.nytimes.com/interactive/2009/07/19/technology/20090719-driving-game.html?_r=2&

Environment and Task Complexity

As the environment or task increases in complexity, the attentional demands will undergo a corresponding increase, reducing the amount of attentional space available for additional tasks. For instance, sufficient processing space appeared to be available in the example of reading a magazine while walking on a treadmill. However, these same two tasks would likely interfere with one another if, rather than a treadmill, the performer were walking on a crowded sidewalk. Practitioners may want to decrease the complexity of the environment or task so that attentional limits will not be exceeded, enabling learners to allocate the necessary attentional resources toward the task being learned. Placing Aaron in a distraction-free setting, for example, would help him concentrate on the task at hand. Likewise, an optimal environment for a first-time driver would be a large, empty parking lot instead of a city street during rush hour. Similarly, by removing defenders when individuals are learning skills such as layups, dribbling, and offensive plays, a basketball coach can ensure that attentional capacity is not likely to be exceeded.

Clinicians should also consider attentional capacity when prescribing assistive devices for functional deficits. For example, research has shown that the attentional demands on an individual can vary according to the type of mobility aid being used and the patient's familiarity with that aid (O'Sullivan, 1988). While both a standard pick-up walker and a rolling walker require the allocation of attention during use, a rolling walker has been found to be less attention demanding.

CEREBRALchallenge   3.1

1. Observe an individual performing a closed skill and another individual performing an open skill. Describe your observations. How do the attentional demands differ for the two performers?
2. For teaching a skill of your choice, explain how you might design the instructional environment in order to reduce the attentional demands imposed on the learner.

Skill Level of Performer

Beginners, characteristically, have difficulty attending to more than one task at a time when learning a new skill. Remember your juggling experience from Chapter 1? Imagine having to carry on a conversation while you were attempting to juggle. You probably needed all your attentional resources to focus on the task at hand. The addition of a conversation would have overloaded your attentional space, and the two tasks would have interfered with one another. A skilled circus performer, on the other hand, can not only juggle and carry on a conversation but can do so while riding a unicycle. When teaching beginners new skills, be sure that they have had sufficient practice on the first task before you teach them additional tasks. Also, highly complex skills with many components are often overwhelming for beginners. Breaking such skills into parts for initial practice may facilitate learning. This strategy will be discussed further in Chapter 9.

Numbers of Cues

Attentional limitations are exceeded when a performer tries to think about too many things when learning or refining a motor skill. This can be remedied with a few simple teaching strategies. First, when teaching a new skill, focus on only a small number of meaningful cues. Recognizing Aaron's frustration and difficulty performing the pegboard task, the occupational therapist should reduce the number of cues and focus his/her attention on only one thing at a time until he becomes more proficient with the movement. Second, when correcting performance by providing feedback, avoid overloading the learner with information. Again, provide only one or two cues for the learner to think about. Finally, most performance situations present an abundance of information. Some of this information is relevant or useful to the task at hand (relevant cues), and some is not (irrelevant cues). Teaching learners to attend selectively to relevant cues and ignore irrelevant ones will reduce the competition for attentional space.

RESEARCH NOTES

Using the volleyball set, Sibley and Etnier (2004) examined the effect of decision making on attention demands and task performance. Twenty intermediate volleyball players participated in the study, which employed a dual-task paradigm in which participants completed a primary and secondary task both individually and simultaneously.

The primary task in this investigation was the volleyball set, received from an underhand toss. Set direction was dictated by ball color, with a blue-and-white striped ball indicating a back set and a white ball indicating a front set. Sets were scored according to their accuracy in dropping through a hoop that was placed parallel to the ground, 12 feet from the participant and at net height. A point value of 3 was assigned if the ball went through the hoop, 2 if it hit the hoop, 1 if it missed within one ball diameter (near misses), or 0 if it missed completely.

The secondary task required participants to respond to an auditory tone by yelling "ball" as fast as possible. Reaction time was measured from the time the tone was sounded until the participant's first auditory response. To examine attentional demands at various points in the ball's flight, tones were sounded: (1) as the ball was tossed, (2) just before the tossed ball reached its peak, (3) just after the tossed ball reached its peak, and (4) just before the participant made contact with the ball. Catch trials were also administered where no tone was given, in order to eliminate anticipation.

continued

All participants were given time to warm up and practice setting to the targets. Baseline measures for both the primary and secondary tasks were then obtained. Following a 5-minute rest period, the two tasks were performed simultaneously in one block of 20 front sets, one block of 20 back sets, and two blocks of 20 choice sets. Four tones at each of the four points of the ball's flight (probe positions) and four catch trials were administered randomly within each block of 20. Blocks were presented in random order.

Results indicated that attentional demand was higher on the choice sets at the first two probe positions, suggesting that "choosing the direction to set the ball and preprogramming the motor portion of the task affected attention during the first half of the ball's flight" (Sibley & Etnier, 2004, p. 105). In addition, when participants were forced to choose set direction, a small but significant decrease in setting performance was found. Results also revealed an increase in attentional demand for the first and last portions of ball flight and a lowered attentional demand mid-flight. This is consistent with the literature, in that visual selective attention is thought to be required to gather information on flight characteristics during the initial portion of a ball's flight in order to intercept it, while visual tracking does not appear to be necessary during the middle phase. As the participant prepares to contact and then does contact the ball, greater attention is likely required in order to process proprioceptive information and make necessary positioning adjustments during contact.

AROUSAL

A critical factor that influences an individual's available attentional resources at any given time is arousal (Kahneman, 1973). Arousal is "a general physiological and psychological activation of the organism that varies on a continuum from deep sleep to intense excitement" (Gould & Krane, 1992, pp. 120–121). It should not be confused with anxiety, which is an emotion result-

COMMON MYTH

The higher the level of arousal, the better the performance.

ing from an individual's perception of a situation as threatening—although changes in anxiety levels do lead to changes in arousal levels. While performance is influenced by level of arousal, it is not as simple as the common myth implies.

Relationship between Arousal and Performance

The relationship between arousal and performance is captured by the inverted-U principle, also known as the Yerkes–Dodson Law (1908). According to this principle, illustrated in Figure 3.2, there is an optimal level of arousal for peak performance.

That optimal level is not a constant, however; it depends on both task and performer characteristics. As a task increases in complexity—due to increased fine motor control, decision making, and attentional requirements—lower levels

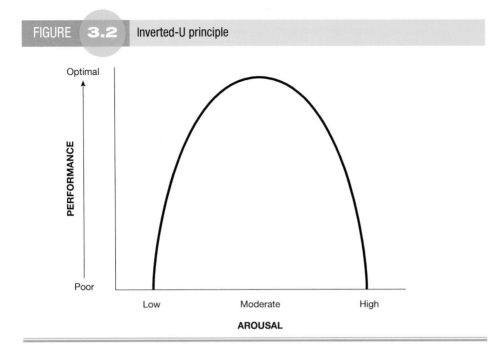

FIGURE 3.2   Inverted-U principle

of arousal will be optimal. On the other hand, higher arousal levels are appropriate for tasks involving gross movements, minimal decision making, and low attentional demands. In other words, the level of arousal for optimal performance is quite different when conducting a delicate surgical procedure versus executing a power clean. Watch the first 3 minutes of the video on the website listed on the right, paying close attention to the answer given at 2:05 minutes to see how a low level of arousal is critical for optimal performance in rock climbing.

www

INTERVIEW WITH FREE SOLO CLIMBER ALEX HONNOLD FROM "60 MINUTES"

www.youtube.com/watch?v=SR1j
   wwagtaQ

A second factor is the performer. Individual differences exist with respect to arousal and anxiety. The natural arousal level for one individual may be significantly higher than that of another individual (known as trait anxiety, an individual's propensity to perceive situations as threatening or nonthreatening). In addition, if an individual perceives a situation as threatening (e.g., possible performance failure), given the relationship between arousal and anxiety mentioned earlier, the person's arousal level will rise. These factors—a naturally high level of arousal and perception of the situation as threatening—combine to make an individual more susceptible to exceeding an optimal level of arousal.

Arousal and Movement Preparation

The cue utilization hypothesis (Easterbrook, 1959) provides an explanation for the relationship between arousal and performance. According to this hypothesis,

FIGURE **3.3**

A higher arousal level is optimal for peak performance of a power clean

changes in attentional focus occur according to arousal levels (Figure 3.4). Under low arousal conditions, a performer's attentional focus is relatively broad. If attentional focus becomes too broad, both task-relevant and -irrelevant cues become available to the performer. Because of our limited attentional capacity, as we saw earlier, a competition for attentional resources will occur, resulting in response delays and a corresponding decrement in performance. In other words, performers are more likely to become distracted by irrelevant environmental cues such as a taunting fan, the actions of players on the sideline, or even the appearance of the playing facility; the consequence will be failure to attend to relevant performance information, such as a shift in the opponent's defensive formation (Wrisberg, 2007).

As arousal approaches optimal levels, attentional focus narrows, enabling the performer to concentrate on task-relevant cues while ignoring irrelevant ones. These are the conditions necessary for quick and accurate decision making; the individual is considered to be in the zone of optimal functioning (Hanin, 1980), the range of arousal levels that leads to optimal performance. As arousal continues to increase, perceptual narrowing—the narrowing of attentional focus with increasing levels of arousal—continues, and at some point

FIGURE **3.4** Relationship between level of arousal and attentional focus

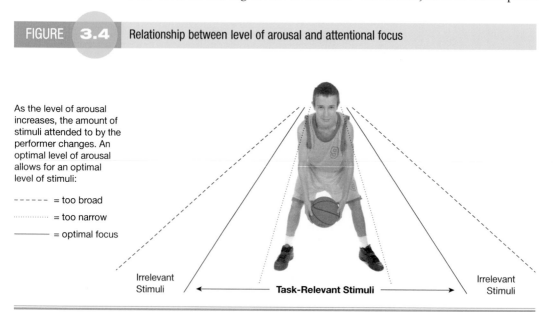

As the level of arousal increases, the amount of stimuli attended to by the performer changes. An optimal level of arousal allows for an optimal level of stimuli:

- - - - - - = too broad

.... = too narrow

———— = optimal focus

Irrelevant Stimuli

← Task-Relevant Stimuli →

Irrelevant Stimuli

attentional focus becomes so narrow that the performer may no longer be capable of effectively scanning the environment. This could lead to potentially significant stimuli being left undetected. This phenomenon is frequently seen in the opening minutes of a major championship. Players might become over aroused, and their attentional focus becomes so narrow that they are not able to detect the cues needed for appropriate decision making. Fans are then baffled, for example, by how a quarterback fails to spot a wide-open receiver.

Perceptual narrowing has greater implications than simply missing a scoring opportunity. For lifeguards, medical personnel, firefighters, police officers, air traffic controllers, and military personnel, learning to control arousal levels is paramount.

CEREBRALchallenge 3.2

1. The focus of a performer whose arousal levels are too low may become too broad. As a result, s/he will direct some attention to irrelevant stimuli. One example of such irrelevant stimuli is a heckler in the stands. From your own experience, list other examples of irrelevant stimuli that might attract the attention of an individual with low arousal and affect overall performance.
2. An emergency room physician who is overly excited may experience perceptual narrowing to the degree that s/he becomes susceptible to making poor decisions. Give specific examples of other professions or situations that may lend themselves to perceptual narrowing and resultant poor decision making. Fully explain your answer.

CEREBRALchallenge 3.3

Are team pep talks before a game beneficial for performance? Fully explain your answer.

Practical Implications

Numerous techniques are available to assist students, athletes, clients, and patients in managing their arousal levels. Strategies to increase arousal include increasing the rhythm and rate of breathing, listening to upbeat music prior to play, and increasing physical activity. Practice and rehabilitation sessions should be designed to include a wide variety of activities to keep learners motivated (Martens, 2004).

To decrease arousal, encourage slow and controlled breathing, progressive muscular relaxation (which involves alternately contracting and relaxing various muscle groups), positive self-talk (where negative thoughts are replaced with constructive ones), visualization, and focusing on performance rather than outcome. For a more comprehensive review, see Weinberg and Gould (2015).

SELECTIVE ATTENTION

As stated earlier, the performance environment is teeming with information, some of it relevant and some irrelevant to the impending response. Because attentional capacity appears to be limited, successful performance depends on the performer's ability to attend to meaningful information. Fortunately, we have the capacity to do this through selective attention.

The classic example that demonstrates our ability to attend to or focus on one specific item in the midst of countless stimuli is what is known as the *cocktail party phenomenon* (Cherry, 1953). Let's say that you are at a large tailgate party in the midst of many other tailgate parties. Although countless conversations are taking place around you, you are able to attend selectively to the conversation in which you are engaged. Of further interest is the fact that if you hear your name mentioned in another conversation, this will divert your attention to the individual who said your name. For another example of selective attention, try Exploration Activity 3.1.

exploration ACTIVITY 3.1

Selective Attention

Read the bold print in the following paragraph:

Somewhere **among** hidden **the** in **most** the **spectacular** Rocky Mountains **cognitive** near **abilities** Central City **is** Colorado **the** an **ability** old **to** miner **select** hid **one** a **message** box **from** of **another**. gold. **We** Although **do** several **this** hundred **by** people **focusing** have **our** looked **attention** for **on** it, **certain** they **cues** have **such** not **as** found **type** it **style**.

What conclusions can you draw regarding selective attention? Include what you remembered about the regularly printed text in your response.

From www.mtsu.edu/~sschmidt/Cognitive/attention/
attention.html#Broadbent

Directing Attentional Focus: Attentional Styles

The process of selectively attending to or concentrating on specific environmental information is known as attentional focus. Nideffer (1993) initially identified two intersecting dimensions of attentional focus: width and direction. *Width* refers to the amount of information and size of the perceptual field to which a performer attends (Roberts, Spink, & Pemberton, 1999). It ranges from a broad focus, in which the performer attends to a large quantity of information, to a narrow focus, in which attention is directed to only one or two cues. An Ultimate Frisbee player needs a broad focus to scan the field for an open teammate; once

FIGURE 3.5 Four attentional styles based on the interaction of two dimensions: direction (internal to external) and width (broad to narrow)

EXTERNAL

Broad External

Used to **assess** the external environment/ situation, e.g., a bicycle courier maneuvering in traffic

Narrow External

Used to focus exclusively on one or two external cues to **perform** the motor response, e.g., a volleyball player executing a set

BROAD ←——————————————————→ NARROW

Broad Internal

Used to **analyze** and **plan** strategy or the impending motor response, e.g., a billiards player taking a shot

Narrow Internal

Used to monitor internal cues and mentally **rehearse** an upcoming performance, e.g., a high jumper visualizing her performance prior to performance

INTERNAL

one is located, the passer must focus his or her attention on that individual (narrow focus) to execute the pass (Roberts et al., 1999). The other dimension, *direction*, may be either external or internal. When adopting an external focus, the performer attends to information in the environment, such as the opponent, or to movement effects, such as motion of a golf club. When a performer focuses on his/her thoughts, body movements that create the effect (such as the arm motion in the golf swing), or internal cues, he/she has adopted an internal focus. As Figure 3.5 shows, width and direction interact to create four types or styles of attentional focus: broad–external, broad–internal, narrow–external, and narrow–internal.

Different performance situations place different attentional demands on the performer. Success is often contingent on the performer's ability to employ the appropriate attentional focus for a given situation. For instance, situations requiring proficient environmental awareness and assessment, such as a bicycle courier maneuvering through New York City traffic, necessitate the use of a broad–external attentional focus. On the other hand, employing a broad–internal focus is necessary in situations where strategic analysis is required, such as when a billiards player plans the next shot. Mentally rehearsing the impending action, such as visualizing one's performance in the high jump prior to actually performing it, requires a narrow–internal focus; a volleyball player executing a set is an example of a narrow–external focus.

It is important to understand that many situations require performers to shift their attentional focus continually throughout the performance. For example, a soccer player performing a penalty kick will likely use all four attentional focus styles. She must assess the environment (goalie position, wind, etc.) through a broad–external focus. Once she has gathered this information, her focus shifts to broad–internal as she decides what shot to take. A narrow–internal focus is necessary as she mentally rehearses the shot to be executed. During its execution, she adopts a narrow–external focus (Nideffer & Sagal, 2001).

The example just given may seem to indicate that attentional switching follows a certain pattern or sequence, but this assumption is inaccurate. In the performance of open skills, for example, performers must be able to shift their attentional focus quickly and accurately according to the demands of the situation. If, rather than making a penalty kick, the soccer player was executing a pass and a defender suddenly appeared in the vicinity of her open teammate, she would have to revert quickly from a narrow–external to a broad–external focus.

Practical Implications

Performers who know where, when, and how to focus their attention are able to disregard irrelevant information that would cause response delays. Practitioners should not assume that learners will inherently be able to do this (Wilson, Peper, & Schmid, 2001). By teaching them to recognize the attentional demands of their sport or movement, as well as by providing ample practice opportunities, practitioners can help learners sharpen their attentional switching skills.

Practitioners should also be aware that they can inadvertently cause learners to shift their attentional focus in the wrong direction (Ziegler, 2002). For example, a physical therapist might tell a patient who is undergoing gait training to learn to walk with a new prosthesis: "Don't think about falling." The thought of falling has now been planted in the patient's mind, changing his attentional style from the desired narrow–external focus to a narrow–internal one, which will likely disrupt performance (Ziegler, 2002). Similarly, a coach who tells a hurdler not to worry about hitting the hurdles will trigger a disruptive attentional response. Binsch, Oudejans, Bakker, and Savelsbergh (2010) examined this phenomenon by tracking the gaze behavior of competitive soccer players during the execution of a stationary penalty kick when instructed to either shoot as accurately as possible, shoot as accurately as possible being careful not to shoot within reach of the keeper, or shoot as accurately as possible being careful to shoot into the open space. They found that when trying not to kick the ball within reach of the goalkeeper, 44 percent of players showed ironic effects (Wegner, 1994) whereby the action that they were trying to avoid was actually carried out. In addition, significantly shorter final fixations on the open goal (actual target) were noted either because the kicker "disengaged their gaze from the keeper [the to-be-avoided area] later, that is, closer to kicking the ball, or because they showed an extra fixation on the keeper prior to kicking the ball" (Binsch et al., 2010, p. 287). To maximize performance, practitioners should therefore be careful to use language that elicits positive attentional responses rather than directing attention to what the learner should not do.

RESEARCH NOTES

Woodman, Barlow, and Gorgulu (2015) conducted two experiments to examine ironic effects while anxious. In the first experiment, 40 university hockey players performed a shooting task under both low and high anxiety conditions. Prior to the task players were informed that they would get 1 point for hitting the target zone, no points for hitting outside the target zone, and that they would lose a point if they hit to the right of the target zone. Specifically they were told: "Try to hit the target zone. Be particularly careful not to hit the ball to the right of the right-hand post, as you will score minus 1 point each time you do." (Woodman et al., 2015, p. 215). Results revealed that when anxious, players hit significantly more shots in the "to be avoided" zone and significantly fewer shots in the target zone. In experiment two, a dart-throwing task was used to not only examine the incidence of ironic effects but the precision of those errors. Once again, a designated zone was identified as to be avoided and the following instruction provided: "Please try to hit the target zone, or as close to the target zone as possible, in order to gain maximal points but be particularly careful not to hit the [top right quarter] of the dart board, as you will score zero points each time you do" (p. 218). Results supported those of experiment one in that anxiety led to greater ironic errors and also revealed that dart strikes were not only significantly farther from the target zone but also significantly farther into the ironic error zone.

Dr. Woodman discusses ironic effects and shows an example of an experimental design at www.youtube.com/watch?v=l8tE0nvn_Pk.

In other instances, it may be advantageous to disrupt attentional focus. A coach may call time out before an opponent's free throw or pivotal field goal attempt in the hopes of creating a distraction that will negatively influence performance (Ziegler, 2002). Or fans will try to disrupt an opponent's attentional focus by yelling, heckling, waving, and calling out players' names.

Attentional Focus and Instruction

Where should learners focus their attention when learning and practicing a skill? A growing body of evidence calls into question the common practice of instructing learners to focus their conscious attention on their own body movements. Numerous studies have consistently demonstrated that adopting an internal attentional focus can have a degrading effect on skill acquisition (see Wulf, 2013, for a review). Instead, studies indicate that when instructions induce an external focus, whereby the learners' attention is directed to the effects of their movements, learning and performance are enhanced. Advantages of adopting an external focus of attention have been demonstrated for both

CEREBRALchallenge   3.4

1. Describe the attentional shifts that would be required to perform the following successfully:

    a. Maneuvering through a restaurant in a wheelchair
    b. Cooking using a new recipe

2. On your next trip to the grocery store, notice the attentional shifts that occur from the time you enter the store to the time you leave the parking lot. Describe them.

movement effectiveness and movement efficiency across a variety of skills including pitch shots in golf (Wulf, Lauterbach, & Toole, 1999; Wulf & Su, 2007), dart throwing (Marchant, Clough, Cranshaw, & Levy, 2009; Sherwood, Lohse, & Healy, 2014), basketball free throws (Zachry, Wulf, Mercer, & Bezodis, 2005; Perreault & French, 2016), rowing (Schücker, Jedamski, Hagemann, & Vater, 2015), running/sprinting (e.g., Porter, Wu, Crossley, Knopp, & Campbell, 2015), standing long jump (e.g., Porter, Anton, Wikoff, & Ostrowski, 2013), tennis stroke (Wulf, Mc-Nevin, Fuchs, Ritter, & Toole, 2000), throwing (Southard, 2011), vertical jump (Wulf, Dufek, Lozano, & Pettigrew, 2010), volleyball serves and soccer passes (Wulf, McConnel, Gãrtner, & Schwarz, 2002), and a number of balance tasks (e.g., Totsika & Wulf, 2003; Wulf & McNevin, 2003; Landers, Wulf, Wallmann, & Guadagnoli, 2005).

These findings imply that the wording of instructions and feedback can influence motor skill acquisition and performance (Lohse, Wulf, & Lewthwaite, 2012). For example, if a physical therapist is working with a patient on elbow extension in a reach-to-grasp movement, instructions to "reach closer toward the cup" on the next attempt rather than saying "straighten your elbow as you reach" may better elicit the desired behavior (Durham, Van Vliet, Badger, & Sackley, 2009). Attentional focus and instruction will be discussed in more detail in Chapter 8.

Directing Attentional Focus: Visual Search

Skilled decision making and anticipation are dependent on the learner's attunement to affordances or awareness of relevant informational variables in the environment. Successful performance therefore depends on the visual search strategies or gaze behavior the performer employs to scan the environment to locate critical regulatory cues. During this active scan, our gaze may land on numerous objects; this is known as *gaze fixation*. By observing the characteristics of those fixations, such as their order, location, and duration, we can infer how and to what information the performer attends (Kluka, 1999). You can experience visual search in Exploration Activity 3.2.

exploration ACTIVITY   3.2

Visual Search

Find the letter B in the following diagrams.

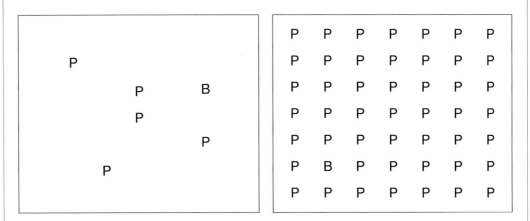

From http://psychology.wikia.com/wiki/Visual_search, contributed by Dr. Joe Kiff (licensed under the Creative Commons Attribution-Share Alike License).

QUESTIONS

1. What strategy did you use to complete the task?
2. What features in the box on the right made the task more difficult?
3. How might this relate to visual search in movement activities?

Additional visual search activities are available at
www.youtube.com/watch?v=XreVWeMdYk0
&feature=youtu.be and at www.psytoolkit.org/lessons/experiment_visualsearch.html.

Quiet Eye

One variable in particular, called the *quiet eye* (Vickers, 1996), has enhanced our understanding of how performers use vision to control their movements. The quiet eye is defined as the final fixation located on a specific target or object before the initiation of movement. Research has shown that the quiet eye of elite performers is significantly longer, has an earlier onset, and is of more optimal duration for the task at hand relative to that of near-elite or lower-skilled performers (for reviews see Rienhoff, Tirp, Strauß, Baker, & Schorer, 2016 and Vickers, 2016). This means that higher-level performers are able to see critical regulatory cues sooner, and they have more time to process the information.

Targeting Skills

Targeting skills typically involve accurately propelling an object toward a target (Vickers, 2007). Examples include archery, rifle shooting, putting a golf ball, a basketball free throw, serving a volleyball, and throwing or kicking a ball to a receiver. According to Vickers (2007), targets may be fixed, abstract, or moving, and they present different gaze-control constraints.

Fixed targets, such as a basketball hoop, are stable and predictable in position and require a performer to fixate on a specific location prior to executing a response. An example of an abstract targeting task is the golf putt. In putting, the performer must account for the slope of the green when aiming. Although the target itself (the hole) is fixed in space, the optimal aiming location is more difficult to detect. The final category, moving target tasks, requires the performer to anticipate the target's impending location. Examples include passing or kicking an object to a receiver or attempting to strike an opponent in elusive sports such as fencing, boxing, and martial arts (Vickers, 2007).

Researchers have found systematic differences in visual search behavior for targeting tasks between skilled performers and their less-skilled counterparts. (For a review of the quiet eye specific to targeting skills see Vine, Moore, & Wilson, 2012.) In basketball, for example, not only did expert shooters turn their head toward the basket sooner, but they had longer fixations on the target (hoop region) than did novices (Ripoll, Bard, & Paillard, 1986). Vickers (1996) further noted that the duration of final fixation prior to the initiation of the free throw was significantly longer for experts.

Similar findings have been demonstrated in abstract targeting tasks. Quiet eye durations were found to be longer for expert pool players, who fixated on the cue and the target ball longer than novices did (Williams et al., 2002). In putting, high-skilled golfers were found to fixate for a longer duration on the hole, had a more precise scan path, and displayed longer quiet eye durations than lower-skilled putters (Vickers, 1992). In addition, the less-skilled putters often tracked the movement of the club head on the backswing, whereas the high-skilled golfers maintained their gaze on the top or back of the ball. To see the differences in quiet eye during good and bad putts watch the video at www.youtube.com/watch?v=WVPrzxffcsQ. The quiet eye during free throw performance can be viewed at www.youtube.com/watch?v=voi00-xDiJw.

Interceptive Skills

Interceptive skills are complex in nature, as they require the performer to track a moving stimulus, decide when and/or where the stimulus will arrive, and determine and execute the appropriate limb movement to intercept it. Examples are skills involving striking, catching, creating or avoiding a collision, and landing. In other instances, such as a volleyball spike that is going out of bounds or a ball that is outside of the strike zone, the ability to inhibit the response to intercept is equally important for successful performance (Müller & Abernethy, 2012).

One variable critical to successful performance of interceptive skills is the prediction of time to contact. Time-to-contact information is determined via a single optic variable, tau, which is determined by taking the size of the retina image at any position of an object's approach and dividing it by the rate of change of the image (Lee, 1976, 1980). As an object approaches, its retinal image enlarges. The rate at which this enlargement occurs is directly related to the speed of the object's approach and is, therefore, indicative of time to contact. In other words, the faster the enlargement occurs, the faster the object is approaching.

A question of interest in interceptive skills is whether the performer must visually track a moving object until contact. Several studies indicate that continuous tracking before contact is unlikely. For example, Bahill and La Ritz (1984) studied skilled baseball hitters tracking a pitch. Their findings suggested that the athletes did not "keep their eyes on the ball" until contact and that they were unable to track the ball closer than 5 feet from home plate. Vickers and Adolphe (1997) also found that elite and near-elite volleyball players tracked the ball until contact during the forearm pass on only 7 percent (elite) to 8 percent (near-elite) of trials, respectively. The researchers concluded that although tracking to contact was possible, it was not favored. The more prevalent response during ball reception and passing was to leave one's gaze in front. For elite table tennis players, Ripoll and Fleurance (1988) also found that players did not track the ball throughout its entire trajectory. In another example, Land and McLeod (2000) demonstrated that cricket batters tracked the ball for the initial 100 to 200 ms and then quickly moved their eyes to the point where they anticipated that the ball would bounce on the ground. These anticipatory saccades, where a performer's gaze jumps to an anticipated location, have also been reported in baseball (Bahill & La Ritz, 1984), cricket (Mann, Spratford, & Abernethy, 2013), table tennis (Ripoll, Fleurance, & Cazeneuve, 1987; Rodrigues, Vickers, & Williams, 2002), and catching a self-tossed wall-bounced ball (Mennie, Hayhoe, Stupak, & Sullivan, 2005).

WWW

VISUAL TRACKING IN BASEBALL

www.sciencedaily.com/releases/2006/
04/060411223044.htm

Vickers (2016) suggests that pursuit tracking differs according to the predictability of an object's flight. When anticipatory judgments can be made by extracting task-relevant information from an opponent's preparatory actions, for example, continuous tracking does not appear to be necessary. However, marked differences exist between expert and novice performers in knowing where to look to detect these relevant indicators and when. For example, when waiting to receive a serve, beginning tennis players spend more time looking at the region around the server's head than do experts (Singer, Cauraugh, Chen, et al., 1994). Shank and Haywood (1987) found that expert hitters fixated on a pitcher's release point, whereas novices tended to move their eyes before the release of the ball, alternating their fixations between the release point and the pitcher's head; this resulted in poorer pitch identification. In badminton and squash, Abernethy (1991) found that experts were better than novices at using earlier-occurring cues from the opponent's arm to predict the speed and direction of the forthcoming shot. Also examining expert-novice differences in badminton Alder, Ford, Causer, and Williams (2014) found that expert players fixated on movement kinematics more frequently and for a longer duration enabling them to better differentiate between serve types compared to novices. In soccer, as a kicker approached the ball, the focus of experienced goalkeepers progressed from the kicker's head to the non-kicking foot, to the kicking foot, and finally to the ball, whereas novice goalkeepers focused more on the kicker's trunk, arms, and hips (Savelsbergh, Williams, van der Kamp, & Ward, 2002). Finally, while viewing a setter receive a pass then set it either forwards or backwards, elite volleyball players' were found to perform fewer visual fixations of greater duration, shifting their gaze from the initial trajectory of the pass to the hands of the setter, and ignoring ball flight. Novices, on the other hand, tracked the ball both before and after the setter redirected it (Piras, Lobietti, & Squatrito, 2010). The researchers concluded that their findings support the contention that experts are more proficient in extracting task-relevant information from each fixation than their less skilled counterparts, a conclusion supported by Piras, Lobietti, and Squatrito (2014) in a follow-up study.

Tactical Skills

Tactical skills require quick and accurate situational decision making, selective attention to relevant environmental cues, and pattern recognition. Expert–novice differences in gaze behavior again shed light on the role of vision in the performance of sport skills. Experts have been shown to be faster and more accurate at decision making than their non-elite counterparts (Mann, Williams, Ward, & Janelle, 2007; Abernethy, Farrow, Gorman, & Mann, 2012).

exploration ACTIVITY   3.3

Visual Occlusion

Visual occlusion is a technique used by researchers to examine expert–novice differences in visual attention and the use of visual-perceptual information for anticipation and decision making. In a typical paradigm, video footage of an opponent performing a skill, such as a tennis serve, is shown from the receiver's perspective to the viewer. At some point during the opponent's action sequence, the video is blackened out to block visual information. By occluding the viewer's vision at various points in the action sequence (temporal occlusion), or blocking out certain sections of the display (spatial occlusion), researchers can determine when the receiver extracts key anticipatory information and which features of the opponent's movements (kinematics) were attended to respectively (Müller & Abernethy, 2012). To see an example of expert novice differences when vision is occluded, check out the video of Cristiano Ronaldo at www.youtube.com/watch?v=TR_uyPT-_aw. Then try it yourself at www.youtube.com/watch?v=ZuJ0u19A4K8. Can you correctly anticipate where the ball is going?

Differences in the location and duration of fixations have also been found. For example, inexperienced soccer players tend to focus more frequently on the ball and the player passing the ball rather than on the positions and movements of the other players, which was found to be the focus of experienced players (Williams, Davids, Burwitz, & Williams, 1994; go to www.youtube.com/watch?v=U_eub88aq7I to see an example of visual scanning in soccer). Expert soccer players were also shown to fixate more often on their opponents' knee and hip regions, suggesting that the information in these areas is important in anticipating an opponent's next move (Nagano, Kato, & Fukuda, 2004). Successful soccer goalkeepers have also been shown to predict the height and direction of the kick more accurately, wait longer to initiate their response, and spend more time fixated on the non-kicking leg (Savelsbergh et al., 2002). In rugby, Mori and Shimada (2013) found that experienced players were superior to novices in responding to the direction changes of a running opponent fixating mainly on their opponent's hip and leg areas, while novices looked more at the opponent's chest. Similar findings were reported by Alhosseini, Safavi, and Zadeh (2015), who showed that skilled handball players focused their visual attention on their rival's trunk hand, ball, and belly area to anticipate ball situations whereas novices focused only on the opponents hand and ball.

Practical Implications

Vision clearly plays an integral role in the performance of skilled movement. Consequently, numerous visual training programs have been created in an effort to improve sports performance. Practitioners should be cautious when examining the claims of such programs. Generalized visual training programs, often referred to as sports vision training and offered by optometrists, lack research support for their effectiveness in developing on-field improvement (Abernethy & Wood, 2001). Sport-specific perceptual and decision-training programs, however, have been shown to be effective (see Causer, Janelle, Vickers, & Williams, 2012 for a review). Examples include tennis (e.g., Smeeton, Williams, Hodges, & Ward, 2005), badminton (e.g., Hagemann, Strauss, & Cañal-Bruland, 2006), basketball (e.g., Oudejans, 2012), European handball (Abernethy, Schorer, Jackson, & Hagemann, 2012), putting (Moore, Vine, Cooke, Ring, & Wilson, 2012), soccer (e.g., Savelsbergh, Van Gastel, & Van Kampen, 2010; Ryu, Kim, Abernethy, & Mann, 2013), and table tennis (e.g., Raab, Masters, & Maxwell, 2005). Try the pitch recognition sample drill on the site listed in the margin.

www

> **PITCH RECOGNITION SAMPLE DRILL**
> www.sportseyesite.com

Pinder, Davids, Renshaw, and Araújo (2011) proposed that two critical components must be considered when designing training activities to enhance perceptual-cognitive skills. First, the constraints that are presented for the performer to act upon must replicate those that occur in the performance environment (functionality). Second, the task has to allow the performer to respond in the same manner as he or she would in the performance environment (action fidelity). In other words, "there should be a high level of similarity between training and real-life performance when designing perceptual-cognitive skills training" (Broadbent, Causer, Williams, & Ford, 2015, p. 322). For example, Bruce, Farrow, and Young (2004) caution that reactive agility tasks that involve quickly responding to a coach's directive (e.g., www.youtube.com/watch?v=kkl-mhWOWgY) or to flashing lights (e.g., www.youtube.com/watch?v=-j_DSncq3FI) may not transfer well to a game situation. Instead they recommend the use of small sided games that present the same perceptual information sources that occur in the real game.

Magill (1998) also offers several practical tips to help learners develop effective visual search strategies. First, instruction and verbal feedback should direct learners to information-rich areas where critical cues occur. For instance, rather than instructing a novice hitter to look at how the ball leaves the pitcher's hand, the practitioner should direct the learner's visual attention to the area where the ball is released. Second, practitioners should design appropriate learning experiences that provide extensive practice opportunities in situations that contain common task-relevant cues. For example, providing opportunities to make connections between cues and ultimate event outcomes can facilitate the development of anticipatory skills. Finally, the context of learning situations should include a great deal of variability while still requiring learners to search for the same cues on each attempt. This variability will prepare learners to generalize their visual-search strategies for performance or game situations.

CEREBRALchallenge 3.5

1. To what information-rich area(s) would you suggest that beginning drivers direct their visual attention?
2. Play the game at http://vv.carleton.ca/games/html/escape.html. Describe the changes in your visual search strategies as a result of this experience.
3. Evaluate the pros and cons of the visual training activities in the following videos:

   a. www.youtube.com/v/n6r_OwlxUiY
   b. www.youtube.com/watch?v=hWEjX8c_XK4

PUTTING IT INTO PRACTICE

Learning Situation: Learning the Indirect Pass in Hockey

Jennifer has determined that the poor indirect pass performance observed in a game situation is the result of below-average anticipation skills when passing. Her assistant suggests the following drill (Figure 3.6).

 **FIGURE** **3.6**   Puck carrier skates around the net and makes an indirect pass off the wall to meet the receiver in the shaded area

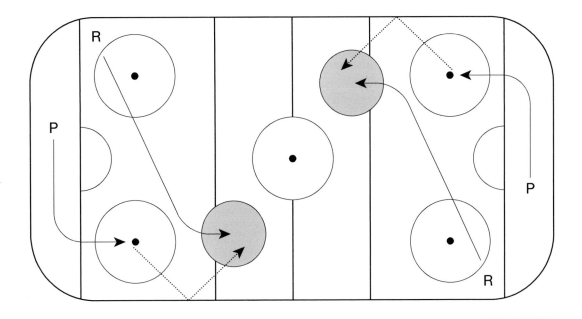

P = Puck carrier; R = Receiver

Test Your Knowledge

Review the drill outlined above. Would you recommend that Jennifer adopt this drill? Why or why not? Compare your answer with the sample response provided at www.routledge.com/cw/coker.

A LOOK AHEAD

The next chapter will add to your knowledge of movement production. It discusses theoretical information regarding how responses are organized, executed, and controlled once the decision has been made as to how to respond.

FOCUS POINTS

After reading this chapter, you should know:

- A limit exists as to how many things an individual can pay attention to or process at any given time. When that limit is exceeded, those items compete for attentional resources and interfere with one another, and performance declines.
- An optimal level of arousal exists for each performer. When that level is too low, attentional focus is too broad, and the learner attends to both relevant and irrelevant cues. When arousal is too high, the learner may no longer be capable of scanning the environment effectively due to perceptual narrowing, which may cause him to miss potentially significant cues.
- Selective attention is the ability to attend to or focus on specific aspects of the environment while ignoring others.
- Successful performance is often contingent on whether the learner can employ the appropriate attentional focus (attend to relevant information while ignoring what is irrelevant) for the situation. Performers must also be able to shift that focus according to the changing demands of the task, to avoid response delays.
- Instructions that focus the learner on the effects of a movement (external focus) rather than on the movement itself (internal focus) are typically more effective.
- Visual search is the manner by which the performer directs his or her attention while trying to locate critical regulatory cues.
- Experts and novices differ in how they use visual search strategies which affects their decision making speed and accuracy.
- Training activities to enhance perceptual-cognitive skills should be sport specific.

lab

To complete the labs for this chapter, visit routledge.com/cw/coker and select **Lab 3a, Attentional Capacity** and **Lab 3b, Visual Search**.

REVIEW QUESTIONS

1. According to an HLN Morning Express News report on September 19, 2012, "In the United States, someone is killed or injured once every five minutes on average in a crash that happens while a driver is texting and driving." Discuss the data with respect to attention and provide suggestions for stopping this behavior. Then go to www.youtube.com/watch?v=sMNGCHRIjTs&feature=player_embedded to see what 80 percent of teenagers surveyed suggested.

2. Recall the scenario from Chapter 2: You are driving along a road when a deer-crossing sign catches your eye. When you look back to the road, you notice the illuminated brake lights of the vehicle in front of you. A car is approaching in the opposite lane, and there is a ditch on your right.

   a. What attentional style(s) are necessary to avoid a collision?

   b. Discuss how arousal may be a factor in this situation.

3. What implications do ironic effects have for coaching? Rehabilitation?

4. Define fixation. How can we use fixations to infer visual attention?

5. What is the quiet eye? How does it differ between expert and novice performers and what are the implications for performance?

6. Compare and contrast targeting, interceptive, and tactical skills and describe the different visual requirements and strategies needed for successful performance in each.

7. Two components, functionality and action fidelity, should be considered when designing training activities to enhance perceptual-cognitive skills. Explain what these two components are and provide an example using a skill of your choice.

REFERENCES

Abernethy, B. (1991). Visual search strategies and decision-making in sport. *International Journal of Sport Psychology, 22,* 189–210.

Abernethy, B., Farrow, D., Gorman, A., & Mann, D. L. (2012). Anticipatory behaviour and expert performance. In N. J. Hodges & A. M. Williams (Eds.), *Skill acquisition in sport: research, theory and practice* (pp. 287–305). Oxford: Routledge.

Abernethy, B., Schorer, J., Jackson, R. C., & Hagemann, N. (2012). Perceptual training methods compared: The relative efficacy of different approaches to enhancing sport-specific anticpation. *Journal of Experimental Psychology: Applied, 18*(2), 143–153. doi:10.1037/a0028452.

Abernethy, B. & Wood, J. (2001). Do generalized visual training programmes for sport really work? An experimental investigation. *Journal of Sports Sciences, 19,* 203–222.

Alder, D., Ford, P. R., Causer, J., & Williams, A. M. (2014). The coupling between gaze behavior and opponent kinematics during anticipation of badminton shots. *Human Movement Science, 37,* 167–179.

Alhosseini, N. Z., Safavi, S., & Zadeh, M. N. (2015). Effect of skill level and indirect measurements in the attack situations in handball. *Journal of Neuroscience and Behavioral Health, 7*(2), 8–14.

Bahill, A. T. & La Ritz, T. (1984). Why can't batters keep their eyes on the ball? *American Scientist, 72,* 249–253.

Binsch, O., Oudejans, R. R., Bakker, F. C., & Savelsbergh, G. J. (2010). Ironic effects and final target fixation in a penalty shooting task. *Human Movement Science, 29*(2), 277–288.

Broadbent, D. P., Causer, J., Williams, A. M., & Ford, P. R. (2015). Perceptual-cognitive skill training and its transfer to expert performance in the field: Future research directions. *European Journal of Sport Science, 15*(4), 322–331.

Bruce, L., Farrow, D., & Young, W. (2004). Reactive agility—the forgotten aspect of testing and training agility in team sports. *Sports Coach, 27*(3), 34–35.

Causer, J., Janelle, C. M., Vickers, J. N., & Williams, A. M. (2012). Perceptual expertise: What can be trained? In N. J. Hodges & A. M. Williams (Eds.), *Skill acquisition in sport: Research, theory and practice.* New York, NY: Routledge.

Cherry, E. C. (1953). Some experiments on the recognition of speech, with one and two ears. *Journal of the Acoustical Society of America, 25,* 975–979.

Drews, F. A., Yazdani, H., Godfrey, C. N., Cooper, J. M., and Strayer, D. L. (2009). Text messaging during simulated driving. *Human Factors, 51,* 762–770.

Durham, K., Van Vliet, P. M., Badger, F., & Sackley, C. (2009). Use of information feedback and attentional focus of feedback in treating the person with a hemiplegic arm. *Physiotherapy Research International, 14*(2), 77–90.

Easterbrook, J. A. (1959). The effect of emotion on cue utilization and the organization of behavior. *Psychological Review, 66,* 183–201.

Gould, D. & Krane, V. (1992). The arousal-performance relationship: Current status and future directions. In T. S. Horn (Ed.), *Advances in sport psychology* (pp. 119–142). Champaign, IL: Human Kinetics.

Hagemann, N., Strauss, B., & Cañal-Bruland, R. (2006). Training perceptual skill by orienting visual attention. *Journal of Sport and Exercise Psychology, 28,* 143–158.

Hanin, Y. L. (1980). A study of anxiety in sports. In W. F. Straub (Ed.), *Sport psychology: An analysis of athlete behavior* (pp. 236–249). Ithaca, NY: Mouvement.

Kahneman, D. (1973). *Attention and effort.* Englewood Cliffs, NJ: Prentice-Hall.

Kluka, D. A. (1999). *Motor behavior: From learning to performance.* Englewood, CO: Morton.

Kluka, D. A. & Knudson, D. (1997). The impact of vision training on sport performance. *Journal of Health, Physical Education, Recreation and Dance, 68*(4), 17–24.

Land, M. F. & McLeod, P. (2000). From eye movements to actions: How batsmen hit the ball. *Nature Neuroscience, 3,* 1340–1345.

Landers, M., Wulf, G., Wallmann, H., & Guadagnoli, M. A. (2005). An external focus of attention attenuates balance impairment in Parkinson's disease. *Physiotherapy, 91,* 152–185.

Lee, D. N. (1976). A theory of visual control of braking based on information about time to collision. *Perception, 5,* 437–459.

Lee, D. N. (1980). Visuo-motor coordination in space-time. In G. E. Stelmach & J. Requin (Eds.), *Tutorials in motor behavior* (pp. 281–295). Amsterdam: North-Holland.

Lohse, K. R., Wulf, G., & Lewthwaite, R. (2012). Attentional focus affects movement efficiency. In N. J. Hodges & A. M. Williams (Eds.), *Skill acquisition in sport: Research, theory and practice* (pp. 40–58). London: Routledge.

Magill, R. A. (1998). Knowledge is more than we can talk about: Implicit learning in motor skill acquisition. *Research Quarterly for Exercise and Sport, 69*(2), 104–110.

Mann, D. L., Spratford, W., & Abernethy, B. (2013). The head tracks and gaze predicts: How the world's best batters hit a ball. *PLoS ONE 8*(3): e58289. doi:10.1371/journal.pone.0058289.

Mann, D. Y., Williams, A. M., Ward, P., & Janelle, C. M. (2007). Perceptual-cognitive expertise in sport: A meta-analysis. *Journal of Sport & Exercise Psychology, 29*(4), 457–478.

Marchant, D. C., Clough, P. J., Crawshaw, C. M., & Levy, A. (2009). Novice motor skill performance and task experience is influenced by attentional focusing instructions and instruction preferences. *International Journal of Sport and Exercise Psychology, 7,* 488–500.

Martens, R. (2004). *Successful coaching.* Champaign, IL: Human Kinetics.

Mennie, N. N., Hayhoe, M. M., Stupak, N., & Sullivan, B. (2005). Sources of information for catching balls [Abstract]. *Journal of Vision, 5*(8), 383.

Miyasike-daSilva, V., Allard, F., & McIlroy, W. E. (2011). Where do we look when we walk on stairs? Gaze behaviour on stairs, transitions, and handrails. *Experimental Brain Research, 209,* 73–83.

Moore, L. J., Vine, S. J., Cooke, A., Ring, C., & Wilson, M. R. (2012). Quiet eye training expedites motor learning and aids performance under heightened anxiety: The roles of response programming and external attention. *Psychophysiology, 49* (7), 1005–1015.

Mori, S. & Shimada, T. (2013). Expert anticipation from deceptive action. *Attention, Perception, & Psychophysics, 75*(4), 751–770. doi:10.3758/s13414-013-0435-z.

Müller, S. & Abernethy, B. (2012). Expert anticipatory skill in striking sports: A review and a model. *Research Quarterly For Exercise & Sport, 83*(2), 175–187.

Nagano, T., Kato, T., & Fukuda, T. (2004). Visual search strategies of soccer players in one-on-one defensive situations on the field. *Perceptual and Motor Skills, 99,* 968–974.

Nideffer, R. M. (1993). Attention control training. In R. N. Singer, M. Murphy, & L. K. Tennant (Eds.), *Handbook of research on sport psychology* (pp. 542–556). New York: Macmillan.

Nideffer, R. M. & Sagal, M. S. (2001). Concentration and attention control training. In J. M. Williams

(Ed.), *Applied sport psychology: Personal growth to peak performance* (pp. 312–332). Mountain View, CA: Mayfield.

O'Sullivan, S. (1988). Clinical decision making: Planning effective treatments. In S. O'Sullivan & T. Schmitz (Eds.), *Physical rehabilitation: Assessment and treatment*. Philadelphia: FA Davis.

Oudejans, R. D. (2012). Effects of visual control training on the shooting performance of elite female basketball players. *International Journal of Sports Science & Coaching*, 7(3), 469–480.

Perreault, M. E. & French, K. E. (2016). Differences in children's thinking and learning during attentional focus instruction. *Human Movement Science*, 45, 154–160.

Pinder, R. A., Davids, K., Renshaw, I., & Araújo, D. (2011). Representative learning design and functionality of research and practice in sport. *Journal of Sport & Exercise Psychology*, 33(1), 146–155.

Piras, A., Lobietti, R., & Squatrito, S. (2010). A study of saccadic eye movement dynamics in volleyball: comparison between athletes and non-athletes. *Journal of Sports Medicine and Physical Fitness*, 50(1), 99–108.

Piras, A., Lobietti, R., & Squatrito, S. (2014). Response time, visual search strategy, and anticipatory skills in volleyball players. *Journal of Ophthalmology*, 2014. doi:10.1155/2014/189268.

Porter, J. M., Anton, P. M., Wikoff, N. M., & Ostrowski, J. B. (2013). Instructing skilled athletes to focus their attention externally at greater distances enhances jumping performance. *Journal of Strength and Conditioning Research*, 27(8), 2073–2078.

Porter, J. M., Wu, W. F., Crossley, R. M., Knopp, S. W., & Campbell, O. C. (2015). Adopting and external forcus of attention improves sprinting performance in low-skilled sprinters. *Journal of Strength & Conditioning Research*, 29(4), 947–953.

Raab, M., Masters, R. S. W., & Maxwell, J. P. (2005). Improving the "how" and "what" decisions of elite table tennis players. *Human Movement Science*, 24, 326–344.

Rienhoff, R., Tirp, J., Strauß, B., Baker, J., & Schorer, J. (2016). The "Quiet Eye" and motor performance: A systematic review based on Newell's Constraints-Led Model. *Sports Medicine*, 46(4), 589–603.

Ripoll, H., Bard, C., & Paillard, J. (1986). Stabilization of head and eye movements on target as a factor of successful basketball shooting. *Human Movement Science*, 5, 47–58.

Ripoll, H. & Fleurance, P. (1988). What does keeping one's eye on the ball mean? *Ergonomics*, 31(11), 1647–1654.

Ripoll, H., Fleurance, P., & Cazeneuve, D. (1987). Analysis of the visual strategies involved in the execution of forehand and backhand strokes in table tennis. In J. K. O'Regan & A. Levy-Schoen (Eds.), *Eye movements: From physiology to cognition* (pp. 234–265). Amsterdam: Elsevier Science.

Roberts, G. C., Spink, K. S., & Pemberton, C. L. (1999). *Learning experiences in sport psychology: A practical guide to help students understand important concepts in sport psychology*. Champaign, IL: Human Kinetics.

Rodrigues, S. T., Vickers, T. N., & Williams, A. M. (2002). Head, eye and arm coordination in table tennis. *Journal of Sports Sciences*, 20, 187–200.

Ryu, D., Kim, S., Abernethy, B., & Mann, D. L. (2013). Guiding attention aids the acquisition of anticipatory skill in novice soccer goalkeepers. *Research Quarterly For Exercise & Sport*, 84(2), 252–262.

Savelsbergh, G. J. P., Van Gastel, P. J., & Van Kampen, P. M. (2010). Anticipation of penalty kicking direction can be improved by directing attention through perceptual learning. *International Journal of Sport Psychology*, 41, 24–41.

Savelsbergh, G. J. P., Williams, A. M., van der Kamp, J., & Ward, P. (2002). Visual search, anticipation and expertise in soccer goalkeepers. *Journal of Sports Sciences*, 20, 279–287.

Schücker, L., Jedamski, J., Hagemann, N., & Vater, H. (2015). Don't think about your movements: Effects of attentional instructions on rowing performance. *International Journal of Sports Science & Coaching*, 10(5), 829–839.

Shank, M. D. & Haywood, K. M. (1987). Eye movements while viewing a baseball pitch. *Perceptual and Motor Skills*, 64, 1191–1197.

Sherwood, D. E., Lohse, K. R., & Healy, A. F. (2014). Judging joint angles and movement outcome: Shifting the focus of attention in dart-throwing. *Journal of Experimenta Psychology: Human Perception and Performance*, 40(5), 1903–1914. doi:10.1037/a0037187.

Sibley, B. A. & Etnier, J. (2004). Time course of attention and decision making during a volleyball set. *Research Quarterly for Exercise and Sport*, 75, 102–106.

Singer, R. N., Cauraugh, J. H., Chen, D., Steinberg, G. M., Frehlich, S. G., & Wang, L. (1994).

Training mental quickness in beginning/inter-mediate tennis players. *The Sport Psychologist, 8,* 305–318.

Smeeton, N. J., Williams, A. M., Hodges, N. J., & Ward, P. (2005). The relative effectiveness of various instructional approaches in developing anticipation skill. *Journal of Experimental Psychology: Applied, 11,* 98–110. doi:10.1037/1076–898X.11.2.98.

Strayer, D. L., Drews, F. A., & Crouch, D. J. (2006). A comparison of the cell phone driver and the drunk driver. *Human Factors, 48,* 381–391.

Totsika, V. & Wulf, G. (2003). The influence of external and internal foci of attention on transfer to novel situations and skills. *Research Quarterly for Exercise and Sport, 74,* 220–225.

Vickers, J. N. (1992). Gaze control in putting. *Perception, 21,* 117–132.

Vickers, J. N. (1996). Visual control when aiming at a far target. *Journal of Experimental Psychology: Human Perception and Performance, 22,* 342–354.

Vickers, J. N. (2007). *Perception, cognition and decision training: The quiet eye in action.* Champaign, IL: Human Kinetics.

Vickers, J. N. (2016). The Quiet Eye: Origins, controversies, and future directions. *Kinesiology Review, 5*(2), 119–128.

Vickers, J. N. & Adolphe, R. A. (1997). Gaze behaviour during a ball tracking and aiming skill. *International Journal of Sports Vision, 4*(1), 18–27.

Vine, S. J., Moore, L. J., & Wilson, M. R. (2012). Quiet eye training: The acquisition, refinement and resilient performance of targeting skills. *European Journal of Sport Science, 14,* S235–S242. doi: 10.1080/17461391.2012.683815.

Wegner, D. M. (1994). Ironic processes of mental control. *Psychological Review, 101,* 34–52.

Weinberg, R. S. & Gould, D. (2015). *Foundations of sport and exercise psychology* (6th ed.). Champaign, IL: Human Kinetics.

Wickens, C. D. (1984). Processing resources in attention. In R. Parasuraman & D. R. Davies (Eds.), *Varieties of attention* (pp. 63–102). New York: Academic Press.

Williams, A. M., Davids, K., Burwitz, L., & Williams, J. G. (1994). Visual search strategies in experienced and inexperienced soccer players. *Research Quarterly for Exercise and Sport, 65*(2), 127–135.

Williams, A. M., Singer, R. A., & Frehlich, S. (2002). Quiet eye duration, expertise and task complexity

in a near and far aiming task. *Journal of Motor Behavior, 34,* 197–207.

Wilson, V. E., Peper, E., & Schmid, A. (2001). Strategies for training concentration. In J. Williams (Ed.), *Applied sport psychology* (5th ed., pp. 404–422). New York: McGraw-Hill.

Woodman, T., Barlow, M., & Gorgulu, R. (2015). Don't miss, don't miss, D'oh! Performance when anxious suffers specifically where least desired. *Sport Psychologist, 29*(3), 213–223.

Wrisberg, C. A. (2007). *Sport skill instruction for coaches.* Champaign, IL: Human Kinetics.

Wulf, G. (2013). Attentional focus and motor learning: a review of 15 years, *International Review of Sport and Exercise Psychology, 6:1,* 77–104.

Wulf, G., Dufek, J. S., Lozano, L., & Pettigrew, C. (2010). Increased jump height and reduced EMG activity with an external focus. *Human Movement Science, 29,* 440–448.

Wulf, G., Lauterbach, B., & Toole, T. (1999). The learning advantages of an external focus of attention in golf. *Research Quarterly for Exercise and Sport, 70*(2), 120–126.

Wulf, G., McConnel, N., Gärtner, M., & Schwarz, A. (2002). Feedback and attentional focus: enhancing the learning of sport skills through external-focus feedback. *Journal of Motor Behavior, 34,* 171–182.

Wulf, G. & McNevin, N. (2003). Simply distracting learners is not enough: More evidence for the learning benefits of an external focus of attention. *European Journal of Sport Science, 3*(5), 1–13.

Wulf, G., McNevin, N., Fuchs, T., Ritter, F., & Toole, T. (2000). Attentional focus on complex skill learning. *Research Quarterly for Exercise and Sport, 71*(3), 229–239.

Wulf, G. & Su, J. (2007). An external focus of attention enhances golf shot accuracy in beginners and experts. *Research Quarterly for Exercise and Sport, 78,* 384–389.

Yerkes, R. M. & Dodson, J. D. (1908). The relation of strength of stimulus to rapidity of habit-formation. *Journal of Comparative Neurology and Psychology, 18,* 459–482.

Zachry, T., Wulf, G., Mercer, J., & Bezodis, N. (2005). Increased movement accuracy and reduced EMG activity as a result of adopting an external focus of attention. *Brain Research Bulletin, 67,* 304–309.

Ziegler, S. G. (2002). Attentional training: Our best kept secret. *Journal of Physical Education, Recreation and Dance, 73,* 26–30.

Behavioral Theories of Motor Control

4

We watch in awe as elite athletes perform incredible feats: the pole-vaulter who becomes one with the pole while being projected into the sky, the trapeze artist who completes a flip and is caught at just the right moment, and the swimmer with an above-the-knee amputation completing the race in record time. We look with equal wonder at the patient with Parkinson's disease who is able to take a drink despite having difficulty raising a glass, or an accident victim who must relearn how to walk. Indeed, the human body and its ability to perform both simple and complex movements are truly fascinating. How the nervous system organizes the muscles to perform skilled movements is a complex puzzle that continues to challenge movement scientists.

In this chapter, we will examine theories of the organization and execution of skilled movements. Understanding theory is important for practitioners, as it is the foundation on which all instructional decisions should be made. After all, how can we design and implement effective instruction—whether in classrooms, gymnasiums, coaching, or clinical settings—if we don't understand how people learn?

COORDINATION AND CONTROL

The human body has many joints, each of which is capable of moving in various directions. Hence, due to its anatomical structure, the human body has numerous independent elements, or degrees of freedom, that afford abundant action possibilities. To produce a specific, coordinated movement, all of these independent elements must be controlled.

To illustrate this concept, highlight the word "coordination" in the heading above. To accomplish this task, you must somehow manipulate your highlighter (or your finger if using a tablet) and produce a limb movement that corresponds with the dimensions and location of the word on the page. The process of organizing a system's available degrees of freedom (in this case your arm and highlighter/finger) into an efficient movement pattern to achieve a specific goal effectively is known as coordination (Turvey, 1990; Sparrow, 1992). But this alone does not solve the movement problem. What if you were asked to highlight only the first five letters, or what if your highlighter was running low on ink?

Variables within the movement pattern, such as how hard to push, where to start and finish, and how fast to complete the movement, must also be resolved to achieve the goal of the task. The manipulation of variables within a movement to meet the demands of a given situation is known as control. Performing a skilled movement, therefore, requires that the learner coordinate the available degrees of freedom while also controlling the resulting movement. How we coordinate and control the available degrees of freedom to produce a particular movement is known as the degrees of freedom problem (Bernstein, 1967)—a problem that has plagued not only human movement scientists but

www

DEGREES OF FREEDOM

www.youtube.com/watch?feature=
endscreen&v=nvoC9h7K3JA&NR=1

ASIMO ROBOT

www.youtube.com/watch?v=uUiZ8r
Z8wzl

also robotic engineers, whose work in humanoid development is limited by the gaps in our understanding of human movement. To learn more about degrees of freedom and to see how closely a humanoid can replicate purposeful human movement, watch the videos at the adjoining websites.

SKILLED MOVEMENT: COMMAND CENTER OR DYNAMIC INTERACTION?

Currently, two predominant theoretical approaches offer explanations of how skilled movement is coordinated and controlled. The first, motor program theories, suggest the existence of a command center in the brain that is thought to make all decisions regarding the movement. When a decision to act is made, an appropriate movement plan is retrieved from memory, and instructions are sent to the rest of the body to carry out the action.

Dynamic interaction theories, on the other hand, contend that a plan created by a command center could not possibly account for all variations and adjustments in skilled movement; the load on memory would be too great. Instead, skilled movement results or "emerges" from a dynamic interaction of numerous variables in the body, the environment, and the skill.

MOTOR PROGRAM THEORIES

The mechanism at the core of the command center–based construct is the motor program. A motor program is an abstract representation of a movement plan, stored in memory that contains all motor commands required to carry out the intended action.

Early Theories

Early motor program theories proposed that, for each movement to be made, a separate motor program existed and was stored in memory. When a specific action was required, the appropriate program was simply retrieved from memory and executed. As the idea of motor programs was examined more closely, however, researchers noted two inherent problems. The first involved storage. If a motor program existed for each and every possible movement and movement variation, one's memory would require limitless storage space. The second problem lies in the production of novel responses. If a movement or variation of a movement has never been performed before, where does the program for that specific action come from?

Generalized Motor Program

Unlike the authors of earlier motor program theories, Schmidt (1975) proposed that every movement does not require a separate motor program for its execution; instead, the motor program is more general in nature. This generalized motor program represents a class of actions or pattern of movement that can be modified to yield various response outcomes. Some elements of the generalized motor program (called invariant features) are thought to be relatively fixed from trial to trial, defining the motor program itself, while others (called parameters) are more flexible and define the program's execution (Schmidt, 1985). See if you can identify some of these features in Exploration Activity 4.1.

According to early motor program theories, each of these variations of your signature would have its own separate motor program stored in memory. Those theories were modified to suggest that the motor program is a more general representation of a class of actions and consists of both elements that are relatively fixed and elements that can be modified.

Which aspects of the above instructions and your corresponding responses were flexible and defined how to execute the motor program? Which aspects were relatively fixed from trial to trial?

Invariant Features

Regardless of how you wrote your name in Exploration Activity 4.1, some underlying features of your signature remained constant. These underlying features, or invariant features, are similar to fingerprints. Just as our fingerprints can identify each of us, each motor program can be identified by its invariant features. To date, researchers have identified three possible invariant features: the sequence of actions or components, relative timing, and relative force.

Sequence of Actions

In Exploration Activity 4.1, regardless of how you signed your name, you spelled your name the same way each time. For example, if your name is Kim,

exploration ACTIVITY   4.1

Signature Analysis: Fixed versus Flexible Features

Using a blank sheet of lined paper, complete your signature eight times, according to the following instructions:

1. Write with your dominant hand.
2. Write with your non-dominant hand.
3. Hold the pen or pencil in your mouth.
4. Hold the pen or pencil between your toes.
5. Press down very hard.
6. Press very softly.
7. Write slowly, while maintaining legibility.
8. Write quickly, while maintaining legibility.

the "i" always follows the "K" and precedes the "m." Any disruption of that specific order would result in both an error in your signature and the creation of a different name. Similarly, in a volleyball spike, regardless of where the ball has been set, certain actions (i.e., the approach, the jump, the arm swing, and ball contact) must be sequentially executed. The sequence of actions, or the order of components, is an invariant feature.

Relative Timing

Relative timing has been suggested as another invariant feature of the generalized motor program, with supporting evidence offered from a variety of activities, including walking (Shapiro, Zernicke, Gregor, & Diestal, 1981), throwing (Roth, 1988), hurdling (Hay & Schoebel, 1990), and gait initiation (Brunt, Lafferty, McKeon, et al., 1991). In essence, relative timing refers to the internal rhythm of the skill. The arm movement in the freestyle stroke, for example, can be broken down into five components. Of the total time needed to complete one cycle, let's say that 35 percent is accounted for by the entry, 13 percent by the catch, 8 percent by the mid-pull, 12 percent by the finish, and 32 percent by the recovery. Because relative timing is considered invariant, these percentages will remain the same regardless of whether the athlete is swimming quickly or slowly. See Figure 4.1 for an illustration. This concept is similar to adjusting a recipe to yield more servings. In order to double the recipe, the cook must double all ingredients (retaining their proportional relationship) or the end result will not be the same (personal communication, Matthew Dancosse, Oct. 23, 2011).

FIGURE 4.1 Illustration of relative timing in the 100 m freestyle (a) for a 61-second performance and (b) for a 70-second performance

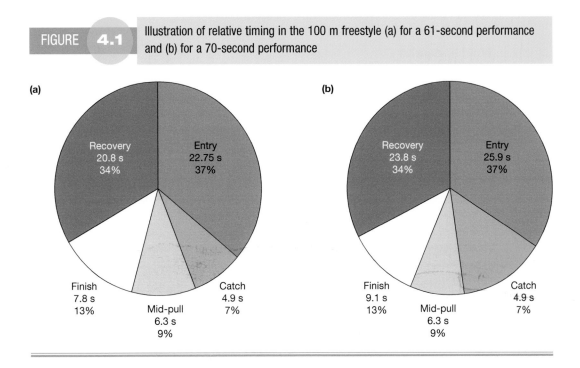

(a)

Recovery 20.8 s 34%
Entry 22.75 s 37%
Finish 7.8 s 13%
Mid-pull 6.3 s 9%
Catch 4.9 s 7%

(b)

Recovery 23.8 s 34%
Entry 25.9 s 37%
Finish 9.1 s 13%
Mid-pull 6.3 s 9%
Catch 4.9 s 7%

Relative Force

An invariant relationship has also been proposed with respect to ratios of force. When the overall force used to execute a movement changes, as would occur when a patient performed a leg lift with different amounts of weight, the actual force characteristic of each component should change proportionately. In other words, the tension created in each muscle throughout the movement should remain proportionate, even though the force increases as the weight increases. This concept is known as relative force and has received some attention as an invariant feature.

RESEARCH NOTES

Shapiro, Zernicke, Gregor, and Diestal (1981) tested the notion of relative timing by having subjects walk on a treadmill at different speeds. Hypothetically, the relative timing of the components of the walking cycle should not change as the overall speed of the treadmill increases. The results showed that for speeds up to 6 km/h, the relative timing of the step-cycle components did indeed remain intact. As the speed increased to 8 km/h and beyond, however, the relative timing changed. Since members of a class of actions share similar characteristics in relative timing, we can infer that above 8 km/h, a different motor program is controlling the action. The shift in relative timing characteristics corresponded to the participants' shift from walking to running.

Parameters

The features of a motor program that are flexible and define how to execute the program are termed *parameters*. Parameters are easily modified from one performance to another to produce variations of a motor response without altering the fundamental movement pattern. This "adaptability" of parameters enables a center fielder to throw to third base from different areas of the field and allows an individual to walk up and down steps of varying heights. Four parameters have been proposed: overall duration, overall force, movement direction, and muscle selection (Schmidt, 1985; Schmidt & Wrisberg, 2008).

Overall Duration

One aspect of a movement that can be easily varied is the overall duration or speed at which a skill is performed. Swimmers can increase the speed of their stroke as they approach the finish line, runners manipulate their pace during a race, and hitters can swing with varying bat speeds, all without changing the underlying pattern of the movement.

Overall Force

Similarly, the overall force or amplitude (size) of a movement can be modified. Patients can learn to lift off plastic container lids of various sizes (e.g., the lid on a margarine container and the lid on a yogurt container), individuals can perform sit-to-stand motions from varying seat heights, and soccer players can make both long and short passes, depending on the situation.

Movement Direction

Variations in movement direction can also be made to accomplish a movement goal. A darts player can throw the dart to various locations on a board, a lacrosse player can propel a shot or goal to a top or bottom corner of the net, and a shopper can reach for a can on a supermarket shelf that is slightly to the right or left of his position, all without altering the invariant features of the motor program (Schmidt & Wrisberg, 2008).

Muscle Selection

Different limbs or muscles may be used to perform movements. This was demonstrated in Exploration Activity 4.1, where you used your hand, foot, and mouth to write your name. Additionally, many bilateral skills exist—skills in which the performer may execute the task with either the dominant or the non-dominant side. Examples include dribbling

FIGURE **4.2**

A swimmer can increase overall stroke speed without changing the invariant features of the motor program

CEREBRALchallenge   4.1

1. The use of over-weight implements is a common training method for conditioning in many sports. Throwers use heavier shots, discuses, and javelins than are normally used in competition; pitchers throw heavier baseballs; and hitters swing heavier-than-normal bats. Does this technique involve a manipulation of invariant features or parameters? Can you think of a situation or condition where the use of over-weight implements could hinder the development of correct technique? What signs should a practitioner look for to avoid this problem?

2. Another training technique is to practice when the athlete is fatigued. Based on your understanding of invariant features and parameters, is this a good idea? Why or why not?

in basketball and soccer, movement patterns in dance, and manipulating buttons and zippers. In each instance, the underlying movement pattern remains intact.

Schema

According to the generalized motor program theory, a shortstop is able to throw to different bases from various positions on the field by assigning appropriate parameter values, such as throwing speed, to the program. How does the performer know exactly how fast the ball should be thrown in each situation? The answer lies in another aspect of Schmidt's theory (1975, 1985), the development of a schema.

A schema is an abstract representation of a rule or set of rules governing discrete movement. More specifically, it is the rule or relationship that directs decision making when a learner is faced with a movement problem. A schema develops as the result of accumulated experiences within a class of actions. Each movement attempt provides the learner with information about the movement, which is translated into a relationship that will be used to guide future attempts. The more movements a performer has executed, the more developed the rule will become.

Let's say you go to the state fair and come across a ball-toss game. The objective of the game is to toss a softball into a peach basket in such a way that the softball does not bounce out. Feeling confident that you can accomplish this goal, you purchase three chances. Having assessed the tosses of some of the previous players, you decide that the best approach will be an underhand toss. On your first toss, the ball ricochets off the bottom of the basket. On your second attempt, you decide to lean over the barrier and adjust the toss, decreasing the height of the arch and aiming more toward the front of the basket. Again, the ball bounces out of the basket, but this time with less force. On your final attempt, you lean over the barrier as far as possible and throw the same low-arched toss, but with a little less force. Unfortunately, the ball bounces out of the basket again, just barely.

According to the schema concept, on each attempt you subconsciously abstract four pieces of information:

1. *Initial conditions* are the conditions that are present at the start of the movement, including limb and body position and the environmental conditions when the movement was begun. Leaning over the barrier as far as possible is an example of initial condition information.
2. *Response specifications* are the parameter values used in the execution of the movement, such as the speed and force of your throw.
3. *Sensory consequences* include the response-produced sensory information or sensory feedback of the movement. What the throw felt like is an example.
4. *Response outcome* is the success of the response obtained, in relation to the originally intended goal or outcome. Although none of the three attempts stayed in the basket, the response outcome for each of the three tosses was

different. In the first attempt, the ball ricocheted out of the basket, suggesting that your toss had a great deal of force. In subsequent attempts, the magnitude of that force was reduced, indicating that the movement was approaching that which was necessary to achieve the goal.

These four sources of information are briefly stored in memory after a movement attempt, allowing the performer to abstract some relationship among them. For example, in the first ball toss, the initial conditions (e.g., starting position), the response specifications (whatever parameter values were assigned to the program), the sensory consequences (what the performer's sensory system perceived), and the response outcome (the ball ricocheting out of the basket)—and the relationship of each source of information with the others—are all assessed, leading to an inference about how to perform the task successfully. The schema has begun to develop. Not only does this process occur for each additional attempt, but the resulting relationship from each attempt becomes incorporated with the relationship already developed in the existing schema. Hence, the strength of the overall relationship increases with practice. The result is the development of the motor response schema, which is thought to be composed of two relationships, the recall schema and the recognition schema (Schmidt, 1985).

Recall Schema

The recall schema is responsible for organizing the motor program that initiates and controls the desired movement. When an individual attempts to perform a movement, she considers the desired outcome for that movement and the initial conditions. A recall schema is then subconsciously selected; this is based on the relationship between actual outcomes and response specifications that has developed through experiences with similar movements. From this relationship, the performer determines the specifications that will be required to achieve the intended outcome. She then executes the motor program according to these movement parameter values.

Recognition Schema

The recognition schema is responsible for the evaluation of a movement attempt. It is formulated based on the relationship among the initial conditions, past actual outcomes, and past sensory consequences. A set of expected sensory consequences representing the best estimate of the sensory consequences of the correct movement is generated, based on the relationship between actual outcomes and sensory consequences. By comparing the actual sensory feedback from the initiated movement with the expected sensory feedback, the performer assesses the correctness of the movement. When a mismatch occurs between feedback and the reference of correctness, an error signal is generated. Error signals provide the performer with information that is used to update the recall schema. Additional information from the teacher or coach also serves to update the recall schema.

FIGURE **4.3**

With practice and subconscious abstraction of information regarding the initial conditions, the response specifications, the sensory consequences, and the response outcome on each attempt, you develop a schema for the skill

By continually revising its estimates of the expected sensory consequences and response specifications, the recall schema updates the instructions to the muscles; this in turn leads to more accurate responses on subsequent attempts. Through this process, the schema becomes more established, and the performer can more accurately select appropriate response specifications or parameter values to accomplish a movement goal.

Executing the Motor Program

Once a learner decides what movement to execute in a given situation, he subconsciously retrieves the appropriate generalized motor program from memory, based on the existing schema, and adds to it the estimated parameter values that will achieve the desired outcome. The details of the desired movement are, therefore, organized in advance by the motor program and sent to the rest of the body to be carried out. How is the movement controlled once the motor program initiates it? Does the motor program contain all of the information needed to carry out the action from start to finish, or are continuous adjustments made to the movement based on response-produced feedback? The answer to these questions lies in the details of the initial movement commands.

Before you can start your workout on a stair-climbing fitness machine, you have to select from a number of program options, such as the hill profile or interval training. Once you select the desired program, it will be executed for the amount of time you specify. It cannot sense that you don't like the program you have selected or that it is too easy or too difficult for you. It simply runs its course. Email operates in a similar fashion. Once the message leaves your outbox, it is automatically sent. You cannot change it; it will be sent exactly as it was when it left the outbox. These two examples illustrate the notion of *open-loop control*.

Open-loop control mechanisms function through a two-level hierarchy, as seen in Figure 4.4(a). An executive level or command center generates action plans that contain all of the information necessary to complete a response. These action plans are carried out at the second level—the effector level—by the limbs and muscles (the effectors) without modification. Applying this to human movement, input is perceived via processes in the brain. A decision as to how to respond is made, instructions to execute that response are sent to the muscles via the nervous system, and the response is performed. Feedback is constantly

CEREBRALchallenge   4.2

A hockey coach uses the following teaching strategy. Having taught her players the slapshot and after giving them an opportunity to develop a basic understanding of the movement, coach X gives her players these instructions:

"Using the slapshot technique that we have been learning, perform the actions listed below from each of these four locations:

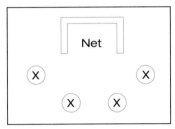

First, shoot the puck so that it misses the net to the right.

Second, shoot the puck so that it misses the net to the left.

Third, shoot the puck so that it goes in the net."

Will this experience help or hinder the athletes' technique development for the slapshot? Why or why not? Use the schema theory to support your answers.

present during movement, but it comes too late to adjust the ongoing movement. Once the pre-structured commands are initiated (sent to the nervous system), the action has to run as planned. The feedback received regarding this trial can be used only to modify subsequent attempts.

A second kind of control mechanism allows adjustments to be made after a program has been initiated. This is known as closed-loop control (see Figure 4.4(b)). A thermostat that regulates room temperature is a good example of a closed-loop system. The heating system, once set, continuously monitors the actual room temperature and compares it to the desired temperature. If a discrepancy is detected (the room becomes too hot or too cold), the system makes the corresponding adjustments automatically by turning the heater off or on, respectively.

Like open-loop systems, closed-loop systems function in a hierarchical fashion, with one important distinction—they involve feedback modifying an ongoing action. Instead of having to generate all of the information needed to complete the response, the command center must generate only an action plan that initiates the movement. Sensory information resulting from the movement's progress (response-produced feedback) is then continually compared to the desired movement, and any detected discrepancies are sent to the command

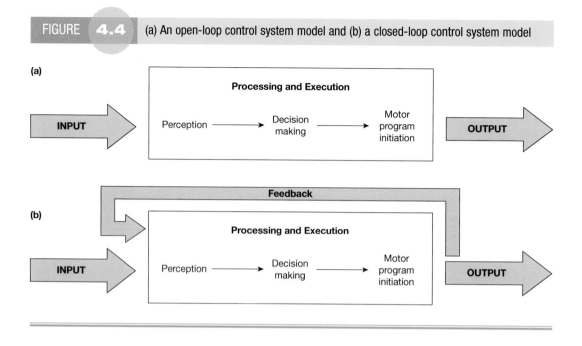

FIGURE **4.4** (a) An open-loop control system model and (b) a closed-loop control system model

center for correction. This cycle continues until the response is completed. The distinction between open- and closed-loop systems, then, is that the feedback that accompanies a movement can be used to modify an ongoing action in a closed-loop system, but it cannot be used until the next response in an open-loop system.

Open- and closed-loop systems served as precursors to current motor program–based theory. Present-day theories consider motor control as a function of both open- and closed-loop mechanisms, with motor programs operating in an open-loop fashion. Basically, skilled movements are believed to be planned in advance, initiated, and carried out with limited modification, unless time permits the incorporation of response-produced feedback. Consequently, in rapid movements, the pre-structured motor program will control the movement from start to finish, because there is not enough time to process response-produced feedback and make the corresponding adjustments. For movements where there is enough time to process feedback, open-loop mechanisms control the initiation of the skill, but closed-loop control is used to continue the movement to its completion. It should be noted that initial skill acquisition is governed predominantly by closed-loop control. As skill proficiency increases, a shift occurs to more automatic open-loop control processes characteristic of skilled performance.

Evidence Supporting Motor Program Control

Three lines of evidence support the notion of motor program control. First, if the motor program organizes the details of the desired movement in advance,

CEREBRALchallenge   **4.3**

1. Compare and contrast open and closed skills with open- and closed-loop control systems.
2. Provide an explanation for what transpires in the video found at www.youtube.com/watch?v=lPLFSuoDacQ.

it seems logical that, as a task increases in complexity, the amount of time needed to organize the motor program must also increase. Henry and Rogers (1960) tested this notion by measuring the reaction time of subjects performing three tasks that varied in complexity. The tasks, moving from the lowest level of complexity to highest, were: (1) lifting the finger from a switch being pressed down, (2) lifting the finger from the switch and then reaching and grasping a tennis ball that hung 30 cm away, and (3) lifting the finger from the switch, striking the tennis ball, reversing direction to push a button, and finishing by reversing direction again to grasp another tennis ball. Results showed that, as the complexity of the movement increased, reaction time increased (165 ms, 199 ms, and 212 ms, respectively). Since reaction time measures the time from the onset of a stimulus to the initiation of a response (see Chapter 2), these findings support the idea that movements are planned in advance.

A second experimental approach used to test the notion of motor programs involved deafferentation. Deafferentation is a technique in which the sensory nerves of a limb, for example, are surgically severed so that response-produced feedback cannot reach the central nervous system. Early studies of this type examined the motor behaviors of monkeys before and after deafferentation (Taub & Berman, 1968; Polit & Bizzi, 1978). In the Polit and Bizzi study, three monkeys were trained in a pointing task prior to undergoing deafferentation of their arm. After deafferentation, they were retested on the same pointing task. Results revealed that after deafferentation and the loss of sensory feedback from the limb, the monkeys were still able to move their arm and point to the target accurately, further supporting the notion of motor program control.

Experiments exploring the effects of a limb being unexpectedly blocked during movement are the basis of the third line of research supporting motor program control. Using electromyography (EMG), researchers compared the electrical activity in muscles during limb movements to the electrical activity in those same muscles when the limb movements were suddenly and unexpectedly blocked (Wadman, Dernier van der Gon, Geuze, & Mol, 1979). Researchers inferred that if a motor program does indeed organize all of the instructions for carrying out a movement prior to the movement's initiation, without regard for feedback, then the EMG of the blocked muscle should temporarily display a similar pattern to that of the muscle that was not blocked. Comparisons of the two limb movement conditions (unblocked and blocked) revealed that this was in fact the case.

Many baseball and softball players, much to their dismay, have probably experienced a real-world example of this concept. The change-up has left many accomplished hitters looking foolish while standing at the plate. An effective change-up is designed to look like a regular-speed pitch but is manipulated just prior to release, so that the ball leaves the pitcher's hand much more slowly than the hitter is anticipating from the windup. In this situation, the hitter selects the motor program for the swing, assigning to it the parameter values that will successfully contact a regular-speed pitch. Once that program is organized and initiated, it will run its course even if the hitter recognizes that the pitcher has thrown a change-up. According to motor program–based theory, to change the tempo of the swing, the hitter must not only recognize that an error has been made in parameter selection but also reorganize and initiate the corrected program in order to meet the demands of the task. Because hitting is a rapid movement, often there is not enough time to do this, and the hitter swings prematurely.

Summary of Generalized Motor Program Theory

Schmidt's "schema" theory (1975, 1985) is an open-loop theory of motor control that combines the basic idea of a schema (an abstract representation of rules governing movement) and the idea of a generalized motor program. The theory proposes that, for a given class of actions such as the overhand throw, we abstract different pieces of information from every throwing experience we've ever had that involved an overhand pattern (Magill, 1993). We then construct schemas that will enable us to use the overhand throw in a number of situations and circumstances.

The schema theory proposes that movements are generalized and are run by complex rules that are revised with each movement experience. The stronger the

CEREBRALchallenge 4.4

Slater-Hammel (1960) provided a good illustration of the difficulty we have in stopping a planned movement. Subjects were asked to lift their finger from a response key at the same instant that the sweep hand of a clock they were watching passed over the number 8. However, if the sweep hand stopped prior to reaching the 8, subjects were instructed to continue to press down on the response key. Results showed that when the sweep hand was stopped less than 140 ms before reaching the target, subjects had a difficult time not lifting their finger. In most cases, subjects could not stop the action of lifting their finger in trials where the sweep hand stopped 50 to 100 ms before reaching the 8.

Can you think of other real-life examples where you start a movement and then recognize that you shouldn't do it but have difficulty stopping? Describe one example.

CEREBRALchallenge   4.5

Answer the following questions according to Schmidt's schema theory:

1. You are coaching an athlete who has a major competition in three weeks. You have noticed a flaw in her performance. Should you correct the flaw? Why or why not? What questions must you ask to help you make your decision?

2. You are coaching an eighth-grade volleyball team and are receiving complaints about the soreness in the players' forearms from bumping the ball. To help the athletes, you decide to let them wear wristbands on their forearms in practice. Is this a good idea? Why or why not?

3. You are teaching a unit on basketball—specifically the free throw—to middle school students. Unfortunately, there are 28 students in your class and only four baskets in your gymnasium. In addition to the lack of baskets, there are only 10 functional basketballs. You remember reading an article in college that encouraged you to be creative and use substitute equipment to increase time on task. You come up with the idea to use playground balls in addition to the basketballs, and to tape targets on the wall at the height of a normal basket. Are these good ideas? Why or why not?

rule (schema), the more skilled the performance. The task of the instructor, once the fundamental movement pattern has been achieved, is to provide the learner with appropriate activities designed to strengthen the schema.

DYNAMIC INTERACTION THEORIES

Proponents of dynamic interaction theories argue that motor program–based theories fall short in accounting for the control of complex movements. They contend that a plan created by a command center couldn't possibly account for all variations and adjustments in skilled movement. They further note that the fact that movements occur in response to a dynamic interaction of the person and the environment is not accounted for.

Dynamic Systems Theory

The Dynamic Systems Theory (also termed the Dynamic Pattern Theory) suggests that—rather than functioning in a hierarchical manner, with a command center issuing instructions that are carried out by the limbs and muscles—movement patterns emerge or self-organize as a function of the interacting, ever-changing individual (learner), environmental, and task constraints. In other words, the arrangement of a movement pattern will emerge from the dynamic interaction of the learner, the environment, and the task, rather than being generated by a motor program (see Figure 4.5 and complete Exploration Activity 4.2).

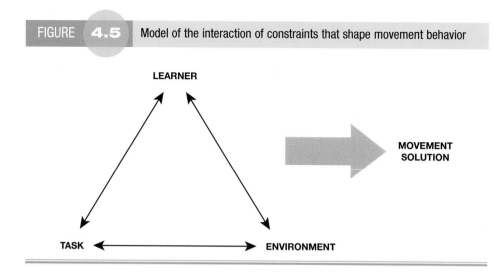

FIGURE **4.5**   Model of the interaction of constraints that shape movement behavior

exploration ACTIVITY   4.2

Self-Organization

To demonstrate the concept of self-organization, perform the following activities over a 10-meter distance and then observe another person performing the same activities.

a.   Walk at a normal pace wearing running shoes.
b.   Walk at a normal pace wearing the running shoes on the opposite feet.
c.   Walk at a normal pace wearing a pair of running shoes that are at least two sizes too large.
d.   Walk at a normal pace wearing a pair of running shoes that are at least two sizes too small.

QUESTIONS

1.   Based on your experience and observations, discuss the concept of self-organization.
2.   Speculate as to what changes you might see in someone's gait pattern when the person is walking (a) on ice, (b) on a sandy beach, (c) across a log, and (d) with a condition/injury such as plantar fasciitis or hip flexor strain. Include the concept of self-organization in your response.

Constraints

The optimal pattern of any movement is determined by the interaction of internal constraints placed on the performer by the state of the body's subsystems and external constraints imposed by the movement that is to be executed and by the environment within which that movement will take place (Caldwell & Clark, 1990). Constraints, then, are defined as the boundaries that have a bearing on an individual's movement capabilities (Newell, 1986; Clark, 1995). Although the term seems to imply a limiting or negative factor, this is not always the case. Constraints should instead be thought of as all of the factors, both limiting and enabling, within the practice environment that influence skill acquisition and performance (Araújo, Davids, Bennett, et al., 2004).

Individual Constraints

Individual constraints (also known as *organismic constraints*) include a person's biological and functional characteristics (Newell, 1986). Examples include body attributes (e.g., shape, height, weight, and body composition), personality characteristics (e.g., high or low trait anxiety, motivation, confidence), fitness variables (e.g., flexibility, power, strength, speed, endurance, aerobic capacity, agility), and perceptual and decision-making skills (e.g., spatial and temporal anticipation capability). Other examples of individual constraints include amputations, juvenile arthritis, or obesity (Getchell & Gagen, 2006). Complete Exploration Activity 4.3 to learn more about individual constraints.

Environmental Constraints

Gravity, temperature, and natural light are examples of physical environmental constraints. In the javelin throw, for example, the force and direction of the wind place an environmental constraint on the performer. Failure to take the wind into account will therefore negatively influence the throw. An environmental constraint that should be considered with respect to falls risk in older adults is lighting. Remember that constraints can be limiting or enabling. Falls risk increases in dim lighting but is reduced in brightly illuminated conditions. In other words, simply turning on the lights can positively influence mobility.

Social environmental factors also serve as constraints. These include societal expectations, cultural norms, and the presence and characteristics of spectators, as well as family and peer networks (Haywood & Getchell, 2014). Exploration Activity 4.3 explores environmental constraints.

Task Constraints

The task itself imposes constraints on motor skill acquisition and performance. Three categories of task constraints have been proposed (Newell, 1986):

1. *Goal.* All tasks are governed by goals that relate to the product or outcome of the action. For example, the goal of the long jump is to maximize horizontal displacement, and the goal of a tennis serve is to gain an advantage over one's opponent.
2. *Rules.* Sport skills typically have rules that dictate the specific coordination pattern that must be produced. For example, in collegiate fastpitch softball, the pitcher's feet must remain in contact with the pitching rubber

exploration ACTIVITY   4.3

Individual, Environmental, and Task Constraints

Perform the following activities to develop a greater understanding of the role of constraints.

INDIVIDUAL CONSTRAINTS

1. Attempt the following:

    a. Jump up and touch the ceiling.
    b. Perform the splits.

    Were you able to do each of these tasks? What individual constraints enabled you to accomplish each task or prevented you from doing so?

2. Median nerve loss simulation (Perry, Rohe, & Garcia, 1992):

    For this activity, you will need a pair of latex-free exam/surgical gloves.

    a. Place a quarter and a nickel in your pocket. Put your bare hand in your pocket and find the quarter.
    b. Now turn one hand of the gloves inside out and cut the little and ring fingers off. Put both gloves on the same hand, and reach into your pocket to retrieve the quarter while simulating median nerve functional loss at the wrist level.

    Did your strategies for identifying and retrieving the coins differ in the two tasks? Relate your findings to the concepts of individual constraints and self-organization.

ENVIRONMENTAL CONSTRAINTS

Equipment Needed

*   2 pieces of paper
*   A small electric fan

With the pieces of paper, make two identical paper airplanes. Mark a starting point on the ground to ensure the same starting position for each trial. Place the fan perpendicular to the direction of throw, on your throwing side, and approximately 3 meters in front of the starting line, as depicted in the image.

Turn on the fan and throw your first plane straight ahead, so that it must pass through the stream of air created by the fan. Note the resulting flight path. Now, turn off the fan and throw your second plane using the same throwing motion you used to throw the first plane. Again, note the resulting flight path.

Path of paper airplane

3 meters

STARTING LINE

continued

exploration ACTIVITY   4.3

What influence did the fan's airstream have on the flight path of the first airplane? The second? What adjustments would have to be made to get the plane to land directly in front of you when the fan is turned on?

TASK CONSTRAINTS

Equipment Needed

- 1 tennis ball or baseball
- 1 partially deflated volleyball
- 1 basketball
- 1 large playground ball
- Large open field or area

Using a mature overhand throwing pattern, throw each ball as far as possible into the open area. If possible, have a friend capture a video recording of each attempt.

Compare and contrast the attempts. How did each ball influence the distance of the throw? Did you use the same techniques to throw each ball? What compensations did you make, and why? Did any individual constraints also influence the task?

throughout the initiation of the pitch (until her weight is transferred forward). This rule prevents the pitcher from taking a step backward prior to the pitch, which would allow the pitcher to generate added momentum and create an unfair advantage. If the pitcher breaks contact with the rubber at any time during the onset of the pitch, the base umpire will charge her with an illegal pitch. The performer must carry out the specific pattern of coordination for the movement to be called a legal pitch.

Other rules do not specify the performer's pattern of coordination but instead specify the range of response dynamics that can be performed to achieve the desired outcome. For example, in volleyball the ball must pass over the net when served and land within the boundaries of the court. Three types of serves—underhand, overhand, and jump—and a variety of movement patterns can accomplish this; as a result, the optimal pattern of coordination for a given individual becomes the prominent issue (Newell, 1986). Since interactions of internal and external constraints determine the optimal movement coordination and control, individual differences must be considered—no "one size fits all" strategy exists. Because individuals often interpret the constraints differently, one individual may generate one type of response while another will produce a different movement for the same set of task constraints. Thus, two people may be placed in a situation with identical environmental and task constraints but produce entirely different movement patterns because of their bodies' internal constraints.

FIGURE **4.6**

Fitness equipment constrains movement possibilities

www

BALANS MULTI-CHAIR
www.fully.com/variable-balans-by-varier.html

3. *Implements or machines.* The third category of task constraints results from the interaction of the individual with an implement or a machine. Examples include stepping on a stair climber machine, walking on a treadmill, using crutches, snow or water skiing, kayaking, opening a can with a can opener, and performing core-stability exercises on a therapeutic ball. The size, dynamics, and weight of sporting equipment relative to the body size of the individual constrain the optimal coordinated movement. For example, if a client sets the seat for a stationary bike too high, this will reduce the efficiency of the exercise, and over time could lead to an injury. The task constraint activity in Exploration Activity 4.3 should help you gain a better understanding of how the characteristics of various implements or equipment can affect the resulting movement pattern.

Constraints and the Emergence of Movement Patterns

As indicated earlier, movement patterns are thought to emerge or spontaneously conform as a function of the ever-changing constraints placed on the learner. Movement, then, is a function of the system spontaneously self-organizing and compressing the available degrees of freedom into a single functional unit that is designed to carry out a specific task. In other words, the arrangement of a movement pattern will be the result of the constraints imposed by a given situation rather than from specific commands or instructions provided by pre-existing motor programs. This concept was demonstrated in the task-constraint portion of Exploration Activity 4.3, where the movement pattern used to perform the overhand throwing motion changed as a function of the type of ball being used.

RESEARCH NOTES

The Balans Multi-Chair (BMC) is designed with a forward-tilted seat and a padded rest for the lower legs, enabling the user to assume a semi-kneeling position. To examine the resulting postural control induced by this design, Shenoy and Aruin (2007) compared the electrical activity of muscles (using EMG) of the trunk and legs when subjects were seated on a standard stool (identified as REG in the study) and the BMC. Nine participants were seated with their arms extended toward a wooden horizontal piece mounted at shoulder level. A force sensor was attached to the palm of the dominant hand. When an auditory tone was sounded, participants were to produce a brief pulse of force against the wooden piece with both hands, creating a self-initiated perturbation (body disturbance). Six force applications against the wooden frame were performed, in four directions: (1) horizontal forward push, (2) horizontal pull, (3) upward vertical push, and (4) downward vertical push. Electromyographic data were recorded before and during perturbations. Results indicated that sitting on both types of chair was associated with using anticipatory activation of postural muscles; the magnitude of activation depended on the direction of the self-initiated perturbation. In addition, anticipatory activation of distal muscles was found for sitting in the REG chair but not for sitting in the BMC chair, suggesting that the body position induced by the BMC's design may not allow for effective activation of the lower leg muscles to preserve body stability. Shenoy and Aruin (2007) concluded that "these findings stress the important role of chair designs in the control of sitting posture" (p. 309).

QUESTION

How does the concept of constraints relate to the findings of this study?

CEREBRALchallenge   4.6

1. Categorize each of the following as an individual (I), environmental (E), or task (T) constraint:

    a. Height of the curb that an individual in a wheelchair needs to overcome
    b. Catching a pop fly while looking into the sun
    c. Having poor flexibility
    d. Taunting fans who are trying to distract a basketball player about to attempt a free throw
    e. Using a regulation size football with 10-year-olds
    f. Lack of motivation
    g. Center-of-mass differences between females and males (go to www.youtube.com/watch?v=MW0ZTvRCS1o for an example)

2. One approach that coaches use for skill development is to copy the techniques used by current champions. Given your understanding of constraints, justify or refute this practice.

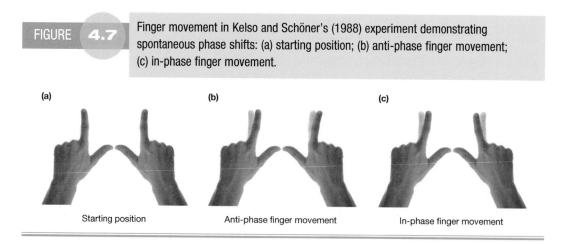

FIGURE 4.7 Finger movement in Kelso and Schöner's (1988) experiment demonstrating spontaneous phase shifts: (a) starting position; (b) anti-phase finger movement; (c) in-phase finger movement.

(a)   (b)   (c)

Starting position   Anti-phase finger movement   In-phase finger movement

DYNAMIC SYSTEMS DEMONSTRATION

www.youtube.com/watch?v=4m-9VweerAg&feature=relmfu

The concept is further supported by empirical evidence provided by Kelso and Schöner (1988). In this study, participants were asked to place their hands on a table, beginning with the position shown in Figure 4.7a. They were then asked to move their index fingers, keeping in beat with a metronome, so that both fingers pointed to the left or right at the same time. This movement pattern was labeled as an anti-phase pattern, because the two fingers were actually performing opposite movements (one in adduction and the other in abduction), as illustrated in Figure 4.7b. As the speed of the metronome was gradually increased, a sudden phase shift occurred, and the fingers spontaneously began to perform the same movement pattern (in-phase pattern), illustrated in Figure 4.7c and demonstrated in the video at the site listed in the margin. Because a motor program should have been trying to keep the fingers moving out of phase, the motor program theory falls short in explaining the spontaneous shift to in-phase behavior. From a dynamic systems perspective, the change in speed (task constraint) causes the system to self-organize, and a new behavior emerges.

Changes in Movement Patterns

Systems prefer states of stability. These preferred states of stability or patterns are known as attractors and play a role in the self-organizing process. When a change is imposed on a system, the stability of that system is endangered. If the magnitude of the change is high enough, the state of stability of the system will be altered, and the system will reorganize into a new form within the boundaries established by the constraints (Thelen & Ulrich, 1991). In the task-constraint section of Exploration Activity 4.3, the size of ball acted as a control parameter. Control parameters are variables that, when changed, lead to corresponding changes in the collective behavior of the system. They can push an unstable

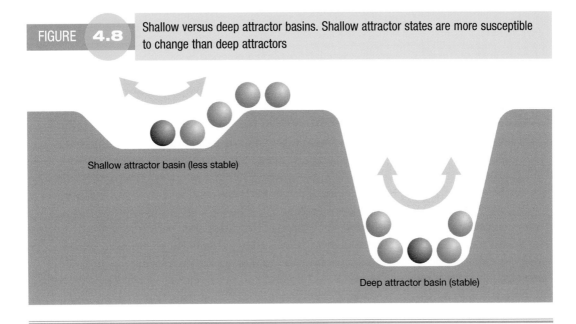

FIGURE **4.8** Shallow versus deep attractor basins. Shallow attractor states are more susceptible to change than deep attractors

Shallow attractor basin (less stable)

Deep attractor basin (stable)

system to a new, more stable state or vice versa (Clark, 1995; Wallace, 1996). Direction, force, speed, and perceptual information are some examples of control parameters. Constraints can also hinder or hold back the ability of the system to change. When variables function in this capacity, they are known as rate limiters. A strength deficiency due to an injury would act as a rate limiter on the performer's ability to effectively grasp objects. Through an appropriate strength-building program, however, grip strength levels can be increased. With these increased strength levels, there is a corresponding decrease in the stability of the current attractor state. Once grip strength reaches a critical level, the system will self-organize and a new form of behavior emerges, seen in the performer's improved ability to grasp objects.

Ennis (1992) suggests that attractors function much like basins or wells in which observable behaviors pool, and their depth is an indication of the stability of the system (see Figure 4.8). Deep attractor basins are characteristic of stable systems. Stable patterns are difficult to change. Conversely, shallow basins are less stable and are more susceptible to change.

Changes in movement behavior are the result of a series of transitions in a system's state of stability. These transitions are called phase shifts. When an attractor state is shallow, a phase shift can occur abruptly. For example, by replacing a bat that is too heavy for the learner with one that is more developmentally appropriate, a change in movement pattern will likely be immediate. On the other hand, in order to change a well-learned movement (a deep level attractor state), intervention strategies have to cause instability to an already deep attractor (the current technique). As instability is created, an increase in

RESEARCH NOTES

One challenge faced by individuals with Parkinson's disease is difficulty using eating utensils. Ma, Hwang, Chen-sea, and Sheu (2008) examined the task constraint of spoon-handle size when scooping water (simulating soup) on the movement kinematics of individuals with Parkinson's disease. Using spoons with three different-sized handles, 18 individuals with Parkinson's and 18 age-matched healthy participants transported 10 continuous scoops of water from a large bowl positioned in front of them and then back and into a small, closer bowl. The researchers gathered three-dimensional kinematic data in addition to subjective reports about whether the spoon was comfortable to use. Results indicated that, for those participants with Parkinson's disease, the small- or medium-sized handle elicited faster and smoother movements than did the larger handle. In contrast, no significant differences in movement kinematics were found for handle size for the healthy control group. In addition, those with Parkinson's disease had a significantly smaller hand aperture and used more fingers to hold the spoons than their healthy counterparts. In other words, for individuals with Parkinson's disease, handle size (a task constraint) "affects not only the grip pattern and movement time, but also the kinematics of spoon-use movement" (p. 525).

CEREBRAL challenge   4.7

1. According to Haywood and Getchell (2014), two rate limiters for early walking are muscular strength and balance. Speculate as to why these would be considered rate limiters on walking until critical levels of each are developed.
2. Develop a list of potential rate limiters for walking in older adults.
3. Identify activities of daily living (ADLs) for which a paretic upper limb (a limb with partial paralysis) might serve as a rate limiter.

variability of the movement will occur (Harbourne & Stergiou, 2009). For example, when a student-athlete moves from high school to college, the new coach might attempt to change a well-learned technique in order to improve future performance. As a result of the changes imposed, the movement pattern will begin to break down, becoming a combination of the new and the old technique. Over time, the pattern will reorganize, the new technique will begin to take over, and a phase shift will occur to a new attractor state. Initially, this new attractor will be somewhat shallow; with continued practice, however, it will gain stability.

Non-Linear Pedagogy and the Constraints-Led Approach

Predicated on the concepts of the dynamic systems theory and the notion that interacting constraints shape movement behavior is the theoretical framework known as non-linear pedagogy. According to this view, learners search through a range of potential movement solutions for the optimal movement strategy that will satisfy the imposed constraints (Newell, 1991; Davids, Araújo, & Shuttleworth, 2005). Critical to this search process is the exploration of what is known as the perceptual-motor workspace (Shumway-Cook & Woollacott, 2012; see also Figure 4.9). According to Davids (2006), "The perceptual-motor workspace represents the practice context for the learner" (p. 1004). When an individual explores perceptual information sources and the range of movement possibilities to discover task solutions unique to that individual, she is involved in exploring her perceptual-motor workspace. Shumway-Cook and Woollacott (2012) offer an excellent illustration of this concept. A patient who is re-learning how to reach for and lift a glass of milk must match relevant perceptual cues— such as the location of the glass in relation to the body, the size and texture of the glass, and how full the glass is—to the available movement possibilities to determine the optimal movement solution to accomplish the goal. This movement solution will differ according to the constraints imposed by the situation. For example, when the glass is perceived as full, the optimal movement solution will differ in speed and trajectory from the optimal solution were it half full.

Given that learners generate specific movement solutions to satisfy the unique combination of constraints imposed on them, non-linear pedagogy advocates a constraints-led approach to skill acquisition (Chow, Davids, Button, et al., 2007; Davids, Button, & Bennett, 2008). The constraints-led approach involves the purposeful manipulation of key task, performer, and environmental constraints during practice in an effort to "channel the acquisition of movement

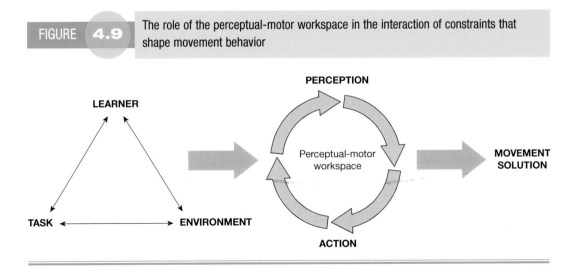

FIGURE 4.9 The role of the perceptual-motor workspace in the interaction of constraints that shape movement behavior

skills and decision making behaviors" (Renshaw, Chow, Davids, & Hammond, 2010, p. 117). It further advocates the concept of the hands-off practitioner (Handford, Davids, Bennett, & Button, 1997; Davids, Button, & Bennett, 2008). This concept redefines the role of the practitioner as a facilitator—rather than as an information provider. Information providers dictate the correct movement response through verbal instructions, practice structure, and feedback. In contrast, the role of the practitioner as facilitator is one of identifying and manipulating key constraints to guide the learner's search for optimal movement solutions (Davids, Araújo, Shuttleworth & Button, 2003; Araújo et al., 2004).

Research supports the assertion that "the manipulation of constraints by educators can lead to the production of successful motor patterns, decision-making behavior, and intentions that guide the achievement of task goals" (Chow et al., 2007, p. 259). For example, Chow, Davids, Button, and Koh (2008) examined the influence of manipulating task constraints, specifically the task criteria, on the acquisition of a soccer chipping task. The task was to kick a ball over a height barrier to different target positions. No other instruction was provided. Results revealed improved outcome scores and more consistent kicking patterns as a result of practice. In addition, each participant showed a different progression of change in levels of joint involvement in the kicking leg, highlighting individual differences in coordination and control as participants searched for functional movement solutions based on the interaction of key constraints.

Nakayama (2008) examined the effect of playing-area size on the passing skills of young soccer players. In the practice task, three attackers attempted to retain possession of the ball while one defender tried to take it away (3 vs. 1). Play was conducted in three playing areas of different sizes: 8 m by 8 m, 10 m by 10 m, and 12 m by 12 m. Results indicated clear differences in play as a result of play area size. The 12 m area permitted greater distance between the attacker and the defenders and yielded the highest percentage of pass success. The 10 m and 8 m areas had similar play aspects, but the 8 m area required speedier play. The author concluded that a wide area would reinforce player success, while a narrow area would reinforce skill development and enhance decision making.

Jackson (2011) examined the use of standard vs. body-scaled badminton rackets on the serving patterns of children. The data indicated that using equipment fitted to body size resulted in improved serving performance and the adoption of a more mature sequential movement pattern. Similar improvements in performance and technique have been reported in tennis (Gagen, 2003; Farrow & Reid, 2010; Larson & Guggenheimer, 2013; Buszard, Farrow, Reid, & Masters, 2014), catching (Payne & Koslow, 1981), and basketball (Chase, Ewing, Lirgg, & George, 1994).

Finally, Correia, Araújo, Duarte, et al. (2012) demonstrated that decision-making behaviors emerged as a function of the relative positioning between defenders (initial distance apart). In their study, 12 experienced youth players performed 80 trials of a 1 (attacker) vs. 2 (defenders) rugby practice task in which the starting distance between defenders was systematically decreased. Their findings indicated that shorter starting distances between defenders were associated with a higher frequency of effective tackle outcomes, slower perform-ance speeds, and subsequently longer time periods between the first crossover and the end of the trial. These data further support the notion that manipulating key constraints in practice design can shape decision-making behavior in team sports training.

RESEARCH NOTES

To examine the influence of manipulating individual, task, and environmental constraints, Rose and Clark (2000) designed a biofeedback-based, computerized intervention program for individuals with a history of repeated falls due to postural instability. Forty-five older adult participants (mean age 78.5 years) who had sustained two or more falls requiring medical treatment within the previous year and who had no medical diagnosis to account for the falls were assigned to either a control or an intervention group. Following the assessment of multiple dimensions of balance using the Pro Balance Master® force plate system and the administration of the Berg Balance Scale and the Timed Up and Go tests, the members of the control group were instructed to maintain their pre-study daily activities while participants assigned to the intervention group attended two 45-minute balance-training sessions per week for 8 weeks. All intervention group participants performed the same set of balance-training exercises; however, the spatial (e.g., distance and/or direction) and temporal (e.g., pacing) requirements of each task, as well as the support surface characteristics (e.g., amount and type of movement or compliance), were manipulated to accommodate each individual's physical capabilities (e.g., muscular strength, range-of-motion). Reassessment following the intervention program revealed significant improvements in dynamic balance, sensory integration, and the two clinical measures of balance and mobility (Berg Balance Scale and Timed Up and Go test) for the intervention group only. The authors concluded that rehabilitation programs that focus on manipulating the interaction of individual, task, and environmental constraints can significantly improve an older adult's ability to control body orientation.

Practical Implications

Strategies for creating effective learning environments are limited only by the practitioner's imagination. Game and context-related skills should be emphasized to encourage learners to explore potentially important sources of infor-mation to hone their decision-making capabilities and develop functional movement patterns. Questioning strate-gies can further guide learners in their search process. Challenges can also be developed to encourage learners to adapt movement behaviors to meet task requirements. By imposing rule modifications, scaling equipment, altering

www

TEACHING GAMES FOR UNDERSTANDING

Coaching
www.youtube.com/watch?feature= player_embedded&v=xx25KgDdHmQ
Invasion Games
www.youtube.com/watch?v=k2l2as qzCtg&feature=related

playing area dimensions, manipulating situational factors during performance such as the relative positioning of players or the number of attackers and defenders (Passos, Araújo, Davids, & Shuttleworth, 2010), and/or changing task criteria, practitioners can create action possibilities that allow for the emergence of desired behaviors through the process of guided discovery (Williams, 2003). Finally, Teaching Games for Understanding (TGfU), a pedagogical method used in physical education, might be considered as it reflects the constructs outlined under the constraints-led approach. (See Chow, Davids, Button, et al., 2009, for additional information, and visit the adjoining websites to see TGfU examples in coaching and invasion games.)

Summary of Dynamic Systems Theory, Non-Linear Pedagogy, and the Constraints-Led Approach

The complexity of human behavior has led to the development of the dynamic systems approach, which emphasizes the dynamic interaction of the learner, the task, and the environment. The notion that interacting constraints shape movement behavior has also led to the development of a theoretical framework for understanding and facilitating skill acquisition, known as the constraints-led approach. Human behavior is seen as complex and representing a compression of degrees of freedom. This compression of degrees of freedom allows behavior to emerge in a self-organizing fashion that accounts for the cooperation of the many subsystems in a task context. New movements self-organize, and movement variability—where patterns stabilize and destabilize as a function of the changing constraints on the system—is an integral part of the learning process. A patient who is learning to walk again after sustaining an injury, for example, will display a given gait pattern as a result of the constraints imposed on her system. If her leg strength reaches a critical level, a new movement solution (gait pattern) will emerge. The instructor's task in this process is to identify and manipulate constraints in a manner that facilitates the learner's discovery of functional movement patterns.

CEREBRALchallenge   4.8

1. Fear often serves as a rate limiter (a constraint that hinders the ability of the system to change). In hurdling, for example, beginners are often afraid that they will not clear the hurdle and will be injured. If you were teaching hurdles, what strategies would you use to overcome this rate limiter? What other rate limiters might be involved? Discuss your answer in terms of the dynamic systems theory.

2. Explain how orthotics function from a constraints perspective.

3. Given what you have learned about dynamic systems, can the speed at which a sit-to-stand transfer is executed influence performance? Fully explain your answer.

PUTTING IT INTO PRACTICE

Learning Situation: Rehabilitation of an Ankle Sprain

Assessment of Darren's progress indicates that he is ready for balance and proprioceptive activities to be incorporated into his rehabilitation program. Before doing so however, the physical therapist needs to develop a more comprehensive situational profile.

Test Your Knowledge

What individual constraints must be taken into consideration when designing a balance/proprioception program for Darren? Will these change over time? How will those changes influence program design? Compare your answer with the sample response provided at www.routledge.com/cw/coker.

A LOOK AHEAD

In this and previous chapters, we explored theoretical constructs underlying the coordination and control of human movement from a behavioral perspective. In the remaining chapters, we will revisit these theories, because practitioners must consider theories in order to make effective instructional decisions. In the next chapter, we will examine movement from a neurological perspective; we will consider the role the nervous system plays in movement and the clues it offers movement scientists about the human movement puzzle.

FOCUS POINTS

After reading this chapter, you should know:

- Skilled movement requires the learner not only to condense the available degrees of freedom (coordination) but also to control the resulting movement.
- Two prominent theories, motor program theory and the dynamic systems theory, offer explanations of how movement is coordinated and controlled.
- A generalized motor program is an abstract representation of a class of actions that can be modified to yield various response outcomes.
- Some elements of the generalized motor program (invariant features) are thought to be relatively fixed from trial to trial, defining the motor program itself; others (parameters) are more flexible, defining the program's execution.
- Parameters for a given situation are specified according to one's schema, an abstract representation of rules governing movement. It is a rule or relationship that is developed through practice and directs decision making.
- Motor control is thought to be a function of both open- and closed-loop mechanisms, where movements are planned in advance, initiated, and carried

out with limited modification, unless time permits the incorporation of response-produced feedback.

• The dynamic systems theory argues against the notion of a central command center and suggests instead that movement emerges or self-organizes as a function of the constraints imposed on the system at any given time.

• Three categories of constraints have been identified: individual, environmental, and task.

• According to the constraints-led approach, the learner searches through a range of potential movement solutions for the optimal movement strategy that will satisfy the imposed constraints.

• The role of the practitioner is one of identifying and manipulating key constraints to guide the learner's search for optimal movement solutions.

lab

To complete the lab for this chapter, visit www.routledge.com/cw/coker and select **Lab 4a, Motor Programs and Lab 4b, Constraints**.

REVIEW QUESTIONS

1. Define the terms *coordination* and *control.* Explain their relationship.

2. Explain the degrees of freedom problem.

3. What two major flaws were identified in early motor program theories? How does Schmidt's schema theory solve these problems? How does the dynamic systems theory solve them?

4. What is a schema? How do the recall schema and recognition schema work together?

5. What is the relationship between parameters and schema?

6. How could you determine whether snow skiing and waterskiing share the same motor program? Explain your answer, using motor learning terminology and providing specific examples.

7. What three lines of evidence suggest the existence of motor program control?

8. Compare and contrast open- and closed-loop systems.

9. What is a constraint? List the three types of constraints and provide an example of each.

10. Discovery learning is emphasized in the constraints-led approach. What is discovery learning, and how can the practitioner design practice to create it?

REFERENCES

Araújo, D., Davids, K., Bennett, S. J., Button, C., & Chapman, G. (2004). Emergence of sport skills under constraints. In A. M. Williams & N. J. Hodges (Eds.), *Skill acquisition in sport: Research, theory and practice* (pp. 409–433). London: Routledge, Taylor and Francis.

Bernstein, N. (1967). *The coordination and regulation of movements*. Oxford, UK: Pergamon.

Brunt, D., Lafferty, M. J., McKeon, A., Goode, B., Mulhausen, C., & Polk, P. (1991). Invariant characteristics of gait initiation. *American Journal of Physical and Medical Rehabilitation, 70*(4), 206–212.

Buszard, T., Farrow, D., Reid, M., & Masters, R. W. (2014). Modifying equipment in early skill development: A tennis perspective. *Research Quarterly For Exercise & Sport, 85*(2), 218–225.

Caldwell, G. & Clark, J. E. (1990). The measurement and evaluation of skill within the dynamical systems perspective. In J. E. Clark & J. H. Humphrey (Eds.), *Advances in motor development research* (pp. 165–199). New York: AMS.

Chase, M., Ewing, M., Lirgg, C., & George, T. (1994). The effects of equipment modification on children's self-efficacy and basketball shooting performance. *Research Quarterly for Exercise and Sport, 65*(2), 159–168.

Chow, J. Y., Davids, K. W., Button, C., & Koh, M. (2008). Coordination changes in a discrete multi-articular action as a function of practice. *Acta Psychologica, 127*(1), 163.

Chow, J. Y., Davids, K. W., Button, C., Renshaw, I., Shuttleworth, R., & Uehara, L. A. (2009). Nonlinear pedagogy: Implications for teaching games for understanding (TGfU). In Hopper, T. A. J. & Butler, J. (Eds.), *TGfU: Simply good pedagogy: Understanding a complex challenge* (pp. 131–143). Ottawa, ON: Physical and Health Education Canada.

Chow, J. Y., Davids, K., Button, C., Shuttleworth, R., Renshaw, I., & Araújo, D. (2007). The role of non-linear pedagogy in physical education. *Review of Educational Research, 77*, 251–278.

Clark, J. E. (1995). On becoming skillful: Patterns and constraints. *Research Quarterly for Exercise and Sport, 66*(3), 173–183.

Correia, V., Araújo, D., Duarte, R., Travassos, B., Passos, P., & Davids, K. (2012). Changes in practice task constraints shape decision making behaviours of team games players. *Journal of Science and Medicine in Sport, 15*, 244–249.

Davids, K. (2006). Perceptual-motor workspace. In R. Bartlett, C. Grafton, & C. Rolf (Eds.), *Encyclopedia of international sports studies* (p. 1004). London: Taylor and Francis.

Davids, K., Araújo, D., & Shuttleworth, R. (2005). Applications of dynamical systems theory to football. In T. Reilly, J. Cabri, & D. Araújo (Eds.), *Science and football: The proceedings of the 5th world congress on sports science and football* (pp. 537–550). London: Routledge, Taylor and Francis.

Davids, K., Araújo, D., Shuttleworth, R., & Button, C. (2003). Acquiring skill in sport: A constraints-led perspective. *International Journal of Computer Sciences in Sport, 2*, 31–39.

Davids, K., Button, C., & Bennett, S. (2008). *Dynamics of skill acquisition: A constraints-led approach*. Champaign, IL: Human Kinetics.

Ennis, C. (1992). Reconceptualizing learning as a dynamical system. *Journal of Curriculum and Supervision, 7*(2), 115–130.

Farrow, D. & Reid, M. (2010). The effect of equipment scaling on the skill acquisition of beginning tennis players. *Journal of Sports Science, 28*, 723–732.

Gagen, L. M. (2003). Choosing a racket for striking tasks in elementary school. *Journal of Physical Education, Recreation, & Dance, 74*(7), 39–40.

Getchell, N. & Gagen, L. (2006). Adapting activities for all children: Considering constraints can make planning simple and effective. *Palaestra, 22*, 20–27.

Handford, C., Davids, K., Bennett, S., & Button, C. (1997). Skill acquisition in sport: Some applications of an evolving practice ecology. *Journal of Sports Sciences, 15*, 621–640.

Harbourne, R. T. & Stergiou, N. (2009). Movement variability and the use of nonlinear tools: Principles to guide physical therapist practice. *Physical Therapy, 89*(3), 267–282.

Hay, L. & Schoebel, P. (1990). Spatio-temporal invariants in hurdle racing patterns. *Human Movement Science, 9*, 37–54.

Haywood, K. M. & Getchell, N. (2014). *Life span motor development*. Champaign, IL: Human Kinetics.

Henry, F. M. & Rogers, D. E. (1960). Increased response latency for complicated movements and the "memory drum" theory of neuromotor reaction. *Research Quarterly, 31*, 448–458.

Jackson, S. (2011). Biomechanical analysis of badminton serves using standard and body scaled equipment: A perception-action perspective. *Arkansas Journal, 46*(1), 31–36.

Kelso, J. A. S. & Schöner, G. (1988). Self-organization of coordinative movement patterns. *Human Movement Science, 7,* 27–46.

Larson, E. J., & Guggenheimer, J. D. (2013). The effects of scaling tennis equipment on the forehand groundstroke performance of children. *Journal of Sports Science & Medicine, 12*(2), 323–331.

Ma, H. I., Hwang, W. J., Chen-Sea, M. J., & Sheu, C. F. (2008). Handle size as a task constraint in spoon-use movement in patients with Parkinson's disease. *Clinical Rehabilitation, 22*(6), 520–528.

Magill, R. (1993). *Motor learning: Concepts and applications.* Dubuque, IA: W. C. Brown.

Nakayama, M. (2008). The effects of play area size as task constraints on soccer pass skills. *Football Science, 5,* 1–6.

Newell, K. M. (1986). Constraints on the development of coordination. In M. G. Wade & H. T. A. Whiting (Eds.), *Motor development in children: Aspects of coordination and control* (pp. 341–360). Dordrecht: Martinus Nighoff.

Newell, K. M. (1991). Motor skill acquisition. *Annual Review of Psychology, 42,* 213–237.

Newell, K. M. (1996). Changes in movement and skill: Learning, retention and transfer. In M. L. Latash & M. T. Turvey (Eds.), *Dexterity and its development.* Mahwah, NJ: Lawrence Erlbaum.

Newell, K. M., Liu, Y. T., & Mayer-Kress, G. (2001). Time scales in motor learning and development. *Psychological Review, 108*(1), 57–82.

Passos, P., Araújo, D., Davids, K. W., & Shuttleworth, R. (2010). Manipulating task constraints to improve tactical knowledge and collective decision-making in rugby union. In I. Renshaw, K. W. Davids, & G. J. P. Savelsbergh (Eds.), *Motor learning in practice: A constraints led approach,* pp. 120–130. London: Routledge (Taylor & Francis Group).

Payne, V. G. & Koslow, R. (1981). Effects of varying ball diameters on catching ability of young children. *Perceptual and Motor Skills, 53,* 739–744.

Perry, J. F., Rohe, D. A., & Garcia, A. O. (1992). *The kinesiology workbook.* Philadelphia: F. A. Davis.

Polit, A. & Bizzi, E. (1978). Processes controlling arm movements in monkeys. *Science, 201,* 1235–1237.

Renshaw, I., Chow, J. Y., Davids, K. W., & Hammond, J. (2010). A constraints-led perspective to understanding skill acquisition and game play: A basis for integration of motor learning theory and physical education praxis? *Physical Education & Sport Pedagogy, 15*(2), 117–137.

Rose, D. J. & Clark, S. (2000). Can the control of bodily orientation be significantly improved in a group of older adults with a history of falls? *Journal of the American Geriatrics Society, 48*(3), 275–282.

Roth, K. (1988). Investigations on the basis of the generalized motor programme hypothesis. In O. G. Meijer & K. Roth (Eds.), *Complex movement behavior: The motor action controversy* (pp. 261–288). Amsterdam: North-Holland.

Schmidt, R. A. (1975). A schema theory of discrete motor skill learning. *Psychological Review, 82*(4), 225–260.

Schmidt, R. A. (1985). The search for invariance in skilled movement behavior. *Research Quarterly for Exercise and Sport, 56*(2), 188–200.

Schmidt, R. A. & Wrisberg, C. A. (2008). *Motor learning and performance: A situation based learning approach.* Champaign, IL: Human Kinetics.

Shapiro, D. C., Zernicke, R. F., Gregor, R. J., & Diestal, J. D. (1981). Evidence for generalized motor programs using gait pattern analysis. *Journal of Motor Behavior, 13,* 33–47.

Shenoy, S. & Aruin, A. S. (2007). Effect of chair design on feed-forward postural control in sitting. *Motor Control, 11,* 309–321.

Shumway-Cook, A. & Woollacott, M. H. (2012). *Motor control: Translating research into clinical practice.* Philadelphia: Lippincott Williams & Wilkins.

Slater-Hammel, A. T. (1960). Reliability, accuracy and refractoriness of a transit reaction. *Research Quarterly, 31,* 217–228.

Sparrow, W. A. (1992). Measuring changes in coordination and control. In J. J. Summers (Ed.), *Approaches to the study of motor control and learning* (pp. 147–162). North Holland: Elsevier Science.

Taub, E. & Berman, A. J. (1968). Movement and learning in the absence of sensory feedback. In S. J. Freedman (Ed.), *The neuropsychology of spatially oriented behavior* (pp. 173–192). Homewood, IL: Dorsey.

Thelen, E. & Ulrich, B. D. (1991). Hidden skills: A dynamical systems analysis of treadmill walking in infants. *Monographs of the Society for Research in Child Development, 56,* serial #223.

Turvey, M. T. (1990). Coordination. *American Psychologist, 45,* 938–953.

Wadman, W. J., Dernier van der Gon, J. J., Geuze, R. H., & Mol, C. R. (1979). Control of fast goal-directed arm movements. *Journal of Human Movement Studies, 5,* 3–17.

Wallace, S. A. (1996). A dynamic pattern perspective of rhythmic movement: An introduction. In H. N. Zelaznik (Ed.), *Advances in motor learning and control* (pp. 155–193). Champaign, IL: Human Kinetics.

Williams, A. M. (2003). Learning football skills effectively: Challenging tradition. *Insight: The FA Coaches Association Journal, 6*(2), 37–39.

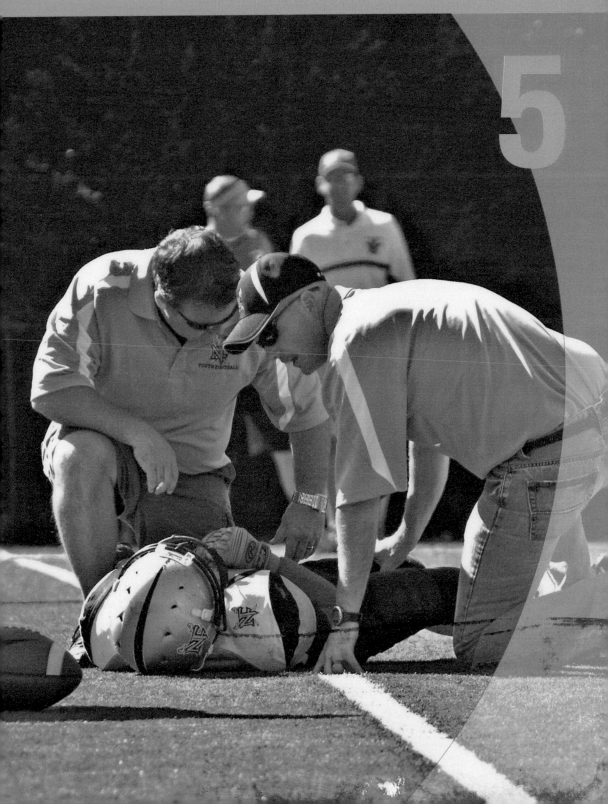

Neural Mechanisms: Contributions and Control

5

It was a seemingly normal play in the Buffalo Bills' season opener, but a player was down. Medical teams rushed onto the field. The news was not good. Tight end Kevin Everett was rushed to the hospital; it was later reported that he had sustained a fracture and dislocation of his cervical spine while trying to make a tackle. Initial reports indicated that it was unlikely he would walk again. But on December 23, 2007, four months after the accident, Everett walked again in public for the first time, at Ralph Wilson Stadium before the Bills' final home game against the New York Giants. In July 2008, at the ESPY awards, he received a standing ovation as he walked onto the stage and accepted the Jimmy V award for perseverance. While he will never be 100 percent, Kevin Everett refused to give up on his recovery.

THE NERVOUS SYSTEM

The nervous system is responsible for the processes that underlie movement preparation, execution, and control. It may be subdivided into two primary components: the central nervous system (CNS) and the peripheral nervous system (PNS). Within the CNS (which consists of the brain and the spinal cord), sensory information is integrated, decisions are made, and signals are generated and sent to the effectors (muscles and glands) to carry out responses. The PNS consists primarily of nerves that extend from the brain and spinal cord, linking the body and the CNS. The PNS may be further subdivided into a sensory or afferent division, which detects changes in the environment and conducts nerve impulses from the various sensory receptors toward the CNS, and a motor or efferent division, which transmits impulses away from the CNS to the effectors.

Sensory Receptors

We are constantly bombarded with stimuli, which are detected through components of the nervous system known as *sensory receptors*. Numerous forms of stimuli exist, as do a variety of sensory receptors, each of which is sensitive to a particular stimulus. A useful method of classifying these various receptors is by location or, more specifically, by the location of the stimuli to which they respond. Exteroceptors detect stimuli outside the body and provide information about the environment. They are located at or near the body's surface and include receptors for pressure, pain, touch, temperature, vibrations, hearing, vision, smell, and taste. Interoceptors detect stimuli from the internal viscera and provide information about the internal environment, leading to feelings such as hunger and nausea. Finally, proprioceptors, which are located in the muscles, tendons, joints, and internal ear, provide information regarding body position and movement by detecting changes in muscle tension, joint position, and equilibrium.

Sensory Contributions to Movement

The information that sensory receptors relay to the CNS for processing and interpretation allows us to interact with our environment. Of particular importance in the acquisition and performance of skilled movement are vision and proprioception. We now move on to exploring how these two sources of information contribute to the selection of a movement, its regulation, and even its correction when necessary.

VISION

Among our numerous sensory receptors, the visual system predominates. In fact, as is demonstrated in Exploration Activity 5.1, our dependence on vision is so strong that we may ignore information from other sensory receptors in its favor (Lee & Aronson, 1974). This dominance of the visual system is also reflected in estimates that 70 percent of the human body's sensory receptors are located in the eyes. Furthermore, 40 percent of the cerebral cortex is thought to be involved in some aspect of processing visual information (Marieb, Mallatt, & Wilhelm, 2017). It is not surprising, then, that interest in the role of vision in the production of skilled movement has not only increased but has also led to the development of a sub-discipline known as *sports vision*, which focuses on investigating visual contributions to performance and emphasizes vision care, visual correction, visual enhancement and performance training, and injury (Kluka, 1999; Erickson, 2007).

Our capacity to see objects clearly, at variable distances and under various conditions of light, depends on the actions of a complex arrangement of structures in and around our eyes, shown in Figure 5.1. After entering the eye, light rays are manipulated and focused onto the retina, forming an image that is converted into nerve impulses by light-sensitive cells called photoreceptors.

The two types of photoreceptor are rods and cones. Rods are more numerous, do not detect wavelength (color), and are specialized for vision in dim light. They enable us to see shapes and movements, and they discriminate between different shades of light and dark, making them the primary receptor used in night vision, as is demonstrated in Exploration Activity 5.2. Cones, on the other hand, operate best in bright light and are specialized for color vision and visual acuity (sharpness of vision). Cones are most densely concentrated in the fovea, the area of maximal visual acuity. Given the location of the fovea, our vision is most clear and sharp when we look directly at an object.

The electrical signals generated by the photoreceptors are sent to the brain via optic nerves. At one point, known as the optic chiasm, some fibers from each of the optic nerves cross, as illustrated in Figure 5.2. Because of this crossing, visual sensations from the left side of the visual field are sent to the right side of the brain for processing, while those from the right are sent to the left side.

exploration ACTIVITY   5.1

Visual Dominance

ACTIVITY 1

Equipment Needed:
- Pencil
- Mirror
- Piece of cardboard (20 x 20 cm or 8" x 8")

Procedure:
Position a mirror so that the diagram below is visible in the mirror. Now, place the tip of your pencil in between the two lines. You may start anywhere. Using the cardboard, cover the hand using the pencil so that you can see your hand and its movements only through the mirror in front of you. Using only the image in the mirror, trace the diagram by moving the pencil around the shape while staying between the lines. You may move in either direction.

How did you do? Were you able to stay in the lines and move around the shape efficiently?

ACTIVITY 2

You will need a partner for this activity. Hold your arms straight out in front of you so that they are parallel with the floor. Now, cross your arms over one another. From this position, turn your palms so that they are facing one another, and interlock your fingers. Pull your hands down and toward your chest. Continue this rotation until your knuckles are facing the sky. Once you are in position, ask your partner to point to one

continued

exploration ACTIVITY   5.1

of your fingers. It is important that the person only point to it and not touch it. Your task is simply to move the finger that your partner
pointed to.

Do you think the result would have been different if your partner had touched the finger to be moved while your eyes were closed? Try it.

In both of these activities, a sensory conflict between vision and proprioception is created. Our vision is so dominant that even when we know the visual information we are receiving is not accurate, such as when the image is reversed in a mirror, we will often rely on it anyway. The consequence is poorer performance. Lee and Aronson (1974) demonstrated visual dominance in their moving wall study. Subjects stood in a special room where the walls could be moved but the floor remained stationary. The study found that the subjects adjusted their posture to compensate for changes in visual information even though proprioceptive information did not change. The results of this study not only support the notion of visual dominance but also provide insight into the role vision plays in the maintenance of posture.

FIGURE **5.1**   Basic structures of the eye

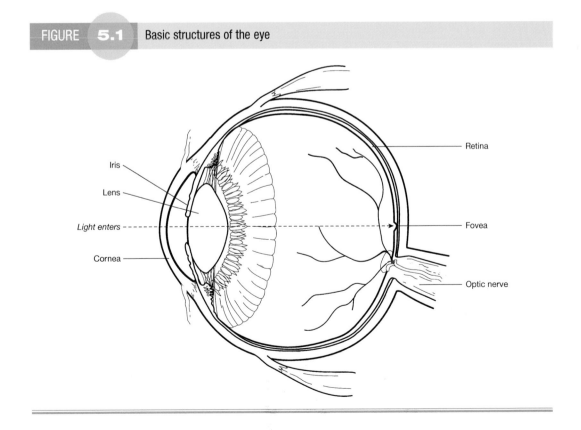

exploration ACTIVITY   5.2

Night Vision

In recent years, headlamps used for hiking and exploring have added a new feature—the ability to select between a red and a white light. The purpose of the added red light is to assist in preserving night vision. Your rods typically take 15 to 30 minutes to become fully adapted for night vision after moving from a well-lit environment. You experience this waiting period when you turn on a bright flashlight or headlamp. The red light in the headlamp, however, is detected not by rods but by cones, since they are the photoreceptors specialized for color vision. By using a red lamp headlight, our night vision is unaffected and we can enjoy the stars and landscape around us.

Try the following activities to demonstrate the role of rods and cones at night.

TEST YOUR NIGHT VISION

Place a patch over one eye for at least 45 minutes while sitting or standing outdoors in bright light. After the time has passed, go into a dimly lit room, such as a basement, and remove the eye patch. Alternate opening and closing one eye at a time. The eye that had been covered by the patch should have retained its night vision and will interpret the room as bright while the other eye adjusts to the dim light.

SEEING COLOR AT NIGHT

For this activity you will need a couple of friends and enough index cards and crayons (with the wrappers removed) for everyone. Have everyone go outside at night, as far removed as possible from street lights and other light sources. After 20 to 40 minutes, distribute the index cards and crayons. Using the crayons, your friends should write on the index cards (1) their name and (2) the color they believe the crayon they are using to be. Collect the crayons and cards and go back inside to see how they did. Can you explain the results?

From Susan Caplan McCarthy, "Night Vision Activities," http://suite101.com/article/night-vision-activities-a138968. Used with permission

Focal and Ambient Vision

The existence of two separate visual pathways to the brain has led to the theory that two separate but parallel-functioning visual systems exist. The focal system, which involves the fovea, functions to identify objects primarily located in the central region of the visual field. In other words, it serves a "what is it" role in the organization and execution of movement. Focal vision operates under conscious control (voluntary) and as a result "must be directed rapidly to the (potentially) most 'meaningful' parts of the [visual] field, so that the objects located there can be identified with minimal delay" (Müller & Krummenacher, 2006). Its function is hampered in low-light conditions.

FIGURE   **5.2**   Visual fields of the eyes and associated neural pathways

Optic chiasm

Retina

Right visual field

Left visual field

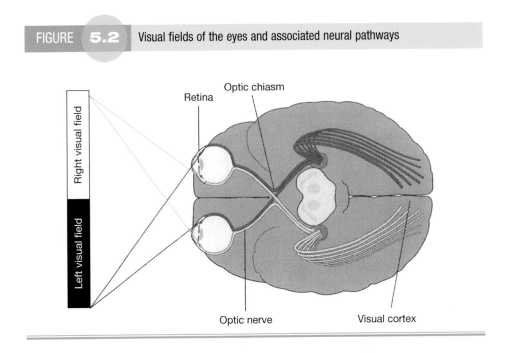

Optic nerve

Visual cortex

FIGURE   **5.3**   A mountain biker uses focal vision to identify changes in the trail, while awareness of the trees off to the side is acquired through ambient vision

In contrast, the ambient system, which functions at a subconscious level, is thought to be responsible for spatial localization and orientation. It serves a "where am I/where is it" function in the organization and execution of movement and provides information about the speed and direction that you are moving, the stability and balance of your movements, movements of other objects in the environment and time to contact information (Wrisberg, 2007). Consequently, ambient vision plays a key role in visually guiding movements such as reaching and grasping, as well as postural control, locomotion and interceptive actions. Unlike focal vision, it involves the entire retina, both the central and peripheral visual fields, and is not affected by changes in light level.

During movement, we most likely process information obtained through both systems simultaneously. While mountain biking through a forest, for example, a rider is rarely aware of the type of trees that are on the side of the trail, but he does need to be aware of where those trees are so he can avoid collisions and successfully follow the trail. Ambient vision serves the rider in this task as it allows for rapid adjustments to movement due to automatic processing of information in the visual field as a result of optic flow. At the same time, the rider uses focal vision to identify changes in the trail, such as a fallen tree across it, or a rider in front of him. It changes from moment to moment according to the visual search process the rider adopts to focus on specific features in the environment. The rider's ability to identify such objects will be hampered because of a decrease in focal sensitivity when the forest is very dense or if the tint of his sunglasses is too dark. Try Exploration Activity 5.3 to experience the use of ambient versus focal vision.

Vision and Performance

Vision is used throughout all aspects of performance. Not only do we use it to detect environmental stimuli, which we subsequently use to make movement decisions; it also provides important feedback that we use to guide our resulting action. Therefore, the role of various visual abilities in performance warrants exploration.

Eye Dominance

Information is not processed and transmitted to the brain by both eyes equally. One of your eyes, the dominant one, carries out these actions a few milliseconds faster. Those individuals whose dominant eye is on the same side of the body as their dominant hand are considered same-side dominant, while those whose dominant eye is opposite that of their dominant hand are considered cross-domi-nant. Exploration Activity 5.4 provides a simple method for discovering which eye is dominant.

Eye dominance has received attention with respect to hitting performance in baseball and softball. It has been suggested that cross-dominant hitters have an advantage because their dominant eye is closer and more in line with the

exploration ACTIVITY   5.3

Ambient versus Focal Vision

ACTIVITY 1

Try walking around the room while reading this book. You should be able to accomplish this without running into furniture because of the combined efforts of focal and ambient vision. You use focal vision to read, while ambient vision allows you to locate obstacles and successfully move about the room.

ACTIVITY 2

Now perform the task again while wearing a pair of sunglasses. What influence did the sunglasses have on your performance? How can these results be explained?

ACTIVITY 3

For the final activity, you will need a piece of three-hole paper. Hold the paper horizontally about one inch from your face so that you can see through the middle hole. Wrap the rest of the paper around to touch the sides of your head. Now walk around the room again. Explain the results.

Source: Shea, Shebilske, and Worchel, 1993

exploration ACTIVITY   5.4

Eye Dominance

Find a small object, such as a clock, on a wall. Stand directly in front of it, approximately 10 feet away. Once you are in this position, create a small triangular window with your hands by overlapping your thumbs and fingers. Stretch your arms in the direction of the wall so that you can see the object through your triangular window, as in the illustration. Now, close one eye, and then open it. Repeat with the other eye. Your dominant eye is the one where the object remained in the triangular window.

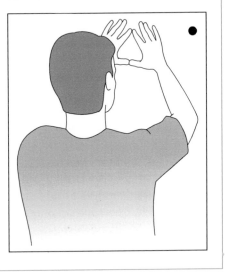

pitcher. Although research has not substantiated this claim (Milne, Buckholz, & Cardenas, 1995), turning the head to give both eyes a clear view of the pitch has been advocated (Kluka & Knudson, 1997). Evidence does exist, however, for a cross- dominant advantage in dueling sports such as fencing, boxing, and table tennis (Azémar, Stein, & Ripoll, 2008). Researchers suggest that a contra- lateral relationship between the dominant eye and the responding hand (cross- dominant) allows for a more direct pathway to the motor area of the brain; this differs from an ipsilateral relationship (same side dominant) where an inter- hemispheric transfer must occur, requiring additional processing time (Azémar et al., 2008).

Spotting

Spotting is a technique used in the performance of rotational skills (e.g., in dance, diving, gymnastics, and figure skating) to reduce the dizziness associated with spinning and to keep the performer oriented. In spotting, the rotation of the head is delayed relative to the body's rotation. This is accomplished by focusing or fixating one's visual attention on a specific spot. Once the individual's body has turned to where he or she begins to lose sight of the mark, the head quickly turns to the opposite side to re-focus on the target spot. The BallroomDancers.com link in the adjoining margin offers more information and a demonstration of spotting.

SPOTTING DEMONSTRATION

www.ballroomdancers.com/Learning_Center/Lesson/2/Default.asp?page=5

Locomotion

For safe travel over various terrains, vision provides information that is used to regulate locomotion on both a step-by-step basis and for route planning (Patla, 1997). As we move through our world, the objects and surfaces within our field of vision flow around us. For example, as you approach and pass a sign when driving, it seems to become larger as it moves from the center of your vision to the side until it is no longer in view. This perceived visual motion of objects as observers move relative to them is known as optic flow. Optic flow helps us judge how close we are to certain objects and how quickly we are approaching them, and we rely on it to guide locomotion (Gibson, 1950; Warren, Kay, Zosh, Duchon, & Sahuc, 2001).

We also rely on the feedforward function of vision in the regulation of locomotion. As Vickers (2007) noted, "during locomotion the visual field in front changes constantly, and within each visual field there are a number of visual targets and locations that must be attended to in order to navigate safely" (p. 144). Feedforward control allows information, such as the dimension of an object or details of the terrain, to be sent ahead of the movement to prepare or adjust the movement in advance. For example, when a person is walking up a steep hill, he or she makes adjustments to stride length, body lean, and arm swing in advance to negotiate the terrain and slope of the hill (Kluka, 1999).

Feedforward control is used both to contact and to avoid objects. Lee, Lischman, and Thomson (1982) demonstrated how long jumpers used *tau* to adjust their stride length during the long jump approach. In addition to using *tau*, performers used vision to provide predictive information for obstacle negotiation by fixating on objects well in advance of reaching them (Hollands, Patla, & Vickers, 2002; Patla & Vickers, 1997). Patla and Vickers also found that fixation duration and frequency were a function of object height when the task involved stepping over an obstacle. Predictive information regarding surface compliance characteristics has also been shown to cause alterations in foot placement, body posture, and velocity (Patla, Prentice, & Unger-Peters, 1993). For a more complete review of the role of vision in controlling locomotion, see Patla (1997).

RESEARCH NOTES

Given that visual information is considered critical for the safe navigation of our environment, Miyasike-daSilva, Allard, and McIlroy (2011) were interested in where we look when we walk up and down stairs. Specifically, they were interested in gaze behavior relative to transitions between ground level and stairs, the detection of handrails, and the difference between familiar and unfamiliar environments. Eleven participants performed five trials in which they approached and walked up and down a set of stairs with seven steps while wearing a head-mounted eye tracker. Contrary to the researchers' hypothesis, no difference was found in fixation frequency between transitions (the two top and bottom steps) and the middle steps of the staircase. This finding suggests that stair transitions do not require increased gaze behavior for their negotiation. Further, handrails were rarely a target of fixation, and familiarity with the environment had no effect. Participants did, however, use gaze fixations to extract information to guide stepping. During stair descent, they directed their gaze within four steps ahead of their location; during ascent their gaze remained between two to four steps ahead in the travel path.

Reaching and Grasping

Two tasks, manual aiming and prehension, allow us to interact with our environment. Manual aiming involves transporting the hand to a target location while prehension includes reaching for, grasping, and manipulating an object to achieve a goal. Both involve vision for movement coordination and control. Initially, vision is used to assess the regulatory conditions of the situation, such as the target or object's location as well as the size, position, and orientation of the object to determine reach trajectory. As the hand is initially projected towards the target, limb speed and displacement is monitored and time to contact information (tau) obtained. In the final stage of aiming movements, visual feedback enables the performer to judge the movement's accuracy and make any adjustments needed to achieve the task (e.g., tapping an icon on your smartphone). When the action goal requires grasping and object manipulation, vision aids in determining the grip characteristics including the size and shape of the hand (aperture) needed for successful performance.

Studies have shown that grip formation is not only dependent on the characteristics of the object, as mentioned earlier, but also on the intended activity to be performed (Jeannerod, 1996; Castiello, 2005). In other words, reach and grasp movements will differ according to task constraints and task goals. Consequently, practitioners should not only include a variety of objects of different sizes, shapes, weights, and textures into a patient's reach and grasp re-education program, but also a variety of tasks. For example, patients might manipulate dominoes into different patterns, relocate Cheerios from a flat surface into a bowl, reach for an item on a countertop and place it on a shelf or in a shopping cart, or reach and grasp a bean bag and throw it at a target. Go to www.youtube.com/watch?v=M7ovIDE8vhY to view a video of a patient performing other reach and grasp tasks.

FIGURE	5.4

Proprioception helps a backpacker make adjustments while walking across a log

PROPRIOCEPTION

Proprioception is the continuous flow of sensory information that is received from receptors located in the muscles, tendons, joints, and inner ear regarding movement and body position. Multiple receptors are involved. **Golgi tendon organs**, for example, are proprioceptors located at the junction of a tendon with a muscle. When tension is applied to a tendon, Golgi tendon organs relay the corresponding sensory information (intensity of the contraction) to the CNS. One of their functions is to protect tendons and their associated muscles from damage due to excessive tension.

Muscle spindles, another type of proprioceptor, are found between the skeletal muscle fibers in the muscle belly. When a muscle is stretched, the spindle sends a signal to the CNS indicating how much and how fast the muscle's length is changing. Muscle spindles can also cause a reflexive contraction known as a *stretch reflex*, which contributes to the contractile force that can be generated during a skill. The stretch reflex is created when a muscle is put on stretch just prior to contracting. For example, as in many striking skills, the tennis forehand is preceded by a backswing that stretches the involved muscles and sets up a stretch reflex. Lack of this stretch reflex would change the dynamics of the skill, and practitioners should keep this in mind when designing learning experiences.

Joint kinesthetic receptors, located in and around synovial joints, respond to pressure, acceleration and deceleration, and excessive strain on a joint. Joint receptors provide feedback about whether movements are too slow, too fast, or in the wrong direction (Kreighbaum & Barthels, 1996).

Finally, the vestibular apparatus is a collective group of receptor organs in the inner ear that respond to changes in posture and balance. The otolithic organs monitor the position of the head, providing sensory information regarding static equilibrium and the maintenance of body position when motionless. They also contribute to dynamic equilibrium, which is the maintenance of body position in response to movement, by monitoring changes in linear acceleration. You have experienced dynamic equilibrium while moving in an elevator, when you feel that you are descending as the elevator starts to ascend. A second aspect of dynamic equilibrium involves angular acceleration of the head, such as when a figure skater does a spin. The cristae in the semicircular ducts of the inner ear are responsible for monitoring changes in the angular acceleration of the head. To better understand proprioception, complete Exploration Activity 5.5 and view the video at www.youtube.com/watch?t=2&v=A1BVp5aivtA.

What would happen if we did not have proprioception? One British man, Ian Waterman, knows firsthand. When he was 19, a rare virus attacked his nervous system, rendering his proprioception useless. His muscles still worked, but he could no longer sense body position and movement without looking directly at his joints and limbs (Cole, 1995; Azar, 1998). He has had to learn to rely on his vision to control his movements, as this has become his only source of feedback. In order to judge the weight of an object he is picking up, for example, Waterman has to watch how his hand reacts instead of receiving feedback from his proprioceptors about the amount of stretch caused in the

exploration ACTIVITY 5.5

Proprioception

1. To demonstrate the use of proprioception, close your eyes and hold your arms out to the side, forming a T. Now touch your nose with the index finger of your dominant hand. Repeat with your non-dominant hand. Speculate as to why this exercise is sometimes used to test drivers suspected of being intoxicated.

2. Again, close your eyes. Raise your leg so that your thigh is parallel to the floor. Open your eyes and check your leg's position. Repeat the exercise, bringing your arm to a position parallel to the floor. How accurate was your positioning? How did you accomplish this activity in the absence of vision?

3. Research an appropriate progression of therapeutic exercises to improve proprioception for a specific population or injured area. Create a presentation to share with the class.

www

MIXED UP IN SPACE

https://science.nasa.gov/science-
news/science-at-nasa/2001/ast07
aug_1

tendons and muscles as a result of the weight. The faster and higher his hand moves, the lighter the object. This adaptation was also demonstrated in a study that required an individual deprived of proprioceptive information to judge different weights (Fleury, Bard, Teasdale, et al., 1995). When vision was available, the individual could discriminate between weights within 10 g. When his eyes were closed, the person's ability to judge the weights was significantly impaired. Similar adaptations are made by astronauts in space. Without gravity, the vestibular system has difficulties sensing which way is up! To learn more, visit the adjoining site.

RESEARCH NOTES

To evaluate how visual and proprioceptive information are integrated and modified throughout the learning process, five neurologically normal subjects and one deafferented subject (deprived of proprioception) performed a mirror-tracing task (Lajoie, Paillard, Teasdale, et al., 1992). Subjects were instructed to trace a six-pointed star pattern as fast and accurately as possible while viewing it in a mirror (similar to Exploration Activity 5.1). Normal subjects demonstrated difficulties when drawing oblique lines and changing direction while attempting to trace the star pattern. These difficulties were, however, overcome with practice. These difficulties were not evident in the tracing performance of the deafferented subject, as all trials were consistent in their execution. Because the star is viewed in a mirror, a conflict between visual and proprioceptive information is created for the normal subjects. This conflict does not exist for the deafferented subject. The results of this study demonstrate that there is a tight coupling between visual and proprioceptive feedback in the execution of visuomotor tasks.

Proprioception and Performance

Combined, proprioceptors function to "make the motor control system more efficient and flexible for the regulation of goal-directed movements" (Park & Toole, 1999, p. 645). Before a movement is initiated, proprioception provides the information about initial body and limb position that serves as the basis for the programming of motor commands. Once initiated, the movement is continuously evaluated for correctness by comparing proprioceptive feedback to the intended goal. If the two do not correspond, an error is detected. At that point, the adjustments needed to correct the movement must be determined, initiated, and accomplished prior to the completion of the response. As we saw with open- and closed-loop systems (see Chapter 4), the success of this process depends on the time available. If a movement is too rapid, response-produced feedback will be used to make adjustments on the next trial.

As indicated earlier, the intended goal of the movement serves as a frame of reference for error detection, but a learner's level of understanding of that goal depends on her skill level. Because a beginner is still trying to develop an idea of how a movement should be executed, her frame of reference for correct movement has yet to be developed. In contrast, the instant the ball leaves the hands of a skilled free-throw shooter, he can tell whether the shot was good by the way it felt at release. To assist beginning learners in developing their frame of reference, practitioners should provide opportunities for learners to experience a variety of positions and movements in a broad assortment of environments (Kreighbaum & Barthels, 1996). In addition, practitioners should focus learners' attention on the feelings associated with a movement. Because we can often see our limbs relative to the environment, we have information regarding movement and body position not only through proprioception but also through visual feedback. Learners often rely too heavily on visual feedback when judging a movement's correctness. Kinesthetic feedback should be stressed for optimal learning.

CEREBRALchallenge 5.1

1. Speculate as to why many practitioners incorporate strategies that focus a learner's attention on the feelings associated with a movement.
2. One such strategy is the use of weighted implements (bats, shots, baseballs). List other devices designed to enhance the feelings associated with movement.

CEREBRALchallenge 5.2

A popular method of teaching a youngster how to swing a bat is to stand next to him or her and manually guide the batter through the movements. This technique, appropriately termed *manual guidance*, is also frequently used in a therapeutic setting. The idea of manual guidance is to move the learner through the desired pattern or range of motion so that he or she can experience the feeling associated with it.

This technique, however, presents an inherent problem. Speculate as to what that problem might be. Try the strategy yourself prior to formulating your response. Based on your response, what conditions might you adhere to when employing this strategy?

Balance and Postural Control

Postural control involves multiple sensory inputs that tell the CNS where the body is in space. These information sources include the vestibular apparatus, the somatic senses (touch), and proprioception from the feet and ankles. Vision also provides information regarding vertical orientation, but it is not absolutely necessary—we are capable of maintaining our balance with our eyes closed.

FIGURE 5.5

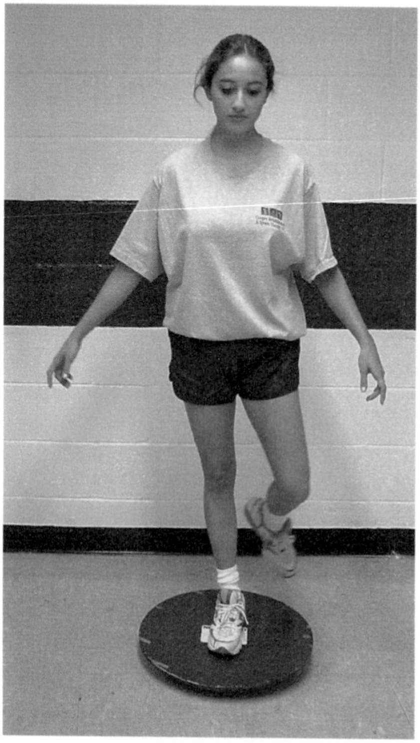

Balance board exercises assist in reestablishing proprioception

During quiet stance, maintaining one's equilibrium requires postural adjustments that may be either compensatory or anticipatory (Bleuse, Cassim, Blatt et al., 2005). Compensatory (feedback) postural adjustments occur after an external perturbation or loss of desirable posture. Anticipatory postural adjustments are activated before a voluntary movement (feedforward control) to counteract a potential loss of stability. For example, a shift in a person's center of gravity will occur when he or she reaches forward from a standing position to lift a weight from a table. Without the activation of anticipatory mechanisms, a loss of stability would occur.

Rehabilitation and Proprioception Training

According to Lepart (2004) and Prentice (2011), the reestablishment of proprioception should be a primary concern for rehabilitation programs. Consequently, athletic trainers commonly include proprioception training in rehabilitation programs following a lower-limb musculoskeletal injury. The intent is to help patients regain movement and balance sense that are lost as a result of inactivity or immobilization following an injury or surgery (Leach, 1982; Prentice, 1999). Failure to reestablish proprioception can result in functional instability that may impair performance and predispose an athlete or patient to recurrent injury (Laskowski, Newcomer-Aney, & Smith, 1997). Hence, functional progressions that incorporate balance and proprioception training (e.g., one-legged standing, double-arm balancing, and wobble board exercises) and sport-specific exercises (e.g., cutting and defensive slide drills) are important components of any rehabilitation program designed to return athletes or patients to pre-injury performance levels and prevent the reoccurrence of injury (for an example of a balance board training program, see Verhagen, van der Beek, Twisk, et al., 2004).

RESEARCH NOTES

Taping is often used to counter the proprioceptive deficit that occurs as a result of joint injuries such as ankle sprains. While its use has been shown to be effective in reducing the risk of future sprains, its effects on proprioceptive acuity (ability to sense joint

continued

position and movement) remain unclear. To determine whether taping improves proprioceptive acuity, Refshauge, Raymond, Kilbreath, and colleagues (2009) examined the movement detection capabilities of 16 participants with recurrent ankle sprains with and without the ankle taped. Participants were seated such that the hip was neutrally rotated and in the middle of the abduction/adduction range and the knee was flexed at approximately 60 degrees. The test foot was placed on a metal footplate with the ankle in the middle of both the plantar flexion/dorsiflexion range and the inversion/eversion range. Movement detection was measured at three velocities (0.1°/s, 0.5°/s, and 2.5°/s) and two directions (inversion and eversion), with the order of testing the taped and untaped conditions randomized. Contrary to the hypothesis, the application of the tape significantly decreased the ability to detect movements of the ankle in the inversion/eversion plane, adding to the conflicting findings regarding taping and proprioceptive acuity. The authors suggest that clinicians continue taping, as studies have found it effective in reducing the reoccurrence of ankle sprains.

TRANSMISSION OF INFORMATION: THE SPINAL CORD

The continuous flow of information from the receptors to various levels of the CNS is achieved via the conduction of afferent or sensory nerve impulses. Once the information has been perceived and a decision made as to how to respond, signals are sent by efferent or motor neurons to the muscles telling them to carry out the desired action. An integral component in this process is the spinal cord.

The spinal cord performs two major functions. First, it serves as a route for impulse conduction. Sensory impulses travel up the spinal cord to the brain via ascending pathways, while motor impulses travel in the opposite direction along descending pathways. However, not all signals travel to the brain for interpretation. The spinal cord's second function is to integrate some impulses at various levels and to serve as an integrating center for spinal reflexes.

FIGURE 5.6

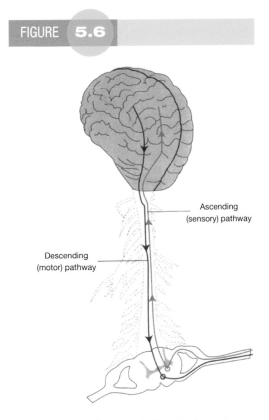

Ascending (sensory) pathway

Descending (motor) pathway

Transmission of afferent and efferent information between the body and the brain via the spinal cord

Sensory and Motor Pathways

Sensory information travels up the spinal cord to the brain via two major routes (ascending pathways) on either side of the cord: the spinothalamic pathway and the posterior or dorsal column pathway. The spinothalamic pathway conducts impulses associated with pain, temperature, crude touch, and deep pressure. Proprioception, discriminative touch, lighter pressure, and vibrations travel to the brain via the dorsal column pathway.

The two descending pathways, which transmit motor impulses to the skeletal muscles that will execute movement, are the pyramidal and extrapyramidal pathways. Nerve impulses that control skilled voluntary movements travel down the pyramidal pathway. The extrapyramidal pathway conducts nerve impulses that result in more subconscious control of body movements, such as the control of motor activities associated with posture and balance.

Spinal Reflexes

As noted above, not all impulses travel to the brain for integration. In some cases, the integration of sensory information occurs at the level of the spinal cord. The result is an automatic, involuntary response to stimuli called a reflex. Because information is integrated at the spinal cord, reflexes allow the individual to react to a stimulus faster than if conscious thought were involved.

> **COMMON MYTH**
>
> All sensory messages must go to the brain for integration.

The simplest pathway by which a reflex occurs is known as the reflex arc. Its basic components include (1) the receptor, (2) the sensory neuron, (3) the integrating center, (4) the motor neuron, and (5) the effector. When a sensory receptor detects a change in the internal or external environment, a sensory neuron is stimulated; this carries an impulse to the integrating center in the spinal cord (or brain stem). The integrating center then triggers an impulse in a motor neuron, which subsequently stimulates a response in a muscle or gland.

Several types of reflexes exist and are distinguished by the characteristics of the integrating center.

Monosynaptic Reflex

The simplest reflex involves a single synapse. Hence, a sensory neuron communicates directly with a motor neuron. Because it involves only one synapse, this type of reflex is called a *monosynaptic* or *stretch reflex*. The knee-jerk reflex illustrated in Figure 5.7 is one example of a monosynaptic reflex. When an unexpected stretch of the quadriceps occurs, there is a corresponding stretch of the muscle spindles. As we learned earlier, when a muscle spindle is stretched, it sends a signal to the CNS—more specifically, the spinal cord—indicating how much and how fast the muscle's length is changing. A single synapse is then made, which prompts an adjustment by increasing the contraction of the quadriceps,

Monosynaptic reflex loop

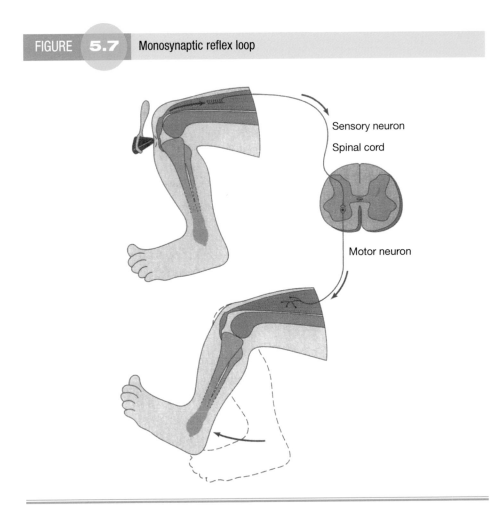

Sensory neuron

Spinal cord

Motor neuron

exploration ACTIVITY   5.6

Knee-Jerk Reflex

ACTIVITY 1

Have a partner sit on a chair and cross his or her legs so that the lower knee fits into the hollow at the back of the upper knee. Now, using the edge of your open hand, firmly tap the soft part just below your partner's kneecap. You may have to try a few times to find the spot that initiates the reflex. Switch places with your partner.

ACTIVITY 2

Repeat the above activity, but this time try to prevent your reflex from occurring. Can you do it?

resulting in an extension of the leg at the knee. Because only one synapse is involved, the monosynaptic reflex is very fast. Its function in counteracting changes in muscle length, especially those that occur unexpectedly, contributes to our ability to maintain posture and position our limbs. This reflexive action is demonstrated in Exploration Activity 5.6.

Polysynaptic Reflexes

A more common reflex pathway, known as a *polysynaptic reflex arc*, consists of one or more interneurons that lie between a sensory neuron and a motor neuron in a reflex arc (Marieb et al., 2017). Because polysynaptic reflexes involve more than one synapse, they are not as fast as monosynaptic reflexes but still function more quickly than if they required conscious control. The withdrawal reflex, in which we pull back from danger, is a polysynaptic reflex. The classic example of the withdrawal reflex occurs when an individual touches a hot stove. Impulses are generated by heat and pain receptors and sent via sensory neurons to the spinal cord. A synapse occurs there with an interneuron, which in turn synapses with a motor neuron that signals the muscles to withdraw your hand from the hot stove.

| FIGURE | 5.8 | Withdrawal and crossed extensor reflex arc |

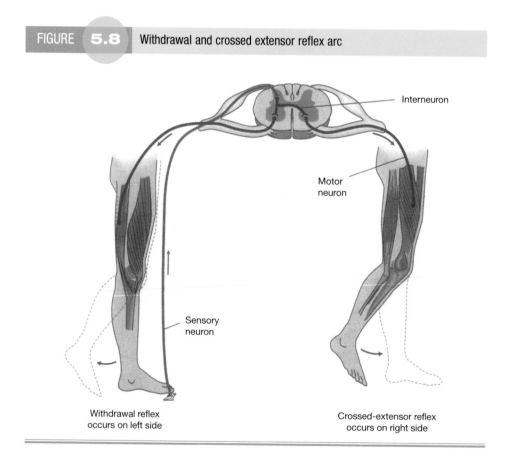

Withdrawal reflex occurs on left side

Crossed-extensor reflex occurs on right side

Another polysynaptic reflex, often associated with the withdrawal reflex, is the crossed extensor reflex. In addition to an interneuron stimulating the motor neuron responsible for the withdrawal signal, a collateral axon conducts an impulse to the opposite side of the spinal cord to a motor neuron that innervates the muscles on that side of the body, causing them to extend. In other words, when the withdrawal reflex occurs in one limb, the crossed extensor reflex may be initiated to cause the opposite limb to extend. The crossed extensor reflex is illustrated in the shifting of one's body weight to prevent a fall. For example, as illustrated in Figure 5.8, if you were walking along the beach and accidentally stepped on a broken shell, the withdrawal reflex would occur in response to the painful stimuli, while the crossed extensor reflex would cause the opposite leg to extend, creating a weight shift and preventing a fall.

Damage to the Spinal Cord

Damage to the spinal cord can result in loss of function and/or sensation (feeling). Two factors determine the effects of a spinal cord injury: the type of injury and the level at which the injury occurred.

Type of Injury

Spinal cord injuries may be classified as either complete or incomplete. In a complete injury, function and sensation are lost below the level of the injury on both sides of the body. In an incomplete injury, partial damage occurs to the spinal cord, and the effects depend on the area (front, back, side) of the spinal cord affected. Some function and sensation will remain below the level of the injury, and it is possible that the different sides of the body will be affected differently. If damage occurs to the ascending pathways, sensations arising from receptors below the level of the injury will be lost. If nerve fibers in the descending tracts are cut, the result will be loss of motor functions.

Level of Injury

The level or location of the injury also determines impairment. In general, the higher up the spinal cord the injury occurs, the greater the extent of disability. An injury to the lower segment of the cord (lumbar and sacral areas), for example, will affect the lower extremities. A cervical (neck) injury, on the other hand, may result in paralysis in both the arms and the legs, as well as loss of many vital involuntary functions, such as breathing.

THE BRAIN

Composed of about 100 billion neurons, the brain is highly complex in both structure and function. As shown in Figure 5.9, it is divided into four main parts: (1) brain stem, (2) diencephalon, (3) cerebrum, and (4) cerebellum. The brain

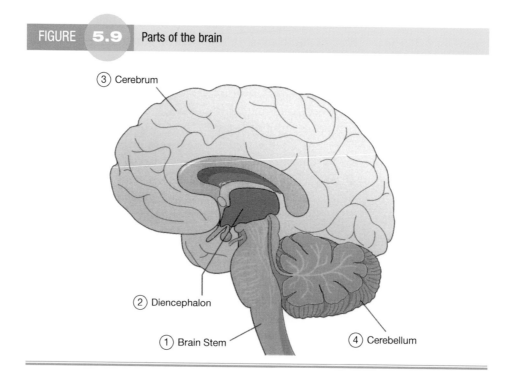

FIGURE **5.9** Parts of the brain

③ Cerebrum

② Diencephalon

① Brain Stem

④ Cerebellum

stem and diencephalon serve many vital functions; their major roles with respect to movement production and control include serving as a reflex center and relaying sensory and motor information between different parts of the brain and between the brain and the spinal cord. The cerebrum and cerebellum, however, contribute more extensively to movement, and they will receive greater attention in the following discussion.

Cerebrum

The cerebrum is the largest portion of the brain. It is divided into left and right cerebral hemispheres, each of which is concerned with the sensory and motor functions of the opposite side of the body. The outermost layer of the cerebrum, the cerebral cortex, is where we find the centers responsible for higher brain functions.

Cerebral Cortex

The cerebral cortex can be subdivided into three functional areas: (1) sensory areas, (2) motor areas, and (3) association areas. Each of these areas can be further subdivided as depicted in Figure 5.10. The following discussion will focus on those areas associated with movement production and control. It should be noted that these areas do not function independently, and a detailed examination is beyond the scope of this text.

FIGURE **5.10**   The functional areas of the cerebral cortex

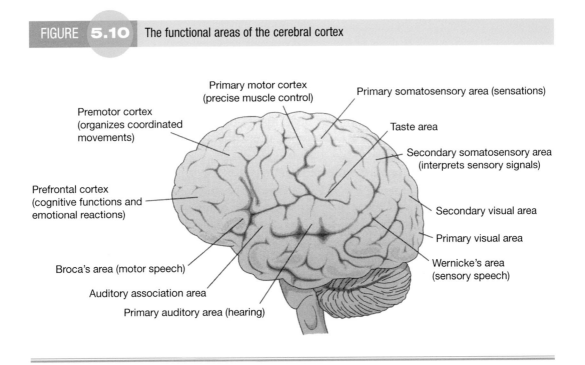

Primary motor cortex
(precise muscle control)

Primary somatosensory area (sensations)

Premotor cortex
(organizes coordinated
movements)

Taste area

Secondary somatosensory area
(interprets sensory signals)

Prefrontal cortex
(cognitive functions and
emotional reactions)

Secondary visual area

Primary visual area

Broca's area (motor speech)

Wernicke's area
(sensory speech)

Auditory association area

Primary auditory area (hearing)

Sensory Areas

The sensory areas interpret information received from the various sensory receptors. The primary somatosensory area receives sensations from cutaneous
receptors (touch, pressure, temperature, pain) and proprioceptors in the periphery
of the body. In this area, information is processed and an individual becomes
consciously aware of not only the sensation itself but also the exact location from
which the sensation arose. Primary somatosensory area damage from a stroke,
for example, will eliminate one's conscious ability to feel and localize touch
and pressure on the skin. This in turn will affect grip and object manipulation
(Leonard, 1998). In addition, the individual will experience a loss in joint
position awareness, as he or she will no longer be able to perceive accurate
sensory feedback associated with movement. Movements will, therefore, become
uncoordinated.

In contrast, the secondary somatosensory area serves to integrate and
interpret sensory signals. If damage were to occur in this area of the cerebral
cortex, sensory information that would normally be associated with object
manipulation would no longer be available. For example, your ability to identify
that your hand is feeling a golf ball versus a racquetball would be impaired. In
addition, because signals to the secondary area are partly processed in the
primary somatosensory area before being relayed, impairments similar to those
described above for the primary somatosensory area will be manifested.

Given the role of vision in movement, the visual areas deserve attention.
These can also be subdivided into primary and secondary areas. The primary

RESEARCH NOTES

It is believed that in baseball, a batter's chance of getting a hit increases if the previous few batters hit successfully and reach base. In other words, baseball theorists have long suggested that "hitting is contagious." Gray and Beilock (2011) investigated this notion, specifically asking what effect observing a successful hit just prior to one's own attempt to hit a baseball would have on performance. Given the discovery of mirror neurons in the premotor cortex of the brain, they predicted that a stimulus viewed just before one's turn at bat would in fact influence both hitting success and the direction the ball traveled. Mirror neurons fire both when an individual performs an action and when he or she watches it being performed by someone else (see Chapter 8 for more detail). In other words, this distinctive class of neurons is thought to "mirror" movement, as though the observer were the one performing the action.

Twelve junior college baseball players and 12 who played in competitive recreational leagues participated in the study. Following one practice round of 25 pitches to acquaint them with the batting simulation, participants completed 30 "at bats" in which they attempted to hit a simulated pitched ball after viewing one of three inducing stimuli or receiving no prompt. The stimuli were presented with three different prompt directions (right, left, and center) and were (1) a ball traveling to a particular location on the field, (2) a stationary ball sitting in a particular location on the field, and (3) a written message indicating the location where the ball landed. Results supported the researcher's predictions, as both groups of batters significantly improved their performance when they viewed a successful outcome prior to hitting. Based on these findings, the researchers suggest that activating the mirror neurons by showing a batter a video of the baseball successfully being hit to the desired location prior to an "at bat" should result in superior hitting outcomes than the traditional method of verbal instructions or hand signals.

visual area receives visual information regarding the image formed on the retina. Whereas this area detects light and dark spots and determines the orientation of the visual field, the secondary visual area interprets what one is seeing.

Motor Areas

The motor areas coordinate and initiate voluntary movements of skeletal muscles. The primary motor cortex is the region responsible for initiating skilled voluntary movements, including those required for performing fine motor skills. Decisions regarding how to initiate those movements are a function of the premotor cortex, which lies just anterior to the primary motor cortex. More specifically, the premotor cortex organizes learned coordinated movements that involve complex sequencing of muscles. For example, if a performer decides to take a step, decisions regarding which muscles to contract, in what order, and to what degree are made in the premotor cortex (Seeley, Stephens, & Tate, 1997). Impulses are then sent to the primary motor cortex, which initiates each planned movement.

Association Areas

Association areas are concerned with the analysis and interpretation of sensory information. For this function, it appears that new sensory inputs are associated with past experiences. The prefrontal cortex's role involves emotional reactions and cognitive functions. Attentiveness, the ability to make accurate judgments, planning for future events, and the motivation to practice depend on prefrontal cortex functioning.

A second area, known as the *general interpretive area*, plays a primary role in complex thought processing. Situations are interpreted as a result of the integration of sensory information in this region. The interpretation is then sent to the prefrontal cortex, where it is linked with emotion and a decision on how to respond is made.

CEREBRALchallenge   5.3

Damage to the primary visual area results in functional blindness. Speculate as to the consequences of damage to the secondary visual area.

Basal Ganglia

The basal ganglia, a group of functionally related nuclei, lie deep within the cerebrum. Extensive communication occurs between the basal ganglia and both the cerebral cortex and the brain stem, creating a loop of information flow that is relayed through the thalamus. The basal ganglia are important in the initiation and control of subconscious gross body movements, such as swinging the arms while walking (Tortora, 1997), and play a key role in regulating the intensity (scaling) of movement parameters. One can see the importance of scaling movement parameters through the functional changes that occur in two different degenerative conditions of the basal ganglia. The first, Parkinson's disease—characterized by slow, uncontrollable shaking (tremor) of the limbs and difficulty in initiating voluntary movements—is the result of understimulating the basal ganglia. Huntington's disease, on the other hand, is the result of overstimulating the basal ganglia. An individual with this condition will display uncontrollable jerking movements of the limbs and/or facial muscles.

Cerebellum

The cerebellum monitors movement by comparing the intended movement, programmed by the motor areas, to what is actually taking place. In other words, it compares the sensory input it receives from proprioceptors and visual receptors to the expected sensory consequences. Consequently, the cerebellum plays a key role in detecting and correcting errors, and it works in conjunction with the

CEREBRAL challenge   5.4

A patient who was not wearing a helmet suffers brain damage as a result of a serious biking accident. The part of the brain affected is the cerebellum. Speculate as to what behaviors this patient will display as a result of trauma to the cerebellum.

motor cortex to produce smooth coordinated movements. The cerebellum is also important in the maintenance of posture and balance.

Traumatic Brain Injuries and Concussions

WWW

CONCUSSIONS

Everything we know—and don't know—about concussions
www.statnews.com/2015/12/17/
everything-know-dont-know-
concussions/

Sports-Related Concussion Testing and ImPACT Testing Program
www.nebsportsconcussion.org/
impact/sports-related-concussion-
testing-and-impact-testing-
program.html

Impact Testing and Concussions
www.youtube.com/watch?v=MB
Y12KJTeDk

Traumatic brain injury (TBI) is the disruption of normal brain function as a result of an external mechanical force (Marion, 1999). Depending on the nature of the TBI, temporary or lasting cognitive and/or motor impairments can result; physical therapists may have to design programs to help restore motor function, strength, coordination, balance, endurance, and/or movement. Approximately 75 percent of TBIs that occur each year are concussions or other forms of mild TBI (Centers for Disease Control and Prevention, 2003), and an estimated 3.8 million of those occur as a result of sport and physical activity (Broglio et al., 2014). A *concussion* is the temporary impairment of brain function caused by a bump, blow, or jolt to the head or by a rotational force (Cartwright & Pitney, 2011). Visit the websites listed in the margin below for an overview of concussions, their causes, symptoms, and rate of occurrence in the NFL by year and by team, and learn more about the ImPACT test—a computerized concussion-evaluation system that athletic trainers use to evaluate the concussed athlete's post-injury condition objectively and track recovery for a safe return to play.

Neural Plasticity

It was once thought that after the brain developed during a critical period in early childhood, it remained relatively unchangeable with fixed neuronal circuits in adulthood. Research has shown however, that this is not the case but rather the human brain has the ability to reorganize itself by forming new neuronal connections in response to injury, learning, and practice. This ability to change its organization and ultimately its function throughout the lifespan is known as neural plasticity (Kolb, Gibb, & Robinson, 2003). A good illustration of how the brain is thought to rewire itself, known as cortical remapping, can be viewed at www.youtube.com/watch?v=iAzmyB9PFt4.

TABLE 5.1	Ten principles of experience-dependent plasticity relevant to skill acquisition and rehabilitation
PRINCIPLE	**DESCRIPTION**
1. Use it or lose it	Lack of use of neural circuits can degrade brain function.
2. Use it and improve it	Skill training can evoke plasticity in specific regions of the brain.
3. Specificity	Specific forms of neural plasticity and ultimately function are dependent on specific kinds of experiences.
4. Repetition matters	Repetition is necessary to evoke lasting changes.
5. Intensity matters	Sufficient training intensity is needed to evoke lasting changes.
6. Time matters	Different forms of plasticity occur at different times during training with some appearing dependent on others.
7. Salience matters	Plasticity is dependent on the level of engagement and motivation of the learner or on the salience of the training.
8. Age matters	While experience dependent plasticity can be induced throughout the lifespan, neural adaptations are less profound and/or slower as one ages.
9. Transference	Plasticity resulting from one training experience can facilitate the acquisition of similar behaviors.
10. Interference	Plasticity resulting from one training experience can inhibit the acquisition of other behaviors.

Adapted from Kleim and Jones (2008).

Neuroplasticity is experience dependent (Kolb et al., 2003). Table 5.1 lists 10 principles of experience-dependent plasticity identified by Kleim and Jones (2008) relevant to skill acquisition and rehabilitation. While they offer considerations for designing interventions to promote brain reorganization and function in both the intact and damaged brain, many of which underlie strategies that will be discussed in upcoming chapters, much about how to best exploit the plasticity of the brain has yet to be determined (Novak, 2016). For more information on neural plasticity in general, and related to both motor skill acquisition and clinical applications specifically, see Kolb and Gibb (2014), Dayan and Cohen (2011), and Cramer et al. (2011) respectively.

RESEARCH NOTES

Complex regional pain syndrome type 1 (CRPS1) is a chronic pain condition most often affecting one of the limbs (arms, legs, hands, or feet), usually after an injury or trauma to that limb (National Institute of Neurological Disorders and Stroke, 2015). Because it

continued

MEMORY

An exploration of the brain and motor skill acquisition and performance would be incomplete without a discussion about memory. Memory is the ability to store and retrieve information. That information might be a friend's phone number, or it might represent past movement experiences that help with decisions about what motor response to make and how to make it. Several changes have to occur in the CNS in order for an experience to become represented in memory. Portions of the brain—including the association cortex of the frontal, parietal, occipital, and temporal lobes; parts of the limbic system; and the diencephalon—are known to be associated with memory, but much about its function remains unknown.

Memory Model

Atkinson and Shiffrin (1968, 1971) offered a popular and influential model of memory, the Multi-Store Model. This model proposed that memory is composed of three distinct systems—the sensory memory, short-term memory, and long-term memory—each defined by its storage and processing characteristics. Over time, however, the model was viewed as too simplistic, and Baddeley and Hitch (1974) offered a more comprehensive modification, substituting a three-component working memory for short-term memory. The resulting model is seen in Figure 5.11.

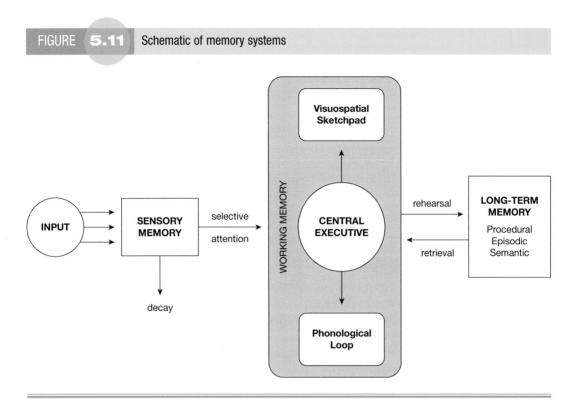

FIGURE **5.11** Schematic of memory systems

Sensory Memory

The first stage of memory, the point at which information enters the nervous system through the sensory system, is called sensory memory. We are constantly exposed to information through our sensory receptors. Sensory memory retains a brief impression of a sensory stimulus even after the stimulus itself has ceased. This brief period, lasting only a few hundred milliseconds, allows just enough time for an individual to decide whether the incoming sensory information demands further attention (Plotnik & Kouyoumdjian, 2011). Information we choose to selectively attend to is processed further, while the rest will be lost.

Working Memory

Working memory is a set of interacting information-processing components that actively stores and manages information required to carry out complex cognitive tasks such as learning, decision making, reasoning, and comprehension (Becker & Morris, 1999). Current views of working memory involve a central executive and two short-term storage systems that are defined by their function: the phonological loop and the visuospatial sketchpad (Baddeley, 2003). The phono-logical loop deals with short-term storage of spoken and written material, while the visuospatial sketchpad is responsible for temporary storage and manipulation of spatial and visual information. The central executive, the most important but

exploration ACTIVITY   5.7

Short-Term Storage Test

Try the short-term storage test at http://faculty.washington.edu/chudler/stm0.html. Attempt all six trials.

How do your results compare to the limited capacity of seven plus or minus two items? What strategies did you use to remember the letters?

For more memory games and strategies to improve your memory, go to www.exploratorium.edu/memory/dont_forget/index.html.

least understood component of Baddeley's (2003) working memory model, serves to control the flow of information between the two storage systems, regulates information processing (including retrieval from long-term memory), and governs attentional activities.

With respect to its storage function, working memory retains many features of the previous conception of short-term memory. It has a limited capacity and can hold only seven, plus or minus two, items or chunks of information at a given time (Miller, 1956). In addition, the information is retained in this temporary storage space for only 20 to 30 seconds unless it is given further attention through processing activities such as repetition, association, or rehearsal (Adams & Dijkstra, 1966). Active processing is also necessary to transfer the information for more permanent storage in long-term memory (LTM). Without this transfer, effective learning is not possible. Try Exploration Activity 5.7 to explore the capacity of your own working memory.

As we have learned, there is more to memory than simply the storage of information. Working and long-term memory work together to integrate information about the current situation and past experiences, which in turn enables a performer to make, execute, and evaluate strategic and movement decisions. For example, a racquetball player must combine information about the current situation (e.g., the position of the opponent and her level of fatigue) with information retrieved from LTM about past experiences (e.g., the opponent's strengths, weaknesses, and probable responses) in order to decide what serve to use. Furthermore, once the serve has been selected, additional information and integration are needed for its execution. These integrative processes take place in working memory.

Long-Term Memory

Long-term memory is characterized as having a seemingly limitless capacity and duration. Three types of LTM exist: procedural memory and two types of declarative memory, semantic and episodic (Tulving, 1985). Procedural memory retains information regarding how to perform different skills and actions and is fundamental to our ability to achieve movement goals. Riding a bike, tying your shoes, and taping an ankle with a closed basketweave are all examples of procedural memories. Declarative memory is our memory for facts or events and is commonly broken down into two types—episodic and semantic memory. Episodic memory contains information about personal experiences and events that are associated with a specific time and context. The date you graduated from high school is an example of knowledge represented by episodic memory. Semantic memory, on the other hand, represents general knowledge that is developed by our experiences but not associated with time. Factual knowledge, such as your school colors, and conceptual knowledge, such as your concept of success, are included in semantic memory. Consequently, episodic and semantic memory store information that we use to decide what to do in a given situation.

Forgetting

Through practice, learners can transfer increased information into LTM. However, all performers, regardless of skill level, are vulnerable to the phenomenon of forgetting. Two theories have been proposed to explain forgetting. The first, known as the *decay theory*, suggests that forgetting occurs as a result of the passage of time. A second theory, the *interference theory*, proposes that forgetting can be attributed to either proactive or retroactive interference. In proactive interference, old memories interfere with the retention of newly presented information that is to be remembered. Retroactive interference occurs when learning something new interferes with the retention of older memories. Figure 5.12 illustrates these two types of interference, using the example of an individual who took surfing lessons over the summer and is learning how to snowboard this winter. If this person experiences difficulties in remembering a snowboarding movement because of experiences with surfing, then proactive interference has occurred. On the other hand, if the learner forgets how to perform a surfing movement as a result of interference from newly learned snowboarding skills, this is retroactive interference.

Practical Implications

Because of limitations in memory capacity, keep instructions, verbal cues, and feedback short and simple. Repeat key learning points, and provide ample opportunities for physical rehearsal. Since learners more easily retain meaningful information, relate the skill being learned to their previously learned skills. Use meaningful verbal labels and analogies to strengthen associations. For example, the knee examination stress test known as the tibial drop back or posterior sag test is so named because "the tibia 'drops back' or sags back on the femur because of gravity if the posterior cruciate ligament is torn" (Magee, 2008, p. 773). Similarly, in tennis, learners are instructed to "shake hands" with the racket rather than given a less memorable, detailed explanation to convey the grip. Finally, grouping or "chunking" several movements together into a single unit

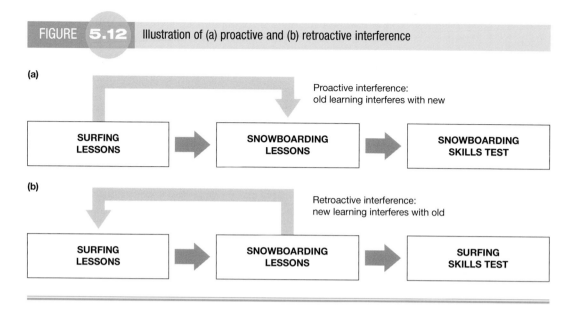

FIGURE 5.12 Illustration of (a) proactive and (b) retroactive interference

(a)

Proactive interference: old learning interferes with new

SURFING LESSONS → SNOWBOARDING LESSONS → SNOWBOARDING SKILLS TEST

(b)

Retroactive interference: new learning interferes with old

SURFING LESSONS → SNOWBOARDING LESSONS → SURFING SKILLS TEST

exploration ACTIVITY 5.8

Chunking

Below is a list of 21 letters. Study the letters for 15 seconds and then cover the list. Based on what you remember, write down as many letters as you can.

TRY

CHU

NKI

NGT

HEL

ETT

ERS

How did you do? What strategies did you use to remember the letters?

One strategy that you may have used to recall the letters in this activity is called *chunking*. If you look at the first three letters, they spell the word *try*. By grouping the letters into a word, you now only have to remember one word instead of three individual letters. Since short-term storage is limited in capacity to seven plus or minus two items, chunking can increase the amount of information that can be remembered. In fact, as you may have realized, the letters spell out the following: **TRY CHUNKING THE LETTERS**. If you had noticed this trick, remembering all 21 letters would have been easy!

is an effective method of reducing the amount of information a learner must remember, as demonstrated in Exploration Activity 5.8.

PUTTING IT INTO PRACTICE

Learning Situation: Rehabilitation of an Ankle Sprain

Darren doesn't think an ankle sprain is a big deal. The swelling is down and he asks his physical therapist why he can't just wear a brace instead of doing all of the balance exercises.

Test Your Knowledge

If you were Darren's physical therapist would you agree to let him wear the brace? Why or why not? Compare your answer with the sample response provided at www.routledge.com/cw/coker.

A LOOK AHEAD

At this point, the complexity involved in movement production should be apparent. Numerous receptors provide information to various levels of the CNS via afferent pathways for integration. Reflexes are integrated at the spinal cord, while information requiring conscious thought travels up the spinal cord to various locations of the brain, where it is integrated and interpreted. Through the collective efforts of numerous brain structures, including the cerebral cortex and basal ganglia, movements are organized and signals sent to the effectors to produce the output, which is continuously monitored by the cerebellum.

Chapters 1 through 5 have focused on the behavioral and neurological processes that influence performance. We will now build on this foundational knowledge of how skilled movements are produced to examine the processes involved in their acquisition and refinement. The next chapter begins this discussion by examining the characteristics of learners as they progress from novice to expert.

FOCUS POINTS

After reading this chapter, you should know:

* The nervous system is responsible for the processes that underlie movement preparation, execution, and control.
* Sensory receptors can be classified as exteroceptors, interoceptors, and proprioceptors.
* Vision is the dominant sensory system.

- The focal system functions to identify objects primarily located in the central region of the visual field, while the ambient system is responsible for spatial localization and orientation.
- The focal and ambient systems work in conjunction to process visual information during movement.
- Proprioceptors provide information regarding body position and movement by detecting changes in muscle tension, joint position, and equilibrium through Golgi tendon organs, muscle spindles, joint kinesthetic receptors, and the vestibular apparatus.
- Proprioception provides information about initial body and limb position. This serves as the basis for the programming of motor commands, evaluates ongoing movements by comparing proprioceptive feedback to the intended goal, and provides response-produced feedback that can be used to make adjustments on the next trial.
- The spinal cord serves as a reflex center and a pathway for the transmission of sensory and motor information.
- The cerebral cortex plays a significant role in movement production and control through three major functional areas (sensory, motor, and association) where interpretive and integrative processes occur.
- The cerebellum plays a key role in error detection and correction and in the maintenance of posture and balance.
- The brain is capable of changing its organization and ultimately its function throughout the lifespan.
- Learning occurs when information is moved into long-term memory.

lab

To complete the lab for this chapter, visit www.routledge.com/cw/coker and select **Lab 5, Balance**.

REVIEW QUESTIONS

1. Which photoreceptor is specialized for vision in dim light? Which one is specialized for visual acuity?

2. Compare and contrast focal and ambient vision. Which one deals with peripheral vision?

3. Compare and contrast Golgi tendon organs, muscle spindles, joint kinesthetic receptors, and the vestibular apparatus.

4. Explain how vision is used during prehension.

5. What functional problems would be associated with damage to the dorsal column pathways? The extrapyramidal pathway?

6. What are the five components of a reflex arc? Explain why reflexes are faster than voluntary movements.

7. What is the significance of neuroplasticity?

8. What are the three memory systems? Compare each with respect to capacity and duration.

9. Explain why phone numbers have traditionally consisted of seven digits. Many regions of the country now use 10-digit dialing. Do you foresee any problems with the new system? If so, what strategies will callers use to overcome them?

10. What are the two functions of working memory?

REFERENCES

Adams, R. & Dijkstra, S. (1966). Short-term memory for motor responses. *Journal of Experimental Psychology, 71,* 314–318.

Atkinson, R. C. & Shiffrin, R. M. (1968). Human memory: A proposed system and its control processes. In K. W. Spence & J. T. Spence (Eds.), *The psychology of learning and motivation (Vol. 2)* (pp. 89–195). Orlando, FL: Academic Press.

Atkinson, R. C. & Shiffrin, R. M. (1971). The control of short-term memory. *Scientific American, 225,* 82–90.

Azar, B. (1998). Why can't this man feel whether or not he is standing up? *APA Monitor Online, 29*(6).

Azémar, G., Stein, J. F., & Ripoll, H. (2008). Effets de la dominance oculaire sur la coordination oeil-main dans les duels sportifs. *Science & Sports, 23* (6), 263–278.

Baddeley, A. D. (2003). Working memory: Looking back and looking forward. *Nature Reviews: Neuroscience, 4,* 829–839.

Baddeley, A. D. & Hitch, G. (1974). Working memory. In G. H. Bower (Ed.), *The psychology of learning and motivation: Advances in research and theory (Vol. 8)* (pp. 47–89). New York: Academic Press.

Bahill, A. T. & La Ritz, T. (1984). Why can't batters keep their eyes on the ball? *American Scientist, 72,* 249–253.

Becker, J. T. & Morris, R. G. (1999). Working memory. *Brain and Cognition, 41,* 1–8.

Bleuse, S., Cassim, F., Blatt, J., Defebvre, L., Derambure, P., & Guieu, J. (2005). Vertical torque allows recording of anticipatory postural adjustments associated with slow, arm-raising movements. *Clinical Biomechanics, 20*(7), 693–699S.

Broglio, S. P., Cantu, R. C., Gioia, G. A., Guskiewicz, K. M., Kutcher, J., Palm, M., & Valovich McLeod, T. C. (2014). National Athletic Trainers' Association position statement: Management of sport concussion. *Journal of Athletic Training (Allen Press), 49*(2), 245–265.

Cartwright, L. & Pitney, W. (2011). *Fundamentals of athletic training* (3rd ed.). Champaign, IL: Human Kinetics.

Castiello, U. (2005). The neuroscience of grasping. *Nature Reviews Neuroscience, 6*(9), 726–736. doi:10.1038/nrn1744.

Centers for Disease Control and Prevention (CDC), National Center for Injury Prevention and Control. (2003). *Report to Congress on mild traumatic brain injury in the United States: Steps to prevent a serious public health problem.* Atlanta, GA: Author.

Cole, J. (1995). *Pride and a daily marathon.* Cambridge, MA: MIT.

Cramer, S. C., Sur, M., Dobkin, B. H., O'Brien, C., Sanger, T. D., Trojanowski, J. Q., & Vinogradov, S. (2011). Harnessing neuroplasticity for clinical applications. *Brain: A Journal of Neurology, 134*(6), 1591–1609. doi:10.1093/brain/awr039

Dayan, E. & Cohen, L. (2011). Neuroplasticity subserving motor skill learning. *Neuron, 72*(3), 443–454. doi:10.1016/j.neuron.2011.10.008

Erickson, G. B. (2007). Sports vision: vision care for the enhancement of sports performance. Oxford, UK: Butterworth-Heinemann.

Fleury, M., Bard, C., Teasdale, N., Paillard, J., Cole, J., Lajoie, Y., & Lamarre, Y. (1995). Weight judgment: The discrimination capacity of a deafferented subject. *Brain, 118,* 1149–1156.

Gibson, J. J. (1950). *Perception of the visual world.* Boston: Houghton Mifflin.

Gray, R. & Beilock, S. L. (2011). Hitting is contagious: Expertise and action induction. *Journal of Experimental Psychology: Applied, 17*(1), 49–59.

Hollands, M. A., Patla, A. E., & Vickers, J. N. (2002). Look where you are going! Gaze behavior associated with maintaining and changing direction. *Experimental Brain Research*, *143*, 221–230.

Jeannerod, M. (1996). Reaching and grasping: Parallel specification of visuomotor channels. In H. Heuer & S. W. Keele (Eds.), *Handbook of perception and action. Vol. 2: Motor skills* (pp. 405–460). San Diego: Academic Press.

Kleim, J. A. & Jones, T. A. (2008). Principles of experience-dependent neural plasticity: implications for rehabilitation after brain damage. *Journal of Speech, Language, and Hearing Research: JSLHR*, *51*(1), S225–S239.

Kluka, D. A. (1999). *Motor behavior: From learning to performance.* Englewood, CO: Morton.

Kluka, D. A. & Knudson, D. (1997). The impact of vision training on sport performance. *Journal of Health, Physical Education, Recreation and Dance*, *68*(4), 17–24.

Kolb, B. & Gibb, R. (2014). Searching for the principles of brain plasticity and behavior. *Cortex; A Journal Devoted to the Study of the Nervous System and Behavior*, *58*, 251–260. doi:10.1016/j.cortex.2013.11.012

Kolb, B., Gibb, R., & Robinson, T. (2003). Brain plasticity and behavior. *Current Directions in Psychological Science*, *12*(1), 1–5.

Kreighbaum, E. & Barthels, K. (1996). *Biomechanics: A qualitative approach for studying human movement.* San Francisco: Benjamin Cummings.

Lajoie, Y., Paillard, J., Teasdale, N., Bard, C., Fleury, M., Forget, R., & Lamarre, Y. (1992). Mirror drawing in a deafferented patient and normal subjects: Visuoproprioceptive conflict. *Neurology*, *42*(5), 1104–1106.

Laskowski, E. R., Newcomer-Aney, K., & Smith, J. (1997). Refining rehabilitation with proprioception training: Expediting return to play. *The Physician and Sportsmedicine*, *25*(10), 89–102.

Leach, R. E. (1982). Overall view of rehabilitation of the leg for running. In R. P. Mack (Ed.), *Symposium on the foot and leg in running sports.* St. Louis: Mosby.

Lee, D. N. & Aronson, E. (1974). Visual proprioceptive control of standing in human infants. *Perception and Psychophysics*, *15*, 527–532.

Lee, D. N., Lischman, J. R., & Thomson, J. A. (1982). Regulation of gait in long jumping. *Journal of Experimental Psychology: Human Perception and Performance*, *8*, 448–459.

Leonard, C. T. (1998). *The neuroscience of human movement.* St. Louis, MO: Mosby-Year Book.

Lepart, S. (2004). Reestablishing neuromuscular control. In W. E. Prentice (Ed.), *Rehabilitation techniques in sports medicine* (4th ed., pp. 100–120). Dubuque, IA: WCB/McGraw-Hill.

Magee, D. J. (2008). *Orthopedic Physical Assessment.* St. Louis, MO: Saunders Elsevier.

Marieb, E. N., Mallatt, J., & Wilhelm, P. B. (2017). *Human anatomy.* Washington, D.C.: Pearson Education.

Marion, D. (1999). *Traumatic brain injury.* New York: Thieme Medical.

Miller, G. A. (1956). The magical number seven, plus or minus two: Some limits on our capacity for processing information. *Psychological Review*, *63*, 81–97.

Milne, C., Buckholz, E., & Cardenas, M. (1995). Relationship of eye dominance and batting performance in baseball players. *International Journal of Sports Vision*, *2*(1), 17–21.

Miyasike-daSilva, V., Allard, F., & McIlroy, W. E. (2011). Where do we look when we walk on stairs? Gaze behaviour on stairs, transitions, and handrails *Experimental Brain Research*, *209*, 73–83.

Moseley, G. L. (2006). Graded motor imagery for pathologic pain: a randomized controlled trial. *Neurology*, *67*(12), 2129–2134.

Müller, H. J. & Krummenacher, J. (2006). Visual search and selective attention. *Visual Cognition*, *14*, 389–410.

National Institute of Neurological Disorders and Stroke (2015). Complex Regional Pain Syndrome Fact Sheet. Retrieved from www.ninds.nih.gov/disorders/reflex_sympathetic_dystrophy/detail_reflex_sympathetic_dystrophy.htm

Novak, M. R. (2016). Promoting neuroplasticity in a developing brain: Integrated neurorehabilitation (INRA) for children with cerebral palsy—A protocol description and case report. *Journal of Neurology and Stroke*, *4*(4), 00137. doi: 10.15406/jnsk.2016.04.00137

Park, S. & Toole, T. (1999). Functional roles of the proprioceptive system in the control of goal-directed movement. *Perceptual and Motor Skills*, *88*(2), 631–647.

Patla, A. E. (1997). Understanding the roles of vision in the control of human locomotion. *Gait and Posture*, *5*, 54–69.

Patla, A. E., Prentice, S., & Unger-Peters, G. (1993). Accommodating difference compliant surfaces in the travel path during locomotion. In *Proceedings of the Fourteenth International Society for Biomechanics Conference.* Paris. 11: 1010–1011.

Patla, A. E. & Vickers, J. N. (1997). When and where do we look as we approach and step over an obstacle in the travel path? *NeuroReport*, *8*(17), 3661–3665.

Plotnik, R. & Kouyoumdjian, H. (2011). *Introduction to Psychology*. Belmont, CA: Wadsworth/Cengage Learning.

Prentice, W. E. (1999). Using therapeutic exercise in rehabilitation. In W. E. Prentice (Ed.), *Rehabilitation techniques in sports medicine* (3rd ed., pp. 226–243). Boston: WCB/McGraw-Hill.

Prentice, W. E. (2011). *Arnheim's principles of athletic training: A competency based approach*. New York: McGraw-Hill.

Raab, M., Masters, R. S. W., & Maxwell, J. P. (2005). Improving the "how" and "what" decisions of elite table tennis players. *Human Movement Science, 24,* 326–344.

Refshauge, K. M., Raymond, J., Kilbreath, S. L., Pengel, L., & Heijnen, I. (2009). The effect of ankle taping on detection of inversion-eversion movements in participants with recurrent ankle sprain. *American Journal of Sports Medicine, 37*(2), 371–375.

Seeley, R., Stephens, T., & Tate, P. (1997). *Anatomy and physiology* (3rd ed.). St. Louis: Mosby-Year Book.

Shea, C. H., Shebilske, W. L., & Worchel, S. (1993). *Motor learning and control*. Englewood Cliffs, NJ: Prentice-Hall.

Tortora, G. J. (1997). *Introduction to the human body: The essentials of anatomy and physiology*. Mountain View, CA: Benjamin Cummings.

Tulving, E. (1985). How many memory systems are there? *American Psychologist, 40,* 385–398.

Verhagen, E., van der Beek, A., Twisk, J., Bouter, L., Bahr, R., & van Mechelen, W. (2004). The effect of a proprioceptive balance board training program for the prevention of ankle sprains: A prospective controlled trial. *The American Journal of Sports Medicine, 32,* 1385–1393.

Vickers, J. N. (2007). *Perception, cognition and decision training: The quiet eye in action*. Champaign, IL: Human Kinetics.

Warren Jr., W. H., Kay, B. A., Zosh, W. D., Duchon, A. P., & Sahuc, S. (2001). Optic flow is used to control human walking. *Nature Neuroscience, 4,* 213–216.

Witt, J. K. & Proffitt, D. R. (2005). See the ball, hit the ball: Apparent ball size is correlated with batting average. *Psychological Science, 16*(12), 937–938.

Wrisberg, C. A. (2007). *Sport instruction for coaches*. Champaign, IL: Human Kinetics.

Growing up in the White Mountains of New Hampshire, Jenny was introduced to skiing at the age of five and has been carving turns ever since. Now 11 years old, her parents have signed her up for race camp and she couldn't be more excited. This is the first step to fulfilling her dream of becoming a World Cup Champion like her idol Lindsey Vonn!

What does it take to go from nursery slopes to elite downhill racer? Reaching the high caliber of skill demonstrated by world-class athletes requires underlying ability as well as countless hours of hard work and practice—practice that is grounded in the underlying principles that affect skill acquisition and control, and practice that is designed to accommodate the changing needs of the learner as he or she moves through the learning process.

MODELS OF STAGES OF LEARNING

When developing motor skill proficiency, regardless of whether in alpine skiing or re-learning how to walk after a serious accident, learners progress through various stages. Several models have been proposed, each examining the progression from beginner to expert from a different perspective. These models can assist practitioners in defining the needs of their learners throughout the learning process and, in turn, enable practitioners to select appropriate instructional activities. As you learn about each model, you should take three considerations into account. First, although the models present each stage as distinct, in reality one stage blends gradually into the next and transitions between learning stages cannot be clearly delineated (Fitts & Posner, 1967; Christina & Corcos, 1988). Second, a learner can be in different stages for different skills. A soccer player, for example, might be considered highly skilled in dribbling but only a novice for heading the ball, if the latter skill is just being introduced. Finally, stages of learning are not dependent on age. Just ask Landon Shuffett, professional billiards player who was considered an expert when he was only 7 years old! (You can learn more about him at the adjoining website.)

WWW

VIDEO STORY OF LANDON SHUFFETT

www.youtube.com/watch?v=7bAvWs1PX2s

Fitts and Posner's Three-Stage Model

To facilitate skill acquisition, practitioners must understand what is happening during the learning process from the learners' perspective. One popular model, which psychologists Fitts and Posner proposed in 1967, suggests that learners pass through three distinct stages. These stages are defined by the behavioral tendencies learners display at various points throughout the learning process, as shown in Figure 6.1.

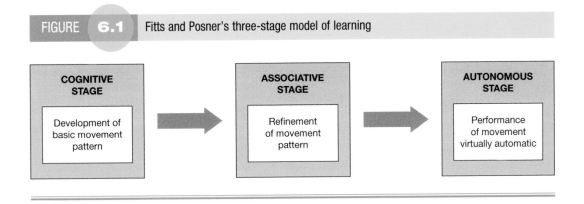

FIGURE 6.1 Fitts and Posner's three-stage model of learning

COGNITIVE STAGE	**ASSOCIATIVE STAGE**	**AUTONOMOUS STAGE**
Development of basic movement pattern	Refinement of movement pattern	Performance of movement virtually automatic

Cognitive Stage

The first stage, the cognitive stage, is named for its high degree of cognitive activity. During this stage, the learner is first introduced to the new motor skill, and his or her primary task is to develop an understanding of the movement's requirements or, said another way, the basic pattern of coordination (Newell, 1985). A learner in this stage may have many questions. Think back to your experience with juggling in Chapter 1. Questions such as How do I hold on to the balls? How and when do I let go? How high do I throw them? What is the pattern of movement? and countless others likely came to mind. To discover the answers to these questions, learners will often attempt numerous techniques and strategies through a trial-and-error approach. In addition, past movement experiences will be reformulated in an effort to solve the current movement problem. The resulting movements lack synchronization and appear choppy and deliberate. In addition, throughout this process the attentional demands are high and are limited to movement production. Consequently, difficulties will be apparent when learners are required to time their movements in conjunction with an external object or event. Performance at this stage is inconsistent and characterized by numerous errors, which are typically gross in nature.

Through effective verbal instructions and demonstrations, and/or the purposeful manipulation of task and environmental constraints practitioners can facilitate a learner's progression through this stage. Instructions should take into account the fact that learners can more easily reformulate past movement experiences into new patterns if the similarities and differences between them are pointed out. Furthermore, whereas a trained observer may easily recognize the errors being made, the learner lacks the capability to determine the specific cause of an error and is unable to make necessary adjustments. Practitioners play a key role not only in detecting and correcting errors but also in helping the learner to do the same.

Associative Stage

The second stage, the associative stage, is characterized by marked performance improvements. Having attempted numerous possible movement strategies, a learner at this stage becomes committed to refining one particular movement pattern. Performance becomes more consistent, and errors are gradually reduced. A setter in the early part of the associative stage would, for example, be able to execute a clean pass but may not always do so with the desired accuracy. The ability to time movements with external objects and events also improves as the attentional demands of performing the movement itself decrease; this allows learners to begin attending to other things. This results in an increased ability to make movement adjustments in accordance with various environmental conditions. In this stage, the learner becomes more and more capable of detecting the cause of errors and then developing appropriate strategies to eliminate them.

Given the learner's changing characteristics, the practitioner's role at this stage shifts from one of predominantly providing instruction to one of designing constructive practice experiences. For open skills, those experiences should help develop visual search strategies as learners become increasingly able to direct their attention toward aspects of the performance environment. Finally, throughout this stage the provision of effective feedback continues to play an important role, not only to guide skill refinement but also to further develop learners' error detection and correction capabilities.

Autonomous Stage

Transition to the final stage in Fitts and Posner's model, the autonomous stage, requires countless hours of practice. In fact, not all learners will reach this final stage. In the autonomous stage, performance reaches the highest level of proficiency and becomes automated. Learners' attention during this stage is reallocated to strategic decision making. In addition, learners can perform multiple tasks simultaneously. Finally, learners in this stage are consistent and confident, make few errors, and can generally detect and correct those errors that do occur.

CEREBRALchallenge   6.1

Create a chart with column headings as shown below. Choose a skill or task and generate a list of practical tips practitioners could follow based on Fitts and Posner's description of the behavioral characteristics of the learner for their three-stage model.

SKILL/TASK

COGNITIVE	ASSOCIATIVE	AUTONOMOUS

exploration ACTIVITY 6.1

Stage of Learning Analysis

ACTIVITY 1

Observe and compare the forearm pass performance for each individual at the following web links:

> www.youtube.com/watch?v=dLyraHkLnrg
>
> www.youtube.com/watch?v=fxr63BfDG8Y
>
> www.youtube.com/watch?v=7_CW6jHRYuo
>
> www.youtube.com/watch?v=lFwltz8xAgE

Based on your observations, use Fitts and Posner's model to determine which stage of learning each performer is in; list the specific behavioral characteristics that led you to your decision.

ACTIVITY 2

Observe a youth sport competition or practice in a skill of your choice. Choose five individuals to watch closely. Based on your observations, determine which stage of learning each performer is in and list the specific behavioral characteristics that led you to your decision.

One might falsely assume that when a learner has reached this stage, the role of the practitioner is minimal at best. It is important to remember, however, that while skill proficiency has reached the highest levels, room for improvement still exists. The practitioner is still responsible for practice design and error detection and correction. Performance improvements are difficult to obtain at this level, and advances occur so gradually that learners can become discouraged and lose the motivation necessary to strive to obtain them; the practitioner must act as motivator to help learners reach their potential. Use Exploration Activity 6.1 to apply Fitts and Posner's stages to real-world performers.

Gentile's Two-Stage Model

Rather than simply describing the characteristics of the learner in each phase of the learning process, Gentile (1972, 2000) approached the identification of learning stages from the learner's perspective. More specifically, Gentile's model, illustrated in Figure 6.2, emphasizes the learner's goal and the influence of task and environmental characteristics on that goal.

"Getting the Idea of the Movement" Stage

The first stage of learning in Gentile's model is termed "getting the idea of the movement." According to Gentile, after a learner is introduced to a new motor

FIGURE **6.2** Gentile's two-stage model of learning

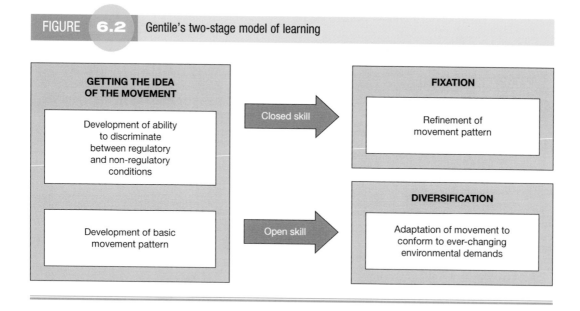

FIGURE **6.2** Gentile's two-stage model of learning

skill, his or her goal is, first, to develop an understanding of the movement requirements that are necessary to meet the demands imposed by the characteristics of the task and the environment in which the task is to be performed, and then to organize a corresponding movement. Paramount to the learner's success in achieving this goal is the ability to discriminate between regulatory conditions and non-regulatory conditions. As you will recall from Chapter 1, regulatory conditions are environmental conditions that specify the movement characteristics necessary to perform the task. In contrast, non-regulatory conditions are those factors that are not inherently related to producing the appropriate motor response. To produce a movement pattern that meets the demands imposed by task and environmental conditions, the learner must be able to selectively attend to relevant information while ignoring irrelevant information.

Instruction and practice during the initial stage of learning should facilitate the development of a basic movement pattern. To accomplish this, the practitioner must clearly communicate the task's goal to the learner, using verbal instructions and demonstrations and/or guided discovery. In addition, the practitioner must convey to the learner those environmental features that are regulatory and those that are non-regulatory and direct his or her attention and visual search toward relevant stimuli.

Fixation/Diversification Stage

Once the learner has acquired a general idea of the requisite movement, he or she advances to the second and final stage, fixation/diversification. During this stage, the learner's goal is one of refinement. The nature of that refinement is a function of the predictability of the environment in which the skill is to be performed. Consequently, the learner's objective will be different for closed versus open skills. Closed skills—such as taping an ankle, performing a balance beam routine, or playing a musical instrument—are performed in a fixed, stable environment. Successful performance of such skills requires that the learner be able to replicate the movement pattern consistently and accurately (fixation). Open skills, on the other hand, are performed in an unpredictable, ever-changing environment. Accordingly, a performer must be able to adapt responses continually to conform to these ever-changing demands (diversification). With open skills, the learner's objective is to diversify the movement pattern. An individual confined to a wheelchair, for example, must be able to change directions, traverse various surfaces and inclinations, and negotiate obstacles. Similarly, a hockey player must be able to shoot the puck from countless angles, distances, and positions, as well as negotiate around the movements of teammates and defenders.

Once the learner has reached the fixation/diversification stage, the instructional strategies employed will depend on whether the skill is open or closed. For a closed skill—such as the free throw, where the regulatory conditions remain fixed during each successive performance attempt—practice should reflect these fixed conditions (basket is same height, shot is taken from behind the free throw line, etc.), while also subjecting the learner to the variety of non-regulatory cues that would normally occur (crowd noise, importance of the shot). If the regulatory conditions change across trials—as is the case of the golf putt, a closed skill with inter-trial variability—learners should practice under the various regulatory conditions that may occur in the criterion condition (e.g., putt from various locations and distances on the green, including different slopes).

Practice for open skills should also reflect various regulatory conditions. Because learners performing open skills must be able to respond proficiently

CEREBRALchallenge   6.2

1. Determine which strategy, fixation (F) or diversification (D), would be more appropriate for practicing each of the following skills:

    a. Free throw
    b. Guarding (soccer, basketball, etc.)
    c. Moving from sitting to standing position
    d. Floor routine in gymnastics
    e. Ascending and descending stairs
    f. Diving

2. Revisit the integrative model for facilitating motor learning and performance introduced in Chapter 1. Explain why stage of learning is an important component of the situation profile.

CEREBRALchallenge 6.3

Create a chart with column heads as shown below. Choose a skill or task and generate a list of practical tips practitioners could follow based on Gentile's two-stage model of learning.

SKILL/TASK

GETTING THE IDEA OF THE MOVEMENT	FIXATION	DIVERSIFICATION

under ever-changing and often unpredictable environmental conditions, variations that simulate possible criterion conditions should be systematically introduced in practice. This approach not only helps the learner to acquire a larger repertoire of movement possibilities but also aids in the development of vital decision-making skills. Because decision making depends on the learner's ability to detect regulatory cues and ignore non-regulatory stimuli, practitioners should continue to highlight those features of the environment that are regulatory and non-regulatory and direct the learner's attention and visual search toward relevant stimuli.

LEARNER AND PERFORMANCE CHANGES

As indicated previously, it is difficult to determine with any certainty the exact moment when a learner makes a transition to the next stage. How, then, can we tell that learning has occurred? One of the most common methods of assessing an individual's progress is to note changes in observable motor behavior over time. This section discusses a number of performance indicators that have been identified through the study of novice versus expert performers and can provide clues for the practitioner as to the progress of the learner.

Movement Pattern

www

WALKING FOLLOWING A STROKE

www.youtube.com/watch?v=bAV3 w3nlyE8

It would not be difficult to distinguish between a professional baseball player's swing and that of a novice. While both may be able to achieve the goal of the task—hitting the ball—the movement pattern they produce to do so will be quite different. As the novice hitter's skill level improves, however, these differences will diminish. Similarly, a post-stroke individual re-learning how to walk will move from slow, deliberate steps (as seen in the adjoining video) to a more coordinated, efficient gait.

Increase in Coordination and Control

A learner's progression in skill acquisition characteristically results in several changes related to movement production; perhaps the most notable changes are in coordination and control. As we learned in Chapter 4, organizing a movement pattern that will effectively achieve the goal of the task requires that the learner coordinate and control numerous independent elements or degrees of freedom. In the early stages of skill acquisition, the learner attempts to accomplish this by freezing or fixing the possible movements of a joint so that the limb(s) will function as a single unit or segment. In other words, novices will reduce the available degrees of freedom to a more manageable quantity in order to accomplish a task's goal. This strategy, termed freezing the degrees of freedom (Bernstein, 1967; Whiting, 1984), results in stiff, rigid, inefficiently timed movements. As learners progress in skill development, the once-constrained degrees of freedom will be gradually released and collectively reorganized into a new movement pattern that is smoother, faster, and more closely resembles the correct movement.

Consider the swing pattern of a novice racquetball player compared to that of a highly skilled player. The novice will attempt to control the swing by restricting the movement that occurs at each joint. Consequently, the novice will initially use a straight-arm swing in which the racquet is simply treated as a rigid extension of the arm (see Figure 6.3a). Furthermore, it is likely that the lower body will remain inactive. The pattern of coordination exhibited by a highly skilled player, depicted in Figure 6.3(b), incorporates multiple and sequential joint action (both upper and lower body); because of its biomechanical efficiency, the movement is significantly faster. Support for this resulting increase in velocity, as well as the notion of freezing and then gradually releasing or unfreezing the available degrees of freedom, has been found in studies investigating the acquisition of the forehand shot in racquetball (Southard & Higgins, 1987), kicking in soccer (Anderson & Sidaway, 1994), learning a slalom skill on an indoor ski apparatus (Vereijken, van Emmerik, Whiting, & Newell, 1992), and comparing the preferred and non-preferred kicking feet in the drop punt (Ball, 2011).

The notion of moving from freezing to freeing degrees of freedom during skill acquisition, however, has come into question; it has been suggested that the emergence of a particular pattern of coordination depends on the task (Newell, Broderick, Deutsch, & Slifkin, 2003). In fact, studies have reported that novices may demonstrate larger ranges of motion initially and then experience a freezing of the degrees of freedom as a result of practice. One example is a case study by Hodges, Hayes, Horn, and Williams (2005), in which coordination changes were examined for a ball-kicking task. Specifically, the task required a scoop-like movement over a low barrier to a target. With practice, range of motion (ROM) of the knee and ankle joints decreased, whereas an increased ROM was found at the hip. Chow, Davids, Button, and Koh (2007), investigating movement patterns that emerged as a function of the interaction between task

| FIGURE | 6.3 | Kinematic illustration of (a) freezing and (b) freeing the degrees of freedom for the arm and racket during a racquetball kill shot |

(a) Freezing   **(b)** Freeing

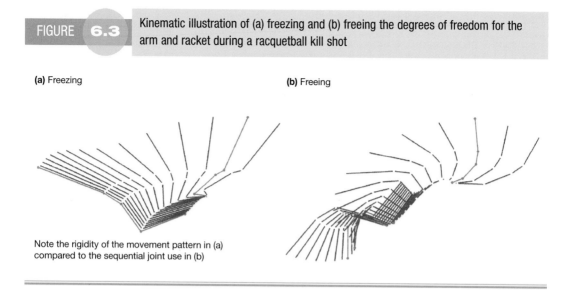

Note the rigidity of the movement pattern in (a) compared to the sequential joint use in (b)

constraints and stage of learning for a kicking task, reported similar findings. For a soccer chip shot, they reported a movement pattern that involved greater ROM at the distal joints with less joint involvement at the proximal segments for skilled and intermediate players, versus the larger ranges of motion of the kicking leg that novices demonstrated. The authors suggested that "it is possible that skilled and intermediate players are better able to optimize the intersegmental dynamics about the hip and knee to allow a functional movement to emerge" (p. 477). In other words, the optimal movement solution for the imposed task constraints, which was not discovered until later stages in learning, required greater ROM at one joint and less ROM at another.

Additional research is necessary to explore the interaction of task constraints and skill level for variations in coordination. Regardless, practitioners must be highly proficient not only in their knowledge of skill-specific performance indicators but also in skill analysis.

More Fluid Muscle Activity

Accompanying the reorganization of the system to produce a new coordination pattern is a change in muscular activity. As the learner becomes more proficient, the number of activated muscles needed to produce a movement will be reduced to only those that are fundamental for correct performance. In addition, the timing and sequence in which the muscles are activated will be altered. Skilled movement is the result of cooperative actions of muscle groups (Hall, 2006), but early in the learning process the cycle of muscle activation is mistimed. This has been found to be the case in sport skills (e.g., Jaegars, Peterson, Dantuma, et al., 1989; Lay, Sparrow, Hughes, & O'Dwyer, 2002), rapid finger and arm movement tasks (e.g., Schneider, Zernicke, Schmidt, & Hart, 1989;

RESEARCH NOTES

Using the soccer in-step kick, Anderson and Sidaway (1994) examined changes in coordination as a result of practice. Six novices, who were enrolled in a beginning soccer class, were given an initial demonstration of the skill. They then performed 15 to 20 shots for each of 20 practice sessions. Performance was videotaped before and after the practice period, and hip and knee peak angular velocities, timing variables, and joint range of motion were analyzed, along with maximum linear velocity of the foot (using motion analysis software). Results of the kinematic analysis revealed a change in the fundamental pattern of coordination for the skill as a result of practice. A corresponding increase in the maximum resultant linear velocity of the foot was also found, indicating the adoption of a more effective movement pattern.

Gabriel & Boucher, 1998; Carson & Riek, 2001), and aiming tasks (e.g., Shemmell, Tresilian, Riek, et al., 2005). With practice, correct activation patterns are achieved and movements become more fluid.

More Efficient Energy Expenditure

Unlike experts, whose movements appear effortless, beginners are mechanically inefficient. This can be readily seen with beginning swimmers who are learning to flutter kick. Because of poor mechanics, many beginners will initially lack forward progress, and some will even move backward in the water! Puzzled by their lack of movement across the pool, they will quite often kick harder, but to no avail. Fatigue will eventually set in, and they will have to rest before attempting the skill again.

Understandably, beginning swimmers will expend a great deal of energy (and frustration) in their efforts. We know, however, that with practice comes improved coordination, the use of only necessary muscles, and increased accuracy of muscle activation. You can observe this firsthand by visiting a local pool and answering the questions in Exploration Activity 6.2. Through practice, movements become more efficient, and the amount of energy needed to perform them will be reduced. Eventually, this decreased energy

FIGURE **6.4**

A professional cyclist uses only the essential muscles needed to create a skilled, fluid movement that appears effortless

exploration ACTIVITY 6.2

Observation: Expert versus Novice Swimmers

Visit a local swimming pool.

a. Watch a beginning swimmer performing the freestyle stroke for several minutes. Describe his or her technique. List the muscles that are involved in accomplishing this technique. Now watch an individual who is more proficient at freestyle. Describe his or her technique. Again, note the muscles involved in the performance.

b. What physical differences did you observe between the two learners' execution of the freestyle stroke?

expenditure will allow a once-frustrated swimmer to travel greater distances with fewer rest periods. For more information on the energetics of human movement, see Sparrow (2000).

Increased Consistency

Another means of assessing a learner's progress is through changes in performance consistency. Recall from Chapter 1 that learning is defined as a relatively permanent change in a person's capability to execute a motor skill, as a result of practice or experience. Increased consistency is indicative of a relatively permanent change (Yang & Scholz, 2005). It should be noted, however, that although a learner may be able to reproduce an action consistently, this does not necessarily mean that he or she is performing the skill correctly. Practitioners should consider several performance variables prior to making a judgment about learning.

While increased consistency can be a sign of learning, practitioners can also look at the onset of *inconsistent* performance for clues about skill acquisition. As suggested above, a learner may develop a consistent movement pattern that is fundamentally flawed. Unless the movement is corrected, future progress will be impeded. To change a fundamentally flawed movement, the learner must learn new invariant characteristics, which means learning a new motor program. In the terms of the dynamic systems theory (see Chapter 4), the learner must move from one state of stability to a new state of stability (a phase shift). This transition, regardless of how it is described, will be characterized at first by increased inconsistency as the learner tries to abandon the old movement for the new coordination pattern. Eventually, with practice, the learner will begin to produce the new movement with continued practice, the movement will become consistent.

RESEARCH NOTES

Using a rowing task, Lay, Sparrow, Hughes, and O'Dwyer (2002) examined the effects of practice on coordination and control, metabolic energy expenditure, and muscle activation. Six physically fit male volunteers with no rowing experience rowed an ergo-meter at a predetermined constant power output of 100 W for ten 16-minute sessions. The data revealed improved movement economy based on a significant decline of oxygen consumption and perceived exertion. In addition, the researchers found significantly less variance in the peak forces applied to the ergometer handle as well as a considerable decrease in stroke rate. Furthermore, electromyographic data indicated decreased muscle activation and increased coordination based on changes in activation patterns. Consequently, these results demonstrated reduced metabolic energy cost of performance and improved coordination and control as a result of practice.

CEREBRALchallenge   6.4

Having just introduced a beginning soccer class to dribbling, the teacher designs a drill in which the learners pair up and one dribbles to the other end of the field while avoiding the other player, who tries to take away the ball. Will this be an effective drill? Justify your answer.

Attention

Changes in both the amount of conscious attention focused on movement exe-cution and the allocation of visual attention also accompany skill development. These changes lead to quicker and more accurate movement preparation and a corresponding reduction in response times.

Attention to Skill Execution

Initially, learners concentrate on how to perform each technical component of a skill, focusing their undivided attention on the skill's execution. As they develop their skill proficiency, their need to attend consciously to each aspect of the movement decreases; eventually (after a great amount of practice) perform-ance becomes more or less automatic. Conscious thought is no longer required to perform the movement. Throughout this transition, overt performance shifts, and an initial hesitancy with a robotic appearance becomes a smooth, free-flowing, and apparently effortless performance.

Once a learner reaches the point where the skill can be performed with little or no conscious control, two consequences emerge. First, the learner can now reallocate attentional resources to other factors of performance. For example, in the volleyball spike, the learner can focus on game strategy (e.g., where to

exploration ACTIVITY   6.3

Automatic Behaviors

Each able-bodied person has a walking pace that is natural for him or her. If able, determine your natural pace by walking down a hallway several times.

QUESTIONS

1. Describe what happened when you tried to determine your natural walking pace.
2. When a practitioner asks a patient to walk naturally across the clinic in order to evaluate the patient's gait, would you expect to see similar results? Give suggestions to help ensure an accurate assessment.

FIGURE 6.5

When undergoing gait analysis, a patient may become conscious of his movements and change his natural walking pattern

place the ball in the opponent's court) rather than concentrate on the technique that will successfully result in ball contact. The learner becomes better able to focus on and evaluate the environmental context and, hence, able to respond more quickly and appropriately to performance conditions.

Now observe what happens in Exploration Activity 6.3. From this activity, you can see a second consequence of automaticity; once it is achieved, conscious control of the movement may actually be detrimental to performance. When a performer consciously focuses on the specifics of a well-learned skill that is normally performed automatically, the information needed to coordinate the muscle pattern is slowed (Byers, 2000). The resulting performance becomes hesitant and choppy. Adopting a "non-awareness" strategy, in which the performer simply "lets the movement happen," is recommended.

Allocation of Visual Attention

As we saw in Chapter 3, differences exist between experts and novices with respect to where their visual attention is allocated. Recall the study by Shank and Haywood (1987) showing that expert hitters direct their visual attention toward information-rich areas while ignoring non-regulatory cues. Beginners, on the other hand, pay attention to too many things and have difficulty discriminating between relevant environmental cues and those that are irrelevant to performance. A superior visual attention allocation strategy, combined with extensive knowledge of

RESEARCH NOTES

To explore differences in attentional mechanisms as a function of skill level, Beilock, Carr, McMahon, and Starkes (2002) examined the dribbling performance of novice and experienced soccer players through a slalom course under a dual-task condition and a skill-focused condition. The dual-task condition involved dribbling through the course while concurrently monitoring a list of words and repeating the target word out loud each time it was heard. In the skill-focused condition, participants were prompted to focus on a specific component of the dribbling task. Participants performed the task under both conditions with both their dominant and non-dominant foot. As expected, for dominant-foot dribbling, novices were distracted during the dual-task condition and performed at a lower level than they did in the skill-focused condition, which was designed to draw their attention to the performance of the movement. The opposite pattern of results was found for the experienced players, whose performance declined when they focused on skill execution.

the sport, enables highly skilled performers to recognize, predict, and respond to performance situations more accurately and rapidly than their less-skilled counterparts (Abernethy, 1997).

Knowledge and Memory

It stands to reason that changes in a learner's knowledge base regarding the activity would accompany performance changes. Quite simply, accomplished performers know more about the skill than do their less-proficient counterparts. Experts not only know what to do in a wide variety of situations; they also know how and when to apply this knowledge (Singer & Janelle, 1999). They have higher levels of both declarative knowledge (e.g., rules) and procedural knowledge (e.g., what to do in a given situation), giving them a larger knowledge base from which to draw (Thomas & Thomas, 1994).

The structure of that knowledge base (specific to the activity) has been found to be more complex in skilled performers and organized in a manner that facilitates pattern recognition and recall. This was demonstrated by Allard, Graham, and Paarsalu (1980), who found expert basketball players to be superior to novices in a recall study. Participants were shown two sets of slides depicting basketball game situations; one set displayed structured situations and the other unstructured situations. At the end of a four-second viewing period, participants were asked to recreate the slide using magnets representing players on a magnet board representing a half basketball court. The experts were found to be superior to the novices at recalling the structured situations only. Since the experts' superiority was evident only in the game condition, it appears that experts are able to build a better representation of the problem because of their ability to organize or chunk information into meaningful units (Allard, 1982). This ability, along with a larger knowledge base, enables them to access information more

CEREBRALchallenge   6.8

List examples of declarative and procedural knowledge for a skill of your choice.

Skill: _____

Declarative knowledge: _____

_____

_____

Procedural knowledge: _____

_____

_____

efficiently, focus on higher-level concepts, make more connections between concepts, and solve problems more quickly and with fewer errors (Thomas, French, & Humphries, 1986; McPherson & Thomas, 1989). Similar results have been found in chess (Chase & Simon, 1973), snooker (Abernethy, Neal, & Koning, 1994), and dance (Smyth & Pendleton, 1994). For a review of knowledge development in sport, see Iglesias, García-González, García, et al. (2010).

Error Detection and Correction

Another indicator of skill development is the learner's increased ability to detect and correct performance errors. With practice, learners develop the capability to monitor and interpret the exteroceptive and proprioceptive feedback that the various sensory receptors provide. This information can be used either to make corrections during a movement (time permitting) or to direct future attempts.

As their error detection and correction capabilities improve, learners will become less dependent on practitioners. Questions such as "What did I do that time?" will decrease, and the questions will become more specific. Learners will also display behaviors indicating that they know they have made an error. For example, when serving a tennis ball, if the ball toss is off, less-skilled learners will likely attempt to hit it anyway, jeopardizing the outcome; more proficient learners will be able to recognize a bad ball toss and will let the ball drop so they can try again.

Self-Confidence

As learners become more skilled, their confidence in their ability to perform the skill will increase. With increased confidence comes increased motivation to improve further. Consequently, when designing learning experiences, practitioners should ensure that each learner experiences some degree of success during each practice period. Chase, Ewing, Lirgg, and George (1994) provide support for this strategy; when children were learning to shoot a basketball, modifying the height of the basket from the regulation 10 feet to 8 feet had a positive influence on their self-efficacy and shooting performance.

MEASURING PROGRESS

In addition to evaluating an individual's progress subjectively by observing variations in performance over time, practitioners may use a number of objective assessment measures to evaluate the effectiveness of training or instructional strategies. These techniques allow practitioners to document changes in proficiency by quantifying learning based on performance indicators such as time, distance, and frequency to demonstrate improvement, persistence, consistency, and/or adaptability.

Performance Curves

A performance curve is obtained by systematically plotting the results from repeated measurements of a specific performance variable across time. The resulting graph offers the practitioner two pieces of information. First, the general direction of the curve is indicative of improvement. Second, by examining successive trials, the practitioner can make inferences about consistency.

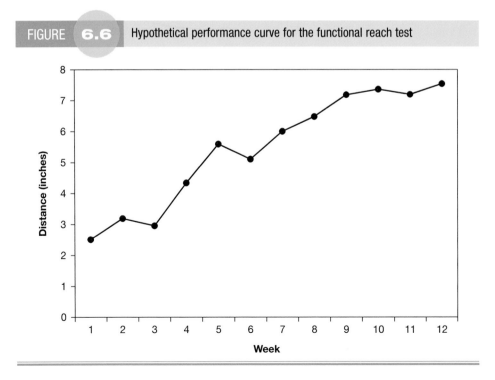

FIGURE 6.6 Hypothetical performance curve for the functional reach test

To construct a performance curve, first select an evaluable performance variable that is an appropriate indicator of skill. For example, the functional reach test (Duncan, Weiner, Chandler, & Studenski, 1990) may be used to evaluate the impact of a rehabilitation program designed to assist a patient in regaining postural control. To perform the test, the patient stands with feet shoulder-width apart and one shoulder flexed to 90 degrees, so that the arm is parallel to the floor. The patient then reaches as far forward as possible while maintaining balance. The distance reached is measured and recorded. In the hypothetical performance test shown in Figure 6.6, the patient was tested once a week for a period of 12 weeks. On the graph, the distance reached (in inches) is plotted on the y-axis and the number of weeks in the performance test is plotted on the x-axis.

FIGURE **6.7**   Types of performance curves

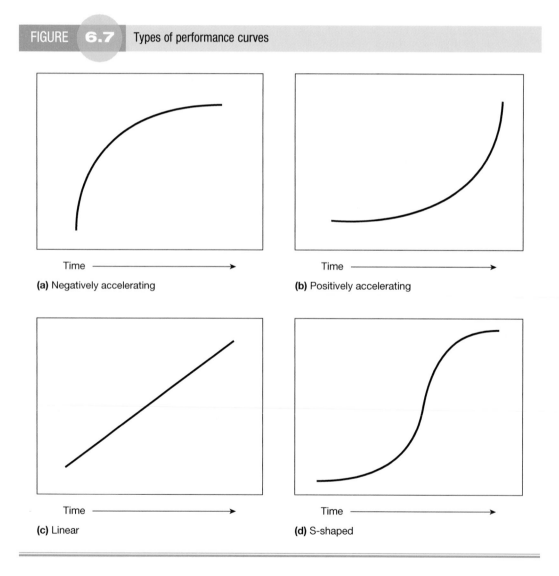

Time ⟶

(a) Negatively accelerating

Time ⟶

(b) Positively accelerating

Time ⟶

(c) Linear

Time ⟶

(d) S-shaped

Types of Performance Curves

Performance curves generally follow one of four patterns (see Figure 6.7):

1. A *negatively accelerating curve* reflects the power law of practice. When learning a new skill, individuals tend to demonstrate a large initial improvement in performance, which slows later in practice (Newell & Rosenbloom, 1981). This is the most common performance curve.
2. A *positively accelerating curve* is characterized by little initial improvement but larger gains occurring later.
3. A *linear curve* reflects a direct relationship between performance and time.
4. An *S-shaped curve* is a combination of the negative and positively accelerating curves.

When reading performance curves, keep in mind that the nature of the curve depends on what is being measured. For example, if the performance variable being measured is time, and a decrease in the time required to execute the skill indicates improved performance, then the curve will be reversed.

Limitations of Performance Curves

Although a popular method of documenting progress, performance curves do possess several limitations. To understand the first limitation, we must review the characteristics that distinguish between performance and learning. Recall that learning results in a relatively permanent change in a person's capability to execute a motor skill, whereas performance is simply the act of executing a skill. Because the measures for performance curves are taken while an individual is practicing a skill, these measures represent temporary effects and cannot establish relative permanence. It is for this reason they are labeled performance curves rather than learning curves.

A second limitation comes from calculating the mean of several trials in a particular session to obtain the measurements used to construct the curve. Two individuals learning how to juggle may have the same mean number of catches, for example, but their performances for each trial could be very different. Examine the data of two learners' juggling performance as shown in Table 6.1, for example. Each learner performed 10 trials in one session, and their resulting means for the 10 trials are equal: 4.5. However, learner A's performance is relatively consistent across trials, whereas learner B displays a much broader range of scores. If we look only at the mean, we might lose valuable information regarding the learning process. Recall that improved performance consistency is an indicator of learning. The standard deviation of the two learners' juggling performance confirms that learner A ($SD = 0.53$) has less performance variability than learner B ($SD = 4.77$) indicating greater skill proficiency. Consequently, multiple measures of performance allow for better conclusions about learning.

TABLE 6.1	Individual juggling data (number of catches per trial in a 10-trial session) for two different learners		
TRIAL	**LEARNER A**	**LEARNER B**	
1	5	1	
2	5	6	
3	4	0	
4	4	11	
5	5	3	
6	4	6	
7	5	2	
8	5	2	
9	4	14	
10	4	0	
MEAN	4.5	4.5	

CEREBRALchallenge 6.6

Three learners were asked to practice juggling 10 minutes per day for 10 consecutive days. The mean number of catches per day was calculated by dividing the total number of catches by the number of trials. The mean number of catches per day for each learner is graphed below.

1. Categorize each participant's performance curve based on the four patterns depicted in the graph below.
2. What conclusions can you make based on the data presented?

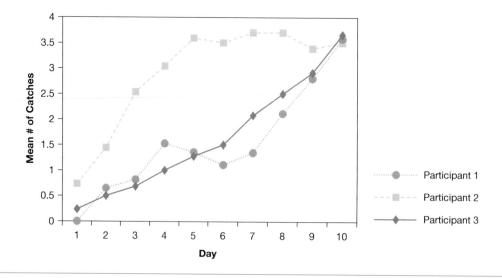

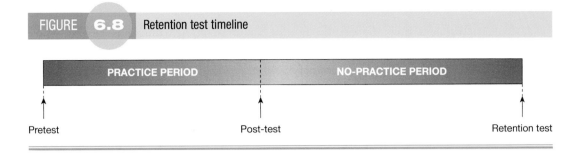

FIGURE **6.8**   Retention test timeline

PRACTICE PERIOD	NO-PRACTICE PERIOD

Pretest   Post-test   Retention test

Retention and Transfer Tests

Retention and transfer tests are used to infer that a relatively permanent change in a performance has occurred. In other words, they are used to see whether the patient, student, athlete, or client really did learn. A retention test measures the persistence of improved skill performance. Unlike a post-test, which is administered directly following a practice period (which could be one session or multiple sessions) and is used to find out what a learner can do after practicing a skill, a retention test is given after a period in which the learner has not engaged in any practice (see Figure 6.8). The resulting performance level is compared to the initial performance level of that same skill (the pretest administered before the practice period). If the comparison indicates a high degree of improvement, you can infer that learning has occurred.

Since a major goal of practice is being able to retain what was learned for later use, retention tests can also be used as a pre-assessment tool. For example, in the autumn, an elementary physical education class completed a unit targeting the refinement of fundamental locomotor skills, including sliding and skipping. Later, in the spring, sliding and skipping will be foundational for the learning of more complex, specialized skills in a dance unit. Through a retention test, the teacher can determine if the students did indeed retain skill proficiency in sliding and skipping before beginning the new unit. If retention does not meet the expected level, the teacher will need to review what were thought to be previously learned skills before introducing the dance unit and attempting to build on those skills (personal communication, Lynn V. Johnson, March 27, 2012).

A second type of assessment that can be used to distinguish between temporary and permanent performance changes is a transfer test. A transfer test measures the degree to which a learner can adapt the practiced skill to a different performance situation. Variations in the skill itself or the environment in which it is performed can serve to test adaptability and allow the practitioner to infer learning. For example, a transfer test for a patient learning to execute a sit-to-stand movement might involve a new chair height or surface (e.g., firm versus padded). A transfer test for handball volleying might require the learner to strike the ball after it bounces off the back wall instead of the front wall. A useful resource for designing transfer tests is Gentile's (2000) taxonomy, discussed in Chapter 1.

PERFORMANCE PLATEAUS

Practitioners must be careful not to assume that learning has ceased when performance is no longer improving. It might be that the learner is experiencing a performance plateau—a period of time during the learning process in which no overt changes in performance occur. Again, it is import-ant that practitioners be able to distinguish between temporary changes in performance and relatively perma-nent changes, which are indicative of learning.

> **COMMON MYTH**
>
> Unless a learner displays some overt changes in performance, he or she is no longer learning.

Remember that learning is not directly observable. We cannot see what someone perceives, we cannot see what someone is thinking, and we cannot see changes in underlying behavioral and neurological processes. Thomas and Thomas (1994) remind us that "knowing when and how is not synonymous with the execution of the activity" (p. 296). Plateaus often represent transitional periods in the learning process when the integration of task components (and perhaps strategy) is being resolved. Consequently, performance plateaus do not necessarily indicate that the learner has stopped learning; plateaus are instead a normal part of the learning process. Variables such as fatigue, anxiety, or lack of motivation can also temporarily affect performance, resulting in a plateau. Finally, a plateau might be the result of limitations in the performance measurement used. Ceiling and floor effects occur when there is a maximum or minimum achievable score on a task. For example, if a learner's average number of successful free throws out of 10 are plotted on a performance curve, as he or she approaches the ceiling (10), the performance curve will begin to plateau.

PUTTING IT INTO PRACTICE

Learning Situation: Learning the Indirect Pass in Hockey

Jennifer also works with the Squirts (ages 9–10). The indirect pass to a moving target is introduced at this level. Her assistant reminds her of the drill he suggested earlier and thinks it would be a good one to start with after the skill is introduced and demonstrated.

Test Your Knowledge

Go back to the drill outlined at the end of Chapter 3. Does this drill target cognitive or associative stage learners? Should Jennifer start with this drill as her assistance suggested? Justify your answer. Compare your answer with the sample response provided at www.routledge.com/cw/coker.

A LOOK AHEAD

Learners progress through distinct stages of learning as they acquire a skill. Each stage is characterized by both behavioral changes and alterations in the learner's goals. In addition, a number of learner and performance indicators have been identified to assist practitioners' inference of skill development. Understanding the characteristics of each learning stage, in addition to being able to assess a learner's proficiency level, can assist a practitioner's decision making with respect to the delivery of instructions, the design of practice and experiences, and the provision of feedback. The next chapter begins our discussion of how to design appropriate learning environments by examining pre-instructional considerations that influence communication.

FOCUS POINTS

After reading this chapter, you should know:

- According to Fitts and Posner, learners pass through three distinct stages:

  1. Cognitive stage: development of basic movement pattern
  2. Associative stage: refinement of movement pattern
  3. Autonomous stage: virtually automatic performance of movement

- Gentile's two-stage model emphasizes the goal of the learner and the influence of task and environmental characteristics on that goal.

  — Stage 1: getting the idea of the movement
  — Stage 2: fixation (closed skills)/diversification (open skills)

- To infer learning has occurred, the practitioner can assess numerous performance changes, including changes in coordination and control, muscle activity, energy expenditure, consistency, attentional focus, knowledge and memory, error detection and correction, and self-confidence.

- Progress can also be assessed through performance curves, retention tests, and transfer tests.

  — Retention tests measure the persistence of improved skill performance.
  — Transfer tests measure the degree to which the learner can adapt the practiced skill to a different performance situation.

- A performance plateau is a period of time during the learning process in which no overt changes in performance occur. Plateaus often represent transitional periods in the learning process when the integration of task components (and perhaps strategy) is being resolved; they are not necessarily indicative of a cessation in the learning process.

lab

To complete the lab for this chapter, visit www.routledge.com/cw/coker and select **Lab 6, Stages of Learning**.

REVIEW QUESTIONS

1. Explain how the role of the instructor shifts as a learner progresses through Fitts and Posner's three stages of learning.

2. How does Gentile's model differ from that of Fitts and Posner?

3. Define fixation and diversification, and explain their relationship to closed and open skills.

4. List five performance characteristics that can help you infer that learning has occurred.

5. What does "freezing the degrees of freedom" mean?

6. What are the two consequences of automaticity?

7. Explain how expert performers are able to build a better representation of the movement problem.

8. What can you look for to determine whether a learner's error detection and correction capabilities have improved? Do you have any suggestions beyond those listed in the chapter?

9. Why might it be false to assume that someone is no longer learning if the person does not display any performance improvements?

10. Compare and contrast retention tests and transfer tests.

REFERENCES

Abernethy, B. (1997). Motor control adaptations to training. In B. Abernethy, V. Kippers, L. T. Mackinnon, R. J. Neal, & S. Hanrahan (Eds.), *The biophysical foundations of human movement* (pp. 334–353). Champaign, IL: Human Kinetics.

Abernethy, B., Neal, R. J., & Koning, P. (1994). Visual-perceptual and cognitive differences between expert, intermediate and novice snooker players. *Applied Cognitive Psychology*, 8, 185–211.

Allard, F. (1982). Cognition, expert performance and sport. In J. H. Salmela, J. T. Partington, & T. Orlick (Eds.), *New paths of sport learning and excellence* (pp. 22–27). Ottawa: Sport in Perspectives.

Allard, F., Graham, S., & Paarsalu, M. F. (1980). Perception in sport: Basketball. *Journal of Sport Psychology*, 2, 14–21.

Anderson, D. I. & Sidaway, B. (1994). Coordination changes associated with practice of a soccer kick. *Research Quarterly for Exercise and Sport*, 65(2), 93–99.

Ball, K. A. (2011). Kinematic comparison of the preferred and non-preferred foot punt kick. *Journal of Sports Science*, 29(14), 1545–1552.

Beilock, S. L., Carr, T. H., McMahon, C., & Starkes, J. L. (2002). When paying attention becomes counterproductive: Impact of divided versus skill focused attention on novice and experienced performance of sensorimotor skills. *Journal of Experimental Psychology*, 8, 6–16.

Bernstein, N. (1967). *The coordination and regulation of movements*. Oxford, UK: Pergamon.

Byers, B. B. (2000). "Just do it": Commercial slogan or movement principle? *Journal of Physical Education, Recreation and Dance, 71*(9), 16–19.

Carson, R. G. & Riek, S. (2001). Changes in muscle recruitment patterns during skill acquisition. *Experimental Brain Research, 138*(1), 71–87.

Chase, M. A., Ewing, M. E., Lirgg, C. D., & George, T. R. (1994). The effects of equipment modifications on children's self-efficacy and shooting performance. *Research Quarterly for Exercise and Sport, 65*, 159–168.

Chase, W. G. & Simon, H. A. (1973). Perception in chess. *Cognitive Psychology, 4*, 55–81.

Chow, J. Y., Davids, K., Button, C., & Koh, M. (2007). Variation in coordination of a discrete multiarticular action as a function of skill level. *Journal of Motor Behavior, 30*, 463–479.

Christina, R. W. & Corcos, D. M. (1988). *Coaches guide to teaching sport skills*. Champaign, IL: Human Kinetics.

Duncan, P. W., Weiner, D. K., Chandler, J., & Studenski, S. (1990). Functional reach: A new clinical measure of balance. *Journal of Gerontology: Medical Sciences, 45*(6), M192–197.

Fitts, P. M. & Posner, M. I. (1967). *Human performance*. Belmont, CA: Brooks/Cole.

Gabriel, D. A. & Boucher, J. P. (1998). Practice effects on the timing and magnitude of agonist activity during ballistic elbow flexion to a target. *Research Quarterly for Exercise and Sport, 69*, 30–37.

Gentile, A. M. (1972). A working model of skill acquisition with application to teaching. *Quest, Monograph, 17*, 3–23.

Gentile, A. M. (2000). Skill acquisition: Action, movement, and the neuromotor processes. In J. H. Carr and R. B. Shepard (Eds.), *Movement science: Foundations for physical therapy in rehabilitation* (pp. 111–180). Rockville, MD: Aspen.

Hall, S. J. (2006). *Basic biomechanics*. New York: McGraw-Hill.

Hodges, N. J., Hayes, S. J., Horn, R. R., & Williams, A. M. (2005). Changes in coordination, control and outcome as a result of extended practice with the non-dominant foot on a soccer skill. *Ergonomics, 48*, 1672–1685.

Iglesias, D., García-González, L., García, T., León, B., & Del Villar, F. (2010). Expertise development in sport: Contributions under cognitive psychology perspective. *Journal of Human Sport & Exercise, 5*(3), 462–475.

Jaegars, S. M. H. J., Peterson, R. F., Dantuma, R., Hillen, B., Geuze, R., & Schellekens, J. (1989). Kinesiologic aspects of motor learning in dart throwing. *Journal of Human Movement Studies, 16*, 161–171.

Lay, B. A., Sparrow, W. A., Hughes, K. M., & O'Dwyer, N. J. (2002). Practice effects on co-ordination and control, metabolic energy expenditure, and muscle activation. *Human Movement Science, 21*, 807–830.

McPherson, S. L. & Thomas, J. R. (1989). Relation of knowledge and performance in boys' tennis: Age and expertise. *Journal of Experimental Child Psychology, 48*, 190–211.

Newell, K. M. (1985). Coordination, control, and skill. In D. Goodman, R. B. Wilberg, & I. M. Franks (Eds.), *Differing perspectives in motor learning memory and control* (pp. 295–317). Amsterdam: North-Holland.

Newell, K. M., Broderick, M. P., Deutsch, M., & Slifkin, A. B. (2003). Task goals and change in dynamical degrees of freedom with motor learning. *Journal of Experimental Psychology: Human Perception and Performance, 29*, 379–387.

Newell, A. & Rosenbloom, P. S. (1981). Mechanisms of skill acquisition and the law of practice. In J. R. Anderson (Ed.), *Cognitive skills and their acquisition* (pp. 1–51). Hillsdale, NJ: Lawrence Erlbaum.

Schneider, K., Zernicke, R. F., Schmidt, R. A., & Hart, T. J. (1989). Changes in limb dynamics during the practice of rapid arm movement. *Journal of Biomechanics, 22*, 805–817.

Shank, M. D. & Haywood, K. M. (1987). Eye movements while viewing a baseball pitch. *Perceptual and Motor Skills, 64*, 1191–1197.

Shemmell, J., Tresilian, J. R., Riek, S., Barry, B. K., & Carson, R. G. (2005). Neuromuscular adaptation during skill acquisition on a two-degree-of-freedom target-acquisition task: Dynamic movement. *Journal of Neurophysiology, 94*, 3058–3068.

Singer, R. N. & Janelle, C. M. (1999). Determining sport expertise: From genes to supremes. *International Journal of Sport Psychology, 30*, 117–150.

Smyth, M. M. & Pendleton, L. R. (1994). Memory for movement in professional ballet dancers. *International Journal of Sport Psychology, 25*, 282–294.

Southard, D. & Higgins, T. (1987). Changing movement patterns: Effects of demonstrations and practice. *Research Quarterly for Exercise and Sport, 58*, 77–80.

Sparrow, W. A. (2000). *Energetics of human movement*. Champaign, IL: Human Kinetics.

Thomas, J. R., French, K. E., & Humphries, C. A. (1986). Knowledge development and sport performance: Directions for motor behavior research. *Journal of Sport Psychology, 8*, 259–272.

Thomas, K. T. & Thomas, J. R. (1994). Developing expertise in sport: The relation of knowledge and performance. *International Journal of Sport Psychology, 25,* 295–311.

Vereijken, B., van Emmerik, R. E. A., Whiting, H. T. A., & Newell, K. M. (1992). Free(z)ing degrees of freedom in skill acquisition. *Journal of Motor Behavior, 24*(1), 133–142.

Whiting, H. T. A. (1984). *Human motor actions: Bernstein reassessed.* Amsterdam: North-Holland.

Wilson, C., Simpson, S. E., van Emmerik, R. E. A., & Hamill, J. (2008). Coordination variability and skill development in expert triple jumpers. *Sports Biomechanics, 7*(1), 2–9.

Yang, J. F. & Scholz, J. P. (2005). Learning a throwing task is associated with differential changes in the use of motor abundance. *Experimental Brain Research, 163,* 137–158.

At a college track meet, Coach Hernandez talked with Jackson, a pole vaulter, after the latter performed a warm-up vault. The coach wanted to give Jackson verbal instructions to assist in correcting a technical flaw. When Coach Hernandez finished his explanation, he asked whether Jackson understood what he had just said. Jackson replied that he did and returned to the end of the runway. When he got there, he turned to one of his teammates and asked, "Can you show me what Coach was saying?" Once the technique was demonstrated, he understood perfectly.

Perhaps the single greatest factor that influences a learner's ability to understand new concepts and achieve movement proficiency is communication. Practitioners communicate both verbally and non-verbally through instructions, demonstrations, and feedback. Effective communication occurs when messages are clear and concise, and the receiver understands what the sender intended. However, learners differ in how they receive new information and attempt to make sense of it. The teacher, coach, or therapist who recognizes the influence of individual differences (e.g., learning style, past experiences, and level of motivation) on how learners receive information is able to provide instruction and design experiences that are meaningful for each learner.

LEARNING STYLES

All learners have unique preferences for receiving and processing new information. These preferences constitute the person's individual learning style. Research has shown that when instructional style and learning style are initially matched, then secondary or tertiary modes are used to reinforce the newly presented material, greater learning gains are achieved (e.g., Dunn, Beaudry, & Klavas, 1989; Lovelace, 2005; Dunn, 2009). The pole vaulter in the scenario described above, for example, better understood the movement when he saw it demonstrated than when he had heard verbal instructions. Had Coach Hernandez accommodated Jackson's preference for visual information by modeling the correction initially then reinforcing it through verbal instructions, Jackson would not have needed to turn to his teammate for clarification. Designing the learning environment to incorporate a variety of instructional strategies to accommodate all learners can therefore enhance the learning process.

Among the many theories and models regarding individual learning styles—including Gardner's Multiple Intelligences (Gardner, 2006), Kolb's Learning

CEREBRALchallenge   7.1

Discuss the importance of effective communication for teachers, coaches, and therapists. In your discussion, specify those with whom you will have to communicate and when you will use communication throughout the learning process.

Styles Inventory (Kolb, 2005), and Gregorc's Mind Styles Model (Gregorc, 2006)—the Learning Styles Inventory (Dunn, Dunn, & Price, 2000) has often found informal use in a motor skill acquisition setting. Dunn and Dunn (1975, 1992, 1993) contend that an individual's learning style is an integrative collection of multiple levels and may be determined by assessing five areas:

1. *Instructional environment preferences* for sound, light, temperature, and class design
2. *Emotionality preferences*, including motivation, persistence, responsibility, and structure
3. *Sociological preferences* for individual, pair, peer, team, adult, or varied relations
4. *Physiological preferences* regarding perception, intake (e.g., eating, chewing gum), time, and mobility
5. *Psychological preferences* based on analytic mode (moving from details to big picture or vice versa), hemisphericity (associated with right or left brain dominance), and action.

Some elements of the Dunn and Dunn model, such as intake, are not directly related to a skill acquisition setting, but others can easily be accommodated. Bruner and Hill (1992) altered their coaching strategies and redesigned the varsity high school wrestling room layout to accommodate individual preferences for two of the elements in Dunn and Dunn's model: perceptual mode and socio-logical inclination. Bruner and Hill provided learners with opportunities to attempt new skills, as well as videos, handouts, charts, and verbal presenta-tions, based on perceptual preferences. They redesigned the wrestling room to accommodate sociological preferences by providing distinct areas where wrestlers could work alone, in pairs, or in groups. Although no formal research study examined their program, Bruner and Hill (1992) reported positive changes in wrestlers' athletic skill, academic achievement, and self-esteem as a result of their matching instructional style with individual learning styles.

Not only are the individual elements of Dunn and Dunn's model important considerations in designing the learning environment; many have also been found to correlate with two learning profiles that are based on processing preferences—that is, whether an individual is considered a global learner or an analytic learner (or a combination of the two) (Dunn, Cavanaugh, Eberle, & Zenhausern, 1982; Dunn, Bruno, Sklar, et al., 1990). Global learners learn more easily when they are first presented with the big picture and then asked to concentrate on details. Humor, anecdotes, and graphics are helpful for introducing global learners to new information. Analytic learners, on the other hand, prefer to have new information presented in a step-by-step, sequential manner that builds toward the main concept. Rules, guidelines, and procedures are helpful for analytic learners. Interestingly, individuals who work

VARK LEARNING STYLE QUESTIONNAIRE

http://vark-learn.com/the-vark-questionnaire/?p=results

exploration ACTIVITY 7.1

Exploring Your Learning Preferences

Several elements from Dunn and Dunn's learning style model are presented below. For each element, circle the description that better suits your preference when learning new information. See below for an explanation of which type of learner prefers which option.

ELEMENT	OPTION A	OPTION B
Sound	Work best in silence	Work best when there is background noise or music
Lighting	Prefer room to be well-illuminated	Prefer soft lighting
Design	Prefer to work at a desk, table, or other "work-like" setting	Prefer to work in an easy chair, on bed, in another comfortable setting
Persistence	Need to finish a task once started	Need frequent breaks; prefer to work on several tasks simultaneously
Structure	Prefer guidelines, specifications, procedures, and rules	Prefer less structure that allows for creativity
Social	Prefer to learn alone or with a practitioner	Prefer to learn with peers
Intake	Rarely eat, drink, smoke, or have other distracters while learning	Prefer to eat, drink, smoke, or have other distracters while learning

Analytic learners will tend to select responses under Option A, while global learners are more inclined to choose responses provided under Option B. Remember that all learners are different, and some individuals may have a combined profile.

in science-based professions, such as medical personnel, tend to fall within the analytic profile, while most patients do not (Samelson, 1997). Complete Exploration Activity 7.1 and the activities presented at the adjoining website to gain a better understanding of your own learning preferences.

Perceptual Mode

Although a person's learning style consists of many variables, perhaps the easiest to accommodate for motor skill learning is preferred perceptual mode. Perceptual mode is the way information is received and processed. Learners take in and process information in various ways. Their preferred mode is referred to as their modal strength. When giving instructions and designing practice environments, practitioners should consider four types of learner, based on individual modal strength:

1. *Visual learners* understand new concepts better when explanations include visual cue words such as "watch," "see," and "look." Demonstrations, videos, pictures, models, and the use of mirrors are all effective methods for accommodating learners whose modal strength is visual.
2. *Kinesthetic learners* strive to understand what the desired movement feels like. Once they achieve this understanding, they use it as a frame of reference with which to compare future attempts. Instructional strategies such as simulations, guidance, repeated practice, and incorporating cue words such as "feel," "move," and "experience" all help the kinesthetic learner develop a sense of what the correct movement feels like.
3. *Analytic learners* approach the desired movement in a problem-solving fashion. Scientific concepts and principles and cue words such as "analyze," "investigate," and "why" assist the analytic learner in solving the movement problem.
4. *Auditory learners* prefer sounds and rhythms. Cue words such as "hear," "pace," and "tempo" will assist auditory learners in learning the movement pattern. Auditory learners also benefit from verbal descriptions such as the one given by the coach in the story that opened this chapter.

Table 7.1 offers cue words and teaching strategies for each type of learner. Some learners, however, do not have one particular modal strength but instead have multiple modal preferences. To accommodate these learners, combine strategies to target each of the preferred modes.

TABLE 7.1 Examples of cue words and strategies to target each perceptual mode

	VISUAL	KINESTHETIC	ANALYTIC	AUDITORY
Sample Cue Words	see	feel	analyze	hear
	look	touch	think	listen
	watch	sense	examine	detect
	observe	move	compare	tempo
Sample Teaching Strategies	demonstrations	simulations	principles	clapping
	pictures	guidance	testing	music
	video	trial and error	investigating	sound

CEREBRALchallenge   7.2

Go back to the story at the beginning of the chapter about the pole vaulter, Jackson. What was his preferred perceptual mode? Suggest alternative strategies that the coach could have used to better accommodate Jackson's learning style.

Accommodating Your Learners

How do you find out each individual's learning style? Formal testing instruments are available, such as Kolb's Learning Style Inventory (Kolb, 2005) or Dunn, Dunn, and Price's Learning Style Inventory (Dunn et al., 2000). Exercise caution when using such instruments, however, as these were designed for traditional classroom settings; it has been found that learning styles shift depending on whether the task is predominantly a cognitive or a motor one (Coker, 1995, 2000). If you use formal testing instruments, respondents must be instructed to answer the questions as they apply to a motor setting. In other words, direct learners to answer the questions using learning a motor skill as a frame of reference. One inventory that is specific to sports settings is the VARK Questionnaire for Athletes (Dunn & Fleming, 2013). Its questions are framed in a sporting environment; however, Fuelscher, Ball, and MacMahon (2012) note that many are not specific to the learning of motor skills and call for the design and validation of an assessment specific to motor skill acquisition.

Informal assessment is also possible, and it can be a powerful and reliable technique. For informal assessment, pay attention to the clues that learners provide about their learning preference. Listen to the descriptive words they use to

exploration ACTIVITY   7.2

Self-Analysis

This activity will assess your learning-style usage tendencies. First, video record yourself teaching a 10-minute lesson on a skill of your choice. Next, download the Dartfish EasyTag app to your iPhone, tablet, or Android mobile device. Once you have the app, go to www.dartfish.com/easytag to download the instructions for its use. Create a panel that looks like the one at the right.

While reviewing your video, use the app to tabulate the number of cue words and strategies that you use in each of the four perceptual mode categories: visual, kinesthetic, auditory, and analytic. Do you have a tendency to teach in the same way you prefer to learn, as research suggests? Do you incorporate all four modes of presentation, or do you have a tendency to use only one mode? Can you suggest areas where you could have used a different mode? Give a specific example of an alternative cue word or strategy for each area suggested.

Panels	Learning Styles	Export
Show statistics		ON
Visual Cue	Visual Strategy	
Kinesthetic Cue	Kinesthetic Strategy	
Auditory Cue	Auditory Strategy	
Analytic Cue	Analytic Strategy	

assess their performance and the questions they ask. Do the words consistently fall into one of the four perceptual mode categories? Do the learners ask for clarification through a different mode? The athlete in the opening story was a visual learner. When Coach Hernandez verbally explained the technical flaws (auditory mode) and how to fix them, Jackson did not completely understand. As a result, he sought out an alternative way to get the information through his modal strength, vision. His teammate's demonstration gave him all he needed to understand what the coach had been trying to explain to him verbally.

When you use only one presentation style, you deny learners comparable opportunities to understand the information presented. Instead, rearrange the learning environment as Dunn and Dunn suggest (1992, 1993). Get to know your instructional tendencies and make an effort to expand your repertoire to incorporate strategies for all learning styles. Research suggests that an individual's learning style preference influences that person's teaching style. As a result, practitioners will tend to focus almost exclusively on their preferred style when giving instructions, and these natural instructional tendencies may not match the needs of their learners (MacNeil, 1980; Heikkinen, Pettigrew & Zakrajsek, 1985; McDaniel, 1986). Practitioners must make a conscious effort to employ alternate strategies that are compatible with learners' preferences. Try Exploration Activity 7.2 to determine whether your learning-style preferences influence your teaching. When working one-on-one with an individual, the practitioner should provide instruction and feedback through the learner's preferred perceptual mode so as to capitalize on the learner's strengths (return to Table 7.1 for ideas). With large groups of learners, providing instruction and feedback through each individual's preferred mode is not feasible. In this situation, the practitioner should instead use a multimodal approach, as shown in Table 7.2, constantly varying the mode through which information is presented so that all modes are used. Recognizing and accommodating learning styles will result in more meaningful communication and translate to enhanced learning.

TABLE 7.2 Example of multimodal approach for the basketball set shot	
PREPARATION	**ACTION**
Toes and shoulders face the basket (visual)	Knees bend slightly with tension felt in quads (kinesthetic)
Eyes focus on the front of the rim (visual)	Smooth sequential rhythm begins from knees and ends at fingers (auditory)
Feel weight distributed evenly over both feet (kinesthetic)	Force for shot comes from legs [discuss why generating force with legs is more efficient] (analytic)
Position ball between shoulders and eye level (kinesthetic)	See arm extend through the ball (visual)

CEREBRALchallenge 7.3

Below are examples of strategies for accommodating specific modal strengths in physical education, as offered by Reed, Banks, and Carlisle (2004). Determine which modal preference (visual, kinesthetic, analytic, auditory) would best be accommodated by each suggestion.

a.   Demonstrate five patterns of jumping.
b.   Create a fitness plan for you and your family to follow over summer vacation.
c.   Create a series of diagrams that explain a strategy or tactic used in a game.
d.   Design a flow chart that explains _____.
e.   Create a dance that expresses the way you value physical education.
f.   Create a poster of the four most important things a good dribbler does.

TRANSFER OF LEARNING

Another individual difference that the practitioner should consider when enhancing communication and designing optimal learning opportunities is the learner's past experiences. Throughout a person's lifespan one's knowledge accumulates, as do encounters with various skills; the sum of past experiences influences the individual's ability to learn new skills in both positive and negative ways. This phenomenon, where the learning of a new skill or its performance under novel conditions can be influenced by past experience with another skill or skills, is known as transfer.

Types of Transfer

Three types of transfer exist: positive, negative, and zero. Positive transfer occurs when a learner's past experience with one skill facilitates learning a new skill or using a skill in a different context. The zone defenses used in football and basketball, for example, share many commonalities. In this instance, a learner's knowledge of the zone defense in football will likely accelerate the rate at which he or she learns the zone defense in basketball. Negative transfer occurs when a learner's past experience with one skill hinders or obstructs learning a new skill or performing a skill under novel conditions. Despite the fact that swinging a bat in both softball and baseball has similar movement characteristics, tracking the oncoming pitch differs significantly in the two sports. In baseball, the pitcher uses an overarm throwing motion, causing the ball's trajectory to move from high to low. In softball, the pitcher uses an underhand throwing motion, and the ball rises as it approaches the plate. Previous experiences in baseball could, therefore, temporarily interfere with hitting performance in softball. For another illustration of negative transfer watch the video at www.youtube.com/watch?v=MFzDa BzBlL0&feature=youtu.be. Finally, when two skills are completely unrelated, such as swimming the butterfly stroke and goaltending in water polo, zero transfer occurs, because experience with the first skill has no influence on the second.

While practitioners want to capitalize on positive transfer, negative transfer can occur and is often the result of having to learn a new response to a well-learned stimulus. A classic example of negative transfer can be seen when a skilled badminton player decides to learn tennis. In badminton, the forehand drive requires a wrist snap. This is not the case in tennis, where the wrist contribution is minimal. Initially, the badminton player may attempt to incorporate a wrist snap in the tennis forehand. Fortunately, most negative transfer effects are temporary and can be overcome with practice.

Theories of Transfer

Understanding the theoretical underpinnings of transfer will assist the teacher, coach, or therapist in designing learning experiences that foster positive transfer. This understanding will also help the practitioner account for difficulties that individuals might display as a result of negative transfer.

Identical Elements Theory

The identical elements theory originally hypothesized that transfer was based on the number of common elements that two skills might share (Thorndike, 1914). It was thought that the more identical elements shared by two skills, the greater the positive transfer from one skill to the other. Accordingly, we would expect positive transfer to occur between the skills of picking up buttons and picking up coins, whereas the amount of transfer between putting and an instep kick in soccer would be negligible.

Osgoode (1949) amended the identical elements theory by specifying that, rather than identical elements, it was the similarities between the stimulus and response conditions of the two tasks that were fundamental. Consequently, we would expect a high degree of positive transfer when the stimulus and response conditions for the previously acquired task were the same as for the task being learned.

Learning difficulties arise when two skills have opposite stimulus–response requirements. For example, we would predict negative transfer when the skill being introduced has an identical stimulus to a previously learned skill but requires a different response. An individual who purchases a new mountain bike, for example, will experience some temporary frustration if the gear-shifting mechanism is different from a previously owned bike.

Transfer Appropriate Processing Theory

The identical elements theory does not account for all possible transfer conditions. Strategic and conceptual aspects of games or tasks can also transfer.

As a result, the transfer appropriate processing theory was proposed to account for cognitive processing similarities that occur between practice conditions and the performance criterion (Morris, Bransford, & Franks, 1977; Bransford, Franks, Morris, & Stein, 1979; Lee, 1988). According to this theory, we would expect positive transfer when practice conditions require learners to engage in problem-solving processes similar to those that the criterion task requires.

In volleyball, when a spike is hit around a block, the defensive player may use one of the four main defensive skills: the forearm pass, the roll, the dive, or the sprawl. The technique that the defensive player chooses depends on a number of factors that have to be assessed instantaneously. To facilitate the player's ability to choose the appropriate skill and then execute it correctly, proponents of transfer appropriate processing would recommend practicing each defensive skill during the same practice period but in a random order, rather than practicing each skill independently (to make use of a phenomenon known as *contextual interference*). Furthermore, continuously changing the direction, speed, position, and trajectory of the oncoming ball would help assure maximum positive transfer. This practice strategy, known as *variable practice*, forces the learner to engage in realistic cognitive processing, since the learner will never be in exactly the same situation twice. Both contextual interference and variable practice will be discussed in more detail in Chapter 10.

RESEARCH NOTES

Chen, Kang, Chuang, and colleagues (2007) investigated the training effects of a virtual reality intervention on the reaching behaviors of children with spastic cerebral palsy (CP). Wearing a sensor glove, four children practiced three activities (butterfly, pegboard, and pick-and-place blocks) in a three-dimensional virtual environment. They received virtual reality interventions for two hours per week over the course of a month. All three activities were designed to train the reaching and grasping of stationary or moving objects in different directions, and the children were encouraged to reach as quickly as possible toward the virtual object that appeared. Both auditory (e.g., banging sound as hand hit virtual object) and visual feedback (e.g., change in color of object as it came within grasping range) were provided. The results indicated that three of the four children demonstrated some improvement in reaching behavior (kinematics) during the intervention. Those practice effects were partially maintained in a four-week follow-up test. The researchers concluded that participation in the virtual reality training program appeared to improve the quality of reaching in children with CP.

To view how virtual reality simulators train surgeons and quarterbacks go to www.youtube.com/watch?v=1u5BLlX4nG8 and www.youtube.com/watch?v=0XKxvK EFBps, respectively.

Transfer and Instructional Design

Many instructional decisions regarding presentation sequence and the use of instructional aids are based on the principles of transfer. For example, simplified versions of skills, drills, and games serve as precursors to more complex versions that will be introduced in the future. Skill progressions—such as learning to dive into a swimming pool, where learners are first taught to dive from a kneeling position on the side of the pool and then advance to a crouched position, a stride position, and finally a standing position—are based on the assumption that experience with simplified versions will positively transfer to the actual movement, facilitating its acquisition. Similarly, lead-up games—such as T-ball, sideline soccer, five hundred in softball or baseball, keep away in basketball, and three-hit volleyball—have been used to assist the learner.

Other modifications may be made when the skill involves a potential risk of injury or is expensive, when practice facilities are lacking, or when practice in a real-life setting is not possible. Gymnasts first learn complex and potentially dangerous skills with some type of instructional aid, such as a harness, to minimize the risk of injury. Bicycles are equipped with training wheels. Fighter pilots train on flight simulators that allow countless practice trials with minimal risk and expense. Astronauts train underwater, as it simulates the weightless environment they will experience in space. In the clinical environment, the BTE Work Simulation device allows patients to copy activities such as driving, turning a key, pulling a knob, and applying brakes; the Resusci® Anne mannequin (from Laerdal Medical) helps students learn rescue breathing and CPR; and the C-Mill helps patients learn avoidance strategies in a safe and controlled environment (see www.youtube.com/watch?v=65XrJ9DG3 mM#t=11 for a demonstration). All of these modifications attempt to capitalize on positive transfer.

Until recently, much of the support for designing instructional methodology that capitalizes on the notion of positive transfer was anecdotal. In 2011, however, Künzell and Lukas showed that skateboarding lessons positively transferred to learning how to snowboard. A few years earlier, O'Keeffe, Harrison, and Smyth (2007) demonstrated positive transfer effects from practice in the overarm throw, which led to significant learning effects for the badminton

FIGURE **7.1**

Skill progressions assume that experience with simplified versions, such as diving from the side of a pool, will positively transfer to more advanced skill performance, such as diving from a board

FIGURE **7.2**

A Resusci® Anne mannequin allows the learner to simulate CPR

overhead clear and the javelin throw; this supported the idea of positive transfer between fundamental motor skills and sport-specific skills.

Fostering Positive Transfer

The following guidelines, based on the theories of transfer, provide practitioners with a starting point for creating learning experiences that will foster positive transfer.

Analyze the Skill

Given that transfer is based on similarity between skills, the ability to analyze skills effectively is indispensable for designing instructional strategies that will facilitate learning. We can examine four subcomponents of skills to determine their degree of similarity and assess the potential for positive transfer.

1. *The fundamental movement pattern.* The last three steps of the lay-up, for example, are comparable to those of the high jump. A learner who is proficient at the lay-up will have an advantage in learning the high jump if the practitioner associated the two during instruction.
2. *The strategic and conceptual aspects of the game or task.* For example, the "give and go" strategy is used in a variety of sports. If a learner has performed a "give and go" in one sport, pointing out the similarities to a "give and go" in a different sport should facilitate learning. Similar examples include the use of a pelvic tilt in numerous therapeutic and fitness activities, and the influence of head position on balance.
3. *Perceptual elements.* Whitewater kayaking and whitewater rafting may lack similarities with respect to physical skills, but both activities require the person to know how to read the water to choose the best route. The regulatory cues, as well as the visual search strategies used for their detection, would be quite similar in both skills.
4. *Temporal and spatial elements.* Many skills require the performer to make sure that an implement meets an object at the right time and in the right location; these include the racket sports of squash, tennis, and racquetball.

Prior to providing instruction, practitioners should become familiar with their learners' past experience with various motor skills. Those skills should be

FIGURE **7.3** A high degree of similarity exists between the hand position for (a) catching a football above the waist and (b) setting a volleyball

(a)　　　　　(b)

analyzed to determine whether similarities exist in fundamental movement pattern, strategic and/or conceptual aspects, perceptual elements, and temporal and spatial elements between the skill being taught and those with which the learner is familiar. Comparisons, like the one in Figure 7.3, could then be made throughout the instructional process to facilitate understanding. Observe examples of positive transfer by visiting your college or university's athletic training room or a rehabilitation or physical therapy clinic and answering the questions in Exploration Activity 7.3.

Determine the Cost–Benefit Tradeoff

Lead-up games, simulators, and drills should be evaluated for cost effectiveness prior to their use. In other words, the effectiveness of a drill should be evaluated against the degree of potential amount of positive transfer. Unless there is a high degree of similarity between the designed experience and the criterion or target behavior, implementation of some preliminary activities and drills may not be warranted. For example, if the time spent learning a lead up game (cost) exceeds the potential amount of positive transfer to the actual game (benefit), teaching and playing the lead up game would not be an efficient use of instructional time. Similarly, a volleyball drill that requires teammates to form a circle and bump the ball to the next person in a clockwise direction will transfer poorly to a game situation and might in fact teach players the bad habit of swinging their arms to the side rather than facing their target. Practitioners must remember that the purpose of any drill is the transfer of learning to the target movement pattern, game situation, or functional context—"not the improvement of the drill itself" (Jeffreys, 2006, p. 74).

exploration ACTIVITY   7.3

Observation: Transfer

For this activity, arrange to observe at your school's athletic training room or a local rehabilitation or physical therapy clinic.

1. How many examples of equipment, instructions, exercises, and so on can you find that are designed to elicit positive transfer between two skills? List them.
2. For each example on your list, determine which component(s) of the skill will transfer (fundamental movement pattern, strategic and conceptual aspects, perceptual elements, or temporal and spatial elements).

EXAMPLE	FUNDAMENTAL MOVEMENT PATTERN	STRATEGIC AND CONCEPTUAL ASPECTS	PERCEPTUAL ELEMENTS	TEMPORAL AND SPATIAL ELEMENTS
Training Staircase	X	X		X

Get to Know the Learner

Everyone has past learning experiences that influence their ability to learn new skills. Get to know your learners. Find out what types of experiences they have had that you might use to compare with a skill you are introducing. In rehabilitation, for example, patients will see greater success if clinical practice conditions closely match the real-world functional activities in which they will engage (Stevans & Hall, 1998). Determining the real-world demands imposed on each patient is prerequisite to designing an effective rehab program.

Point out Similarities and Differences

Once you have determined the similarities and differences between the skills already learned and the skill about to be learned, point them out to the learner. Learners are not always able to make connections between skills on their own. Stating that inline skating and ice skating are similar is insufficient; you must point out specifically which aspects of the two skills are similar and which are dissimilar. For example, the push-off to start in inline skating and ice skating is comparable, but stopping is very different. With inline skates, the "brake" is located at the back of the boot, and participants must force it in front of them to engage it. In ice skating, participants can stop in several ways, depending on their experience. An individual who learned how to skate in hockey skates will probably stop by turning to the side with the feet parallel. A person who learned

CEREBRALchallenge   7.4

Analyze the following pairs of skills to determine their similarities and differences. Be sure to compare the fundamental movement pattern, strategic and conceptual aspects, perceptual elements, and temporal and spatial elements. Based on your analysis, assess the potential for transfer, either positive or negative, for each pairing. Justify your answer.

a. Cane walking and using a walker
b. Downhill skiing and waterskiing

c. Kickball and baseball
d. Mountain biking and whitewater kayaking.

RESEARCH NOTES

Coldwells and Hare (1994) conducted an experiment to determine whether short tennis skills positively transferred to lawn tennis. Short tennis is a modified version of tennis designed for children. The rackets are smaller and made of plastic, making them lighter and easier to swing. The ball, made of foam, bounces lower and slower. The court is smaller with a lower net, and the rules are simplified.

Sixteen subjects were divided into two groups. The experimental group received 10 hours of short tennis instruction and 10 hours of lawn tennis instruction. The control group received 20 hours of lawn tennis instruction only. A pre- and post-test using the Dyer Backboard test was administered and videotaped. Three experienced coaches then analyzed the videotape, judging each subject's backswing, follow-through, ball placement, and positioning (position of the player relative to the bounce of the ball). Results revealed that the experimental group improved more than the control group on the Dyer Backboard test ($p < .05$). In addition, the video analysis indicated that the experimental group performed significantly better on the backswing and the follow-through, while the control group was significantly better at positioning and ball placement. A second study, limited to eight hours of total instruction and focusing only on ground strokes, revealed no significant differences between groups for the test but found the experimental group to be significantly better on the backswing, follow-through, and placement, and the control group was better at positioning. The authors concluded that because the experimental group was superior in the backswing and follow-through in both experiments, positive transfer of those actions occurred. They further concluded that the positioning superiority of the control group was probably due to greater experience with the bounce of a tennis ball. Consequently, negative transfer for reading ball bounce likely resulted between the foam ball used in short tennis and the tennis ball.

QUESTION

How could this study be redesigned to test the authors' hypothesis regarding the control group's superiority with positioning?

how to skate using figure skates, however, may simply dig the pick into the ice and drag it. Consequently, blanket statements are misleading and may impede initial performance rather than facilitate it.

Make Sure that the Skills You Refer to Have Been Well Learned

Anytime you attempt to capitalize on the use of transfer, it is important to be sure that the skill or concept you refer to has been well learned. Shoveling snow and scooping up a ball in lacrosse share a similar movement pattern, but a person who lives in the southwestern region of the United States will have limited experience with shoveling snow. Another example is comparing the overhead throwing motion to the volleyball serve. If the individual has an immature throwing pattern to begin with, this strategy could backfire. Unless the skill you refer to is well learned, the example will not be meaningful, and the idea you are trying to convey will not be communicated effectively.

Use Analogies

Another technique to elicit positive transfer is the use of analogies. Learners create a mental image of how a skill is to be executed based on the practitioner's explanation. The practitioner can simplify new concepts by relating the new information to a familiar model. For example, to teach the correct grip in tennis, instructors often ask students to "shake hands" with the racquet. This analogy relates the grip to something familiar, a handshake, enhancing the learner's mental picture of the task.

Liao and Masters (2001) suggest that using analogies can be beneficial because the essential rules of the new skill do not need to be explicated. In their study, participants were to hit a table tennis ball to a target area with topspin using a forehand stroke. The researchers, in teaching the topspin, analogized it to a right-angled triangle, telling participants to "strike the ball while bringing the bat [paddle] up the hypotenuse of the triangle" (p. 310). Other participants were given a set of 12 basic techniques for generating topspin. The findings suggest that analogy learning was implicit in nature and was an effective strategy for learning the topspin forehand stroke in table tennis. Similar findings were reported for a modified (seated) basketball shooting task (Lam, Maxwell, & Masters, 2009), the coordination pattern of the breaststroke (Komar, Chow, Chollet, & Seifert, 2014), and the acquisition of the full swing in golf (Schücker, Ebbing, & Hagemann, 2010).

Maximize Similarities between Practice and Performance

When teaching for positive transfer, provide practice opportunities that have a high degree of similarity to the actual performance context. For example, the movement required to step up stairs is one that is used in a variety of situations. A patient learning this motion will use it not only to climb stairs of differing heights but also to step over a curb, step into the bathtub, and step onto an escalator. Similarly, a second baseman needs to be able to throw accurately to first, second, third, and home plate from a number of fielding positions. Providing opportunities to use newly learned skills in a variety of situations and designing drills that simulate actual performance will foster maximum positive transfer.

Consider the Skill Level of the Learner

Transfer is more beneficial for a beginning learner than for one who has intermediate or advanced levels of skill. Comparing aspects of an overhand volleyball serve to a tennis serve can assist a beginner to create a mental image in order to generate initial attempts. Once the learner has demonstrated an understanding of the desired movement, however, he or she must focus on skill-specific cues to improve.

CEREBRALchallenge 7.5

On a separate sheet, for a sport or activity of your choice, list 10 analogies that you could use to assist a learner in creating a mental picture of a corresponding skill.

MOTIVATION

Motivation is an internal condition that incites and directs action or behavior. Motivation is a powerful force as it influences learners' receptivity to instruction and dedication to practice.

Motivation to Learn

Practitioners should recognize that although some individuals are excited to learn, others might be apprehensive, have misconceptions about the skill being introduced, or simply do not see the importance of learning it. The introduction of a new skill should therefore captivate learners' interest. Simply explaining the objective of the skill is not always enough. Learners must be given a reason why

> **COMMON MYTH**
>
> All learners are motivated to learn the skills presented to them.

it is important to learn that particular skill. Some examples are to develop a good foundation on which to build future skills, to gain a competitive edge, or to improve functional movement and independence following an injury. By framing the learning situation as a means to achieve a certain goal, learners might be better able to see its value.

Motivation to Practice

Accordingly to Lewthwaite and Wulf (2012), both the extent and rate of learning are influenced by motivational factors associated with various practice conditions. In fact, motivation serves as one of the cornerstones of their recently proposed theory, the OPTIMAL theory (Optimizing performance through intrinsic motivation and attention for learning), which suggests that learning is optimized when (1) expectations of a positive outcome are enhanced; (2) learners are provided with choices; and (3) attentional focus is directed externally on the intended movement effect (Wulf & Lewthwaite, 2016). Although the predictions of this theory have yet to be fully examined, Wulf, Chiviacowsky, and Cardozo (2014) demonstrated additive benefits of combining enhanced expectancies and giving learners a choice when learning a novel throwing task. Greater learning gains were also found when combining an external focus of attention and enhanced performance expectancies when compared to the provision of one or the other factor alone (Pascua, Wulf, & Lewthwaite, 2015).

RESEARCH NOTES

Given that autonomy support (AS) and enhanced expectancies (EE) have both been shown to benefit learning, Wulf, Chiviacowsky, and Cardozo (2014) were interested in examining their combined effect. Sixty-four high school students were randomly assigned to four groups: AS, EE, AS + EE, and Control (C). The task was to throw colored beach-tennis balls overhand at a hanging, concentric circle target with the non-dominant hand. Participants performed a five-trial pretest followed by a practice phase consisting of six blocks of 10 trials. Average accuracy score feedback was provided after each block. During the practice phase, those groups receiving autonomy support (AS, AS + EE) were given the choice of ball color (red, yellow, blue) before each block while ball color was predetermined for each practice block (blue, red, yellow, blue, red, yellow) for those participants in the other two groups (EE, C). In addition, enhanced expectancy groups (EE, AS + EE) were provided with bogus positive social-comparative feedback designed to prompt the belief that their performance was above average while the feedback given to other two groups (AS, C) was based on actual performance. A retention and transfer test, each consisting of 10 trials, were performed the following day in the absence of feedback and using only a red ball. Self-efficacy was also measured after the pretest and practice phase and before the retention and transfer tests. Results revealed an additive learning advantage for both autonomy support and enhanced expectancies as the AS + EE group demonstrated the greatest throwing accuracy on both the retention and transfer tests. Accuracy scores were also higher for the AS and EE groups compared to the C group. Further, after the practice phase and before the retention and transfer tests, the groups with AS and/or EE manipulations demonstrated higher self-efficacy than the C group. The researchers concluded that giving learners a choice, even a seemingly incidental one, and enhancing their performance expectancies during practice increased self-efficacy and facilitated learning.

Enhanced Expectancies

Although errors are an integral part of skill acquisition, the learning environment should be one where learners are not afraid to make mistakes (Stratton, 1996). Through the establishment of a positive motivational learning climate, practitioners can instill the confidence and increased perceptions of one's ability that can lead to optimal learning and performance (e.g., Valentini & Rudisill, 2006). Such an environment is created when opportunities are provided to demonstrate competence as well as to become successful (Blankenship, 2008). This will lead to feelings of achievement, creating positive expectancies that will further motivate the learner to practice. For example, improved performance and greater intrinsic motivation was found when learners watched edited videos showing only their good performances versus their actual outcomes, both good and bad (e.g., Clark & Ste-Marie, 2007). Learning advantages have also been reported when feedback is focused on relatively successful attempts (Chiviacowsky and Wulf, 2007; Chiviacowsky, Wulf, Wally, & Borges, 2009; Badami, Vaez-Mousavi, Wulf, & Namazizadeh, 2011, 2012; Saemi, Porter, Ghotbi-Varzaneh, Zarghami, & Maleki, 2012). Other examples of strategies that can influence performance expectancies include positive feedback (e.g., Stoate, Wulf, & Lewthwaite, 2012), task enjoyment (Wulf & Lewthwaite, 2016), and an emphasis on personal improvement (Alderman, Beighle, & Pangrazi, 2006).

Control to Choose

Giving learners the autonomy to make decisions about some characteristics of the learning situation has also been found to be a viable motivational strategy (Lewthwaite, Chiviacowsky, Drews, & Wulf, 2015). Self-control learning advantages have been found for practice schedule (Wu & Magill, 2011), amount of practice (Post, Fairbrother, & Barros, 2011), feedback (e.g., Chiviacowsky, Wulf, de Medeiros, Kaefer, & Tani, 2008), model viewing frequency (e.g., Wulf, Raupach, & Pfeiffer, 2005), and level of task difficulty (Andrieux, Danna, & Thon, 2012; see Sanli, Patterson, Bray, & Lee, 2013 for a review). Practical tips for physical education offered by Alderman et al. (2006) include giving students a choice between activities when possible, allowing them to choose the level of difficulty of the task, and giving them the flexibility to modify activities according to their individual needs. A speech and language pathologist could offer a child the choice of what book to read. In the clinic, patients could be given the choice of which exercise to do first, which object to grasp when working on fine motor control, or they could even be given the opportunity to select, from a number of exercises that address their impairment, those that will be included in their home exercise program.

CEREBRALchallenge 7.6

> Think back to the last time you had to learn something that you weren't interested in. Why were you not motivated to learn? How much effort did you put into learning? What other consequences to the learning process resulted from your lack of motivation?

PUTTING IT INTO PRACTICE

Learning Situation: Rehabilitation of an Ankle Sprain

Darren's job requires him to not only hike along wooded trails, but to negotiate a variety of terrains, slopes, and obstacles while carrying a pack and/or equipment (e.g., a chainsaw). Having developed a good static balance foundation, the physical therapist now needs to prepare Darren for returning back to his work in the field.

Test Your Knowledge

Create three balance/proprioception exercises that will positively transfer to Darren's on the job activities. Compare your answer with the sample response provided at www.routledge.com/cw/coker.

A LOOK AHEAD

The learning process is highly dependent on quality practitioner–learner interactions. Recognizing the influence of individual differences—such as learning style, past experiences, and level of motivation—on how learners receive information enables the teacher, coach, or therapist to provide instruction and design experiences that are meaningful for each individual. We will continue to apply these concepts as we explore methods for presenting novel skills in the next chapter.

FOCUS POINTS

After reading this chapter, you should know:

- All learners have unique preferences for receiving and processing new information, which define their learning style.
- Greater learning gains have been shown when the instructional style is matched to the individual's learning style.
- Four perceptual modes should be considered when giving instructions and designing practice environments: visual, kinesthetic, analytic, and auditory.

- When the learning of a new skill or its performance under novel conditions is influenced by the individual's past experience with another skill or skills, transfer is said to occur.
- While practitioners should capitalize on positive transfer, negative transfer is often the result of having to learn a new response to a well-learned stimulus.
- To determine the similarity between two skills and assess the potential for positive transfer, four factors should be compared: fundamental movement pattern, strategic and conceptual aspects of the game or task, perceptual elements, and temporal and spatial elements.
- Considerations for fostering positive transfer include:

  — determining the cost–benefit tradeoff of its implementation
  — understanding the past experiences of learners
  — determining and highlighting the similarities and differences between skills already learned and those being learned
  — making sure that the skills being used for transfer have been well learned
  — using analogies
  — maximizing similarities between practice and performance
  — adjusting instruction to the skill level of the learner

- Motivation is an internal condition that incites and directs action or behavior.
- In order to learn, an individual must be motivated to do so.
- According to the OPTIMAL theory learning is optimized when (a) expectations of a positive outcome are enhanced, (b) learners are provided with choices, and (c) attentional focus is directed externally on the intended movement effect.

lab

To complete the lab for this chapter, visit www.routledge.com/cw/coker and select **Lab 7, Transfer**.

REVIEW QUESTIONS

1. What are the characteristics of effective communication?
2. Define learning style.
3. What is the significance of matching presentation style and learning style?
4. Two major theories have been proposed to account for transfer. Compare and contrast them.
5. What four subcomponents of a skill would you assess to determine the similarities and differences between two skills?

6. Explain why it is important to point out to learners both the similarities and differences between two skills when comparing them for the purpose of transfer.

7. What is motivation, and why is it a pre-instruction consideration?

8. What are two things a practitioner can do to enhance expectancies?

REFERENCES

Alderman, B. L., Beighle, A., & Pangrazi, R. P. (2006). Enhancing motivation in physical education. *Journal of Physical Education, Recreation, and Dance, 77*, 41–45, 51.

Andrieux, M., Danna, J., & Thon, B. (2012). Self-control of task difficulty during training enhances motor learning of a complex coincidence-anticipation task. *Research Quarterly for Exercise and Sport, 83*, 27–35.

Badami, R., VaezMousavi, M., Wulf, G., & Namazizadeh, M. (2011). Feedback after good trials enhances intrinsic motivation. *Research Quarterly for Exercise and Sport, 82*, 360–364.

Badami, R., VaezMousavi, M., Wulf, G., & Namazizadeh, M. (2012). Feedback about more accurate versus less accurate trials: Differential effects on self-confidence and activation. *Research Quarterly for Exercise and Sport, 83*, 196–203.

Blankenship, B. T. (2008). *The psychology of teaching physical education: From theory to practice.* Scottsdale, AZ: Holcomb Hathaway.

Bransford, J. D., Franks, J. J., Morris, C. D., & Stein, B. S. (1979). Some general constraints on learning and memory research. In L. S. Cermak & F. I. M. Craik (Eds.), *Levels of processing in human memory* (pp. 331–354). Hillsdale, NJ: Erlbaum.

Bruner, R. & Hill, D. (1992). Using learning styles research in coaching. *Journal of Physical Education, Recreation and Dance, 63*(4), 26–28.

Chen, Y. P., Kang, L. J., Chuang, T. Y., Doong, J. L., Lee, S. J., Tsai, M. W., Jeng, S. F., & Sung, W. H. (2007). Use of virtual reality to improve upper-extremity control in children with cerebral palsy: A single subject design. *Physical Therapy, 87*, 1441–1457.

Chiviacowsky, S. & Wulf, G. (2007). Feedback after good trials enhances learning. *Research Quarterly for Exercise and Sport, 78*, 40–47.

Chiviacowsky, S., Wulf, G., de Medeiros, F., Kaefer, A., & Tani, G. (2008). Learning benefits of self-controlled knowledge of results in 10-year-old children. *Research Quarterly for Exercise & Sport, 79*(3), 405–410.

Chiviacowsky, S., Wulf, G., Wally, R., & Borges, T. (2009). KR after good trials enhances learning in older adults. *Research Quarterly for Exercise and Sport, 80*, 663–668.

Clark, S. E. & Ste-Marie, D. M. (2007). The impact of self-as-a-model interventions on children's self-regulation of learning and swimming performance. *Journal of Sports Sciences, 25*, 577–586.

Coker, C. A. (1995). Learning style consistency across cognitive and motor settings. *Perceptual and Motor Skills, 81*, 1023–1026.

Coker, C. A. (2000). Consistency of learning styles of undergraduate athletic training students across the traditional classroom vs. the clinical setting. *Journal of Athletic Training, 35*(4), 441–444.

Coldwells, A. & Hare, M. E. (1994). The transfer of skill from short tennis to lawn tennis. *Ergonomics, 37*(1), 17–21.

Dunn, J. L. & Fleming N. (2013). The VARK Questionnaire-Athletes Version. Available at: http://vark-learn.com/the-vark-questionnaire/the-vark-questionnaire-for-athletes/ [accessed December 21, 2016].

Dunn, R., Beaudry, J. S., & Klavas, A. (1989). Survey of research on learning styles. *Educational Leadership, 46* (6), 46–54.

Dunn, R., Bruno, J., Sklar, R., Zenhausern, R., & Beaudry, J. (1990). Effects of matching and mismatching minority developmental college students' hemispheric preferences on mathematics scores. *Journal of Educational Research, 83*(5), 283–288.

Dunn, R., Cavanaugh, D., Eberle, B., & Zenhausern, R. (1982). Hemispheric preference: The newest element of learning style. *The American Biology Teacher, 44*(5), 291–294.

Dunn, R. & Dunn, K. (1975). *Educator's self-teaching guide to individualizing instructional programs.* Nyack, NY: Parker.

Dunn, R. & Dunn, K. (1992). *Teaching elementary students through their individual learning styles.* Boston: Allyn & Bacon.

Dunn, R. & Dunn, K. (1993). *Teaching secondary students through their individual learning styles.* Boston: Allyn & Bacon.

Dunn, R., Dunn, K., & Price, G. (2000). *Learning styles inventory: Grades 5–12.* Lawrence, KS: Price Systems.

Dunn, Z. J. L. (2009). Using learning preferences to improve coaching and athletic performance, *Journal of Physical Education, Recreation & Dance,* 80(3), 30–37.

Fuelscher, I. T., Ball, K., & MacMahon, C. (2012). Perspectives on learning styles in motor and sport skills. *Frontiers in Psychology,* 69, 1–3.

Gardner, H. (2006). *Multiple intelligences: New horizons.* New York: Basic Books.

Gregorc, A. F. (2006). *The mind styles model: Theory, principles, and applications.* Columbia, CT: Gregorc Associates.

Heikkinen, M., Pettigrew, F., & Zakrajsek, P. (1985). Learning styles vs. teaching styles: Studying the relationship. *NASSP Bulletin,* 69(478), 80–85.

Jeffreys, I. (2006). Motor learning: Applications for agility, part 1. *Strength & Conditioning Journal,* 28(5), 72–76.

Kolb, D. (2005). *Learning styles inventory: Version 3.1.* Boston: HayGroup.

Komar, J., Chow, J., Chollet, D., & Seifert, L. (2014). Effect of analogy instructions with an internal focus on learning a complex motor skill. *Journal of Applied Sport Psychology,* 26(1), 17–32.

Künzell, S. & Lukas, S. (2011). Facilitation effects of a preparatory skateboard training on the learning of snowboarding. *Kinesiology,* 43(1), 56–63.

Lam, W. K., Maxwell, J. P., & Masters, R. S. W. (2009). Analogy learning and the performance of motor skills under pressure. *Journal of Sport and Exercise Psychology,* 31, 337–357.

Lee, T. D. (1988). Transfer appropriate processing: A framework for conceptualizing practice effects in motor learning. In O. G. Meijer & K. Roth (Eds.), *Complex motor behavior: The motor action controversy* (pp. 201–215). Amsterdam: Elsevier Science.

Lewthwaite, R., Chiviacowsky, S., Drews, R., & Wulf, G. (2015). Choose to move: The motivational impact of autonomy support on motor learning. *Psychonomic Bulletin & Review,* 22(5), 1383–1388. doi:10.3758/s13423-015-0814-7

Lewthwaite, R., & Wulf, G. (2012). Motor learning through a motivational lens. In N. J. Hodges & A. M. Williams (Eds.), *Skill acquisition in sport: Research, theory & practice* (2nd ed., pp. 173–191). London: Routledge.

Liao, M. & Masters, R. S. W. (2001). Analogy learning: A means to implicit motor learning. *Journal of Sports Sciences,* 19, 307–327.

Lovelace, M. K. (2005). Meta-analysis of experimental research based on the Dunn and Dunn model. *Journal of Educational Research,* 98, 176–183.

MacNeil, R. D. (1980). The relationship of cognitive style and instructional style to the learning performance of undergraduate students. *Journal of Educational Research,* 22, 354–359.

McDaniel, T. R. (1986). A primer on classroom discipline: Principles old and new. *Phi Delta Kappan,* 66(1), 63–67.

Morris, C. D., Bransford, J. D., & Franks, J. J. (1977). Levels of processing versus transfer appropriate processing. *Journal of Verbal Learning and Verbal Behavior,* 16, 519–533.

O'Keeffe, S. L., Harrison, A. J., & Smyth, P. J. (2007). Transfer or specificity? An applied investigation into the relationship between fundamental overarm throwing and related sport skills. *Physical Education and Sport Pedagogy,* 12(2), 89–102.

Osgoode, C. E. (1949). The similarity paradox in human learning: A resolution. *Psychological Review,* 56, 132–143.

Pascua, L. M., Wulf, G., & Lewthwaite, R. (2015). Additive benefits of external focus and enhanced performance expectancy for motor learning. *Journal of Sports Sciences,* 33(1), 58–66.

Post, P. G., Fairbrother, J. T., & Barros, J. C. (2011). Self-controlled amount of practice. Benefits learning of a motor skill. *Research Quarterly for Exercise and Sport,* 82(3), 474–481.

Reed, J. A., Banks, A. L., & Carlisle, C. S. (2004). Knowing me, knowing who? Getting to know your students' preferred learning style. *Teaching Elementary Physical Education,* 15(4), 25–27.

Saemi, E., Porter, J. M., Ghotbi-Varzaneh, A., Zarghami, M., & Maleki, F. (2012). Knowledge of results after relatively good trials enhances self-efficacy and motor learning. *Psychology of Sport and Exercise,* 13, 378–382.

Samelson, T. C. (1997). Getting information across to patients. *Medical Economics,* 74(3), 105–108.

Sanli, E. A., Patterson, J. T., Bray, S. R., & Lee, T. D. (2013). Understanding self-controlled motor learning protocols through the self-determination theory. *Frontiers in Psychology,* 3611. doi: 10.3389/fpsyg.2012.00611

Schücker, L., Ebbing, L., & Hagemann, N. (2010). Learning by analogies: Implications for performance and attentional processes under pressure. *Human Movement,* 11(2), 191–199.

Stevans, J. & Hall, K. G. (1998). Motor skills acquisition strategies for rehabilitation of low back pain. *Journal of Orthopedic Sports Physical Therapy, 28*(3), 165–167.

Stoate, I., Wulf, G., & Lewthwaite, R. (2012). Enhanced expectancies improve movement efficiency in runners. *Journal of Sports Sciences, 30,* 815–823.

Stratton, R. (1996). Motivating your athletes and yourself. *Coaching Youth Sports.* www.Tandl.vt. Edu/rstratto/CYSarchive/CoachSept96.html

Thorndike, E. L. (1914). *Educational psychology.* New York: Columbia University.

Valentini, N. & Rudisill, M. E. (2006). Goal orientation and mastery climate: a review of contemporary research and insights to intervention. *Estudos de Psicologia (Campinas), 23*(2), 159–171. https://dx. doi.org/10.1590/S0103- 66X2006000200006

Wu, W. W. & Magill, R. A. (2011). Allowing learners to choose: Self-controlled practice schedules for learning multiple movement patterns. *Research Quarterly for Exercise & Sport, 82*(3), 449–457.

Wulf, G., Chiviacowsky, S., & Cardozo, P. L. (2014). Additive benefits of autonomy support and enhanced expectancies for motor learning. *Human Movement Science,* 3712–3720.

Wulf, G. & Lewthwaite, R. (2016). Optimizing performance through intrinsic motivation and attention for learning: The optimal theory of motor learning. *Psychonomic Bulletin & Review,* doi:10. 3758/s13423–015–0999–9

Wulf, G., Raupach, M., & Pfeiffer, F. (2005). Self-controlled observational practice enhances learning. *Research Quarterly for Exercise and Sport, 76,* 107–111.

A 34-year-old patient is referred for physical therapy after surgery to repair a torn anterior cruciate ligament (ACL). A component of the rehabilitation program prescribed for this patient is core stability training using a therapeutic ball. Since the patient is unfamiliar with therapeutic ball exercises, the therapist will have to introduce them. How is that best accomplished? Should the therapist use verbal instructions to introduce the exercises? Should he demonstrate them? Or is a hands-off approach better in this case? What must be considered in order to ensure the skills are presented most effectively?

HANDS-ON VERSUS HANDS-OFF

When determining which instructional strategy to employ, practitioners have two main approaches from which to choose: (1) Hands-on and (2) Hands-off (Williams & Hodges, 2005). Hands-on instruction, also known as direct instruction, is the traditional, prescriptive approach where the practitioner provides a movement template for the learner to imitate. This approach is characterized by the use of verbal instructions and demonstrations to convey information to the learner as well as the provision of feedback to guide skill development. In contrast, the hands-off approach emphasizes movement exploration through the purposeful manipulation of key constraints in order to guide the learner in discovering optimal movement solutions. Both approaches will be discussed in this chapter in detail.

HANDS-ON OR DIRECT INSTRUCTION

In the hands-on or direct instruction approach, when introduced to a new movement, skill, or task, the learner uses the information provided in instructions and demonstrations to develop an idea of the movement's requirements. This idea helps the learner formulate a movement plan that serves as a guide during initial attempts of the skill or task. The development of an accurate movement plan depends on the instructor's ability to analyze a skill, determine the important information that must be conveyed, organize that information, and communicate it effectively (Rink, 2009). Before instruction begins, the practitioner must consider two factors that will directly influence learning. First, it is critical to capture learners' undivided attention before introducing the skill. The practitioner can accomplish this by making sure instruction takes place in a location that is free of background distractions. The set-up or formation should allow all of the learners to see and hear the instructor clearly; if instruction takes place outdoors, the learners should be positioned with their backs to the sun. Finally, the instructor should direct learners to place equipment such as balls, hand weights, surgical tubing, and rackets away from the instruction area to eliminate any temptation to play with them. Lack of attention, even for a brief moment, will result in learners missing important information needed for successful skill development (Abernethy, 1993).

The second factor to consider is the introduction of the skill (or *set induction* as it is termed in physical education lesson planning [Rink, 2009]). Once the learners are settled, the instructor should introduce the skill in a manner that stimulates interest. As discussed in Chapter 7, motivated learners are more receptive to instruction. Enthusiasm is contagious! The practitioner should present the skill dynamically and emphasize its importance.

CEREBRALchallenge   8.1

For a motor skill that you teach or will teach in your professional field, list variables that might compete for your learners' attention while you are giving instructions. Then, develop suggestions that you could implement to reduce these attention problems. For example:

* Patient's cell phone is vibrating.
* Student is pestering a peer.

Verbal Instructions

Have you ever tried to teach a child how to tie his or her shoelaces? You probably didn't think it would be that difficult. You have been tying your own shoelaces for years. In fact, you could probably be considered an expert at tying shoelaces. But the ability to provide effective instructions requires more than a thorough understanding of the skill; you also have to be able to convey that knowledge to the learner. Suddenly, a seemingly simple skill like tying your shoelaces becomes incredibly complex when you try to describe it! Test your verbal instruction effectiveness by performing the tasks in Exploration Activity 8.1.

> **COMMON MYTH**
>
> Experts are always the most effective instructors.

Familiarity with the skill being taught is an obvious asset. A thorough understanding of the skill enables the practitioner to determine what information is important for the learner. That same skill familiarity, however, can negatively influence how the instructor conveys that information. The practitioner may unknowingly provide excessive descriptions, use confusing technical terminology, or leave out important details. The result is a frustrated learner who ultimately loses interest. Effective instructions send clear messages to the learner. This can be accomplished only if individual differences are considered in instructional design.

Role of Task Instructions

Task instructions serve two distinct roles. First, they introduce a learner to a new skill. In this capacity, instructions must communicate a general idea of the goal of the skill or task and make learners aware of major technical features or

exploration ACTIVITY 8.1

Verbal Instruction Effectiveness

TASK 1: TYING SHOELACES

Find a partner whose shoes have laces and who is willing to forget temporarily how to tie them. Using verbal descriptions alone, provide instructions for your partner to assist him or her in tying the shoelaces.

TASK 2: REPLICATING A DRAWING

For this activity you will need a partner, a piece of paper, and a pencil. Your partner should sit facing away from you with the paper and pencil. Your task is to describe the adjacent diagram so that your partner can replicate it.

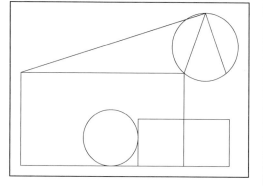

Throughout the exercise, you should not look at your partner's attempt, and your partner should not look at the diagram. Your partner may ask you questions but may not use gestures. Once you have completed your description and your partner has finished his or her interpretation of what you described, compare diagrams.

Perform the exercise again, using the diagram shown (lower right) and switching roles.

This time, the "drawer" is not permitted to ask any questions. Compare diagrams when you are finished.

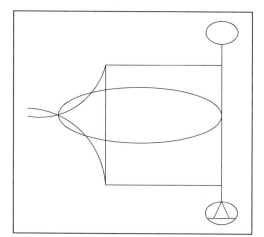

QUESTIONS

1. How accurate was your partner's reproduction of the diagram you described? Do the differences give you any hints about how you communicate?
2. What type of clarification questions did your partner ask? Do these questions give you any information about how you communicate?
3. How did you feel during the second part, when questions were not permitted? Can you generalize any of that information to other learning situations?
4. What changes, if any, could you make to improve your communication effectiveness in the future?

CEREBRAL challenge 8.2

To this point we have focused our attention on characteristics of the learner. Understanding the learner enables us to make more effective decisions regarding instructional design. Based on your understanding of the learner to this point, what do you think are the characteristics of effective instructions? Support your ideas by explaining how each characteristic will accommodate the learner. Continue reading about verbal instructions to see how well you did.

Example: *Characteristic*: Instructions should be brief.
Rationale: Limited capacity of short-term memory storage.

critical elements (Griffey & Housner, 2007). Once this general idea of the movement has been conveyed, the focus of instruction shifts; skill refinement now becomes the goal. Instructions in this capacity serve to develop the learners' skill level so that they can perform the skill under criterion conditions.

Introducing the Skill

As indicated in the previous section, initial instructions should focus learners' attention on the critical elements of the new motor skill (Rink, 2009). Beginners often have difficulty discriminating between relevant and irrelevant stimuli. For example, the juggling activity presented in Chapter 1 provided little direction on how to juggle. If you had not tried juggling before, you probably had many questions about how to perform the task, including "How high do I throw the balls?," "When do I let go?," and "What type of rhythm should I use?" Because the key elements of the juggling task were not pointed out, you probably discovered later, through trial and error, that many of the elements you chose to attend to really had no bearing on learning the task. By drawing the learner's attention to the critical elements of the skill, the instructor does not leave the learner guessing what to focus on, as was the case when you were learning to juggle.

Amount of Information

Keep explanations short and simple. Long, detailed instructions challenge learners' attentional capacity and short-term memory storage; as discussed in Chapter 5, these have a limited capacity. After capturing learners' interest with your introduction, take advantage of it. Learners will be eager to try the skill themselves. Also, supply only the key elements needed to learn the specific skill you're teaching. An explanation about how to grip the bat is appropriate for a first batting lesson, for example, but specific techniques to produce an optimal hip turn for the generation of maximum force are not. Those specifics should be addressed later, when the learner is striving to refine the movement pattern.

CEREBRALchallenge 8.3

Reflect on your juggling experience in Exploration Activity 1.1. What variables did you choose to attend to but later abandon because you discovered they were irrelevant to the task? What variables did you discover were relevant to successful performance? How might your juggling experience have been different had you had an effective instructor?

Precise Language

When giving instructions, be sure to provide learners with enough information to relay the concept while using developmentally appropriate terminology. The phrase "choke up on the bat" might be familiar to some learners, but to a beginner with limited sporting experience it might make little sense. An individual who is learning how to do empty-can exercises for rotator cuff rehabilitation will respond to the direction "raise your arm" with one response, but might respond differently if the direction had been "raise your arm to the point where your upper arm is parallel with the floor."

Lack of specificity can lead to misunderstandings. In one instance, a coach instructed a middle school quarterback to "throw faster" after noticing that the player was short arming his throws, resulting in poor ball speed. Unfortunately, this resulted in the player using an even greater short-arming technique; the athlete's interpretation of the instructions was to release the ball sooner, rather than to use a full range of motion to develop additional velocity. Choose your words carefully. By using specific, developmentally appropriate terminology that matches the learner's skill level, you can significantly increase the likelihood that your instructions will be clearly understood.

RESEARCH NOTES

The superiority of adopting an external attentional focus has also been found using highly skilled athletes. Stoate and Wulf (2011) compared the 25-yard freestyle times of 30 highly trained swimmers under each of three conditions: (1) focusing attention on pushing the water back (external focus), (2) focusing attention on pulling the hands back (internal focus), and (3) no instructions (control condition). They also asked what the swimmers focused on when no instructions were given during the control condition. Swim times for the control and external focus conditions were similar, but those of the internal-focus condition were significantly slower. Furthermore, the control-condition swimmers who focused internally had slower swim times than those who focused on the outcome. The authors concluded that the adoption of a body- or limb-related internal focus hinders performance.

Internal versus External Focus

Interviews of track and field athletes indicated that 84.6 percent of coaches gave instructions related to specific body and limb movements (Porter, Wu, & Partridge, 2010). In a similar study, Durham, Van Vliet, Badger, and Sackley (2009) reported that 95.5 percent of feedback statements that physical therapists gave to stroke patients during treatments were related to body movements (internal focus). Affirmation for this tendency was also provided by Halperin, Chapman, Martin, Abbiss, and Wulf (2016), who analyzed the feedback statements made by boxing coaches during competition. Research suggests, however, that this common practice of directing attentional focus internally, that is on the movements of the body, may not be the most effective approach. Instead, benefits have been shown for both movement effectiveness and efficiency with the adoption of an external focus of attention or attending to the effects of one's actions (see Wulf, 2013 for a comprehensive review). The theory behind this phenomenon is the *constrained action hypothesis* (Wulf, McNevin, & Shea, 2001). According to this theory, when learners adopt an internal focus—as is the case when focusing on the arm movement in Cornhole, for example—they are consciously attempting to control the action. This disrupts the natural flow of the movement. Attending instead to the desired path of the bean bag (adopting an external focus) is thought to promote the use of more automatic control processes, enhancing learning and performance.

What does this mean for the practitioner? WORDS MATTER! Simply changing instruction from turn your shoulders downhill (internal focus) to turn your zipper downhill (external focus) can affect performance. Similarly, direct a tennis player to "finish the stroke with the racket strings facing the side-fence" or "make the ball . . ." instead of focusing attention on the movement of the arm (Regan, 2011). Likewise, instruct a patient to imagine kicking a ball during the terminal swing phase of the gait cycle rather than focusing her attention on heel strike (McNevin, Wulf, & Carlson, 2000). Other examples include instructing a percussionist to focus on the movement of the drumsticks rather

TABLE 8.1	Examples of directing one's focus internally versus externally	
SKILL	**INTERNAL FOCUS**	**EXTERNAL FOCUS**
Landing/plyometrics	Flex your ankle more when you land	Land more softly
Overhead lacrosse throw	Snap your wrist at the target	Throw the stick's basket at the target
Golf putt	Swing your arms using a pendulum motion	Swing the club with a pendulum motion
Block start	Fully extend your leg as you leave the blocks	Push hard against the block behind you
Freestyle swimming	Pull your hand back	Pull the water back
Pelvic tilt	Contract your lower abs to rotate the pelvis posteriorly	Flatten your back into the floor

than those of his wrist, focusing on the target in horseshoes instead of on arm movement, and telling a patient to pay attention to the position of an object to be moved rather than on the hand and finger movements used to move the object (Wulf, 2007). For more examples of directing one's focus internally versus externally see Table 8.1.

CEREBRALchallenge   8.4

Fill in the table below by developing external cues that correspond to the internal cues provided.

SKILL	INTERNAL FOCUS	EXTERNAL FOCUS
Snatch (Weightlifting)	Focus on extending your arms at the top	
Reaching for a cup	Try to stretch your arm further	
Kayaking	Focus on pulling your hand back	
Lengthen one's stride	Push off harder with your foot	
Skiing	Bend your knees more	

RESEARCH NOTES

To study how instructions influence motor skill learning, Wulf, McNevin, and colleagues (2000) compared the relative effectiveness of two effect-related (external) attentional focus conditions. Two groups of 13 subjects hit golf balls, using a 9-iron, toward a target. The "club" group was instructed to focus on the movement of the club, while the "target" group was instructed to direct their attention to the ball's trajectory and the target. More specifically, the club group was asked to concentrate on allowing the club to perform a pendulum motion, and the target group was asked to anticipate the arc of the ball and its outcome relative to the target. Although both groups became more accurate during the 80-shot practice phase, the club group significantly outperformed the target group. This superior performance was also seen in the retention test. The authors concluded that instructions which focus the learner's attention on technique-related effects were more effective for both learning and performance than attentional focus instructions that were related to the outcome of the action.

Awareness of Regulatory Conditions

In open skills, early detection of task-relevant information can reduce response delays and enhance performance. As a result, instructions are commonly given directing the learner's attention toward such information in an attempt to facilitate learning. For example, a person learning to bat might be instructed to look for certain hand positions when a pitcher releases the ball in order to identify or predict the oncoming pitch. Research has shown, however, that this strategy might be unnecessary and might even hinder learning (Hodges & Franks, 2002; Masters & Maxwell, 2004; Masters & Poolton, 2012).

Using a computer-simulated catching task, Green and Flowers (1991) found that participants were able to determine the predictive relationship of ball flight implicitly, without being made aware of it through explicit verbal instructions. Moreover, this implicit learning group showed greater performance improvement than those in the explicit learning group, who were instructed about the underlying rules of the relationship of ball flight. The authors attributed the poorer performance of the explicit learning group to an overload of the available attentional resources—trying to remember the rule and its application along with meeting the demands of performing the movement itself.

Magill (1998) provided additional support for the notion that conscious awareness might not be necessary for acquiring knowledge about the environmental regulatory features of a motor skill. In a tracking study, participants were able to exploit an embedded relationship without being made aware of it through verbal instructions. Sekiya (2009) reported similar findings and evidence continues to mount supporting the implicit motor learning (see Masters & Poolton, 2012). Magill suggests that instructors direct learners' attention at information-rich areas (such as the area where the ball is released) rather than instruct them to look for specific cues (such as how the ball leaves the pitcher's hand). In addition, learners should be exposed to a variety of performance situations that contain the critical environmental regulatory cues to facilitate their acquisition.

Learning Styles

Recall from Chapter 7 that all learners are unique in how they prefer to receive new information, and instructions are more meaningful if delivered through the learner's preferred mode. "See your fingers point to the floor after you release the ball" and "Feel the tension in your wrist after you release the ball" both provide a frame of reference for what the learner should experience if the follow-through in the free throw is performed correctly. The first statement appeals to a visual learner, while the second is more meaningful to a kinesthetic learner. Explanations that accommodate learning preferences enable learners to process information more effectively and achieve greater learning gains (e.g., Ross, Drysdale, & Schulz, 1999).

CEREBRALchallenge 8.6

Performing a task analysis (see Chapter 1) will assist the practitioner in developing verbal cues. First, break down the skill into its phases. Second, determine the key elements of each phase. Finally, develop verbal cues based on the key elements. For example, putting can be broken down into the grip, set-up, and stroke. The table below gives examples of key elements of the stroke and examples of corresponding cues.

KEY ELEMENT	VERBAL CUE
Shoulders, elbows, hands, and putter swing back and forth as a unit	Pendulum swing
Putter accelerates in the front swing	Swing through the ball
Back swing and front swing should move through the same distance	Maintain swing ratio

What cue words could be used to prompt the movements for the ready-to-race position, the forward stroke and the recovery in wheelchair racing, as described in the Special Olympics Athletics Coaches Guide (2007, p. 169)?

WHEELCHAIR RACING

Ready-to-Race Position

Description   *Cues*

1. Athletes must remain seated on the cushion or seat of the wheelchair.
2. Lean upper body forward so shoulders are ahead of hips.
3. Hold knees and feet together in the center of the chair.
4. Grasp wheels or handrails at 11 o'clock position; i.e., just behind highest point of wheel (12 o'clock position) with the thumbs inside and fingers outside.
5. Keep head slightly forward and focus several meters ahead.

Forward Stroke and Recovery

Description   *Cues*

1. From ready-to-race position, push wheels or handrails forward from 11 o'clock position to the 4 o'clock position, and release hands from wheels.
2. Keep moving arms and hands in a circular motion, i.e., past 6 and 9 o'clock positions, and recover to the 11 o'clock position.
3. Keep body and head still during stroke and recovery.

From: Special Olympics Athletic Coaching Guide (2007). Retrieved from http://digitalguides.specialolympics.org/athletics/?#/4/OnePage

Previously Learned Skills

According to the principles of transfer (as discussed in Chapter 7), when a skill is introduced the learner will derive greater meaning from the explanation if it is related to some previous experience. For example, for an individual with extensive volleyball experience, understanding the arm position at contact for a tennis serve will be easier if the instructor compares it to that of the volleyball serve. Such a connection simplifies the new concept for the learner and accelerates the development of an accurate movement plan.

Verbal Cues

Research has shown that the use of verbal cues facilitates learning (e.g., Masser, 1993; Landin, 1994; Fronske, Blakemore, & Abendroth-Smith, 1997; Lorson & Goodway, 2007; McNamee & Steffen, 2007). A verbal cue is a word or concise phrase that focuses the learner's attention or prompts a movement or movement sequence. For example, "Feet shoulder-width apart" focuses the learner's attention on a key element of the skill; "Free ball," used in volleyball, prepares the defense, indicating that the ball will be passed over the net because an attack was not possible. The cue "Step" prompts a movement, and the cue "Right, right, left, together" prompts a movement sequence, the series of foot contacts that occur in the triple jump.

Learners also develop and use cues to guide themselves through an action or movement sequence. This technique is referred to as self-talk or verbal rehearsal, because the learners essentially talk to themselves while performing a task. Thinking "elbow up" to cue a high elbow recovery in the freestyle swimming stroke is a good example. A number of studies have shown that planned instructional self-talk can enhance skill acquisition (e.g., Landin & Hebert, 1999; Perkos, Theodorakis, & Chroni, 2002; Hatzigeorgiadis, Theodorakis, & Zourbanos, 2004).

The following four guidelines can help you develop effective practitioner and self-directed cues:

1. *Cues must be concise.* Self-talk cues are most effective if they contain only one or two words (Ziegler, 1987). For practitioner-directed cues, phrases should, ideally, be no longer than four words (Masser, 1993).
2. *Cues must be accurate.* Unless cues clearly represent skill components, they will be ineffective. To develop critical cues that accurately represent key movement components, you need to be familiar with the skill.
3. *The number of cues should be limited.* Too many cues will not only increase the chances of forgetting but could also interfere with the natural rhythm of the skill. Remember that cues are used to focus the learner's attention. Breaking down a skill into too many components—in an effort to simplify it for the learner—may negatively affect the overall timing of the skill. Learning to drive a car with a manual transmission is a good example.

If the cues "Push in the clutch," "Shift," "Let out the clutch," and "Step on the accelerator" are treated as separate steps, the learner might be surprised when the car stalls or leaps forward!

4. *The same cues should be used repeatedly.* Repetition assists the learner in developing a strong association between the cue and the task. This association will, in turn, have a positive effect on retention.

For other resources to help you in determining activity cues, visit the adjoining website or refer to Fronske (2012).

RESEARCH NOTES

Using 42 college students, McNamee and Steffen (2007) examined the effects of instructional cues on rock-climbing performance. Students were divided into two groups, each of which learned and practiced the same basic techniques of rock climbing over a 14-day period on a 30-foot-tall indoor climbing wall with 12 routes of varying difficulty. The first group (22 students) received 12 instructional cues while the second group (20 students) received no cues during instruction. Participants were pre- and post-tested on their climbing ability using a modified version of the American Sport Climbing Federation's scoring system. Results showed that the group who received the instructional cues significantly outperformed the control group who did not receive any cues. These data support the role of verbal cues in facilitating skill acquisition.

Check for Understanding

Instructions can elicit the desired response only if they are understood. Rather than waiting for learners to attempt to carry out your instructions to assess their understanding of the task at hand, provide them the opportunity to ask questions after the skill presentation. Asking learners to restate the key elements of the skill can help you further assess their comprehension of the instructions. With a quick check for understanding, you will avoid having to reassemble the learners to repeat or clarify instructions.

CEREBRALchallenge   8.6

1. List behaviors or mannerisms which suggest that learners may not have understood the instructions given.
2. Speculate as to whether asking learners if they have any questions or asking them to restate the key elements of a skill will be more effective when checking for understanding. Give reasons for your response.

Demonstrations

Let's revisit the experience of teaching an individual how to tie his or her shoe-laces. It probably didn't take long before you realized that verbally describing shoelace tying in a meaningful way would require a great amount of detail as well as a rather lengthy explanation, neither of which would facilitate learning. In fact, your first instinct when presented with this challenge most likely involved *showing* the learner how to do it. Given the adage *a picture is worth a thousand words*, demonstrations are a preferred instructional method; research supports their use over verbal guidance alone for inducing changes in coordination in early skill acquisition (e.g., Horn, Williams, Hayes, et al., 2007).

Theories of Observational Learning

Demonstrations, also referred to as *modeling* or *observational learning*, rely on the ability of the learner to acquire information through observation of another individual, or model, performing the movement. Neurologically, a newly discovered specialized nerve cell called a *mirror neuron* is thought to account for this ability. Mirror neurons are nerve cells that fire when we perform an action and when we watch someone else perform the same action. In other words, mirror neurons appear to be the neural mechanism through which observational learning occurs (Buccino & Riggio, 2006; Buccino, Vogt, Ritzl, et al., 2004). You can learn more about mirror neurons and their discovery by watching the video at the adjoining website.

WWW

MIRROR NEURONS

http://video.pbs.org/video/161517
3073

While mirror neurons have been shown to be activated during observational learning, how modeling facilitates skill acquisition remains an important question. Two theories offer an explanation.

Social Cognitive Theory of Observational Learning

The social cognitive theory of observational learning (Bandura, 1986) suggests that when a learner observes someone else modeling a movement, the learner processes the information conveyed by the model and transforms it into a cognitive memory representation of the activity. This cognitive representation, formed by symbolic coding and cognitive rehearsal, not only serves to guide the learner's subsequent movement attempts but also provides a frame of reference for error detection and correction.

Dynamic Interpretation of Modeling

The dynamic interpretation of modeling (Scully & Newell, 1985) presents an alternative perspective on how observational learning facilitates skill acquisition. According to this perspective, the key information that the learner acquires from a demonstration is the relative features of the movement pattern or, in other words, the pattern of coordination of the limbs relative to one another. By directly perceiving this information, the learner is able to coordinate body movements to reproduce the observed relative motion. Furthermore, the coordinated motion is scaled according to individual specifications. Consequently, the need to create a cognitive representation of the skill, as Bandura had suggested, is disputed.

Studies also suggest that the type of information obtained from a demonstration might be a function of age. Newell (1985) suggested that watching demonstrations during the early stages of learning was more likely to facilitate the acquisition of modeled coordination patterns rather than the achievement of movement outcomes, such as accurately putting a ball at a target or jumping over an object, because beginners need to focus on acquiring unfamiliar movement dynamics (Ashford, Davids, & Bennett (2007). Studies have shown, however, that this is not necessarily the case for children. For example, Labiadh, Ramanantsoa, and Golomer (2010) found that when children were asked to imitate several jumping tasks modeled by an adult, they replicated the demonstrator's goal but did not necessarily employ the same coordination modes of jumping. According to Ashford et al. (2007), because children's physical and perceptual-motor development differs from adults, they are less likely to have the underlying capacity to perform the necessary movements for imitating the observed form and will instead tend to focus on the movement's goal.

Designing Effective Demonstrations

If a demonstration is to be effective in conveying information that will assist the learner with subsequent movement attempts, the practitioner must make five decisions regarding its design:

1. What should be demonstrated?
2. Who should demonstrate?
3. How should the demonstration be organized?
4. When should the demonstration occur?
5. How often should the demonstration occur?

Content: What Should be Demonstrated?

The demonstration should obviously focus on the skill to be taught, but several additional considerations are important. The specific content of the demonstration is, therefore, the first decision facing the practitioner.

Coordination versus Control: When demonstrations emphasize variables that *control* well-learned patterns of movement, such as speed and force, observational learning has been found to be no more effective than other forms of instruction (Magill, 1998; Williams & Hodges, 2005). Instead, learners seem to benefit most from demonstrations that focus on a new pattern of *coordination*, such as the technique used to cradle a lacrosse ball or to crutch walk (Magill & Schoenfelder-Zohdi, 1996). Studies show that, when one is in the early stages of acquisition, observing a model leads to the adoption of form characteristics similar to the model's relative motion or coordination (see Ashford, Bennett, & Davids, 2006, for a review). As indicated earlier, however, this is not always the case for children who tend to focus on movement outcome. Consequently, Ashford et al. (2007) suggest that, although additional research is needed to understand individual differences in observational learning, children and adult observers "may require a differential emphasis on movement outcomes and movement dynamics" (p. 556).

Entire versus Partial: Since the purpose of the initial demonstration is to provide the learner with a general idea of the movement's requirements, the skill should be performed in its entirety, as it would occur in a competitive or criterion situation. Seeing the whole skill not only gives the learner an idea of the movement and its intended outcome; it also shows the interrelationships among its component parts (Hodges & Franks, 2004). The content of subsequent demonstrations depends on the skill's complexity and the ease with which it can be broken down into its components. After a demonstration of the breaststroke, for example, a swimming instructor might want to focus learners' attention on how to execute the whip kick and perform a demonstration isolating the kick.

Real Time versus Slow Motion: Instructors often use slow motion to direct the learner's attention to a particular aspect of a skill. Its use should be limited, however, because viewing the skill in real time is important for the development of a frame of reference for the skill (Williams, 1986), and it allows the learner to appreciate the natural timing of the movement. Hence, the initial demonstration of the skill should occur in real time; subsequent demonstrations can be done in slow motion to emphasize specific concepts; and once understood, the demonstration can be done again at the original speed.

Characteristics of the Model: Who Should Demonstrate?

The second decision the practitioner must make for a demonstration is determining who should perform it, because the characteristics of the model will affect the demonstration's effectiveness.

Expert versus Learning Model: Learners create a cognitive representation, or "perceptual blueprint" (Lee, Swinnen, & Serrien, 1994), of a skill based on their observation of a demonstration. Since this representation serves to guide the learners' subsequent movement attempts and error detection and correction, it stands to reason that the model should perform the skill correctly. The more a learner sees the skill performed correctly, the stronger the blueprint. The stronger the blueprint, the greater the ability to replicate the skill.

> **COMMON MYTH**
>
> In order for an observer to learn a movement, the demonstration must be performed correctly.

However, increasing evidence challenges the exclusive use of an expert model. Advantages have been shown for the use of a learning model—an unskilled model who is learning the skill. The key elements of this technique are watching another learner practicing the skill, listening to the instructor's feedback, and then watching the individual attempt to correct the errors that were identified (Hebert & Landin, 1994). Support for this strategy has been found for simple timing tasks (McCullagh & Caird, 1990), complex video games (Pollock & Lee, 1992), bimanual coordination patterns (Hirose, Tsutsui, Okuda, & Imanaka, 2004), and sport skills such as tennis (Hebert & Landin, 1994) and weightlifting (McCullagh & Meyer, 1997).

Comparisons of demonstrations by experts versus learning models suggest a significant difference in the degree to which learners are actively engaged in the learning process. Watching an expert model might encourage learners to imitate movements rather than explore movement. On the other hand, after observing a learning model, learners must generate personal movement solutions. This encourages self-discovery through the exploration of a variety of possible task solutions and also increases learners' cognitive effort. Furthermore, learners might better identify with a learning model. Expert and learning models are compared in Table 8.2.

Mixed Observation: Rohbanfard and Proteau (2011) questioned whether observing a combination of skilled and novice models would capitalize on the benefits offered by each compared with viewing an expert or learning model alone. Their findings, as well as those of Andrieux and Proteau (2013, 2014), support the use of this strategy, termed mixed observation. According to Rohbanfard and Proteau (2011) mixed observation better promotes learning because viewing the expert provides the learner with a blueprint of the task while the novice demonstrates errors that may occur. This, according to the findings of Andrieux and Proteau (2014), assists the learner in developing better error detection mechanisms.

TABLE 8.2   Characteristics of expert model versus learning demonstrations

	EXPERT MODEL	LEARNING MODEL
Model Characteristics	• High skill proficiency • High status	• Level of skill proficiency slightly above that of observer • Similar status to observer
Content of Demonstration	• Skill is performed correctly • Verbal cues accompany demonstration • Learner's attention is directed to correctness of performance	• Performance may include both correct and incorrect aspects • Verbal cues plus instructor feedback accompany demonstration • Learner's attention is directed to both correct and incorrect aspects of performance
Outcome	• Passive engagement of observer • Encourages movement imitation	• Active engagement of observer • Encourages movement exploration

From Darden (1997).

Additional research is needed to fully understand the benefits of this modeling strategy and how to best implement it in a practical setting.

Model–Observer Similarity: What influence do variables such as the model's status, age, gender, and similarity to observers have on how well a movement pattern or skill is ultimately learned? In several studies, when participants viewed models whom they perceived as similar to themselves, they performed better than when they viewed models whom they perceived as dissimilar (Gould & Weiss, 1981; McCullagh, 1987). Moreover, when participants view an unfamiliar model, the skill level rather than the status of the model may be more significant to the observer's perception of similarity (Lirgg & Feltz, 1991).

These results may be attributed to increased self-efficacy beliefs (Gould & Weiss, 1981; McAuley, 1985; Schunk & Hanson, 1985). Essentially, when observers view a similar model successfully performing the skill, they have an increased belief that they, too, will be able to reproduce the skill successfully. Consequently, improvements in performance might be the result of increases in observer attention or motivation. Care must be taken when interpreting these results. Note that the increases were found in performance; to date, little direct evidence exists to support the influence of model characteristics on learning.

Alternative Mediums: Practitioners are not limited to the use of live models for demonstrating concepts and movements. The use of video is a viable option and, with advances in technology, practitioners no longer have to rely on commercial products but can create their own custom videos or video podcasts (vodcasts). According to Shumack and Reilly (to whom practitioners should refer for detailed instructions on how to create vodcasts), "the potential opportunities to supplement instruction with vodcasts seem endless" (2011, p. 39). Vodcasts permit learners to view specific aspects of a skill repeatedly, from numerous angles (some of which may be difficult to see during a live demonstration), and

FIGURE **8.1** Images that can be used to convey specific aspects of a movement or technique

(a) Freestyle technique in swimming

(b) Square, closed, and open golf stances

Square   Closed   Open

(c) Closed basketweave ankle taping

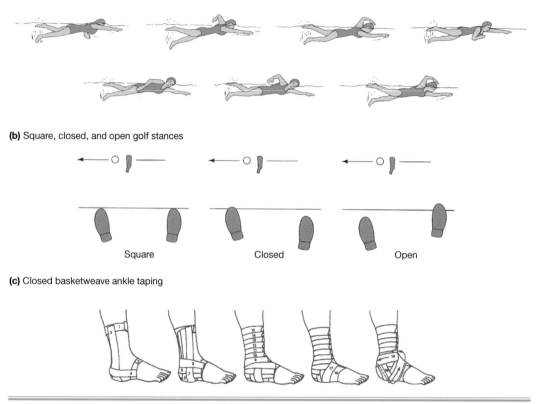

at various speeds; they can also be used to demonstrate plays, rules, strategies, and safety instructions for games and sports. Shumack and Reilly (2011) further point out that vodcasts allow students to review skills outside of the classroom, can be used in conjunction with the mental practice of skills, and can be made available to students who missed class. Additional examples of video capture and editing software programs and phone/tablet applications for practitioners include Camtasia, SportsMotion, Dartfish, SportsCAD, Hudl Technique, Coach My Video, and Coach's Eye.

Another effective way to demonstrate concepts, techniques, and movements is to supplement a live or video model with drawings or still photos. Images such as those in Figure 8.1 allow the instructor to show relationships between performers and implements or opponents, isolate key positions, and highlight hard-to-see aspects of the skill or formation.

Finally, Shea, Wulf, Park, and Gaunt (2001) demonstrated that auditory modeling enhanced learning of the relative-timing features of a task. In other words, highlighting the internal rhythm or tempo of a skill through sound can facilitate skill acquisition. The last five steps in the javelin run-up, for instance, generally have the following rhythm: medium, medium, long, short, short. A live model could reproduce the step pattern for the observer, but clapping the pattern to isolate the rhythm might better increase understanding, especially for auditory learners. Using a metronome in dance is another example. Furthermore, many sport skills have consequent sounds. For example, a different sound results when a softball is caught in the pocket of a glove than when it is caught in the palm. A demonstration of consequent sounds can provide learners with a frame of reference for the correctness of their movements.

Mechanics of Effective Demonstrations: How Should the Demonstration be Organized?

Determining how the demonstration will be organized is the third decision the practitioner must make. The instructor must ensure that all learners have a good viewing angle and that they focus on the key elements of the demonstration. The following guidelines will help you organize effective demonstrations.

Use an Appropriate Formation: All learners must be able to see and hear the demonstration clearly. Some formations lend themselves quite well to this objective, while others are problematic. An example of a problematic formation is a circle with the demonstrator in the center, as in Figure 8.2. Obviously, it will be more difficult for a learner who is positioned to the left of a right-handed demonstrator to attend to the key elements of the skill. Likewise, a learner who

FIGURE **8.2** Circular formation

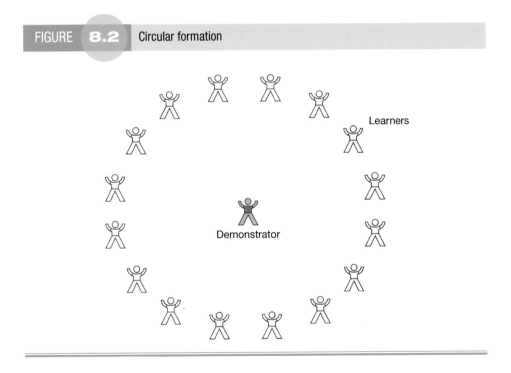

is positioned behind the demonstrator will not be able to hear cues and instructions well. Another problem with a circle is that all learners cannot view the demonstration from the same perspective. Some learners will see it from the front, others from the rear, and others from the side.

Alternative formations designed to resolve these concerns are illustrated in Figure 8.3a. The demonstrator must not be positioned too close to the learners, or the learners at the ends of the formation will have a different viewing angle from those in the center, as illustrated in Figure 8.3b.

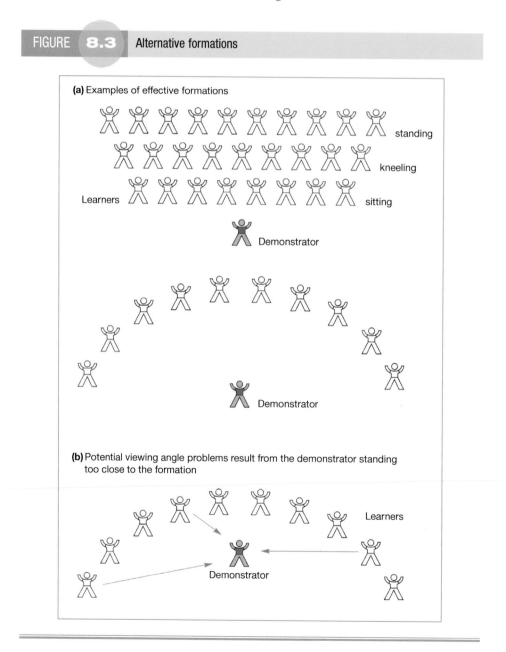

FIGURE **8.3**   Alternative formations

(a) Examples of effective formations

standing

kneeling

Learners   sitting

Demonstrator

Demonstrator

(b) Potential viewing angle problems result from the demonstrator standing too close to the formation

Learners

Demonstrator

Demonstrating a skill from a number of different viewpoints will enhance learners' understanding of the movement requirements. Different viewpoints highlight different aspects of the skill. For example, a patient who is learning to use a walker can see the overall movement pattern from the front, while a side view will provide information about the placement of the walker in relation to the body prior to stepping. Similarly, a side view of the gliding action in the shot put enables learners to focus on the movement of their legs, while a rear view highlights the position of their shoulders. Seeing the demonstration from multiple viewing angles presents a more complete picture of the skill.

Sometimes viewing a skill from the front is problematic. The grapevine in an aerobics class is a good example. If a model demonstrates this skill while facing the group, the learners must reverse what they have just observed in order to perform the steps using the same limbs (right or left), which can be quite confusing. In this situation, viewing the model from behind will aid the learners

FIGURE **8.4**

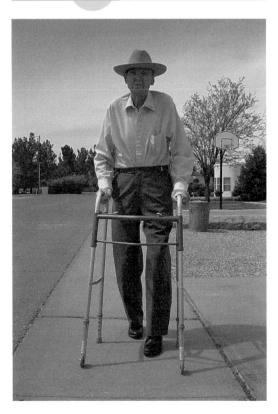

A front view provides information about the timing of the movement

FIGURE **8.5**

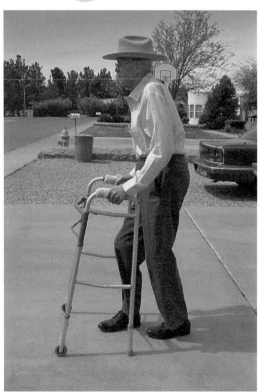

A side view offers a more specific demonstration of the placement of the walker

in imitating the movement. Alternatively, the instructor could present a mirror image by facing the group but performing the skill in the same direction that the group is moving.

Explain How the Demonstration will Proceed and What to Watch For: It has been stressed throughout this chapter that learners must direct their attention to the relevant features of the movement, or instructions are likely to be worthless. To this end, avoid using the phrases "like this" or "like that" in conjunction with the demonstration. These phrases are not specific enough to direct the learners' attention. Instead, tell learners how the demonstration will proceed and what, specifically, to watch for. For example, the initial demonstration of a new skill should encompass the whole skill, as it would be performed in competitive or criterion situations. Since the intent here is to give learners a general idea of the movement's requirements, appropriate instructions would be simply to watch the skill in its entirety. In subsequent demonstrations of either the whole skill or part of the skill, learners should be precued to direct their attention to specific aspects of the movement, such as watching how the toes are pointed during the flutter kick (Weiss & Klint, 1987; McCullagh, Steihl, & Weiss, 1990; Zetou, Tzetzis, Vernadakis, & Kioumourtzoglou, 2002; Janelle, Champenoy, Coombes, & Mousseau, 2003). However, according to Ashford et al. (2007),

> care should be taken when directing a child's attention to relevant cues or particular aspects of the observed motor behavior. If the child does not possess the necessary intrinsic dynamics, directing their attention to replicating movement dynamics could prove detrimental to their motivation and confidence because they will have difficulty satisfying this particular sub-goal (p. 556).

In other words, best practices must be developmentally appropriate.

Avoid Showing the Outcome of the Action: Although the initial demonstration of a new skill should encompass the whole skill, as it would be performed in competitive or criterion situations, subsequent presentations should be designed to avoid showing the outcome of the action. In other words, design the demonstration so that the outcome is eliminated. As humans, we are curious creatures. We want to know if the ball went in, how far the javelin flew, and whether or not the catch was made. Unfortunately, this curiosity often distracts our focus from the key aspects of the movement that produced the outcome (the process). Removing the outcome—throwing a modified javelin into a net, for example—makes learners less likely to track the implement and more likely to focus on the key elements of the movement.

Demonstrate for Both Right- and Left-Limb Dominance: When demonstrating to a group, be aware of the composition of that group with respect to limb dominance. If all learners are right handed, demonstrating the tennis serve with

RESEARCH NOTES

Janelle et al. (2003) examined the effectiveness of different cueing conditions during observational learning on the outcome and form of the inside-of-the-foot soccer pass toward a target. Sixty participants were randomly assigned to one of six groups: discovery learning, verbal instruction, video model with visual cues, video model with verbal cues, video model with visual and verbal cues, and video model only. Each participant performed eight blocks of 10 trials. Blocks 1 and 2 constituted the practice phase, where no manipulation was provided. Blocks 3 through 6 were considered the acquisition phase, as all groups received their corresponding instructional modality (manipulation administered). Finally, 24 hours following the acquisition phase, participants completed blocks 7 and 8, the retention phase, where no manipulation was given. Results indicated that participants who were exposed to video modeling with visual and verbal cueing performed with less error and a more refined movement pattern compared with those who used alternative modeling modalities or learning strategies. These results lend additional support to the notion that the provision of cues during observational learning facilitates skill acquisition.

the left hand may not be necessary. However, if both limb preferences are represented in the group, demonstrate the skill both ways. Telling left-handed learners simply to switch everything that was said to the other side increases the complexity of the task.

Distribution and Frequency: When and How Often Should Demonstrations Occur?

The use of a demonstration to complement initial instructions when introducing a new skill seems intuitive. But practitioners must also decide whether to intersperse additional demonstrations throughout the practice session, and if so, how often? Research exploring this question suggests that, for learning movement form, a schedule that combines viewing a demonstration several times before practicing with inter-practice observations early in the learning process (demonstrations interspersed throughout the practice period) is superior to either pre-practice viewing only or an interspersed-only schedule (Weeks & Anderson, 2000).

To determine the frequency of demonstrations, consider the skill level of the learner and complexity of the task. In general, more experienced learners need fewer demonstrations than inexperienced learners (Wrisberg, 2007). Additional demonstrations will likely be necessary as skills become more complex. To individualize instruction, consider giving learners the opportunity to control their viewing frequency. Research indicates that learners who were able to self-select their model viewing frequency (i.e., see a demonstration when they chose) acquired movement form equally well as those who viewed a model before each practice attempt (Wrisberg & Pein, 2002; Wulf, Raupach, & Pfeiffer, 2005). When learners were given the opportunity to control their model-viewing frequency, they primarily elected to view the model during the early stages of learning, suggesting that demonstrations serve to provide the learner with a "general idea of the movement pattern or perhaps to adjust their movements following an inaccurate performance" (Wrisberg & Pein, 2002, p. 794). Refer to Table 8.3 for a list summarizing demonstration considerations, and complete Exploration Activity 8.2 to assess skill presentation effectiveness.

TABLE 8.3	Demonstration considerations			
WHAT	**WHO**	**HOW**	**WHEN**	**HOW OFTEN**
New pattern of coordination	Expert model vs. learning model	Formation and viewing angle	Introduction of skill	Imposed vs. self-regulated schedule
Whole vs. part	Observer–model similarity	Limb preference	Interspersed throughout practice	
Real time vs. slow motion	Video, still pictures, audio	Direction of movement		
		Avoidance of product options		

exploration ACTIVITY   8.2

Evaluating Skill Presentation Effectiveness

ACTIVITY 1

Using the information presented in this chapter, design an evaluation checklist for determining skill presentation effectiveness.

Examples:

1. Did the practitioner use a clear signal to call the learners together?
2. Did the practitioner demonstrate the skill for both right- and left-limb dominant learners?

ACTIVITY 2

Observe a teacher, coach, or therapist presenting a new skill. Using the checklist you designed in Part A, evaluate the effectiveness of the skill presentation.

ACTIVITY 3

Now record yourself presenting a new skill. Review the video, using the checklist from Part A to evaluate your performance. How might you improve your demonstration effectiveness?

Manual Guidance

In manual guidance—another strategy often used in physical education, sport, and rehabilitation settings—a practitioner or device correctly moves the learner through the goal movement (Sidaway, Ahn, Boldeau, et al., 2008). Examples of manual guidance include a therapist moving a patient's limb through the desired range of motion; the use of a safety belt for diving, gymnastics, and acrobatic stunts; the golf swing ring; and training wheels on a bicycle. The use of manual guidance techniques is based on the assumption that they provide the learner with a clearer understanding of the goal movement, help reduce errors, and allow potentially dangerous movements to be practiced in a safe manner (Wulf, Shea, & Whitacre, 1998).

However, leading a learner passively through a movement presents several potential problems (Wrisberg, 2007). First, one of the premises behind manual guidance is that learners will experience what the correct movement feels like, but assisted movements actually produce different response-produced feedback (feeling) than unassisted ones. Second, learners are likely to be less attentive when they are passively led through a movement. Third, manual guidance eliminates learners' opportunity to detect and correct their own movements.

Given these concerns, practitioners should use this strategy sparingly. In fact, research indicates that while a high frequency of manual guidance facilitates practice performance, it has a detrimental effect on retention (Sidaway et al., 2008; Winstein, Pohl, & Lewthwaite, 1994; Wulf et al., 1998). In other words, marked performance improvements will likely be seen in practice or during treatment, but long-term maintenance of those effects is unlikely (Sidaway et al., 2008). Consequently, although occasions exist where manual guidance may initially be helpful (e.g., injury prevention, developing a basic understanding of a skill), unassisted practice should be introduced as soon as possible.

HANDS-OFF INSTRUCTION

In this method of instruction, learning is promoted through guided discovery and self-exploration (Williams & Hodges, 2005). Rather than dictating how to achieve the action goal, the practitioner shapes movement patterns through the purposeful manipulation of key constraints (Davids, Button, & Bennett, 2008). Learning results from the exploration of action possibilities and adaptation to the constraints imposed on the learner during practice. Although the role of the practitioner shifts to facilitator rather than dictator, it would be a mistake to assume that the practitioner simply assigns tasks for the learner to complete. The practitioner must be actively engaged in the learning process, providing varying degrees of guidance and adjusting constraints based on observed outcomes to increase adaptation opportunities for students (Storey & Butler, 2013). Further, the development of effective instructional activities is challenging as a high level of awareness of the interaction of the learner, the task, and the environment in which the task is performed is needed in order to be attuned to the action possibilities that a task may afford a learner which could subsequently prompt the desired performance change.

Manipulating Task and/or Practice Constraints

Numerous task and practice variables can be manipulated to shape movement patterns and behavior including imposing rule modifications, modifying equipment, altering playing area dimensions, manipulating situational factors during performance, and changing task criteria (Williams, 2003). For example, a soccer coach might alter the playing-area dimensions by reducing the size of the practice space for a dribbling drill "in an attempt to improve the ball control of learners" (Araújo, Davids, Bennett, et al., 2004, p. 413); in volleyball, a rule could be imposed limiting the area to which a ball can be served, passed, or hit, thus forcing players to adapt their movements to accomplish the set goal. Manipulating the relative positioning of players or the number of attackers versus defenders (manipulating situational factors) will force learners to make tactical choices and help them understand concepts like finding open space or reading a pattern of play (Passos, Araújo, Davids, & Shuttleworth, 2010). Scaling equipment, such as adjusting paddle length in canoeing or ski length in skiing can change a learner's movements (Brymer & Renshaw, 2010), and a patient's adoption of different types of grasp can be promoted by manipulating object characteristics such as weight, diameter, size and rigidity. Adaptive changes in skill execution can also be induced by altering various task criteria. During the execution of a side-lying hip abduction exercise, have the client or patient raise a bean bag placed on the ankle to teach correct body position. To encourage students to release the ball closer to the ground when learning the underhand roll, Colombo-Dougovito and Block (2016) suggest focusing students on rolling it under a chair that is placed between them and the target. Finally, as illustrated in the video at www.youtube.com/watch?v=R02GLDfl0Ws, good ski instructors have been using the natural features of the terrain to shape learners' skiing/snowboarding technique for years. This concept was recently formalized into the Terrain Based Learning Program™, which has been adopted by learn-to-ski/ride programs at numerous ski resorts. This program purposefully shapes the snow to create features that control learners' speed and body position, reduce

---

FIGURE 8.6 Examples of task and practice variables that can be manipulated to shape movement patterns

RULES	EQUIPMENT	TASK CRITERIA	SITUATIONAL FACTORS	PLAYING AREA
• Size of playing area	• Size	• Distance	• Relative positioning of players	• Size
• Movement skills used to play the game	• Weight	• Speed	• Number of attackers vs. defenders	• Shape
• Number of players	• Length	• Accuracy	• Terrain, layout and/or conditions of a course	• Position of goals/ shooting areas
• Scoring system	• Grip diameter	• Force		
• Number of contacts	• Texture	• Size of goal or target	• Ball distribution	

CEREBRALchallenge 8.7

1. Predict how the following modifications to an Ultimate Frisbee game would influence the play of (a) the offense and (b) the defense:

    a. Reducing the size of the playing field
    b. Increasing the size of the playing field
    c. Reducing the size of the scoring area
    d. Increasing the size of the scoring area

2. A physical education student teacher decided to use a warm-up activity called builders and bulldozers. For this activity, numerous bowling pins were set up randomly throughout a designated playing area. Next, students were divided into two groups. One group, the bulldozers, ran around tipping over as many buildings (bowling pins) as they could. The builders were to rebuild the fallen buildings by standing the fallen pins back up. As the activity progressed, the student teacher realized that the builders could not keep up with the bulldozers and most of the pins were fallen at any given moment. The builders are quickly losing motivation and stop trying as their task seems impossible to accomplish. Provide suggestions as to how the student teacher might adjust the constraints of the task to improve the activity.

3. You are doing an internship in strength and conditioning and working with athletes on acceleration development from a 3-point stance. You read about a stick drill/acceleration ladder online that might be good to use with your athletes. According to the website, five–seven sticks (tape, cone, etc.) are placed in a ladder formation with the initial mark at a distance of 3 feet from the start line and the remaining "rungs" positioned with a progressive lengthening of 6 inches (see figure below). The goal of the athlete is for foot placement to correspond with each rung as he or she is accelerating.

Start line

| 3ft | 3.5ft | 4ft | 4.5ft | 5ft |

Will you adopt this drill? Fully explain why or why not.

4. You have a patient who presents with shoulder and neck discomfort. During the course of your evaluation, you find out that she recently switched to a standing desk at work and is using a laptop computer. How might this be contributing to her pain? What constraints might be manipulated to alleviate some of her discomfort?

fear and anxiety, and effect change in performance. To learn more watch the video at www.youtube.com/watch?v=wvMkEd_r3Uw.

Refer to Figure 8.6 for additional examples of task and practice variables that can be manipulated to shape movement patterns.

Challenges

Another form of hands-off instruction is the use of challenges. For example, in skiing, learners could be challenged to see how much or how little snow spray they can make. Similarly, they might be challenged to spray the snow uphill, downhill, or towards the side of the trail to work on the timing of edge engagement.

Instruction could also be individualized by giving learners the choice as to the challenge's level of difficulty. Research has shown that self-control of task difficulty results in greater learning gains than when the degree of difficulty of the task is imposed (Andrieux, Danna, & Thon, 2012; Andrieux, Boutin, & Thon, 2016). Further, Andrieux et al. (2012) showed that the decision made regarding task difficulty was dependent on one's own performance on the previous trial. In other words, self-control participants "continuously adjusted the level of task difficulty throughout training, with reference to their own motor capability, to achieve the appropriate condition for optimizing skill acquisition and learning" (Andrieux et al., 2016, p. 57).

An example of this strategy is depicted in Figure 8.7. In this challenge, learners practicing a "J" turn choose the cone around which they will make their turn. Initially they may choose cone C, the easiest of the three, but as they become more proficient, they can adjust the level of difficulty and eventually opt to make the tighter turn around cone A.

Guided Discovery

In guided discovery, the practitioner asks a sequence of questions, each of which elicits a single correct response that the learner needs to discover (Mosston & Ashworth, 1994). This step-by-step process leads to the eventual discovery of the intended concept or principle. To implement this technique, the practitioner must design a series of questions or clues regarding the new movement or concept. The first question is delivered, the learner is given the opportunity to answer, and the practitioner either reinforces the response or redirects the learner. Once the correct answer has been discovered, the practitioner asks the next question in the sequence. For example, while introducing the skill of dribbling a soccer ball, the learner might be asked, "What is the goal of the defenders?" Once the learner identifies the defender's goal as stealing the ball, subsequent questions lead to the learner's discovery of kicking the ball softly and with the side of the foot as opposed to the toe. Gradually, the learner will learn the technique and will also develop an understanding of why that technique is used. Another example is depicted in Figure 8.8 In this relay race, each player

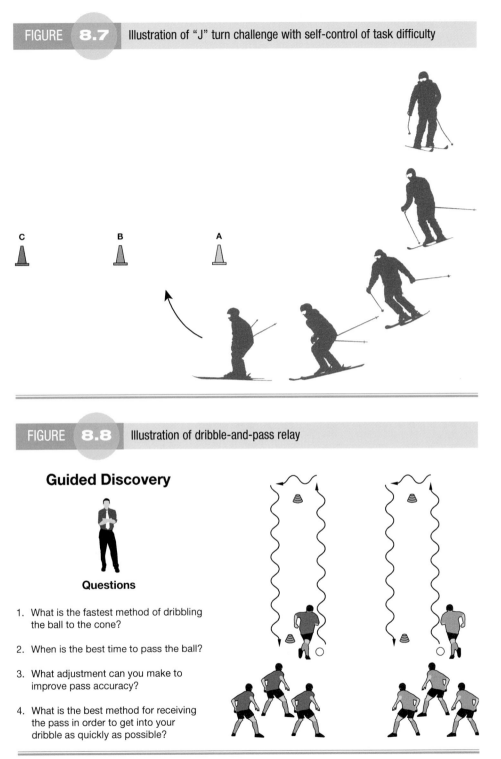

FIGURE **8.7**   Illustration of "J" turn challenge with self-control of task difficulty

C   B   A

FIGURE **8.8**   Illustration of dribble-and-pass relay

Guided Discovery

Questions

1. What is the fastest method of dribbling the ball to the cone?

2. When is the best time to pass the ball?

3. What adjustment can you make to improve pass accuracy?

4. What is the best method for receiving the pass in order to get into your dribble as quickly as possible?

Dribble-and-pass relay drill copyright SoccerHelp.com, used with permission; figure modified from www.top-soccer-drills.com/relay-race—1.html. All reasonable attempts to secure permission for use were made.

must dribble the ball as quickly as possible to the first cone, make the turn, then pass to the next player in line. Through a series of questions, learners advance their understanding of multiple skills including speed dribbling, kicking and passing the ball while running, and the concept that receivers should move to the ball (Soccer Drills That Are Practice Games, 2016). To learn more about guided discovery and how it can be used to teach motor learning concepts, see Rukavina and Jeansonne (2009).

CEREBRALchallenge   8.8

If you were the therapist in the story that opened this chapter, what technique or combination of techniques would you use to teach the patient therapeutic ball exercises? Explain your answer.

PUTTING IT INTO PRACTICE

Learning Situation: Learning the Indirect Pass in Hockey

Instead of trying to explain what to look for in different scenarios to make effective indirect passes, Jennifer elects to use the hands-off instruction approach. She wants to create game-play challenges using 3-on-3 half-ice scrimmages to hone their indirect passing skills.

Test Your Knowledge

What game modifications or conditions might Jennifer impose to help her players learn when to use and where to place their indirect passes? Also, how might guided discovery be used to help players improve their anticipation skills? Compare your answer with the sample response provided at www.routledge.com/cw/coker.

A LOOK AHEAD

When presenting a new skill, the instructor's initial goal is to convey to learners either through direct instruction (hands-on) or guided discovery (hands-off) the information they need in order to develop a basic understanding of the movement's requirements and formulate an initial movement plan. Once this is accomplished, the focus shifts to one of skill refinement. Through carefully designed practice opportunities, maximal gains in skill proficiency can be achieved. Issues related to practice design are the focus of the next chapter.

FOCUS POINTS

After reading this chapter, you should know:

* Hands-on instruction is a direct instruction approach characterized by the use of verbal instructions and demonstrations to convey information to the learner as well as the provision of feedback to guide skill development.
* Hands-off instruction involves the purposeful manipulation of key constraints in order to guide the learner in discovering optimal movement solutions.
* When giving instructions:

    — Keep explanations short and simple
    — Use developmentally appropriate terminology
    — Direct learners' attention to critical elements of the skill during initial instructions
    — Provide learners with a frame of reference for correctness
    — Consider learners' learning styles and previous experiences.

* Words matter. Research suggests that instructions should focus learners on the effects of their actions instead of on specific body movements (internal focus).
* Verbal cues are used to focus learners' attention or prompt a movement or movement sequence and should be concise, accurate, limited in number, and used repeatedly throughout the learning process.
* When planning a demonstration, the practitioner should consider its content, the characteristics of the model performing the demonstration, how the demonstration will be organized, and its distribution and frequency.
* When providing an initial demonstration, the practitioner or model should perform the whole skill in real time to give learners an idea of the movement.
* The use of a learning model encourages movement exploration and active involvement in the learning process.
* For an effective demonstration, all learners should have a good viewing angle and should be focused on the key elements being demonstrated.
* Manual guidance may be used to convey skill requirements and for safety purposes but should be withdrawn as soon as possible.
* Movement patterns and behavior can be shaped by the purposeful manipulation of task and/or practice constraints including imposing rule modifications, modifying equipment, altering playing area dimensions, manipulating situational factors during performance, and changing task criteria.
* Challenges can be designed to individualize instruction and give learners the opportunity to choose task difficulty that has been shown to facilitate skill acquisition.
* Guided discovery gives learners the opportunity to explore possible movement solutions; the practitioner asks a sequence of questions, each of which elicits a single correct response to be discovered by the learner.

lab

To complete the labs for this chapter, visit www.routledge.com/cw/coker and select **Lab 8a, Modeling and Verbal Instructions, Lab 8b, Manual Guidance** and **Lab 8c, Hands Off Practitioner**.

REVIEW QUESTIONS

1. Compare and contrast hands-on and hands-off instruction.

2. Why is it critical to capture learners' attention before skill instruction begins?

3. Explain why practitioners who are highly familiar with their subject matter are not always the most effective instructors.

4. What is the function of a verbal cue?

5. Compare and contrast instructor-directed verbal cues and self-talk.

6. What guidelines should the practitioner follow to optimize the use of cues?

7. What is a learning model? What are some advantages of using a learning model?

8. For a motor skill of your choice, explain what decisions you would make regarding the mechanics of its demonstration. Justify your answers.

9. List the potential problems associated with using a high frequency of manual guidance.

10. List the five categories of task and practice variables that can be manipulated to shape movement patterns.

11. Explain the following statement: It would be a mistake to assume that when implementing hands-off instruction that the practitioner simply assigns tasks for the learner to complete.

REFERENCES

Abernethy, B. (1993). Attention. In R. N. Singer, M. Murphy, & L. K. Tennent (Eds.), *Handbook of research on sport psychology* (pp. 127–170). New York: Macmillan.

Andrieux, M., Boutin, A., & Thon, B. (2016). Self-control of task difficulty during early practice promotes motor skill learning. *Journal of Motor Behavior*, 48(1), 57–65.

Andrieux, M., Danna, J., & Thon, B. (2012). Self-control of task difficulty during training enhances motor learning of a complex coincidence-antici-pation task. *Research Quarterly for Exercise and Sport*, 83, 27–35.

Andrieux, M. & Proteau, L. (2013). Observation learning of a motor task: Who and when? *Experimental Brain Research*, 229,125–137. doi:10.1007/s00221–013–3598-x

Andrieux, M. & Proteau, L. (2014). Mixed observation favors motor learning through better estimation of the model's performance. *Experimental Brain Research*, 232, 3121–3132. doi:10.1007/s00221-014-4000-3

Araújo, D., Davids, K., Bennett, S. J., Button, C., & Chapman, G. (2004). Emergence of sport skills under constraints. In A. M. Williams & N. J. Hodges (Eds.), *Skill acquisition in sport: Research, theory and practice* (pp. 409–433). London: Routledge, Taylor and Francis.

Ashford, D., Bennett, S. J., & Davids, K. (2006). Observational modeling effects for movement dynamics and movement outcome measures across differing task constraints: A meta-analysis. *Journal of Motor Behavior, 38*(3), 185–205.

Ashford, D., Davids, K., & Bennett, S. J. (2007). Developmental effects influencing observational modeling: A meta-analysis. *Journal of Sports Sciences, 25*(5), 547–558.

Bandura, A. (1986). *Social foundations of thought and action: A social cognitive theory.* Englewood Cliffs, NJ: Prentice Hall.

Brymer, E. & Renshaw, I. (2010). An introduction to the constraints-led approach to learning in outdoor education. *Australian Journal of Outdoor Education, 14,* 33–41.

Buccino, G. & Riggio, L. (2006). The role of the mirror neuron system in motor learning. *Kinesiology, 38* (1), 5–15.

Buccino, G., Vogt, S., Ritzl, A., Fink, G. R., Zilles, K., Freund, H. J., & Rizzolatti, G. (2004). Neural circuits underlying imitation learning of hand actions: An event-related fMRI study. *Neuron, 42,* 323–334.

Colombo-Dougovito, A.M. & Block, M. (2016). Make task constraints work for you: Teaching object-control skills to students with Autism Spectrum Disorder. *Journal of Physical Education, Recreation & Dance,* 87:1, 32–37. doi:10.1080/07303084. 2015.1109492

Darden, G. F. (1997). Demonstrating motor skills: Rethinking that expert demonstration. *Journal of Physical Education, Recreation and Dance, 68*(6), 31–35.

Davids, K., Button, C., & Bennett, S. (2008). *Dynamics of skill acquisition: A constraints-led approach.* Champaign, IL: Human Kinetics.

Domingo, A. & Ferris, D. (2009). Effects of physical guidance on short-term learning of walking on a narrow beam. *Gait & Posture, 30*(4), 464–468.

Durham, K., Van Vliet, P. M., Badger, F., & Sackley, C. (2009). Use of information feedback and attentional focus feedback in treating persons with a hemiplegic arm. *Physiotherapy Research International, 14,* 77–90.

Fronske, H. (2012). *Teaching cues for sport skills for secondary school students.* Menlo Park, CA: Benjamin Cummings.

Fronske, H., Blakemore, C., & Abendroth-Smith, J. (1997). The effect of critical cues on overhand throwing efficiency of elementary school children. *The Physical Educator, 54*(2), 88–95.

Gould, D. & Weiss, M. R. (1981). The effects of model similarity and model talk on self-efficacy and muscular endurance. *Journal of Sport and Exercise Psychology, 3,* 17–29.

Green, T. D. & Flowers, J. H. (1991). Implicit vs. explicit learning processes in a probabilistic, continuous fine motor catching task. *Journal of Motor Behavior, 23,* 239–300.

Griffey, D. & Housner, L. D. (2007). *Designing effective instructional tasks for physical education and sports.* Champaign, IL: Human Kinetics.

Halperin, I., Chapman, D. W., Martin, D. T., Abbiss, C., & Wulf, G. (2016). Coaching cues in amateur boxing: An analysis of ringside feedback provided between rounds of competition. *Psychology of Sport & Exercise,* 2544–2550.

Hatzigeorgiadis, A., Theodorakis, Y., & Zourbanos, N. (2004). Self-talk in the swimming pool: The effects of ST on thought content and performance on water-polo tasks. *Journal of Applied Sport Psychology, 16,* 138–150.

Hebert, E. P. & Landin, D. (1994). Effects of a learning model and augmented feedback on tennis skill acquisition. *Research Quarterly for Exercise and Sport, 65*(3), 250–257.

Hirose, T., Tsutsui, S., Okuda, S., & Imanaka, K. (2004). Effectiveness of the use of a learning model and concentrated schedule in observational learning of a new bimanual coordination pattern. *International Journal of Sport and Health Science, 2,* 97–104.

Hodges, N. & Franks, I. M. (2002). Modelling coaching practice: The role of instruction and demonstration. *Journal of Sports Sciences, 20,* 793–811.

Hodges, N. & Franks, I. M. (2004). Instructions and demonstrations: Creating and constraining movement options. In A. M. Williams & N. J. Hodges (Eds.), *Skill acquisition in sport: Research, theory and practice* (pp. 145–174). London: Routledge.

Horn, R. R., Williams, A., Hayes, S. J., Hodges, N. J., & Scott, M. A. (2007). Demonstration as a rate enhancer to changes in coordination during early skill acquisition. *Journal of Sports Sciences, 25*(5), 599–614.

Janelle, C. M., Champenoy, J. D., Coombes, S. A., & Mousseau, M. B. (2003). Mechanisms of attentional cueing during observational learning to facilitate motor skill acquisition. *Journal of Sports Sciences, 21,* 825–838.

Labiadh, L., Ramanantsoa, M., & Golomer, E. (2010). Preschool-aged children's jumps: Imitation performances. *Journal of Electromyography & Kinesiology, 20*(2), 322–329.

Landin, D. (1994). The role of verbal cues in skill learning. *Quest, 46,* 299–313.

Landin, D. & Hebert, E. P. (1999). The influence of self-talk on the performance of skilled female tennis players. *Journal of Applied Sport Psychology, 11,* 263–282.

Lee, T. D., Swinnen, S. P., & Serrien, D. J. (1994). Cognitive effort in learning. *Quest, 46*(32), 328–344.

Lirgg, C. D. & Feltz, D. L. (1991). Teacher vs. peer models revisited: Effects on motor performance and self-efficacy. *Research Quarterly for Exercise and Sport, 62*(2), 217–224.

Lorson, K. M. & Goodway, J. D. (2007). Influence of critical cues and task constraints on overarm throwing performance in elementary age children. *Perceptual & Motor Skills, 105*(3), 753–767.

Magill, R. A. (1998). Knowledge is more than we can talk about: Implicit learning in motor skill acquisition. *Research Quarterly for Exercise and Sport, 69*(2), 104–110.

Magill, R. A. & Schoenfelder-Zohdi, B. (1996). A visual model and knowledge of performance as sources of information for learning a rhythmic gymnastics skill. *International Journal of Sport Psychology, 27,* 7–22.

Masser, L. S. (1993). Critical cues help first grade students' achievement in handstands and forward rolls. *Journal of Teaching Physical Education, 11,* 301–312.

Masters, R. S. W. & Maxwell, J. P. (2004). Implicit motor learning, reinvestment and movement disruption: What you don't know won't hurt you? In A. M. Williams & N. J. Hodges (Eds.), *Skill acquisition in sport: Research, theory and practice* (pp. 207–228). London: Routledge.

Masters, R. S. W. & Poolton, J. M. (2012). Advances in implicit motor learning. In N. J. Hodges & A. M. Williams (Eds.), *Skill acquisition in sport: Research, theory and practice* (pp. 59–75). London: Routledge.

McAuley, E. (1985). Modeling and self-efficacy: A test of Bandura's model. *Journal of Sport Psychology, 6,* 283–295.

McCullagh, P. (1987). Model similarity effects on motor performance. *Journal of Sport Psychology, 9,* 249–260.

McCullagh, P. & Caird, J. K. (1990). Correct and learning models and the use of model knowledge of results in the acquisition and retention of a motor skill. *Journal of Human Movement Studies, 18,* 107–116.

McCullagh, P. & Meyer, K. N. (1997). Learning versus correct models: Influence of model type on the learning of a free-weight squat lift. *Research Quarterly for Exercise and Sport, 68,* 56–61.

McCullagh, P., Steihl, J., & Weiss, M. R. (1990). Developmental modeling effects on the quantitative and qualitative aspects of motor performance acquisition. *Research Quarterly for Exercise and Sport, 61,* 344–350.

McNamee, J. & Steffen, J. (2007). The effect of performance cues on beginning indoor rock climbing performance. *The Physical Educator, 64,* 2–10.

McNevin, N. H., Wulf, G., & Carlson, C. (2000). Effects of attentional focus, self-control and dyad training on motor learning: Implications for physical rehabilitation. *Physical Therapy, 80*(4), 373–385.

Mosston, M. & Ashworth, S. (1994). *Teaching physical education* (4th Ed.). New York: Macmillan.

Newell, K. M. (1985). Co-ordination, control and skill. In D. Goodman, R. B. Wilberg, & I. M. Franks (Eds.), *Differing perspectives in motor learning, memory and control* (pp. 295–317). Amsterdam: North-Holland.

Owens, D. & Bunker, L. K. (1995). *Golf: Steps to success.* Champaign, IL: Human Kinetics.

Passos, P., Araújo, D., Davids, K. W., & Shuttleworth, R. (2010). Manipulating task constraints to improve tactical knowledge and collective decision-making in rugby union. In Renshaw, I., Davids, K. W., & Savelsbergh, G. J. P. (Eds.), *Motor learning in practice: A constraints-led approach* (pp. 120–130). London: Routledge (Taylor & Francis).

Perkos, S., Theodorakis, Y., & Chroni, S. (2002). Enhancing performance and skill acquisition in novice basketball players with instructional self-talk. *The Sport Psychologist, 16,* 368–383.

Pollock, B. J. & Lee, T. D. (1992). Effects of the model's skill level on observational motor learning. *Research Quarterly for Exercise and Sport, 63,* 25–29.

Porter, J. M., Wu, W. F. W., & Partridge, J. A. (2010). Focus of attention and verbal instructions: Strategies of elite track and field coaches and athletes. *Sport Science Review, 19,* 199–211.

Regan, L. (2011). The usefulness of externally-directed instructions for teaching technique and tactics. *Coaching & Sport Science Review,* 537–538.

Rink, J. E. (2009). *Teaching physical education for learning.* New York: McGraw-Hill.

Rohbanfard, H. & Proteau, L. (2011). Learning through observation: A combination of expert and novice models favors learning. *Experimental Brain Research*, 215, 183–197. doi: 10.1007/s00221-011-2882-x

Ross, J. L., Drysdale, M. T. B., & Schulz, R. A. (1999). Learning style in the classroom: Towards quality instruction in kinesiology. *Avante, 5*(3), 31–42.

Rukavina, P. B. & Jeansonne, J. J. (2009). Integrating motor-learning concepts into physical education: Using guided discovery to address NASPE Standard 2. *Journal of Physical Education, Recreation & Dance, 80*(9), 23–30.

Schunk, D. H. & Hanson, A. R. (1985). Peer models: Influence on children's self-efficacy and achievement. *Journal of Educational Psychology, 77*, 313–322.

Scully, D. M. & Newell, K. M. (1985). Observational learning and the acquisition of motor skills: Towards a visual perception perspective. *Journal of Human Movement Studies, 11*, 169–186.

Sekiya, H. (2009). Implicit and explicit learning of tracking patterns. *Asian Journal of Exercise & Sports Science, 6*(1), 1–5.

Shea, C. H., Wulf, G., Park, J., & Gaunt, B. (2001). Effects of an auditory model on the learning of relative and absolute timing. *Journal of Motor Behavior, 33*, 127–138.

Shumack, K. A. & Reilly, E. (2011). Video podcasting in physical education. *Journal of Physical Education, Recreation & Dance, 82*(1), 39–43.

Sidaway, B., Ahn, S., Boldeau, P., Griffin, S., Noyes, B., & Pelletier, K. (2008). A comparison of manual guidance and knowledge of results in the learning of a weight-bearing skill. *Journal of Neurologic Physical Therapy, 32*, 32–38.

Soccer Drills That Are Practice Games (2016). Retrieved from http://soccerhelp.com/soccer_drills/Dribble_Around_Cone_Pass.shtml

Special Olympics Athletic Coaching Guide (2007). Retrieved from http://digitalguides.specialolympics.org/athletics/?#/4/OnePage.

Stoate, I. & Wulf, G. (2011). Does the attentional focus adopted by swimmers affect their performance? *International Journal of Sport Science & Coaching, 6*, 99–108.

Storey, B. & Butler, J. (2013). Complexity thinking in PE: game-centered approaches, games as complex adaptive systems, and ecological values. *Physical Education & Sport Pedagogy, 18*(2), 133–149.

Weeks, D. L. & Anderson, L. P. (2000). The interaction of observational learning with overt practice: Effects on motor skill learning. *Acta Psychologica, 104*, 259–271.

Weiss, M. R. & Klint, K. A. (1987). "Show and tell" in the gymnasium: An investigation of developmental differences in modeling and verbal rehearsal of motor skills. *Research Quarterly for Exercise and Sport, 58*, 234–241.

Williams, A. M. (2003). Learning football skills effectively: Challenging tradition. *Insight: The FA Coaches Association Journal, 6*(2), 37–39.

Williams, A. M. & Hodges, N. J. (2005). Practice, instruction and skill acquisition in soccer: Challenging tradition. *Journal of Sport Sciences, 23*(6), 637–650.

Williams, J. G. (1986). Perceiving human movement: Review of research with implications for the use of demonstrations during motor learning. *Physical Education Review, 9*(1), 53–58.

Winstein C., Pohl, P., & Lewthwaite, R. (1994). Effects of physical guidance and knowledge of results on motor learning: Support for the guidance hypothesis. *Research Quarterly for Exercise and Sport, 65*, 316–323.

Wrisberg, C. A. (2007). *Sport skill instruction for coaches*. Champaign, IL: Human Kinetics.

Wrisberg, C. A. & Pein, R. L. (2002). Note on learners' control of the frequency of model presentation during skill acquisition. *Perceptual and Motor Skills, 94*, 792–794.

Wulf, G. (2007). *Attention and skill learning*. Champaign, IL: Human Kinetics.

Wulf, G. (2013). Attentional focus and motor learning: A review of 15 years. *International Review of Sport & Exercise Psychology, 6*(1), 77–104.

Wulf, G., McNevin, N., & Shea, C. H. (2001). The automacity of complex motor skill learning as a function of attentional focus. *The Quarterly Journal of Experimental Psychology, 54A* (4), 1143–1154.

Wulf, G., Raupach, M., & Pfeiffer, F. (2005). Self-controlled observational practice enhances learning. *Research Quarterly for Exercise and Sport, 76*, 107–111.

Wulf, G., Shea, C., & Whitacre, C. (1998). Physical-guidance benefits in learning a complex motor skill. *Journal of Motor Behavior, 30*, 367–380.

Zetou, E., Tzetzis, G., Vernadakis, N., & Kioumourtzoglou, E. (2002). Modeling in learning two volleyball skills. *Perceptual and Motor Skills, 94*, 1131–1142.

Ziegler, S. G. (1987). Effects of stimulus cueing on the acquisition of groundstrokes by beginning tennis players. *Journal of Applied Behavioral Analysis, 20*, 405–411.

Although it will be two more hours before the sun appears over the horizon, the alarm clock is ringing. It is the dead of winter, and Anna has 30 minutes before she has to be on the deck of the pool warming up for morning practice. In 2008, when Anna was 7, she watched the diving competitions during the Summer Olympics in Beijing. Ever since, she has dreamed of being an Olympic diver—but this morning, that dream is a distant one. She hasn't been diving well recently, and she doesn't feel like practicing. She hits the snooze button and falls back asleep. Five minutes later, her father pokes his head in and says encouragingly, "Come on, Anna, practice makes perfect!"

Several common myths regarding skill acquisition and control have been mentioned throughout this book, but perhaps the most widespread misconception is the old adage, "Practice makes perfect." In reality, practice does not guarantee that a learner will become more proficient. Only when practice is designed that carefully considers the influence of the learner, the task, and the environment can optimal gains in skill proficiency be realized. This chapter will focus on several contributors to effective practice design, including skill progressions, sequencing, and psychological strategies.

BREAKING DOWN SKILLS: PROGRESSIONS AND SEQUENCING

When designing effective practices and rehabilitative experiences, practitioners face several decisions regarding the breakdown of skills. When should a skill be broken down into parts, and when should it be practiced as a whole? How do speed and accuracy influence skill acquisition? How are skills that must be performed with equal proficiency on both the dominant and non-dominant side best learned?

Whole versus Part Practice

Learning a novel motor skill can be a daunting task. Recall that in the early stages of skill development, the functional demands of the task can exceed a learner's attentional capacity. To simplify the learning process, instructors commonly use part practice. The part practice method generally involves breaking down the skill into natural parts or segments, practicing those parts separately until they are learned, and then integrating them to perform the skill in its entirety. This strategy is advantageous in that it (1) simplifies the skill, (2) allows learners to experience early success, leading to increased motivation, and (3) permits practice on problematic components without wasting time on those already mastered. However, separating the skill into parts might not be the most efficient method in all cases. In fact, under certain conditions, the whole practice method—in which the learner practices the complete skill—is favored.

The decision to use whole or part practice in a given situation depends on which method is more likely to result in the greatest amount of positive transfer to the performance of the whole skill (Wightman & Lintern, 1985). To make that judgment, the practitioner must carefully assess the nature of the skill and the capability of the learner.

Nature of the Skill

As we have seen repeatedly, the nature of the skill influences the learning process. Recognizing this, Naylor and Briggs (1963) hypothesized that the effectiveness of part and whole practice depended on two inherent features of the skill. The first, *task complexity*, directly correlates with the number of subcomponents that make up the skill. It is also a function of the information-processing demands imposed by the task. The more components and the greater the attention, memory, and decision-making requirements, the more complex the task. Given this description, it might seem appropriate to use the part practice method to simplify highly complex skills for the learner; however, this judgment would be premature without taking into account a second variable, task organization.

Task organization refers to the degree to which the subcomponents of the skill are interdependent. In other words, how much does the performance of each part depend on the component that precedes it? If the answer is very dependent, as is the case in a cartwheel, the task is considered to be high in organization. Breaking down a highly organized skill into parts would not be effective, as this would change its natural rhythm. Similarly, for gait training using parallel bars or for running the hurdles, the performer must make continuous adjustments according to the positioning of the previous part. If an athlete clears the hurdle too high or hits it, he must make adjustments in his step pattern in order to negotiate the next hurdle successfully. The athlete can acquire this ability only by practicing over several hurdles. Finally, for actions characterized by rapid loading of the muscles, such as a slap shot in hockey, breaking the skill into parts may eliminate the stretch reflex inherent to the task and change its underlying dynamics (Schmidt & Young, 1987). Conversely, the freestyle stroke (in which the kick and arm action are relatively independent) is a skill that is low in organization; it would lend itself quite well to part practice. Table 9.1 provides additional examples of skills classified according to their task complexity and organization.

Once we know the complexity and organization of a skill, how do we determine which technique, the whole or part practice method, will be most effective? Generally, skills that are high in organization and low in complexity are best served through whole practice, whereas part practice is the preferred technique for skills low in organization and high in complexity (Naylor & Briggs, 1963; Fontana, Furtado, Mazzardo, & Gallagher, 2009). Of course, this guideline does not account for all possible combinations of complexity and organization. For example, it does not suggest the optimal method for a skill that is high in both complexity and organization. In these situations, practitioners must decide which segmentation technique will be most efficient in maximizing learning or whether another strategy, such as simplification, which will be discussed later in the chapter, may be more effective.

TABLE 9.1   Examples of skills classified according to their task complexity and organization

		TASK COMPLEXITY	
		High	Low
TASK ORGANIZATION	High	Executing a jump serve in volleyball	Putting a golf ball
	Low	Tying a figure 8 knot	Performing a bicep curl

FIGURE 9.1

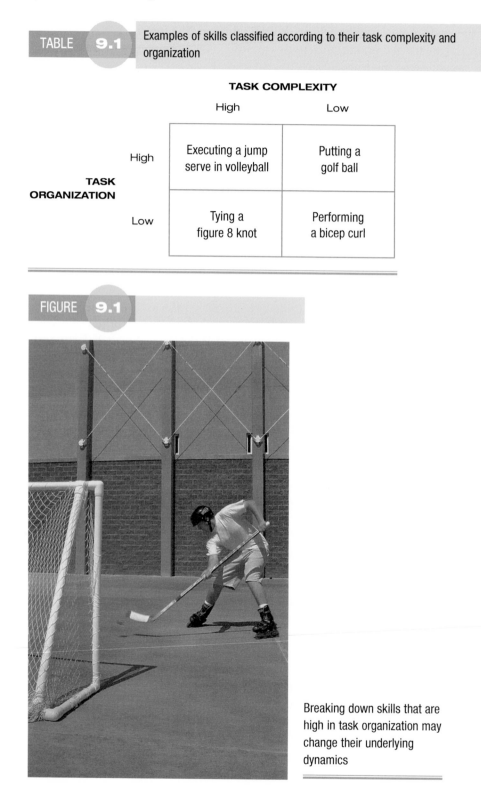

Breaking down skills that are high in task organization may change their underlying dynamics

CEREBRALchallenge   9.1

Using the worksheet below (Coker & Hunfalvay, 2004), conduct a basic task analysis to determine the level of complexity and organization of the following skills:

Fielding a ground ball	_____
Heading a soccer ball	_____
Slalom ski racing	_____
Playing the piano	_____
Transferring from a chair to a wheelchair	_____
Balance beam routine	_____
Reaching and grasping a cup	_____
Walking with crutches	_____
Layup	_____
CPR	_____

PART A: TASK COMPLEXITY

List the motor actions (or steps) required in the skill

1. _____
2. _____
3. _____
4. _____
5. _____

List the decisions needed when performing the skill

1. _____
2. _____
3. _____
4. _____
5. _____

Can these be grouped, that is, can parts of the skill be combined to reduce the number of steps without making the skill too complex for the learner? Describe and justify which actions (or steps) could be grouped.

PART B: TASK ORGANIZATION

Does performance on one part of the skill influence the next skill component?

YES ☐   NO ☐

CEREBRALchallenge   9.2

1. Re-examine each skill presented in Cerebral Challenge 9.1 and indicate whether it would best be served by whole or part practice. Justify your answer.
2. What generalizations, if any, can you make about the use of whole or part practice for skills considered (a) discrete, (b) serial, or (c) continuous?

Capability of the Learner

Although a skill assessment might indicate the use of either whole or part practice, the practitioner should take the capability of the learner into consideration before making a final decision about which method to employ. Learners with limited movement experiences, for example, might be overwhelmed by the demands imposed by the task if it is presented in its entirety. Similarly, if the cognitive or attentional requirements of a task exceed the learner's capacity, using the whole practice method might hinder skill acquisition and leave the learner frustrated. That frustration—the result of a lower success rate—could, in turn, lead to a loss of motivation. In this situation, breaking down the skill into more manageable units will be more effective. Conversely, when learners are highly motivated and have had a variety of movement experiences, gains in skill acquisition can be achieved through the whole method.

Part Practice Techniques

When conditions indicate the use of part practice, the practitioner has several variations from which to choose. Wightman and Lintern (1985) categorized these variations as *segmentation, simplification,* and *fractionization.* It is important to remember that when using part practice—regardless of the variation selected—learners must be taught how the parts are associated with the whole skill. Failure to do this might decrease the transfer to the whole skill. This was demonstrated in an experiment by Newell, Carlton, Fisher, and Rutter (1989); they found that providing learners with part practice, as well as information regarding the goal of the skill, resulted in greater learning gains than were gained by part practice only.

Segmentation

In segmentation, a commonly used part practice technique, the skill is separated into parts according to spatial or temporal elements. The specific structure of this type of practice can take several forms.

1. *Part–whole method.* In this method, the learner practices each part separately until she demonstrates a certain level of proficiency, and then she combines the parts and practices the skill in its entirety. For the football punt, for

example, the catch, approach, drop, and kick would each be practiced separately, and then the parts would be combined and practiced as a unit until the punt is mastered.

2. *Progressive-part method.* In addition to simplifying the skill, this method provides the learner with the opportunity to better understand its underlying timing and integration. The learner begins by practicing two of the parts separately. When he has achieved the criterion level, he combines the parts and practices them together. Once he has mastered these two, the third part is introduced and practiced separately until the learner achieves proficiency. This component is then combined with the other two. This pattern continues until the whole skill is being performed. For the football punt, the learner might practice the catch and approach separately, combine them, practice the drop separately, combine it with the catch and approach, and so on.

3. *Repetitive-part method.* Like the progressive-part method, this method provides the learner with a better understanding of how the parts of a skill fit into the whole. Rather than practicing the new component independently, the learner adds it to the previous part(s) and practices them together. For example, the catch would be practiced first, and then combined with the approach. Once that combination is acquired, the drop would be added, and so on. To view another example using the snatch (weightlifting), go to www.youtube.com/watch?v=L6SjuAOjMEk.

Table 9.2 illustrates the sequence of each part practice strategy for the football punt.

When a skill is broken down using segmentation, the practitioner may also choose to use forward or backward chaining. In forward chaining, the parts are presented and practiced in a sequence progressing from the first to the final part of the skill. The examples given thus far, for the football punt, have employed forward chaining. In backward chaining, the sequence progresses in reverse order,

TABLE 9.2 Implementation of part practice sequences in punting

PART–WHOLE METHOD	PROGRESSIVE-PART METHOD	REPETITIVE-PART METHOD
Catch	Catch	Catch
Approach	Approach	Catch + Approach
Drop	Catch + Approach	Catch + Approach + Drop
Kick	Drop	Catch + Approach + Drop + Kick
Catch + Approach + Drop + Kick	Catch + Approach + Drop	
	Kick	
	Catch + Approach + Drop + Kick	

Reprinted, with permission, from C.A. Coker, 2006. "To break it down or not break it down: That is the question," *Teaching Elementary Physical Education 17*(1): 26–27.

| TABLE 9.3 | Forward and backward chaining combined with the part–whole method for the punt |

FORWARD CHAINING	BACKWARD CHAINING
1. Catch	1. Kick
2. Approach	2. Drop
3. Drop	3. Approach
4. Kick	4. Catch

Reprinted, with permission, from C.A. Coker, 2006. "To break it down or not break it down: That is the question," *Teaching Elementary Physical Education 17*(1): 26–27.

from the final segment to the initial one. For the football punt, the ball could be positioned on a prop or suspended by a string to practice the kick first, the drop would be added, followed by the approach, and finally the catch. See Table 9.3.

Fractionization

In fractionization, skill components that are normally performed simultaneously are partitioned and practiced independently. For example, tacking (changing direction by turning into the wind) on a windsurfer requires simultaneous movements of the arms and legs. The learner would separate these movements, practice them in isolation until they are mastered, and then reassemble them to perform the whole skill. Other examples of fractionization include practicing the movements of each hand separately in playing keyboards or drumming, and practicing the kicking and arm stroke of the breaststroke independently. The effectiveness of this part practice technique remains in question. For rhythmic skills that require bimanual coordination (simultaneous use of the arms) or upper- and lower-limb coordination (simultaneous use of arms and legs), such as playing a musical instrument, fractionization appears to transfer poorly to the whole skill (Klapp, Nelson, & Jagacinski, 1998; Lee, Chamberlin, & Hodges, 2001). Such tasks are high in organization, and whole practice is recommended. When the spatial or temporal movement characteristics of each limb are different, fractionization may be a viable technique. Further research is needed to determine its effectiveness in such situations.

CEREBRALchallenge   9.3

Select a skill for which segmentation would be effective. Outline how you would organize (a) progressive-part practice and (b) repetitive-part practice.

Simplification

Another part practice technique, simplification, reduces the level of difficulty of the task or some aspect of the task. Practitioners can implement this strategy in several ways.

1. *Modify the equipment.* According to Rink (2010), modifying equipment is "one of the most useful ways to reduce the difficulty or complexity of performance in learning skills" (p. 114). (Table 9.4 presents examples of modification strategies.) Oversized striking implements (e.g., larger racket heads, bat barrels, and lacrosse baskets) provide a greater contact surface area. Bigger balls are easier to catch. Shorter or lighter implements are easier to swing. Softer balls with anti-slip surfaces are easier to grasp and catch, and they have lower bounce heights. A broomstick is easier to manipulate than a weighted bar when learning Olympic lifts. Countless occupational training and daily living aids, such as those pictured in Figure 9.2, are available; these include magnetic jewelry clasps, dressing sticks, weighted utensils, nosey cups, rocking-T knives, doorknob grippers, training stairs, and ramp and curb training sets. To learn more about kitchen adaptations for individuals with multiple sclerosis go to www.youtube.com/watch?v=J3PTJK56ZLY.

2. *Reduce the coordination requirements.* The practitioner can reduce task difficulty by manipulating task complexity. It might be possible to reduce or eliminate the need for learners to change location when performing a skill by having them throw, dribble, or kick from a stationary position. When teaching learners how to receive an object, toss, throw, or roll it directly to them. You might be able to manipulate balance, force, speed, and accuracy, provided that the underlying dynamics of the skill (e.g., relative timing) remain intact. For example, training wheels on a bicycle and parallel bars in gait

TABLE **9.4** Equipment modification strategies

MODIFICATION	EXAMPLE	RATIONALE
Size	Larger bat Bigger ball	Easier to contact Easier to catch
Length	Shorter racket	Easier to swing
Weight	Lighter bat	Easier to swing
Grip	Foam grip bat Gator Skin® ball	Easier to hold
Rigidity	Spongy ball	Easier to grasp

Reprinted, with permission, from C.A. Coker, 2006. "To break it down or not break it down: That is the question," *Teaching Elementary Physical Education, 17*(1), 26–27.

FIGURE **9.2** Examples of occupational training and daily living aids

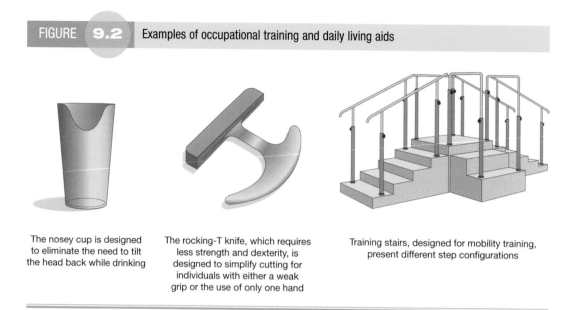

The nosey cup is designed to eliminate the need to tilt the head back while drinking

The rocking-T knife, which requires less strength and dexterity, is designed to simplify cutting for individuals with either a weak grip or the use of only one hand

Training stairs, designed for mobility training, present different step configurations

training assist learners in maintaining balance. When teaching Swiss ball exercises, practice basic positioning initially and make exercises progressively more difficult by decreasing the areas of support, increasing the lever arm length on the ball, and increasing the range of motion (Hoglblum, 2001). Reduce accuracy requirements by increasing the target size. Have learners serve from half court rather than the baseline to reduce the amount of force necessary to get the ball over the net. Permit swimmers with weak kicks to use fins on occasion, so that they can generate enough propulsion to allow them to focus on other aspects of the stroke, such as the arm movement and breathing. Finally, the tempo at which a movement is performed might be decreased by slowing down the overall movement or changing the object being manipulated, such as when juggling scarves are substituted for balls.

3. *Change the complexity of the environment.* The practitioner may manipulate the complexity of the environment to decrease the attentional demands imposed by the task. This can be accomplished by changing the environmental characteristics of an open skill to make it more closed. For example, hitting in baseball or softball might be initially taught as a closed skill, with a stationary ball (placed on a batting tee). Once learners have acquired the basic striking pattern, the skill can be made progressively more open through use of, first, a pitching machine that delivers the ball consistently to a specific location and then a live pitcher who delivers a variety of pitches.

4. *Use skill-building activities and lead-up games.* These activities are a form of simplification, as they allow learners to apply newly acquired skills in a controlled environment. Kickball, one-bounce volleyball, keep away in soccer, and twenty-one in basketball are examples.

5. *Sequence from simple to complex.* Tasks may be modified and sequenced to become progressively more difficult to create the most appropriate challenge for learners. For example, rehab patients might first learn to reach and grasp for a can that is directly in front of them, eventually developing the ability to select a particular can from many. A simple to complex stability ball exercise progression can be created by manipulating range of motion, the size of the base of support, the length of the lever, the speed of movement, the availability of vision, and the use of resistance (Goldenberg & Twist, 2007; see Figure 9.3). Grosse (2009) provides another example, a progression of aquatic exercises that can be viewed online at the adjoining website. Finally, Gentile's taxonomy, found in Chapter 1, is an excellent resource for designing simple to complex progressions.

AQUATIC PROGRESSIONS

www.rehabpub.com/2009/04/aquatic-progressions/

Attention Cueing

A practice option that combines the benefits of both part and whole practice is attention cueing. In attention cueing, the learner directs attention to a specific aspect of the skill while performing it as a whole. Examples include focusing on a high elbow recovery while swimming the freestyle or on the placement of an assisted walking device while traversing a room. This strategy allows the learner to concentrate on one particular task component or movement problem without disrupting the skill's underlying temporal and spatial characteristics.

FIGURE 9.3

1. Pelvic tilt
2. Seated leg raise, hands on hips
3. Seated leg raise, arms at 90 degrees
4. Seated leg raise, arms above head
5. Seated leg raise, arms above head eyes closed

Stability ball exercise progression for seated leg raises

SPEED–ACCURACY TRADEOFF

Movements that require both speed and accuracy in their execution are governed by a basic motor behavior tenet known as the speed–accuracy tradeoff. As the name implies, a tradeoff exists between speed and accuracy such that an emphasis on speed negatively affects accuracy, and vice versa. Through a series of experiments with a rapid aiming task, Fitts (1954) found that performers had to slow their movements as the distance to be moved increased or the size of the target decreased, if they were to perform the task accurately. Try Exploration Activity 9.1 to experience this tradeoff for yourself.

RESEARCH NOTES

To gain a further understanding of the influence of task progressions, Hebert, Landin, and Solomon (2000) examined their influence on students' practice quality and task-related cognition. Eighty-one students enrolled in university beginning tennis classes learned and practiced the serve under one of three conditions. The Criterion group practiced the criterion task, serving using the complete motion from behind the baseline. The remaining two conditions, Part-to-Whole and Extension, practiced using a simple to complex four-step progression that ended with the criterion task. Within this progression, the Part-to-Whole group practiced using segmentation where the skill was broken down into the toss, tossing and hitting from back scratch position, tossing and hitting from hip, and full serve. Learners in the Extension group, on the other hand, were engaged in a simplification practice strategy. Here, the full serve was performed from four different distances on the court starting at the net and ending at the baseline. Data revealed that those instructional conditions that involved easy to difficult progressions (Part-to-Whole and Extension groups) resulted in more successful and appropriate practice trials and enhanced student self-efficacy and motivation. And as reported in a follow-up article (Hebert, Landin, & Solomon, 2004), learners in the Extension group demonstrated greater skill improvement (outcome/accuracy) and superior serving performance in match play as compared to those in the Part-to-Whole or Criterion groups.

CEREBRALchallenge   9.4

1. Review the instructional video of the snatch (www.youtube.com/watch?v=L6SjuAOjMEk) presented under repetitive part practice earlier in the chapter. In addition to segmentation, the coach demonstrates several applications of simplification. What are they and under which category would they be classified?

2. Using the Internet or product catalogs, survey the companies that manufacture equipment for physical education/rehabilitation and list products that are specifically designed for simplification.

3. Read the following progression for the overhead pass and rearrange the items in sequential order from simple to complex by numbering from 1 to 9.

   a. Randomly toss the ball so that the learner is forced to move forward, backward, and side to side. The learner should set the ball back to the individual who tossed it.

   b. Toss the ball to a stationary learner. The learner should catch the ball above the head in the correct position and be facing the individual who tossed it.

   c. The learner sets the ball continuously with a partner.

continued

CEREBRAL challenge—*continued* **9.4**

d. The learner assumes the correct ready position for the set.

e. Toss the ball so that the learner is forced to move forward, backward, and side to side. The learner should catch the ball in the correct setting position and be facing the individual who tossed it. Prior to tossing the ball, indicate to the learner the direction of the toss.

f. Toss the ball to a stationary learner. The learner should set the ball back to the individual who tossed it.

g. Toss the ball to the learner. The learner then sets it to a spiker.

h. Toss the ball so that the learner is forced to move forward, backward, and side to side. The learner should set the ball back to the individual who tossed it. Prior to tossing the ball, indicate to the learner the direction of the toss.

i. The learner assumes the correct ready position for the set, with the ball placed in the hands just above the head. The learner then pushes the ball away using the correct setting motion.

exploration ACTIVITY **9.1**

Speed–Accuracy Tradeoff I

EQUIPMENT

- Piece of paper
- Pen
- Timer or watch with second hand
- Someone to keep time

PROCEDURE

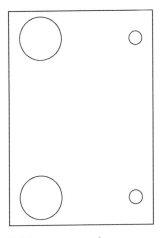

On a piece of paper, draw a circle about the size of a half-dollar coin two inches from the top edge of the paper and a second circle, the same size, two inches from the bottom edge. Draw a second set of circles, about the size of a dime, near the right edge. Your paper should be a full-size version of the one shown in the figure on the right.

Now, place the tip of your pen in the large top-left circle. While someone keeps time for 10 seconds, your objective is to move the pen back and forth between the two large circles as fast as possible, placing a dot inside each one with each pass. (*Note:* Lift the pen off the paper during the movement.) Then repeat the exercise, using the smaller circles, keeping in mind the objective of moving as fast as possible.

What changes did you note between the two tasks? Do your results support the speed–accuracy tradeoff?

Whereas spatial accuracy is governed by the speed–accuracy tradeoff, it appears that temporal accuracy is not. Temporal accuracy, or timing accuracy, concerns *when* a movement should be executed. For example, a tennis player must decide when to swing in order to intercept the ball. Interestingly, research has found that when temporal accuracy is a determining factor in successful skill performance, increasing movement speed decreases timing errors (Schmidt, Zelaznik, Hawkins, et al., 1979). In other words, timing accuracy *improves* when the performer swings faster and/or when movement distance is decreased, violating the speed–accuracy tradeoff. Similar results have been found for spatial accuracy when producing very forceful movements such as hitting a ball off a tee (Schmidt & Sherwood, 1982).

The speed–accuracy tradeoff has several implications for motor skill performance. First, if spatial accuracy is the goal, such as when a patient reaches for an object or when a computer user moves the mouse to click on an icon, accuracy will suffer if the task is attempted with too much velocity. If, on the other hand, the goal is temporal accuracy or the production of a forceful movement, such as a smash in table tennis, speed should be emphasized.

Although these guidelines are useful, they are somewhat limited in applicability for the practitioner. First, they are the product of experiments that employed laboratory tasks. In actual performance, complex motor skills usually involve a combination of spatial and temporal accuracy, as well as the production of forceful movements (Belkin & Eliot, 1997). Second, these experiments examined issues of control rather than skill acquisition. Studies examining the influence of the speed–accuracy tradeoff on the development of complex motor skills found that an emphasis on accuracy during the initial stages of skill acquisition may impede the development of efficient motor patterns. When learners sacrificed velocity to increase accuracy, a constrained movement pattern emerged. Conversely, an emphasis on speed facilitated skill development (Southard, 1989, 2011; Belkin & Eliot, 1997).

These results suggest that during the initial stages of skill acquisition, accuracy should be de-emphasized. Many traditional practice techniques, however, are not structured this way. For example, a technique often used to practice the in-step kick in soccer is to have learners pair up and kick the ball back and forth. Rather than focusing on technique, the goal of the task is for the learner to get the ball to the partner. Because this practice strategy focuses on accuracy, learners may adopt a less efficient kicking pattern in order to get the ball to their partners successfully. Instead, practitioners should either eliminate targets or make them much larger, and instruct learners instead to emphasize speed. Examples include throwing a ball as far across the gymnasium as possible, throwing lacrosse balls into a soccer goal instead of a lacrosse goal, and hitting tennis balls against a backstop rather than into the tennis court (Ciapponi, 2001). To investigate the influence of the speed–accuracy tradeoff in an applied setting, try Exploration Activity 9.2.

CEREBRALchallenge   9.5

The relationship between speed and accuracy is described mathematically by Fitts' Law:

$$MT = a + b[log_2(2A/W)]$$

The law states that movement time (MT) for rapid aiming tasks is linearly related to the distance to be moved (A) and the width of the target (W).

Perform the experiments at www.few.vu.nl/hci/interactive/fitts/. Based on what you learned through the Fitts' Law demonstration, explain how it influences the functions you perform with your computer. How might you redesign your desktop to maximize efficiency?

exploration ACTIVITY   9.2

Speed–Accuracy Tradeoff II

EQUIPMENT

- 2 partners
- 1 tennis ball

PROCEDURE

Position the partners so that they are facing one another at a distance of approximately 5 feet. Have them throw the tennis ball back and forth 10 times. Assess their throwing technique using the characteristics of a mature throwing pattern provided. Next, have them repeat the task from a distance of 25 feet. Again, observe and assess the technique used to accomplish the task. Finally, have one of the two individuals perform hard throws into an open field, and assess the throwing technique.

Reflect on your assessments of the three different situations. Which situation led to the use of a technique that most resembles a mature throwing pattern? What influence did the speed–accuracy tradeoff have in each condition? Based on your observations, speculate as to the optimal practice conditions to elicit a mature throwing pattern. How might you apply this information when teaching a class of 25 students?

CHARACTERISTICS OF A MATURE THROWING PATTERN

1. Side/shoulder toward the target
2. Throwing arm back behind the head
3. Step with the opposite foot toward the target
4. Rotate trunk to face target
5. Follow through.

BILATERAL TRANSFER

The ability to use both limbs with equal proficiency is advantageous in many sport and daily living skills. The question facing the practitioner is how to design practice to best achieve this proficiency. To answer that question, the practitioner must understand a phenomenon known as bilateral transfer. In Chapter 7 we examined the transfer of learning between tasks. Transfer can also occur between limbs, when practice with one limb enhances the rate of skill acquisition using the opposite limb on the same task (e.g., Haaland & Hoff, 2003; Senff & Weigelt, 2011; Stöckel, Weigelt, & Krug, 2011; Teixeira, Silva, & Carvalho, 2003).

Two explanations have been offered to explain the existence of bilateral transfer. The first explanation derives from a motor control perspective. Theoretically, the non-practiced limb would use the same generalized motor program as the practiced limb, because the specification of muscles or limbs to perform the movement is considered a parameter (see Chapter 4 for a review). When a movement is performed with one limb, electromyography (EMG) evidence indicates the presence of sub-threshold electrical activity in the other limb (Hicks, Gualtieri, & Schroeder, 1983), demonstrating the transfer of motor components of a task between the two cerebral hemispheres of the brain.

The second explanation suggests that when a skill is practiced with one limb, the learner acquires important cognitive information about the movement problem, such as the goal of the skill and how to achieve it. When the learner later practices the same skill with the untrained limb, these same cognitive elements apply and are immediately incorporated, and performance with the previously unpracticed limb is enhanced. Kohl and Roenker (1983) provided support for this cognitive explanation, finding that the degree of bilateral transfer was about the same regardless of whether practice was performed physically or mentally. They surmise that an interaction between motor and cognitive components likely accounts for the bilateral transfer phenomenon (see also Chamberlin & Lee, 1993).

Since the training of one limb has been shown to enhance the rate of skill acquisition on the opposite limb, the question of how to sequence practice with the preferred versus non-preferred limb is relevant for the practitioner. The general consensus, according to Magill (2011), is that a greater degree of transfer occurs from the preferred to the non-preferred limb. This recommendation is based on studies that examined the amount of transfer to an untrained limb after practicing with either the dominant or non-dominant limb as well as the potential psychological advantage of experiencing initial success with the preferred limb. However, evidence suggests that a sequential practice schedule—in which the learner practices the task initially with the non-dominant limb and then practices with the dominant limb—leads to greater performance improvements (Senff & Weigelt, 2011; Stöckel et al., 2011). These results suggest that—to achieve maximum transfer effects when training bilateral skills or, for example, when teaching a volleyball player to spike with both hands—the skill should be practiced first with the non-preferred limb and then with the preferred limb.

Additional research is needed to fully understand how the order in which a task is practiced influences skill acquisition.

Clearly, bilateral transfer has practical implications for the acquisition of skills requiring proficient use of both limbs, but learners can also capitalize on bilateral transfer when they have sustained an injury to a limb. In this situation, practicing with the opposite limb might facilitate performance with the injured limb after its rehabilitation (Christina & Corcos, 1988).

RESEARCH NOTES

Liu and Wrisberg (2005) examined the effect of limb preference, age, and gender on the bilateral transfer of throwing accuracy. One hundred and sixty children aged 6, 8, 10, and 12 years were randomly assigned to either an experimental or a control group. The task consisted of projecting a Koosh ball to a target on the floor using a basketball hook shot. Participants performed a 10-trial pretest with either the preferred or non-preferred hand. Hand use was counterbalanced, with half the participants throwing with the preferred hand and the other half with the non-preferred hand.

Following the pretest, those participants assigned to the experimental group practiced the task with the hand not used during the pretest until a designated criterion performance was obtained. The control group performed a balancing activity. Participants then performed an immediate (10 minutes later) and delayed (24 hours later) transfer test under the same conditions as the pretest. Results revealed significantly higher throwing accuracy for the experimental group on both transfer tests, supporting the phenomenon of bilateral transfer.

RESEARCH NOTES

Stöckel, Weigelt, and Krug (2011) examined the sequential effects of bilateral practice on the acquisition of a slalom dribbling task. Fifty-two right-handed school children (mean age = 11.7 years) were randomly assigned to two groups. The first group practiced initially with the dominant hand (D-ND) while the second group trained in the opposite sequence, with the nondominant hand before changing to the dominant hand (ND-D). For eight sessions over a four-week period, each group practiced dribbling as fast as possible around an obstacle course in slalom-like movements. The pre-, post-, and 1-week retention tests were conducted with the right or left hand only, whereas a transfer test was given with both hands alternating and included several cross-over dribbling moves. Significantly larger learning gains for the ND-D group as compared to the D-ND group were found regardless of the respective hand tested. The transfer test also revealed significantly shorter movement times for the ND-D group with both hands alternating.

CEREBRALchallenge   9.6

On a separate sheet, list sport and daily living skills that might lend themselves to bilateral transfer.

PSYCHOLOGICAL STRATEGIES

An important psychological construct for motor skill learning and practice, as discussed in Chapter 7, is motivation. The promotion of goal setting and incorporation of mental practice should also be considered by practitioners as they too can facilitate skill acquisition and performance.

Goal Setting

Perhaps one of the most powerful motivational strategies is goal setting. Goals help to focus learners' attention, encourage learners to develop new skills and strategies to improve performance (Stratton, 1996), and provide a means of monitoring progress or success (Harris & Harris, 1984). Research supporting the effectiveness of goals in enhancing performance is abundant (see Gould, 2006, for additional information on goal setting).

Types of Goals

Based on the nature of the performer's objective, we can divide goals into three categories:

1. Outcome goals are concerned with the final result of a competition relative to one's opponent. Examples are beating the defending champion and performing a skill before a fellow learner performs it. The use of such goals can be problematic. Because the opposition's performance cannot be controlled, a learner can achieve peak performance but still lose a contest and fail to accomplish the goal. Conversely, a learner can perform poorly yet still be victorious.
2. Performance goals are concerned with self-improvement. They focus on improvements in performance based on one's own previous results, such as increasing distance in the long jump or the number of steps that can be taken unassisted. Performance goals tend to be more effective than outcome goals, because they focus on self-improvement, which is under the direct control of the learner.
3. Process goals, which direct one's focus to achieving some technical element during skill execution, may be used to help learners achieve their outcome and performance goals. Examples are maintaining a pelvic tilt position throughout an exercise and pulling the arms in quickly when performing a triple axel. Like performance goals, process goals are favored over outcome goals, as their self-improvement nature tends to enhance motivation.

Research has shown that employing multiple strategies (a combination of outcome, performance, and process goals) leads to superior performance (Filby, Maynard, & Graydon, 1999).

Elements of a Well-Constructed Goal

The benefits of goal setting can be realized only if goals are carefully constructed in accordance to several criteria, which are captured by the acronym SMART—specific, measurable, action-oriented, realistic, and timely.

Specific

A specific goal is one that clearly defines what the performer wants to accomplish. For example, a patient's goal might be to increase the range of motion for right knee extension by 10 percent within two weeks. This directs behavior more precisely than simply telling the patient to do her best. "Best" might have a clear meaning in some situations, but in others, such as driving a golf ball or pitching, the concept is somewhat elusive; in those areas, "best" has yet to be achieved. When goals are specific, the performer is able to evaluate progress toward achieving them.

FIGURE **9.4** Goal setting can motivate a patient to use correct technique when performing rehabilitative exercises

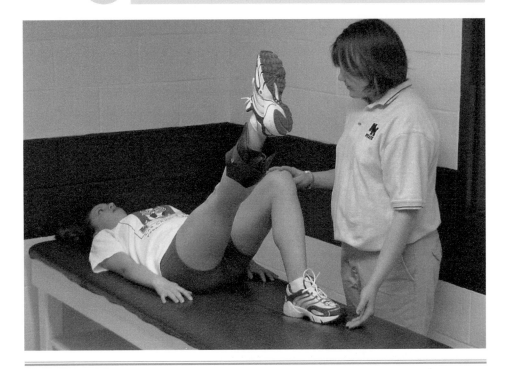

Measurable

Goals should be measurable. The goal of increasing range of motion by 10 percent provides a quantifiable means of tracking progress.

Action-Oriented

Action-oriented goals describe the steps that will be taken to achieve the goal or how the goal will be reached. According to McDonald and Trost (2015), goal commitment is enhanced when the actions that will lead to successful achievement are outlined.

Realistic

Unless a goal is set at an appropriate level of difficulty—one that requires the learner to strive for its attainment—the goal will have little value. Be careful not to exceed the learner's capabilities. This will only result in failure, which will negatively affect learning and performance. A good rule of thumb is to set a goal at a level slightly beyond the learner's reach based on the current level of performance. Basing goals on the existing level of performance allows them to be adjusted according to changing conditions. For example, if the learner progresses faster than expected, the goal can be raised. When an athlete returns to play following an injury, goals might have to be lowered to be realistic.

Timely

Each goal should specify the time for completion, providing a clear target. Without a definite time frame for accomplishment, a learner might lose interest and motivation.

CEREBRALchallenge   9.7

1. Reread the story that opened this chapter. List possible reasons for Anna's lack of motivation. Outline how you might use goal setting to help her refocus.

2. State one thing you would like to accomplish in your sport or professional career (a long-term goal).

   a. Identify three short-term goals that will assist you in achieving your long-term goal.

   b. Analyze your short- and long-term goals to determine whether they are based on outcome, performance, or process.

   c. Analyze your goals to determine whether they meet the SMART criteria.

Goal-Setting Guidelines

When setting goals, establish both short- and long-term goals. Long-term goals may identify the ultimate objective, such as winning a certain championship, but their remoteness makes them less effective. That is not to say that they are inappropriate, but they should be used in conjunction with short-term goals. Short-term goals, because they are more immediate, increase motivation; they allow learners to see performance improvements and serve as stepping-stones for long-term goal achievement. Goals are most meaningful when they account for individual differences, when learners are involved in the goal-setting process, and when they are encouraged to evaluate their progress frequently (Burton & Raedeke, 2008).

Mental Practice

Skill acquisition and performance can benefit from mental practice as well as physical practice. One technique in particular—that of imagery—has received much attention and boasts a variety of applications. Imagery involves the visualization or cognitive rehearsal of a movement in the absence of any physical execution. Studies have shown that imagery can assist in reducing or controlling pre-competitive anxiety, increasing self-confidence, enhancing motivation, and improving selective attention (see Weinberg, 2008, for a review). Athletes also use imagery as an effective preparatory strategy in competition by mentally rehearsing their performance prior to actually executing it (Vealey & Greenleaf, 2006). For example, a figure skater might go over a routine in her mind just before taking to the ice, or a golfer might visualize the successful performance of a strategically placed shot prior to actually hitting the ball. This quote from a successful Olympic diver describes his frequent use of detailed imagery:

> I did my dives in my head all the time. At night, before going to sleep, I always did my dives. Ten dives. I started with a front dive, the first one that I had to do at the Olympics, and I did everything as if I was actually there. I saw myself on the board with the same bathing suit. Everything was the same. I saw myself in the pool at the Olympics doing my dives. If the dive was wrong, I went back and started over again. It takes a good hour to do perfect imagery of all of my dives, but for me it was better than a good workout. I felt like I was on the board.
>
> Orlick & Partington, 1988, p. 112

While often associated with sport psychology and performance as outlined above, the use of imagery has also been shown to facilitate skill learning. Although not a substitute for physical practice, mental practice has been shown to be more effective than no practice at all (Feltz & Landers, 1983; Hird, Landers, Thomas, & Horan, 1991). Furthermore, the combination of physical practice and imagery has been found to be superior to physical practice alone.

RESEARCH NOTES

To explore the effect of mental imagery on skill acquisition, Millard, Mahoney, and Wardrop (2001) randomly assigned 60 competent female swimmers between the ages of 11 and 16 to one of four experimental groups: mental practice, physical practice, combined mental and physical practice, and no practice. The task to be learned was a kayak wet exit. Participants in the mental practice group completed one 30-minute mental practice session daily for three consecutive days. The physical practice group practiced three drills for three consecutive days. The combined group performed the same practice routine as the mental practice group for the first three days and then engaged in the same physical practice as the physical practice group for the next three days. Participants in these three groups were asked to maintain a diary following their practice attempts, where they recorded information such as confidence level and perceived progress. Finally, the no practice group received neither instructions nor practice.

Diary findings indicated that the mental practice and combined groups were confident in their mental ability of the wet exit drill. The mental practice group had higher wet exit ratings than the no practice group. The researchers assert that "the results provide evidence that a combination of mental practice and physical practice are more effective than any single practice type investigated" (p. 982), supporting the notion that novices can benefit from mental and physical practice for skill acquisition.

These findings are not limited to the learning of sport activities. Studies have assessed the efficacy of motor imagery practice on performance and learning in individuals with neurological conditions such as cerebral palsy (Cabral-Sequeira, Coelho, & Teixeira, 2016); stroke, spinal cord injury and Parkinson disease (see Dickstein & Deutsch, 2007); with injured athletes (e.g., Milne, Hall, & Forwell, 2005; Driediger, Hall, & Callow, 2006); for the retraining of upper extremity tasks (see Harris & Hebert, 2015) and of locomotor skills (Malouin & Richards, 2010); for alleviating pain (e.g., Davidson, Snow, Hayden, & Chorney, 2016; and in functional rehabilitation (e.g., Christakou, Zervas, & Lavallee, 2007; Lebon, Guillot, & Collet, 2012). The implication of these findings is that practitioners should consider incorporating imagery in practice to assist in the learning or relearning of a skill or part of a skill. But how should one go about this?

Holmes and Collins (2001) developed the PETTLEP model of motor imagery, which offers practical guidelines to enhance the effectiveness of imagery interventions. Foundational to the model is the notion that imagery intervention should simulate the context of the performance situation as closely as possible. Accordingly, the following factors, corresponding to the acronym, should be considered when implementing imagery interventions: (1) physical, (2) environment, (3) task, (4) timing, (5) learning, (6) emotion, and (7) perspective (see Wakefield, Smith, Moran, & Holmes, 2013 for a review). These factors "describe the physical position of the individual, the environment that has to be imagined, the task involved, the timing or duration of the imagery, the learning or changes involved during imagery, the emotions that are associated with the task, and imagery perspective" (Schuster et al., 2011, p. 2). Improvements found in the performance of bunker shots in golf, especially when combined with physical practice (Smith, Wright, & Cantwell, 2008), penalty shot taking in soccer (Ramsey, Cumming, Edwards, Williams, & Brunning, 2010), kicking accuracy of the non-dominant leg in recreational university soccer players (Finn, Grills, & Bell, 2009), and a turning jump on a gymnastics beam (Smith, Wright, Allsopp, & Westhead, 2007) support the implementation of this approach to facilitate skill development. Specific recommendations offered by Wakefield et al. (2013) to practitioners for using the PETTLEP model to design imagery interventions can be found in Table 9.5. You can try imagery for yourself by performing the tasks outlined in Exploration Activity 9.3.

TABLE 9.5	Recommendations for using the PETTLEP model to design imagery interventions (Wakefield et al., 2013)
FACTOR	**PRACTICAL IMPLICATION**
Physical	The performer should be actively engaged not just relaxing.
Environment	Replicate the actual performance environment trying to incorporate all of the senses (smell the freshly cut grass, hear the roar of the crowd when they score, and focus on how the movement feels). If possible, image in the environment where the performance takes place.
Task	Images should reflect the nature of the task and be adapted and updated as skill level improves.
Time	Perform the imagery in real time.
Learning	As the performers' skill proficiency improves, images should change to reflect their current capabilities.
Emotion	Try to incorporate the emotions typically felt during a game (e.g., joy, adrenaline rush) but avoid those that are debilitative (e.g., fear, panic).
Perspective	Perspective, whether internal (through your own eyes) or external (like watching yourself on video) will be dependent on the purpose of the imagery, the task characteristics and the performer's preference. In general, Holmes and Collins (2001) recommend the use of an internal perspective because it replicates the performance situation but in instances of technique modification, an external focus may be effective.

exploration ACTIVITY 9.3

Mental Imagery I

ACTIVITY 1

Select any object in the room for this activity. Look at its shape and color. Examine it thoroughly, concentrating on every detail. Close your eyes and visualize the object for several seconds. Then open your eyes and compare your mental image to the actual object.

ACTIVITY 2

Close your eyes and imagine that you are in your living room and your roommate or family member is cooking dinner in the kitchen. Can you see your furniture? What color is it? Is the television on? Can you hear it? Are there any other noises? What can you smell? What other details do you notice? (Modified from Weinberg & Gould, 2015).

ACTIVITY 3

Close your eyes and mentally re-create your journey to school today. Did you drive, walk, ride your bike, or take mass transit? See and feel yourself performing the movements associated with your mode of transportation. Visualize the people, environment, and scenery. Are you hot or cold? What are you thinking about? What do you smell?

When you performed this activity, did you see the image through your own eyes or vantage point, or did it seem as if you were watching a movie of yourself? If you felt you were seeing through your own eyes, then you were using internal imagery. If, on the other hand, your perspective was that of an observer, you were using external imagery. The preference for internal or external imagery will vary among individuals, and many will switch back and forth depending on the situation. Try this activity again, but this time use the other perspective.

While everyone has the capacity to perform imagery, not everyone will be equally proficient in its use. Initially, you may have difficulty in creating vivid, controlled images that incorporate all your senses. Practice will help you develop your imagery capability. Start with objects or situations that are familiar, as in these exercises.

Why Does Imagery Work?

Several explanations have been proposed to account for the learning and performance-enhancing effects of mental imagery. According to the cognitive theory, imagery facilitates the acquisition of the cognitive elements of a skill by allowing learners to develop an understanding of a movement's requirements, test solutions to movement problems, and develop performance strategies (Sackett, 1934; Hird et al., 1991). The efficiency of imagery lies in the fact that the learner can practice a skill repeatedly without the risk of injury and without becoming physically fatigued.

The neuromuscular theory postulates that the act of visualizing oneself executing a movement results in the activation of the same motor pathways that would have activated had the movement been physically performed, yet at a subthreshold level. In other words, muscles are innervated in a similar fashion during imagery as when movements are physically practiced. Research supporting this notion has found that muscle activity during imagery, as measured by EMG, was indeed comparable to that during the actual movement, though at a lesser magnitude (Harris & Robinson, 1986; Jacobson, 1931; Jowdy & Harris, 1990; Suinn, 1980). It appears that by rehearsing a skill through imagery, one can strengthen the neural pathways used to perform the actual movement.

More recently, advances in neuroimaging have shown that similar areas in the brain are activated during the mental rehearsal of actions as would be if performing the actual physical movements themselves, a phenomenon termed functional equivalence (Jeannerod, 2001). Accordingly, to maximize the effectiveness of imagery interventions they should mimic actual performance conditions as closely as possible. This is the notion on which the PETTLEP model is based. In addition, studies examining motor imagery using electroencephalography (EEG) and functional magnetic resonance imaging (fMRI) continue to shed light on underlying neural mechanisms that scientists are using to develop technologies that might, some day, be able to help those with neurodegenerative mobility disorders regain function by translating thoughts into actions performed through a computer. Visit www.youtube.com/watch?v=-h3kiws4I54 to learn more.

RESEARCH NOTES

Guillot, Moschberger, and Collet (2013) compared mental imagery performed while motionless versus coupled with actual movement on performance. Participants were 12 national caliber high jumpers between the ages of 16 and 25. Each athlete completed the revised version of the Movement Imagery Questionnaire to determine individual imagery ability. After four warm-up trials, the athletes randomly performed 10 imaged jumps and 10 actual jumps over a bar placed at 90 percent of their personal best. Half of the imaged trials were completed motionless while the other half were performed with associated arm movements. Three performance measures were captured. First, the ability to imagine in real time was determined by comparing actual jump times to mental imagery times captured by the athletes who started a handheld timer when they imaged the first movement and stopped it at the end of the jump. Second, the number of successful attempts was recorded. Third, jump technique was rated by two experts. Results indicated that mental imagery coupled with actual movement enhanced the technical efficiency of the jump, increased the number of successful trials, and was superior in timing congruence between the imaged and actual jumps. Coupling mental imagery with actual movement therefore enhanced performance in this study.

exploration ACTIVITY 9.4

Mental Imagery II*

EQUIPMENT

- 10-inch piece of string
- 1 key

PROCEDURE

Attach the key to the end of the string. Next, place your elbow on a table while holding the other end of the string between your forefinger and thumb so that the key hangs freely. Once the string is still, focus on the key and visualize it moving back and forth like a pendulum.

Were you able to move the key? How do you explain this result?

* Modified from Vealey and Greenleaf, 2006.

PUTTING IT INTO PRACTICE

Learning Situation: Learning the Indirect Pass in Hockey

Although the squirts are in the associative stage for the basic forehand pass and have shown steady improvement, Jennifer knows that the added complexity of banking a pass off of the boards at the right angle and speed to arrive at a desired location and time is a new concept. Until they learn how the puck comes off the boards, passing to a moving target is unrealistic for the squirts who have just been introduced to the indirect pass. She needs to simplify the skill initially.

Test Your Knowledge

How can the indirect pass be simplified for initial practice? Design three activities Jennifer could use to simplify the skill before adding a moving receiver. In what order would you suggest practicing the activities? Explain what strategy you used to simplify the skill and justify your recommended order. Compare your answer with the sample response provided at www.routledge.com/cw/coker.

A LOOK AHEAD

Skill acquisition and performance enhancement result from carefully designed practice opportunities. In this chapter, we examined several strategies, including sequencing and psychological strategies that will help practitioners maximize gains in skill proficiency. We will continue to focus on factors that influence practice effectiveness in the next chapter, as we turn our attention to practice organization and scheduling.

FOCUS POINTS

After reading this chapter, you should know:

- Skills that are high in task complexity and low in task organization are generally best served through part practice, whereas whole practice is preferred for skills low in complexity and high in organization.
- Several part practice methods are available to the practitioner:

  — Segmentation means separating the skill into parts according to spatial or temporal elements. It can be implemented through the part–whole, progressive-part, or repetitive-part methods, and the parts may progress either from the first to the final part (forward chaining) or in reverse order (backward chaining).
  — Fractionization is a part practice technique in which skill components that are normally performed simultaneously are partitioned and practiced independently.
  — Simplification reduces the level of difficulty of the task or some aspect of the task. It can be accomplished by modifying equipment, reducing the coordination requirements of a task, changing the complexity of the environment to make open skills more closed, using skill-building activities and lead-up games, and sequencing from simple to complex.

- Attention cueing directs the learner's attention to a specific aspect of the skill during its performance as a whole, allowing the learner to concentrate on one particular task component or movement problem without disrupting the skill's underlying temporal and spatial characteristics.
- Spatial accuracy is governed by the speed–accuracy tradeoff, in which an emphasis on speed negatively affects accuracy and vice versa.
- Bilateral transfer occurs when practice with one limb enhances the rate of skill acquisition with the opposite limb on the same task.
- A combination of outcome goals, performance goals, and process goals leads to superior performance.
- A well-constructed goal is specific, measurable, action-oriented, realistic, and timely (SMART).
- The combination of physical practice and imagery (the visualization or cognitive rehearsal of a movement) is superior to physical practice alone.

lab

To complete the labs for this chapter, visit www.routledge.com/cw/coker and select **Lab 9a, Segmentation**, **Lab 9b, Simplification**, and **Lab 9c, Speed–Accuracy Trade Off**.

REVIEW QUESTIONS

1. What two task characteristics must you consider when deciding whether to break a skill into parts?

2. Explain the difference between segmentation and fractionization. Illustrate your explanation with an example, using a skill of your choice.

3. What advantage do the progressive-part and repetitive-part practice techniques provide over the part–whole method?

4. Give one example each of backward and forward chaining, with a skill of your choice.

5. Define simplification. List and explain three different simplification strategies for skills of your choice.

6. What is attention cueing? Why is it included in a discussion about whole versus part practice?

7. What condition violates the speed–accuracy principle?

8. What is bilateral transfer? Explain how an athlete who has been injured might be able to capitalize on this phenomenon.

9. What does the acronym SMART stand for?

10. Define imagery. How could imagery be incorporated into a rehabilitation program?

REFERENCES

Belkin, D. S. & Eliot, J. F. (1997). Motor skill acquisition and the speed-accuracy trade-off in a field based task. *Journal of Sport Behavior*, 20(1), 16–28.

Burton, D. & Raedeke, T. (2008). *Sport psychology for coaches*. Champaign, IL: Human Kinetics.

Cabral-Sequeira, A. S., Coelho, D. B., & Teixeira, L. A. (2016). Motor imagery training promotes motor learning in adolescents with cerebral palsy: comparison between left and right hemiparesis. *Experimental Brain Research*, 234(6), 1515–1524. doi:10.1007/s00221–016–4554–3

Chamberlin, C. J. & Lee, T. D. (1993). Arranging practice conditions and designing instruction. In R. N. Singer, M. Murphy, & L. K. Tennant (Eds.), *Handbook of research on sport psychology* (pp. 213–241). New York: Macmillan.

Christakou, A., Zervas, Y., & Lavallee, D. (2007). The adjunctive role of imagery on the functional rehabilitation of a grade II ankle sprain. *Human Movement Science*, 26(1), 141–154.

Christina, R. W. & Corcos, D. M. (1988). *Coaches guide to teaching sport skills*. Champaign, IL: Human Kinetics.

Ciapponi, T. (2001, April). *Speed-accuracy tradeoff in sport skills.* Paper presented at the meeting of the American Alliance for Health, Physical Education, Recreation and Dance. Cincinnati, OH.

Coker, C. A. (2005). Teaching tips for simplification. *Teaching Elementary Physical Education, 16,* 8–9.

Coker, C. A. (2006). To break it down or not break it down: That is the question. *Teaching Elementary Physical Education, 17,* 26–27.

Coker, C. A. & Hunfalvay, M. (April 2004). *Progressions and practice.* Paper presented at the annual meeting of the American Alliance for Health, Physical Education, Recreation and Dance. New Orleans, LA.

Davidson, F., Snow, S., Hayden, J. A., & Chorney, J. (2016). Psychological interventions in managing post-operative pain in children: A systematic review. *Pain,* doi: 10.1097/j.pain.0000000000000636

Dickstein, R. & Deutsch, J. E. (2007). Motor imagery in physical therapist practice. *Physical Therapy, 87,* 942–953.

Driediger, M., Hall, C., & Callow, N. (2006). Imagery use by injured athletes: A qualitative analysis. *Journal of Sports Sciences, 24,* 261–271.

Feltz, D. L. & Landers, D. M. (1983). The effects of mental practice on motor skill learning and performance: A meta analysis. *Journal of Sport Psychology, 5,* 1–8.

Filby, W. C. D., Maynard, I. W., & Graydon, J. K. (1999). The effect of multiple-goal strategies on performance outcomes in training and competing. *Journal of Applied Sport Psychology, 11,* 230–246.

Finn, J., Grills, A., and Bell, D. (2009). A comparison of PETTLEP imagery, physical practice and their combination in the facilitation of non-dominant leg kicking accuracy, in Drust, B., Reilly, T., and Williams, A. M. (Eds.), *International Research in Science and Soccer.* Routledge, NY: 177–189.

Fitts, P. M. (1954). The information capacity of the human motor system in controlling the amplitude of movement. *Journal of Experimental Psychology, 47,* 381–391.

Fontana, F. E., Furtado Jr., O., Mazzardo, O., & Gallagher, J. D. (2009). Whole and part practice: A meta-analysis. *Perceptual & Motor Skills, 109*(2), 517–530.

Goldenberg, L. & Twist, P. (2007). *Strength ball training.* Champaign, IL: Human Kinetics.

Gould, D. (2006). Goal setting for peak performance. In J. Williams (Ed.), *Applied sport psychology: Personal growth to peak performance* (pp. 240–259). New York: McGraw-Hill.

Grosse, S. J. (2009). Aquatic progressions: The buoyancy of water facilitates balance and gait. *Rehab Management, 22*(3), 25–27.

Guillot, A., Moschberger, K., & Collet, C. (2013). Coupling movement with imagery as a new perspective for motor imagery practice. *Behavioral and Brain Functions, 9,* doi:10.1186/1744-9081-9-8

Haaland, E. & Hoff, J. (2003). Non-dominant leg training improves the bilateral motor performance of soccer players. *Scandinavian Journal of Medicine & Science in Sports, 13,* 179–184.

Harris, D. V. & Harris, B. L. (1984). *The athlete's guide to sport psychology: Mental skills for physical people.* Champaign, IL: Human Kinetics.

Harris, D. V. & Robinson, W. J. (1986). The effects of skill level on EMG activity during internal and external imagery. *Journal of Sport Psychology, 8,* 105–111.

Harris, J. E, & Hebert, A. (2015). Utilization of motor imagery in upper limb rehabilitation: a systematic scoping review. *Clinical Rehabilitation, 29*(11), 1092–1107.

Hebert, E. P., Landin, D., & Solomon, M. A. (2000). The impact of task progressions on students' practice quality and task-related thoughts. *Journal of Teaching in Physical Education, 19,* 338–354.

Hebert, E. P., Landin, D., & Solomon, M. A. (2004). The impact of task progressions on college students' skill achievement in tennis. *Journal of Human Movement Studies, 46,* 227–248.

Hicks, R. E., Gualtieri, C. T., & Schroeder, S. R. (1983). Cognitive and motor components of bilateral transfer. *American Journal of Psychology, 96,* 223–228.

Hird, J. S., Landers, D. M., Thomas, J. R., & Horan, J. J. (1991). Physical practice is superior to mental practice in enhancing cognitive and motor task performance. *Journal of Sport and Exercise Psychology, 13,* 281–293.

Hoglblum, P. (2001). *Therapeutic exercise for athletic injuries.* Champaign, IL: Human Kinetics.

Holmes, P. S. & Collins, D. J. (2001). The PETTLEP approach to motor imagery: A functional equivalence model for sport psychologists. *Journal of Applied Sport Psychology, 13,* 60–83.

Jacobson, E. (1931). Electrical measurements of neuromuscular states during mental activities. *American Journal of Physiology, 96,* 115–121.

Jeannerod, M. (2001). Neural simulation of action: A unifying mechanism for motor cognition. *NeuroImage, 14*(1), 103–109.

Jowdy, D. P. & Harris, D.V. (1990). Muscular responses during mental imagery as a function of motor skill level. *Journal of Sport and Exercise Psychology, 12,* 191–201.

Klapp, S. T., Nelson, J. M., & Jagacinski, R. J. (1998). Can people tap concurrent bimanual rhythms independently? *Journal of Motor Behavior, 30,* 301–322.

Kohl, R. M. & Roenker, D. L. (1983). Mechanism involvement during skill imagery. *Journal of Motor Behavior, 15,* 197–206.

Lebon, F., Guillot, A., & Collet, C. (2012). Increased muscle activation following motor imagery during the rehabilitation of the anterior cruciate ligament. *Applied Psychophysiology and Biofeedback, 37*(1), 45–51.

Lee, T. D., Chamberlin, C. J., & Hodges, N. J. (2001). Practice. In R. N. Singer, H. A. Hausenblas, & C. M. Janelle (Eds.), *Handbook of sport psychology* (pp. 115–143). New York: Macmillan.

Liu, J. & Wrisberg, C. A. (2005). Immediate and delayed bilateral transfer of throwing accuracy in male and female children. *Research Quarterly for Exercise and Sport, 76,* 20–28.

Magill, R. A. (2011). *Motor learning: Concepts and applications* (8th ed.). New York: McGraw-Hill.

Malouin, F. & Richards, C. (2010). Mental practice for relearning locomotor skills. *Physical Therapy, 90*(2), 240–251.

McDonald, S. M. & Trost, S. G. (2015). The effects of a goal setting intervention on aerobic fitness in middle school students. *Journal of Teaching in Physical Education, 34*(4), 576–587.

Millard, M., Mahoney, C., & Wardrop, J. (2001). A preliminary study of mental and physical practice on the kayak wet exit skill. *Perceptual and Motor Skills, 92,* 977–984.

Milne, M., Hall, C., & Forwell, L. (2005). Self-efficacy, imagery use, and adherence to rehabilitation by injured athletes. *Journal of Sport Rehabilitation, 14*(2), 150–167.

Naylor, J. C. & Briggs, G. E. (1963). Effects of task complexity and task organization on the relative efficiency of part and whole training methods. *Journal of Experimental Psychology, 65,* 217–224.

Newell, K. M., Carlton, M. J., Fisher, A. T., & Rutter, B. G. (1989). Whole-part training strategies for learning the response dynamics of microprocessor driven simulators. *ActaPsychologica, 71,* 197–216.

Orlick, T. & Partington, J. (1988). Mental links to excellence. *The Sport Psychologist, 2,* 105–130.

Ramsey, R., Cumming, J., Edwards, M. G., Williams, S., & Brunning, C. (2010). Examining the emotion aspect of PETTLEP-based imagery with penalty taking in soccer. *Journal of Sport Behavior, 33*(3), 295–314.

Rink, J. E. (2010). *Teaching physical education for learning.* St. Louis, MO: McGraw-Hill.

Sackett, R. S. (1934). The influences of symbolic rehearsal upon the retention of a maze habit. *Journal of General Psychology, 13,* 113–128.

Schmidt, R. A. & Sherwood, D. E. (1982). An inverted-U relation between spatial error and force requirements in rapid limb movements: Further evidence for the impulse variability model. *Journal of Experimental Psychology: Human Perception and Performance, 8,* 158–170.

Schmidt, R. A. & Young, D. E. (1987). Transfer of motor control in motor skill learning. In S. M. Cormier & J. D. Hagman (Eds.), *Transfer of learning* (pp. 47–79). Orlando, FL: Academic Press.

Schmidt, R. A., Zelaznik, H. N., Hawkins, B., Frank, J. S., & Quinn, J. T. (1979). Motor-output variability: A theory for the accuracy of rapid motor tasks. *Psychological Review, 86,* 415–451.

Schuster, C., Hilfiker, R., Amft, O., Scheidhauer, A., Andrews, B., Butler, J., & Ettlin, T. (2011). Best practice for motor imagery: a systematic literature review on motor imagery training elements in five different disciplines. *BMC Medicine, 9*(1), 75–109. doi:10.1186/1741–7015-9-75

Senff, O. & Weigelt, M. (2011). Sequential effects after practice with the dominant and non-dominant hand on the acquisition of a sliding task in schoolchildren. *Laterality, 16*(2), 227–239.

Smith, D., Wright, C., Allsopp, A., & Westhead, H. (2007). It's all in the mind: PETTLEP-based imagery and sports performance. *Journal of Applied Sport Psychology, 19*(1), 80–92. doi:10.1080/10413200600944132

Smith, D., Wright, C. J., & Cantwell, C. (2008). Beating the bunker: The effect of PETTLEP imagery on golf bunker shot performance. *Research Quarterly For Exercise & Sport, 79*(3), 385–391.

Southard, D. (1989). Changes in limb striking pattern: Effects of speed and accuracy. *Research Quarterly for Exercise & Sport, 60*(4), 348–356.

Southard, D. (2011). Attentional focus and control parameter: Effect on throwing pattern and performance. *Research Quarterly for Exercise & Sport, 82*(4), 652–666.

Stöckel, T., Weigelt, M., & Krug, J. (2011). Acquisition of a complex basketball-dribbling task in school children as a function of bilateral practice order. *Research Quarterly for Exercise & Sport*, 82(2), 188–197.

Stratton, R. (1996). Motivating your athletes and yourself. *Coaching Youth Sports*. www.Tandl.vt.Edu/rstratto/CYSarchive/CoachSept96.html

Stratton, R. (1997). Goal setting: The concept. *Coaching Youth Sports*. www.Tandl.vt.edu/rstratto/CYSarchive/FeatureMay97.html

Suinn, R. M. (1980). Psychology and sport performance: principles and applications. In R. M. Suinn (Ed.), *Psychology in sports: Methods and applications* (pp. 26–36). Minneapolis: Burgess.

Teixeira, L. A., Silva, M. V., & Carvalho, M. A. (2003). Reduction of lateral asymmetries in dribbling: The role of bilateral practice. *Laterality*, 8(1), 53–65.

Vealey, R. S. & Greenleaf, C. A. (2006). Seeing is believing: Understanding and using imagery in sport. In J. Williams (Ed.), *Applied sport psychology: Personal growth to peak performance* (pp. 306–348). New York: McGraw-Hill.

Wakefield, C., Smith, D., Moran, A. P., & Holmes, P. (2013). Functional equivalence or behavioural matching? A critical reflection on 15 years of research using the PETTLEP model of motor imagery. *International Review of Sport and Exercise Psychology*, 6(1), 105–121. doi:10.1080/1750984X.2012.724437

Weinberg, R. S. (2008). Does imagery work? Effects on performance and mental skills. *Journal of Imagery Research in Sport and Physical Activity*, 3(1), 1–20.

Weinberg, R. S. & Gould, D. M. (2015). *Foundations of sport and exercise psychology*. Champaign, IL: Human Kinetics.

Wightman, D. C. & Lintern, G. (1985). Part-task training for tracking and manual control. *Human Factors*, 27(3), 267–283.

Woolfolk, R. L., Parrish, M. W., & Murphy, S. M. (1985). The effects of positive and negative imagery on motor skill performance. *Cognitive Therapy and Research*, 9, 335–341.

10

Mr. Green has had hip replacement surgery and is now waiting for his first physical therapy appointment. He needs to re-learn how to walk using his new hip. He has been warned that it will involve a lot of hard work and practice, but he is up for the challenge. After all, he has a goal: He wants to be able to dance with his granddaughter at her wedding.

The fact that practice is a critical component of learning or re-learning a motor skill is not surprising. Nor is it surprising that the mastery of a skill takes time. To make the most of one's time, practice attempts should be not only maximized but optimized. If Mr. Green's physical therapist has developed a thorough understanding of how practice context and distribution influence learning, his dream of dancing with his granddaughter at her wedding could become reality.

PRACTICE CONTEXT

A common belief in sports is that athletes must master the fundamentals. Coaches who subscribe to this philosophy typically believe that practicing under constant conditions—for example, throwing the same pass or taking the same shot again and again—will lead to superior learning, as the movement pattern will become engrained in memory. What this approach fails to consider is the importance of being able to generalize a skill to a variety of performance situations, including ones that might not have been experienced in the past. A shortstop, for example, will not field ground balls with identical specifications (speed, trajectory, location on the field) repeatedly in a game. Nor will a patient with carpal tunnel syndrome, who is training to regain hand function, button

RESEARCH NOTES

Douvis (2005) examined the effect of variable practice on the forehand drive in tennis by children and late adolescents. Forty male children aged 9 to 10 years and 40 male students aged 18 to 19 years participated in a common instructional program three times a week for six weeks, differing only in practice condition. In the practice phase of each session, participants executed 100 forehand drives from a fixed execution point on the court to no specific target, one target, four targets, or five targets. Following the completion of the training program and a 72-hour rest period, all participants performed 60 transfer trials to a single target point on the court. Deviations in accuracy were recorded. Results revealed that the adolescents executed the shots with greater accuracy than did the children. In addition, children who practiced with four or five targets (variable practice) were significantly more accurate than those who practiced with one or no specific target, and for adolescents variable practice resulted in greater accuracy than practice with no specific target. The variability-of-practice hypothesis was supported, as practicing with four or five targets resulted in greater performance consistency regardless of age group.

the same shirt every day. Buttons come in an assortment of shapes, textures, and sizes, and they are used with an array of fabrics. To accomplish the goal of being able to button a shirt independently, the patient will have to manipulate a variety of buttons under numerous conditions. This inherent variability should, therefore, be the focus of practice.

Support for Variable Practice

The notion that variability in movement and context is a necessary ingredient for skill development and generalizability has strong theoretical underpinnings. In fact, a fundamental prediction of Schmidt's schema theory (refer to Chapter 4) is that variable practice will enhance the development of the learner's schema. This schema, in turn, will enhance the performer's capability to select the appropriate response specifications or parameter values to accomplish a movement goal. Proponents of dynamic systems theory also contend that skill acquisition is best achieved through the modification of constraints, forcing learners to engage in a continuous search for task solutions (Newell & McDonald, 1992).

Several studies support the theoretical prediction that variable practice benefits learning. Shea and Kohl (1991) found that, throughout the practice trials in their study, the constant practice groups (who practiced the same skill variation repeatedly) clearly outperformed the variable practice group (who practiced multiple variations of a single skill) in a force-producing task. The results of the retention test, however, revealed the opposite effect—indicating that greater learning gains were actually achieved by the variable practice group.

To fully understand the significance of these findings, we must revisit the distinction between learning and performance. Recall that learning is defined as *a relatively permanent change in a person's capability to execute a motor skill, as a result of practice or experience.* Performance, on the other hand, is a temporary expression of a skill. Although constant practice has been found to have a greater influence on performance, variable practice has a greater influence on learning. Similar findings have been reported for free throw shooting (Shoenfelt, Snyder, Maue, et al., 2002; Memmert, 2006), an obstacle avoidance task (Cohen, Bloomberg, & Mulavara, 2005), the forehand drive in tennis (Douvis, 2005), and the tennis serve (Hernández-Davo, Urbán, Sarabia, Juan-Recio, & Moreno, 2014).

CEREBRALchallenge   10.1

An argument sometimes made for the use of variable practice is that, in an actual performance context, the same movement is never performed twice. Do you agree or disagree with this statement? Develop an argument to support your position.

Variable Practice Guidelines

To maximize the potential benefits of variable practice, the practitioner must carefully consider how and when to implement variability into the practice session.

How to Implement Variability

According to Gentile (2000), to determine how to implement practice variability one must first assess the nature of the skill being learned and the environment in which it will be performed. Then, depending on that assessment, the practitioner should systematically introduce variations in the regulatory conditions, non-regulatory conditions, or both. For example, in open skills, such as fielding a ground ball, one's response must conform to the demands of an ever-changing environment. For this skill, practice should present variations in both the regulatory conditions (e.g., learner's position on the field, speed and trajectory of the ball) and non-regulatory conditions (e.g., heckling from fans) that might occur in the applied setting. The same approach applies to closed skills that involve inter-trial variability. Variable practice for the sit-to-stand task, for example, might include different chair heights, chairs with and without armrests, variations in seat padding, and various floor surfaces (tile, carpet, linoleum, etc.).

But what about those skills, such as performing a balance beam routine, where the objective of the performance is to replicate a movement pattern consistently and accurately? In such cases, practice should be designed so that the regulatory conditions (e.g., height and width of the beam) remain constant while the learner is subjected to a variety of potential non-regulatory conditions (e.g., distractions).

In addition to manipulating the context in which the skill is performed, skill practice can also be varied through the use of movement concepts and challenges (Boyce, Coker, & Bunker, 2006).

Movement concepts are used in elementary physical education to create movement variations by describing how skills are performed (Graham, Holt/Hale, & Parker, 2013). These concepts include variables such as direction (up/down, forward/backward, etc.), time (fast/slow), force (strong/light), and pathways (straight, curved, zigzagged). For more information and a graphic illustration of how to incorporate movement concepts,

FIGURE **10.1**

For open skills, variations in both regulatory and non-regulatory conditions should be systematically introduced into practice

TABLE **10.1**	Varying practice context for closed and open skills

CLOSED SKILLS	OPEN SKILLS

• Depends on the degree of inter-trial variability (ITV)
 	
  • Closed skills, no ITV
    • Constant regulatory conditions; manipulate non-regulatory conditions
 	
  • Closed skills, with ITV
    • Manipulate both regulatory and non-regulatory conditions
	• Manipulate both regulatory and non-regulatory conditions

practitioners should refer to the Movement Analysis Wheel from Graham and colleagues (2013).

Challenges are variations of a task with a criterion attached that allow learners to test their progress and assess their own performance. According to Shimon (2011), challenges can be created by asking questions such as *How many times, how far or how quickly can you . . . ?* For example, a volleyball player might be challenged to serve 15 balls to the opposing court and see how many different targets she can hit that have been placed on the floor. As another example, when retraining lower limb and ankle proprioception using a wobble board, a series of challenges could be designed that include (1) rock the board front to back as many times as possible in one minute, (2) balance on the wobble board for as long as possible without the edges touching the floor, and (3) rotate the wobble board in a circle without the edge of the board making contact with the floor three times in both directions.

THE PE CENTRAL CHALLENGE TASKS

www.pecchallenge.org/challenges/challengelist.html

When to Implement Variability

Gentile's stages of learning model provides the practitioner with guidelines regarding when to implement variable practice. According to Gentile (2000), the goal of the learner when introduced to a new motor skill is to develop an understanding of the task's requirements. Practice during this initial stage of learning should, therefore, facilitate the learner's development of a basic movement pattern. The practice should be conducted in such a manner as to not overwhelm the novice learner, while providing opportunities for success to enhance his or her confidence. These goals are best achieved through constant practice. Once the learner has acquired the basic movement pattern, variable practice strategies should be introduced.

CEREBRAL challenge 10.2

1. Your patient is Mr. Green, the gentleman in the opening story who is re-learning how to walk after hip replacement surgery. His goal, you will recall, is to dance with his granddaughter at her wedding. Explain how you will incorporate variable practice into his therapeutic program. Describe the variables that you will manipulate and give your reasons for doing so.
2. For a skill of your choice, explain how you would implement variable practice.

CEREBRAL challenge 10.3

A practitioner might decide to continue to use constant practice rather than switch to variable practice once the learner has developed an understanding of the basic movement pattern because the learner will experience greater success during practice. You learned earlier that experiencing success in practice leads to greater motivation. What strategies might you employ to maintain a learner's motivation while incorporating a variable practice schedule?

Organizing the Practice Session: Contextual Interference

Having determined that practice variability is desirable, the practitioner must next decide how to organize the practice session. Whether the learner is learning multiple variations within a single skill (e.g., performing a jump shot from different areas on the court both with and without defenders) or working to acquire a variety of skills (e.g., set shot, lay-up, jump shot, and free throw), the practitioner must decide on an optimum practice sequence. Useful implications can be drawn from a practice phenomenon known as contextual interference.

Contextual interference results from switching from one skill to another or changing the context in which a task is practiced from trial to trial. Although the term "interference" usually carries a negative connotation, contextual interference is a positive learning strategy that has been shown to facilitate skill acquisition (Battig, 1972, 1979). How much contextual interference occurs is a function of how the tasks are integrated within a practice session. On one end of a range of possibilities, low contextual interference results when practice trials are organized in a blocked schedule. In blocked practice, the learner practices one skill or skill variation repeatedly and then moves to another skill or skill variation. For example, in a 30-minute practice, a hockey coach might have his players work on passing for 10 minutes, move on to wrist shots for the next

COMMON MYTH

Long-term retention of a motor skill is best achieved by practicing a skill repeatedly before moving to either a different version of the task or a different task altogether.

10 minutes, and dedicate the final 10 minutes to slap shots. High contextual interference results when multiple tasks or task variations are performed in a random order. In random practice, the hockey coach might have his players perform the same number of repetitions during the 30-minute practice, but the skills would be organized so that no variation (pass, wrist shot, slap shot) was rehearsed twice in a row.

The Contextual Interference Effect

Studies examining the effectiveness of random versus blocked practice for skill acquisition have demonstrated the relatively consistent finding that low contextual interference (blocked practice) often produces superior short-term performance during practice, but practicing multiple skills or skill variations in a random order (high contextual interference) leads to greater long-term learning gains (e.g., Shea & Morgan, 1979). This reversal of results for random practice has been labeled the contextual interference effect.

Researchers have offered two explanations to account for the contextual interference effect. The first, the *elaboration hypothesis*, contends that when random practice is used, working memory simultaneously houses multiple tasks, allowing distinctions between them to be more readily formulated (Shea & Morgan, 1979). These distinctions strengthen the memory representation of each skill, making it more readily available to the learner.

A second proposal, offered by Lee and Magill (1985) and known as the *action plan reconstruction hypothesis*, suggests that random practice facilitates learning by causing temporary forgetting of task solutions between trials. Consequently, learners are required to regenerate a task solution each time they attempt a particular skill variation. In blocked practice, this regeneration would occur only on the first trial of each block. Hence, blocked practice encourages passive learning rather than engaging learners in processing activities that strengthen the motor plan and its retrieval from memory (Patterson & Lee, 2008).

RESEARCH NOTES

To determine whether the contextual interference effect holds true for skilled performers, Hall, Domingues, and Cavasos (1994) examined the influence of different batting practice schedules on the hitting performance of collegiate baseball players. Players participated in two additional batting practice sessions for six weeks, during which they received 15 fastballs, 15 curveballs, and 15 change-ups. The order of pitch presentation depended on group assignment. Players in the blocked group received 15 consecutive pitches of each type in repetitive blocks, and the random group received the same pitches but in random order. When tested under game-like conditions, the players in the random group outperformed those in the blocked group. These results demonstrate that random practice not only benefits beginners but also facilitates performance improvement for skilled performers.

Contextual Interference in Applied Settings

Although the contextual interference effect has been shown to be relatively robust in laboratory settings (e.g., Shea & Morgan, 1979; Lee & Magill, 1983; Wood & Ging, 1991; Tsutsui, Lee, & Hodges, 1998; Li & Wright, 2000; Maslovat, Chua, Lee, & Franks, 2004; Simon, 2007), studies examining its generalizability to applied settings have been less persuasive (see Barreiros, Figueiredo, & Godinho [2007] and Brady [1998, 2004, 2008] for reviews). Superior retention results have been found for random practice in studies using badminton serves (Goode & Magill, 1986; Wrisberg & Liu, 1991), baseball batting (Hall, Domingues, & Cavasos, 1994), forehand and backhand ground strokes in tennis (Hebert, Landin, & Solomon, 1996), the golf putt and pitch shot (Porter, Landin, Hebert, & Baum, 2007), kayak rolling (Smith & Davies, 1995), rifle shooting (Boyce & Del Rey, 1990), and snowboarding skills (Smith, 2002); other investigations have shown no difference between blocked and random practice schedules (e.g., Smith, Gregory, & Davies, 2003; Jones & French, 2007; Zetou, Michalopoulou, Giazitzi, & Kioumourtzoglou, 2007; Žuvela, Maleš, & Čerkez, 2009; Bertollo, Berchicci, Carraro, et al., 2010; Cheong, Lay, Grove, Medic, & Razman, 2012).

These equivocal findings for random practice benefits in applied settings have been attributed to a number of factors. First, the nature of the task appears to influence the contextual interference effect. This notion is based on Magill and Hall's (1990) hypothesis that the probability of eliciting a contextual interference effect depends on whether implemented task variations are governed by the same generalized motor program. Magill and Hall suggest that practicing tasks controlled by different motor programs forces the learner to engage in more cognitive processing, which, in turn, leads to greater interference and enhanced learning. On the other hand, intra-task variations, which require only parameter modifications of the same program, are less likely to generate the critical level of interference to elicit the same effect. Magill and Hall further contend that practicing more dissimilar skills than similar ones would result in greater learning gains. However, several studies have shown that parameter-only modifications can elicit the contextual interference effect (Keller, Li, Weiss, & Relyea, 2006; Landin & Hebert, 1997; Sekiya, Magill, Sidaway, & Anderson, 1994). Further research is needed to resolve this debate.

Learner characteristics, such as age and skill level, are also thought to influence the contextual interference effect. Though limited in number, studies exploring contextual interference and age have found that blocked practice (low contextual interference) generally promotes greater learning for children (Hall & Boyle, 1993; Brady, 1998). Similarly, blocked-practice advantages have been found for novice learners during the early stages of skill acquisition (Del Rey, Whitehurst, & Wood, 1983; Hebert et al., 1996; Landin & Hebert, 1997). Given that a high degree of cognitive processing is needed during the initial stage of learning in order to develop an understanding of the movement, it is likely that the elevated level of interference created by random practice conditions simply overwhelms the learner (Magill & Hall, 1990). Conditions of high interference might, therefore, be effective only after a certain degree of proficiency is achieved (Del Rey et al., 1983; Del Rey, 1989; Hebert et al., 1996).

These results suggest that initial learning should be organized with blocked practice followed by random practice once the learner has gained some degree of proficiency. Based on their findings, however, Landin and Hebert (1997) suggest that moderate levels of contextual interference might be superior in an applied setting. To create moderate contextual interference, the practitioner can use varying degrees of serial practice, where a set sequence of trials is practiced repeatedly. Instead of 10 successive shots at each of four positions (blocked) or one shot from each position over 10 rotations (random), an example of serial practice would be to take one shot from each of the four positions and then repeat the rotation 20 times. Another example would be to take five successive shots at each of the four positions, repeating the rotation twice. This latter form of serial practice, known as repeated blocked practice, combines the advantages of blocked and random practice; it provides the learner the opportunity to make adjustments to each task while still performing several tasks during a practice session (Landin & Hebert, 1997; Proteau, Blandin, Alain, & Dorion, 1994).

TABLE 10.2	Examples of practice variations (blocked, serial, repeated-blocked, and random) for practicing three different hockey skills (pass, slap shot, and wrist shot) in a session

TYPE OF PRACTICE	IMPLEMENTATION
Blocked practice	pass x 20 slap shot x 20 wrist shot x 20
Serial practice	pass x 1 slap shot x 1 } x 20 wrist shot x 1
Repeated-blocked practice	pass x 5 slap shot x 5 } x 4 wrist shot x 5
Random practice	pass, slap shot, wrist shot, slap shot, pass, wrist shot, pass, slap shot, pass, wrist shot, slap shot, wrist shot, pass, wrist shot, slap shot, pass, slap shot, pass, wrist shot, slap shot, wrist shot, slap shot, pass, wrist shot, slap shot, wrist shot, pass, slap shot, pass, wrist shot, pass, slap shot, pass, wrist shot, slap shot, wrist shot, slap shot, pass, slap shot, wrist shot, pass, wrist shot, slap shot, wrist shot, slap shot, pass, wrist shot, pass, slap shot, wrist shot, slap shot, pass, wrist shot, pass, slap shot, pass, wrist shot, pass, wrist shot, slap shot

This strategy also seems advantageous because it would theoretically accommodate the wide range of skill levels typically found in an applied setting (Landin & Hebert, 1997). Although additional research is needed to explore fully the potential of moderate contextual interference in applied settings, Keller and colleagues have reported support for its use (2006). See Table 10.2 for examples of practice schedule variations.

Moderate levels of contextual interference appear to align with ideas forwarded by Guadagnoli and Lee's (2004) challenge point framework (Brady, 2008). According to this framework, an optimal amount of information must be available for learning to occur. That amount is a function of the skill level of the learner and the difficulty of the task being learned (Guadagnoli & Lee, 2004). Accordingly, practitioners should consider the relationship between skill level and task complexity to determine the level of contextual interference that might best facilitate learning.

Consistent with the challenge point hypothesis is a practice schedule that systematically increases the level of contextual interference. Porter and Magill (2010) conducted two experiments examining a practice progression that increased from low to moderate to high contextual interference versus fixed levels (blocked or random only). Systematically increasing the level of contextual interference was found to facilitate the learning of tasks governed by the same motor program (distance variations in putting a golf ball) as well as tasks governed by different generalized motor programs (three different basketball passes: chest, overhead, single arm). Porter and Saemi (2010) reported similar findings; they note that "one reason why a practice schedule that offers gradual increases in CI [contextual interference] may be beneficial is because it challenges learners at the appropriate level by creating an environment that becomes progressively more difficult as the athlete's skill level improves" (p. 69).

Implications of Contextual Interference for Practice Organization

Although further investigations in a variety of sport and movement settings are needed, the available research should encourage practitioners to reconsider deeply rooted traditional practice methods (Coker & Fischman, 2010). Blocked practice appears to be beneficial during early skill acquisition and should be used until learners get the idea of the movement. Once basic proficiency has been achieved, moderate or high levels of contextual interference should be introduced in order to engage the learner in the higher cognitive processing activities that facilitate learning. Practice should be organized using serial, repeated-blocked, and random schedules that combine multiple skills and multiple skill variations. For example, rather than having a tennis player serve to the same spot on each practice attempt, place colored cones in different positions around the court to vary serve placement. Practice the forehand and backhand in the same practice session, and vary the type of ball feed or the area of the court from which the learner hits the ball (Jackson, 2001). In a rehabilitation clinic, design stations where patients can

FIGURE **10.2** Designing practice sessions for contextual interference

To design practice sessions that incorporate high levels of contextual interference:

1. Identify the skills to be practiced.

2. Identify possible skill and performance context variations that will influence how the skill is executed.

3. Design practice where the learner is confronted with different variations and contexts using a randomized schedule.

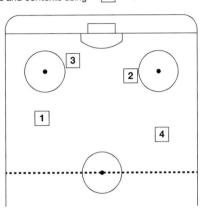

1	Slap shot
2	Wrist shot
3	Backhand shot
4	Slap shot

EXAMPLE: HOCKEY SHOOTING ON GOAL

Shots to be practiced: wrist shot, slap shot, backhand shot.

Variations: distance and angle to the net, with or without defenders, target location on the net, off a pass or possession.

Practice drill: A hockey player skates with puck to station 1 and executes a slap shot. The player then skates to target 2 where a pass is received from another player and a wrist shot is performed. A puck is waiting at target 3, which the player then shoots using a backhand shot. The player then receives a pass from the corner, skates to the center face-off circle, and back to target 4 where another slap shot is executed. As the player is traveling to each shooting location, the coach yells out which corner of the net to shoot to. The drill can be performed with or without a defender.

---

practice different manipulative skills. For patients re-learning to walk, vary the incline, direction, and speed. To teach catching, use multiple objects of various sizes and textures, including balls, rings, beanbags, and rubber chickens. Figure 10.2 offers steps for designing a practice session for contextual interference.

When implementing higher levels of contextual interference, remember that performance during practice might decline. However, a complete breakdown in movement pattern should not be allowed to occur. Practitioners must be vigilant in determining whether the demands of the practice structure are adversely affecting learning and, if necessary, revert to lower levels of contextual interference.

The poorer performance associated with higher levels of contextual interference could lead to decreased motivation. This notion is supported by studies examining learners' estimates of their progress under different levels of contextual interference. When asked to predict how they would do on a retention test, learners who practiced under random conditions underestimated their score, although they more accurately predicted their performance than did their blocked-practice counterparts; these learners were overconfident in their assessment of how much they had learned (Simon and Bjork, 2001; Simon, 2007). Consequently, "the mistaken impression that learning has proceeded worse than it has," as noted by Lee and Wishart (2005, p. 74), could lead to the cessation of practice. When moving from blocked practice to increased levels of contextual interference, learners should be educated about the benefits of practicing under higher contextual interference conditions.

CEREBRALchallenge   10.4

1. How could you combine random and variable practice for the racquetball drive serve, lob serve, and z serve?
2. How could you use random and variable practice to help Mr. Green, from the chapter-opening scenario, re-learn to walk?
3. How would you change your answers to #1 and #2 to implement a repeated-blocked practice schedule in each situation?
4. Recall from the integrative model introduced in Chapter 1 that the design and implementation of the learning experience is dependent on the situation profile. What factors should be taken into consideration before choosing to use blocked, repeated blocked, or random practice to assist Mr. Green in re-learning to walk?

CEREBRALchallenge   10.5

Station work is an excellent way to implement repeated-blocked or random practice. For example, in soccer, six stations could be set up around the field to practice the instep kick, trapping, dribbling, volleying, throw-ins, and heading the ball. At each station, a task card, like the example provided, would describe the activity to be performed and the number of trials to be taken before the learner rotates to the next station.

1. Using a skill or skills of your choice, design a station practice. For each station, specify the rotation to be used, equipment needed, how you will label the station for easy visibility, and what the task card will say.

2. Speculate as to the potential weaknesses of this particular type of practice.

Station 1

Starting on the inside of the first cone, dribble the ball through the cones, using the inside of your foot going up and the outside of your foot coming back. Repeat 10 times and then move to Station 2.

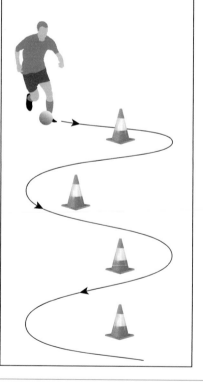

PRACTICE DISTRIBUTION

Thus far, our discussion about organizing the practice sessions has focused on the scheduling of tasks and variations of tasks within a session. Practice organization also includes decisions regarding the duration and frequency of the practice sessions themselves, as well as the allocation of time within a single session. How should these decisions be made to optimize learning?

RESEARCH NOTES

Moulton, Dubrowski, MacRae, and colleagues (2006) examined the influence of practice distribution on the acquisition of a surgical skill, specifically a microvascular anastomosis. Thirty-eight junior surgical residents were randomly assigned to either a massed or a distributed practice schedule. Each group practiced for the same amount of time; the massed group received four training sessions in one day, whereas the distributed group received the same four training sessions spread out over four weeks, one session per week. A one-month retention test and a transfer test to a live, anesthetized rat demonstrated the superiority of distributed practice, as this group significantly outperformed the massed practice group.

Massed versus Distributed Practice

The practitioner can easily manipulate practice distribution, defined in terms of the ratio of time that the learner is physically engaged in practice versus resting. Consequently, whether massed or distributed practice schedules are more beneficial for skill acquisition is a question the practitioner must ask. Massed practice is defined as practice in which the amount of time allocated to rest between sessions or practice attempts is comparatively less than the amount of time the learner is engaged in practice. In distributed practice, the rest component between sessions or practice attempts is equal to or greater than the practice component.

Researchers have examined the influence of massed versus distributed practice schedules on skill acquisition both across and within practice sessions (see Table 10.3). With respect to the duration and frequency of the practice sessions themselves, research indicates a learning advantage for shorter, more frequent meetings (see Baddeley & Longman, 1978 for a classic study). Spacing practice sessions across days, relative to holding all practice sessions within one day, has been shown to enhance both performance and learning (Dail & Christina, 2004; Shea, Lai, Black, & Park, 2001). Therefore, unless the decision as to how often to practice and for how long is out of the practitioner's control, distributed practice is preferred.

TABLE **10.3**	(a) Example of distribution across practice sessions; (b) example of distribution of activity and rest within a practice session

(a)

DAY	PRACTICE TIMES	TYPE OF PRACTICE
Mon.	11:00 a.m.	Technique development
	4:30 p.m.	Lifting
Tues.	6:00 a.m.	Conditioning
	2:00 p.m.	Throwing
Wed.	11:00 a.m.	Technique development
	4:30 p.m.	Lifting
Thurs.	No practice	Active rest
Fri.	11:00 a.m.	Technique development
	4:30 p.m.	**Lifting**
Sat.	10:00 a.m.	Throwing

(b) Lifting Workout

Snatch	5 x 70, 75, 80, 85, 90
Bench	5 x 90, 100, 105, 110, 120
Squat	5 x 150, 160, 175, 185, 195
Split jerks	3 x 12 x 75
Pullovers	3 x 15 x 45
Ab twists	3 x 15 x 25

3-minute rest interval between sets

The optimal practice distribution within a single session remains controversial. Following a review of the practice distribution literature, Lee and Genovese (1988) proposed that distributed practice is beneficial to both performance and learning but more so to performance. García, Moreno, Reina, and colleagues (2008) offered support for this proposal. Furthermore, optimal practice distribution appears to depend on the task (Donovan and Radosevich, 1999; Lee & Genovese, 1988, 1989). For continuous skills—such as cycling or swimming—it seems that distributed practice poses a greater learning advantage than massed practice (Lee & Genovese, 1988). Conversely, discrete skills—such as pitching, punting, or catching—appear best served by massed practice (Carron, 1969; Lee & Genovese, 1988, 1989).

CEREBRALchallenge   10.6

Determine whether you would use massed or distributed practice for the following skills. Justify your answer.

a. Gymnastics vault

b. Free throw

c. Butterfly stroke

d. A dance routine

e. A specific massage technique

f. Maintaining balance with an injured leg while standing on a trampoline (e.g., ankle rehabilitation)

Practical Implications

Research on massed versus distributed practice offers the practitioner several guidelines for the scheduling of practice, training, or rehabilitation sessions. First, learning is enhanced when shorter, more frequent practice sessions are scheduled (distributed practice). It is better to practice three times a week for 30 minutes than once a week for 90 minutes.

Distributed practice should be used to avoid problems associated with high levels of fatigue. Prolonged fatigue can cause the learner to practice incorrect motor patterns, which will have an adverse effect on learning if the boundaries of the generalized motor program are exceeded. In addition, heightened levels of fatigue leave the learner more susceptible to injury. Therefore, shorter, more frequent work periods with adequate rest intervals between sessions are recommended for new and complex skills, continuous tasks, tasks that inherently have high-energy requirements, and tasks whose performance involves some degree of risk. Examples of such tasks include figure skating and rock climbing. This schedule is also recommended for skills practiced in a therapy setting where fatigued learners might fall, such as balancing on a wobble board, and for learners who lack the physical conditioning needed to sustain activity over extended periods of time. Practice should be scheduled so that new skills or those that are highly technical are taught and practiced at the beginning of the session, while the learner is still fresh; conditioning is then done toward the end of practice (Jones, Wells, Peters, & Johnson, 1993).

For massed practice of discrete skills—such as archery or punting a football—practitioners should schedule short rest intervals between trials in order to maximize repetitions and enhance learning. Massed practice can also be effective when used with learners who have acquired basic skills, are motivated, are in good physical condition, and have long attention spans (Christina & Corcos, 1988; Jones et al., 1993). Finally, the fatigue that is often present during competition can be replicated through massed practice. Provided that the level of fatigue remains light to moderate, this strategy could enhance physical conditioning and performance in a game situation (Christina & Corcos, 1988). However, practicing when highly fatigued, as was discussed earlier, can have detrimental effects on learners and should be avoided.

SELF-CONTROL OF PRACTICE VARIABLES

Also consistent with the challenge point framework is self-regulated or self-controlled practice, which gives the learner control to choose some characteristics of the practice situation and has been shown to facilitate learning. One example is self-control of the practice schedule for multiple tasks (Keetch & Lee, 2007; Wu & Magill, 2011). According to Wu and Magill (2011), when learners were given the opportunity to select their own practice schedule, the approach they most often adopted gradually increased the level of contextual interference, and task switching (changing the task to practice) appeared to be regulated by successful performance. In other words, as practice progressed and skill proficiency improved, learners "tended to switch tasks more frequently, creating a practice schedule with more contextual interference" (p. 456).

Self-control advantages have also been reported for the amount and spacing of practice trials. In a study by Post, Fairbrother, & Barros (2011), participants learning to throw a dart for accuracy with their non-dominant hand completed one practice session after being given the incentive that the top performer during testing the following day would receive a $50 gift card. Participants who were given the opportunity to choose when to stop practicing were more accurate during transfer than their counterparts whose practice amount was dictated. Similar findings were reported by Lessa and Chiviacowsky (2015) who found that self-control of the number of practice trials facilitated the learning and performance of a speed cup stacking task in older adults. Finally, giving learners control over both the total number of shots taken and the spacing of shots was beneficial for learning a basketball set shot (Post, Fairbrother, Barros, & Kulpa, 2014).

While additional research is needed to fully understand how learners choose to construct their learning experiences and the implications for practice design, several explanations have been offered to account for the beneficial effects of self-control. Chiviacowsky and Wulf (2002) argued that when given the autonomy to choose characteristics of the practice environment, learners are better able to meet their individual needs. In addition, self-control practice may also create a positive motivational climate for learning through enhanced expectancies (Lewthwaite, Chiviacowsky, Drews, & Wulf, 2015), a notion supported by the OPTIMAL theory proposed by Wulf and Lewthwaite (2016) and discussed in Chapter 7.

MAXIMIZING TIME ON TASK

When a learner is resting, waiting in line, listening to excessive verbal instruction, or participating in a poorly designed drill, precious practice time is wasted. Given the amount of practice needed to become proficient at a skill, and the fact that the time available for such practice is usually limited, wasted time prevents learners from maximizing their learning potential. Fortunately, certain strategies can reduce downtime and maximize time on task.

CEREBRALchallenge   10.7

For a skill of your choice, suggest possible activities that could fill the rest intervals during practice and maximize practice effectiveness.

Rest Intervals

Obviously, given the potentially harmful effects of high levels of fatigue (Godwin & Schmidt, 1971; Arnett, DeLuccia, & Gilmartin, 2000), learners cannot be denied adequate rest. To maximize the utility of rest time, the practitioner can often fill the rest interval with another activity. This technique is commonly used in weight training, where the rest interval for a fatigued muscle group is filled with an activity using a different muscle group. For example, if an athlete's work-out regime calls for three sets of 10 repetitions of bicep curls and triceps extensions, the athlete can alternate continuously between the two exercises. This strategy allows adequate recovery time for the biceps brachii muscle while the triceps are being conditioned. Similar results can be achieved through the use of contextual interference. In repeated-blocked or random practice, recovery is often built into the program and learners do not have to stop activity completely. For example, in volleyball, a rotation could be used in which a player spikes, then moves to the setting position, then goes to the other side of the net to block, then provides coverage behind the block, and finally finishes by shagging a ball.

Equipment Substitutions

Beauchamp, Darst, and Thompson (1990) found that approximately 20 percent of a high school physical education student's time is spent waiting to participate. Similarly, Lacy and Lamaster (1996) found that 22 to 28 percent of time in elementary physical education was spent waiting. One reason is the limitation imposed by an insufficient amount of equipment. A youth soccer coach, for example, may have 20 team members but only eight soccer balls. Similarly, a physical educator teaching putting in a golf unit might have only seven holes on a putting green to which 35 learners must be assigned. The impact on wait time is obvious, but this problem can be remedied by using alternative equipment. In addition to the eight soccer balls, the coach could use playground balls of a comparable size to teach dribbling and kicking skills. The physical educator could give each student a tee to serve as a target; a student who can putt the ball to a tee should be able to get it into the hole. Softballs can serve as substitutes for shot puts, plastic grocery bags for juggling scarves, sand-filled tennis ball canisters for weights, and bicycle inner tubes for surgical tubing. The possibilities are limited only by the practitioner's imagination. Be careful, however, that the alternative equipment does not change the underlying coordination of the movement pattern. If distinct movement pattern changes manifest as a result of the alternative equipment being used, the equipment should be modified or withdrawn.

CEREBRALchallenge 10.8

For a skill of your choice, list possible alternatives that you could use when an inadequate supply of equipment is available.

RESEARCH NOTES

Often, as is the case with the shot put, lack of facilities limits practice as learners must wait their turn. One strategy to reduce wait time is to modify the performance setting. To examine the influence of performance-setting modifications on skill acquisition, Coker (2005) compared a modified practice schedule, in which learners practiced 50 percent of the time in a natural performance setting and 50 percent of the time in a modified setting, to practicing in a natural performance setting 100 percent of the time. Twenty-two college students volunteered to learn the soccer throw-in. They were randomly divided into two groups. Both groups viewed the same instructional video demonstration of a correct throw and performed four blocks of 15 practice throws. The Natural Setting Practice group (NSP) practiced all 60 throws into an open gym where they could see the ball's flight and landing. The Modified Practice Setting group (MPS) alternated each block between the full-view condition and throwing into a trap that was mounted in front of the gym wall (50 percent natural setting and 50 percent modified setting). Feedback on throwing technique was provided. Results indicated that participants in both groups significantly improved their throwing distance. Also, throwing form significantly improved for both groups, according to kinematic analysis. Consequently, participants who spent half of their practice trials performing in the modified setting learned equally well as those who practiced in the natural performance setting 100 percent of the time. The author concluded that alternating between a natural and a modified setting appeared to be a viable strategy for reducing wait time in physical education.

Drill Design

To maximize time on task, the practitioner should design drills to ensure the active participation of all learners. In addition, effective drills should directly target the learning goal. Many traditional drills and activities fail to meet these criteria, however. For example, in volleyball, once a basic movement pattern for bumping and setting has been developed, a common drill is to break the class into two or three large groups (six to eight people) and challenge the learners to see how many times they can hit the ball before it touches the floor. This drill provides learners with the opportunity to practice newly learned skills, promotes

CEREBRALchallenge   10.9

1. Redesign the volleyball drill presented in the Drill Design section. Explain why your drill would be more effective.
2. What is the purpose of learning the weave drill in basketball? Do you think this is effective? Justify your answer.

exploration ACTIVITY   10.1

Time on Task

This activity involves the observation of a team practice or physical education class that is learning a passing or shooting skill (e.g., soccer, field hockey, basketball, etc.). Before doing your observation, download the Dartfish EasyTag app onto your phone or tablet. Create a panel representing each player/student similar to that shown to the right and familiarize yourself with how the app works (view www.youtube.com/watch?v=Hc3GAdFu97I).

Observe several practice activities/drills noting for each the number of times each player/student has an opportunity to perform the task (e.g., shoot, pass, or receive the ball).Then determine the total number of times each individual touched/manipulated the ball and how motivated they appeared during the drill. Determine the value of the drill based on your data, and provide suggestions for how it might be improved.

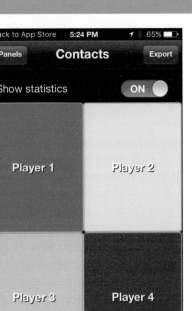

random practice, and enhances motivation, but given the size of the groups each learner will not have many contacts with the ball. Moreover, the learners' goal orientation will be on not letting the ball hit the ground rather than on their form. Consequently, the effectiveness of this activity is questionable. Use Exploration Activity 10.1 to examine the influence of drill design on time on task.

PUTTING IT INTO PRACTICE

Learning Situation: Rehabilitation of an Ankle Sprain

Darren's rehab has been progressing and he is now working on functional balance activities to prepare for going back to field work.

Countless exercises are available to improve balance/proprioception. In addition, numerous variations of those exercises can be prescribed. For example, you can balance on one foot or two, with eyes open or closed, etc. List as many balance exercise variations that you can think of (you may want to refer back to the exercises listed at the end of Chapter 1). Then, design a variable practice program for Darren given his current situational profile. Compare your answer with the sample response provided at www.routledge.com/cw/coker.

A LOOK AHEAD

When planning practices and rehabilitative experiences, the practitioner must decide how to organize practice trials and distribute those trials across and within practice sessions to optimize learning. The practitioner must determine whether random or blocked practice should be implemented, when the use of a massed or distributed schedule is beneficial, and how to maximize time on task. Once the learner begins to practice the skill, the practitioner's focus turns to error correction; before an error can be corrected, however, its cause must be determined. Error detection will be discussed in the following chapter.

FOCUS POINTS

After reading this chapter, you should know:

- When learners are first introduced to a new motor skill, they should engage in constant practice, practicing only a single variation of the task. Once they have acquired the basic movement pattern, they should engage in variable practice strategies, rehearsing multiple variations of the task.
- For open skills and closed skills that involve inter-trial variability, the practitioner should systematically introduce variations in both regulatory and non-regulatory conditions that could be present in an applied setting. For closed skills that do not involve inter-trial variability, learners should be exposed to a variety of potential non-regulatory conditions, while the regulatory conditions of the skill should remain constant.
- Increasing contextual interference—the interference that results from switching from one skill to another or changing the context in which a task is practiced from trial to trial—has been shown to facilitate learning.
- Low contextual interference occurs during blocked practice, when the learner practices one skill or skill variation repeatedly before attempting another skill or skill variation. High contextual interference results when multiple tasks or task variations are performed in random order.
- Initial learning should be organized through blocked practice, and random practice should follow once learners have acquired some degree of proficiency.

- Repeated-blocked practice combines the advantages of blocked and random practice.
- Learning is enhanced when practice sessions are shorter and more frequent.
- Distributed practice is recommended for novel and complex skills, continuous tasks, tasks that inherently have high-energy requirements, and tasks whose performance involves some degree of risk. Massed practice can be effective for learners who have acquired basic skills, are highly motivated, are in good physical condition, and have long attention spans.
- To maximize time on task, the practitioner should carefully consider rest intervals, equipment substitutions, and drill design.

lab

To complete the lab for this chapter, visit www.routledge.com/cw/coker and select **Lab 10, Variable Practice**.

REVIEW QUESTIONS

1. Explain the concept and significance of practice variability. Why is it important to distinguish between learning and performance when answering this question?
2. What variables should the practitioner assess to determine how and when to implement practice variability?
3. Compare and contrast random and blocked practice.
4. What is the contextual interference effect?
5. Describe the two hypotheses that have been proposed to account for the contextual interference effect.
6. What limiting factors have been found to influence the contextual interference effect?
7. What practice strategy can be used to create moderate contextual interference?
8. Compare and contrast massed and distributed practice.
9. Why should prolonged high levels of fatigue be avoided?
10. List and explain three factors that can adversely affect time on task.

REFERENCES

Arnett, M. G., DeLuccia, D., & Gilmartin, K. (2000). Male and female differences and the specificity of fatigue on skill acquisition and transfer performance. *Research Quarterly for Exercise and Sport, 71,* 201–205.

Baddeley, A. D. & Longman, D. J. A. (1978). The influence of length and frequency of training sessions on the rate of learning to type. *Ergonomics, 21*(8), 627–635.

Barreiros, J., Figueiredo, T., & Godinho, M. (2007). The contextual interference effect in applied settings. *European Physical Education Review, 13,* 195–208.

Battig, W. F. (1972). Intra-task interference as a source of facilitation in transfer and retention. In R. F. Thompson & J. F. Voss (Eds.), *Topics in learning and performance* (pp. 131–159). New York: Academic Press.

Battig, W. F. (1979). The flexibility of human memory. In. L. S. Cermak & F. I. M. Craik (Eds.), *Level of processing in human memory* (pp. 23–44). Hillsdale, NJ: Erlbaum.

Beauchamp, L., Darst, P. W., & Thompson, L. P. (1990). Academic learning time as an indication of quality high school physical education. *Journal of Physical Education, Recreation and Dance, 61*(1), 92–95.

Bertollo, M., Berchicci, M., Carraro, A., Comani, S., & Robazza, C. (2010). Blocked and random practice organization in the learning of rhythmic dance step sequences. *Perceptual & Motor Skills, 110*(1), 77–84.

Boyce, B. A., Coker, C. A., & Bunker, L. B. (2006). Pedagogy and motor learning perspectives on variability of practice: Finding a common ground. *Quest, 58,* 330–343.

Boyce, B. A. & Del Rey, P. (1990). Designing applied research in a naturalistic setting using a contextual interference paradigm. *Journal of Human Movement Studies, 18,* 189–200.

Brady, F. (1998). The theoretical and empirical review of the contextual interference effect and the learning of motor skills. *Quest, 50,* 266–293.

Brady, F. (2004). Contextual interference: A meta-analytic study. *Perceptual and Motor Skills, 99,* 116–126.

Brady, F. (2008). The contextual interference effect in sport skills. *Perceptual and Motor Skills, 106,* 461–472.

Carron, A.V. (1969). Performance and learning in a discrete motor task under massed vs. distributed practice. *Research Quarterly, 40,* 481–489.

Cheong, J. P. G., Lay, B., Grove, J. R., Medic, N., & Razman, R. (2012). Practicing field hockey skills along the contextual interference continuum: A comparison of five practice schedules. *Journal of Sports Science & Medicine, 11*(2), 304–311.

Chiviacowsky, S. & Wulf, G. (2002). Self-controlled feedback: Does it enhance learning because performers get feedback when they need it? *Research Quarterly for Exercise and Sport, 73,* 408–415.

Christina, R. W. & Corcos, D. M. (1988). *Coaches guide to teaching sport skills.* Champaign, IL: Human Kinetics.

Cohen, H. S., Bloomberg, J. J., & Mulavara, A. P. (2005). Obstacle avoidance in novel visual environments improved by variable practice training. *Perceptual and Motor Skills, 101,* 853–861.

Coker, C. A. (2005). Practice setting modification and skill acquisition. *The Physical Educator, 62,* 26–31.

Coker, C. A. & Fischman, M. G. (2010). Motor skill learning for effective coaching and performance. In J. M. Williams (Ed.), *Applied sport psychology: Personal growth to peak performance* (6th ed., pp. 21–41). New York: McGraw-Hill.

Dail, T. K. & Christina, R. W. (2004). Distribution of practice and metacognition in learning and long-term retention. *Research Quarterly for Exercise and Sport, 75,* 148–155.

Del Rey, P. (1989). Training and contextual interference effects on memory and transfer. *Research Quarterly for Exercise and Sport, 60,* 342–347.

Del Rey, P., Whitehurst, M., & Wood, J. M. (1983). Effects of experience and contextual interference on learning and transfer by boys and girls. *Perceptual Motor Skills, 56,* 581–582.

Donovan, J. J. & Radosevich, D. J. (1999). A meta-analytic review of the distribution of practice effect: Now you see it, now you don't. *Journal of Applied Psychology, 84*(5), 795–805.

Douvis, S. (2005). Variable practice in learning the forehand drive in tennis. *Perceptual and Motor Skills, 101,* 531–545.

García, J. A., Moreno, F. J., Reina, R. R., Menayo, R. R., & Fuentes, J. P. (2008). Analysis of effects of distribution of practice in learning and retention of a continuous and discrete skill presented on a computer. *Perceptual & Motor Skills, 107*(1), 261–272.

Gentile, A. M. (2000). Skill acquisition: Action, movement, and the neuromotor processes. In J. H.

Carr & R. B. Shepard (Eds.), *Movement science: Foundations for physical therapy in rehabilitation* (2nd ed., pp. 111–180). Rockville, MD: Aspen.

Godwin, M. A. & Schmidt, R. A. (1971). Muscular fatigue and discrete motor learning. *Research Quarterly for Exercise and Sport, 42,* 374–383.

Goode, S. & Magill, R. A. (1986). Contextual interference effects in learning three badminton serves. *Research Quarterly for Exercise and Sport, 57,* 308–314.

Graham, G. M., Holt/Hale, S. A., & Parker, M. A. (2013). *Children moving: A reflective approach to teaching physical education.* Boston, MA: McGraw-Hill.

Guadagnoli, M. A. & Lee, T. D. (2004). Challenge point: A framework for conceptualizing the effects of various practice conditions in motor learning. *Journal of Motor Behavior, 36,* 212–224.

Hall, K. G. & Boyle, M. (1993). The effects of contextual interference on shuffleboard skill in children. *Research Quarterly for Exercise and Sport, Abstracts, 64,* A-74.

Hall, K. G., Domingues, D. A., & Cavasos, R. (1994). Contextual interference effects with skilled baseball players. *Perceptual and Motor Skills, 78,* 835–841.

Hebert, E. P., Landin, D., & Solomon, M. A. (1996). Practice schedule effects on the performance and learning of low- and high-skilled students: An applied study. *Research Quarterly for Exercise and Sport, 67,* 52–58.

Hernández-Davo, H., Urbán, T., Sarabia, J. M., Juan-Recio, C., & Javier Moreno, F. (2014). Variable training: effects on velocity and accuracy in the tennis serve. *Journal of Sports Sciences, 32*(14), 1383–1388.

Jackson, B. (2001, April). *Mixing and matching your repetitions: Contextual interference as a learning opportunity.* Paper presented at the meeting of the American Alliance for Health, Physical Education, Recreation and Dance. Cincinnati, OH.

Jones, B. J., Wells, L. J., Peters, R. E., & Johnson, D. J. (1993). *Guide to effective coaching: Principles and practice.* Madison, WI: WCB Brown and Benchmark.

Jones, L. & French, K. E. (2007). Effects of contextual interference on acquisition and retention of three volleyball skills. *Perceptual and Motor Skills, 105,* 883–890.

Keetch, K. M. & Lee, T. D. (2007). The effect of self-regulated and experimenter-imposed practice schedules on motor learning for tasks of varying difficulty. *Research Quarterly for Exercise & Sport, 78*(5), 476–486.

Keller, G., Li, Y., Weiss, L. W., & Relyea, G. E. (2006). Contextual interference effect on acquisition and retention of pistol shooting skills. *Perceptual and Motor Skills, 103,* 241–252.

Lacy, A. & Lamaster, K. (1996). Teacher behaviors and student academic learning time in elementary physical education. *The Physical Educator, 53*(1), 44–50.

Landin, D. & Hebert, E. P. (1997). A comparison of three practice schedules along the contextual interference continuum. *Research Quarterly for Exercise and Sport, 68,* 357–361.

Lee, T. D. & Genovese, E. D. (1988). Distribution of practice in motor skill acquisition: Learning and performance effects reconsidered. *Research Quarterly for Exercise and Sport, 59,* 277–287.

Lee, T. D. & Genovese, E. D. (1989). Distribution of practice in motor skill acquisition: Different effects for discrete and continuous tasks. *Research Quarterly for Exercise and Sport, 60,* 59–65.

Lee, T. D. & Magill, R. A. (1983). The locus of contextual interference in motor-skill acquisition. *Journal of Experimental Psychology: Learning, Memory, and Cognition, 9,* 730–746.

Lee, T. D. & Magill, R. A. (1985). Can forgetting facilitate skill acquisition? In D. Goodman, R. B. Wilberg, & I. M. Franks (Eds.), *Differing perspectives in motor learning, memory and control* (pp. 3–22). Amsterdam: North Holland.

Lee, T. D. & Wishart, L. R. (2005). Motor learning conundrums (and possible solutions). *Quest, 57,* 67–78.

Lessa, H. T. & Chiviacowsky, S. (2015). Self-controlled practice benefits motor learning in older adults. *Human Movement Science, 40,* 372–380. doi:10.1016/j.humov.2015.01.013

Lewthwaite, R., Chiviacowsky, S., Drews, R., & Wulf, G. (2015). Choose to move: The motivational impact of autonomy support on motor learning. *Psychonomic Bulletin & Review, 22*(5), 1383–1388. doi:10.3758/s13423–015–0814–7

Li, Y. & Wright, D. L. (2000). An assessment of the attention demands of random and blocked practice. *Quarterly Journal of Experimental Psychology, 53A,* 591–606.

Magill, R. A. & Hall, K. G. (1990). A review of the contextual interference effect in motor skill acquisition. *Human Movement Science, 9,* 241–289.

Maslovat, D., Chua, R., Lee, T. D., & Franks, I. M. (2004). Contextual interference: Single task versus multi-task learning. *Motor Control, 8,* 213–233.

Memmert, D. (2006). Long-term effects of type of practice on the learning and transfer of a complex skill. *Perceptual and Motor Skills, 103,* 912–916.

Moulton, C. A., Dubrowski, A. A., MacRae, H., Graham, B., Grober, E., & Reznick, R. (2006). Teaching surgical skills: What kind of practice makes perfect? A randomized, controlled trial. *Annals of Surgery, 244*(3), 400–409.

Newell, K. M. & McDonald, P.V. (1992). Practice: A search for task solutions. In R. W. Christina & H. M. Eckert (Eds.), The Academy Papers, No. 25, Enhancing human performance in sport: New concepts and developments. *Proceedings of the American Academy of Physical Education* (pp. 51–59).

Patterson, J. T. & Lee, T. D. (2008). Organizing practice: The interaction of repetition and cognitive effort for skilled performance. In D. Farrow, J. Baker, & C. MacMahon (Eds.), *Developing sport expertise: Researchers and coaches put theory into practice* (pp. 119–134). London: Routledge.

Porter, J. M., Landin, D., Hebert, E. P., & Baum, B. (2007). The effects of three levels of contextual interference on performance outcomes and movement patterns in golf skills. *International Journal of Sports Science & Coaching, 2*(3), 243–255.

Porter, J. M. & Magill, R. A. (2010). Systematically increasing contextual interference is beneficial for learning sport skills. *Journal of Sports Sciences, 28*(12), 1277–1285.

Porter, J. M. & Saemi, E. (2010). Moderately skilled learners benefit by practicing with systematic increases in contextual interference. *International Journal of Coaching Science, 4*(2), 61–71.

Post, P. G., Fairbrother, J. T., & Barros, J. A. (2011). Self-controlled amount of practice benefits the learning of a motor skill. *Research Quarterly for Exercise and Sport, 82,* 474–481.

Post, P. G., Fairbrother, J. T., Barros, J. A., & Kulpa, J. D. (2014). Self-controlled practice within a fixed time period facilitates the learning of a basketball set shot. *Journal of Motor Learning and Development, 2,* 9–15.

Proteau, L., Blandin, Y., Alain, C., & Dorion, A. (1994). The effects of the amount and variability of practice on the learning of a multisegmented motor task. *ActaPsychologica, 85,* 61–74.

Sekiya, H., Magill, R. A., Sidaway, B., & Anderson, D. I. (1994). The contextual interference effect for skill variations from the same and different generalized motor programs. *Research Quarterly for Exercise and Sport, 65,* 330–338.

Shea, C. H. & Kohl, R. M. (1991). Composition of practice: Influence on the retention of motor skills. *Research Quarterly for Exercise and Sport, 62,* 187–195.

Shea, C. H., Lai, Q., Black, C., & Park, J. H. (2001). Spacing practice sessions across days benefits the learning of motor skills. *Human Movement Science, 19,* 737–760.

Shea, J. B. & Morgan, R. L. (1979). Contextual interference effects on the acquisition, retention and transfer of a motor skill. *Journal of Experimental Psychology, Human Learning and Memory, 5,* 179–187.

Shimon, J. M. (2011). *Introduction to teaching physical education: Principles and strategies.* Champaign, IL: Human Kinetics.

Shoenfelt, E. L., Snyder, L. A., Maue, A. E., McDowell, C. P., & Woolard, C. D. (2002). Comparison of constant and variable practice conditions on free throw shooting. *Perceptual and Motor Skills, 94,* 1113–1123.

Simon, D. A. (2007). Contextual interference effects with two tasks. *Perceptual and Motor Skills, 105,* 177–183.

Simon, D. A. & Bjork, R. A. (2001). Metacognition in motor learning. *Journal of Experimental Psychology: Learning, Memory, and Cognition, 2,* 907–912.

Smith, P. J. K. (2002). Applying contextual interference to snowboarding skills. *Perceptual and Motor Skills, 95,* 999–1005.

Smith, P. J. K. & Davies, M. (1995). Applying contextual interference to the Pawlata roll. *Journal of Sports Sciences, 13,* 455–462.

Smith, P. J. K., Gregory, S. K., & Davies, M. (2003). Alternating versus blocked practice in learning a cartwheel. *Perceptual and Motor Skills, 96,* 1255–1264.

Tsutsui, S., Lee, T. D., & Hodges, N. J. (1998). Contextual interference in learning new patterns of bimanual coordination. *Journal of Motor Behavior, 30,* 151–157.

Wood, C. A. & Ging, C. A. (1991). The role of interference and task similarity on the acquisition, retention and transfer of simple motor skills. *Research Quarterly for Exercise and Sport, 62,* 18–26.

Wrisberg, C. A. & Liu, Z. (1991). The effects of contextual interference on the practice retention and transfer of an applied motor skill. *Research Quarterly for Exercise and Sport, 62,* 406–412.

Wu, W. W. & Magill, R. A. (2011). Allowing learners to choose: Self-controlled practice schedules for learning multiple movement patterns. *Research Quarterly for Exercise & Sport, 82*(3), 449–457.

Wulf, G. & Lewthwaite, R. (2016). Optimizing performance through intrinsic motivation and attention for learning: The optimal theory of motor learning. *Psychonomic Bulletin & Review*. doi: 10.3758/s13423–015–0999–9

Zetou, E., Michalopoulou, M., Giazitzi, K., & Kioumourtzoglou, E. (2007). Contextual interference effect in learning volleyball skills. *Perceptual and Motor Skills, 104,* 995–1004.

Žuvela, F., Maleš, B., & Čerkez, I. (2009). The influence of different learning models on the acquisition of specific athletic throwing skills. *Facta Universitatis: Series Physical Education & Sport, 7*(2), 197–205.

Sally is frustrated. She has spent hours with her tennis coach, working on her backhand. Her technique is flawless, but in competition she consistently contacts the ball too late. Her coach tells her that her technique looks good and that she just needs to swing faster. No matter how hard she tries, though, she just can't fix the problem. She doesn't know what else to do, and her coach has offered no other suggestions.

SKILL ANALYSIS

Practitioners must provide learners with information about the correctness of their performance and prescribe modifications for its improvement. Before they can provide this information, however, practitioners must be able to analyze the performance accurately and determine not only whether an error exists but also the cause of that error and how to fix it. This process is depicted in the second half of the integrated model introduced in Chapter 1. To determine the correctness of a response, the most common approach is simply to observe the performance. For this form of assessment, the practitioner typically compares the learner's technique to technique that is representative of a highly skilled individual. Unfortunately, three potential limitations are inherent in this approach.

First, although it may be natural to try to copy or adopt the technique of a champion athlete, that technique is not necessarily best suited for every learner. Desired outcome can also be achieved through variations of a particular technique and it is not unusual for athletes to adopt their own idiosyncrasies. Practitioners must, therefore, develop a thorough understanding of biomechanics in order to determine the fundamental components of proper technique. In addition, learners might not share the same underlying abilities and attributes as the athlete whom they are trying to emulate. Consequently, certain techniques may be inappropriate due to individual differences.

A second limitation is that the flaw observed is not necessarily indicative of the underlying cause of the error. For example, a practitioner might observe that a volleyball player is hitting the ball into the net on the serve and might try to fix the player's arm swing or the amount of force generated. However, if the player tosses the ball too far out in front of her hitting arm, this too would cause her to hit the ball with too low an angle to clear the net. In this situation, the toss, not the arm swing, should be corrected. Similarly, a right-handed hitter in baseball might be consistently fouling off to the right. One explanation for the error could be a slow swing speed resulting from the athlete taking the bat off his shoulder and implementing a long, swooping swing. However, a second possibility is that the athlete is having difficulty identifying the pitch and delaying the initiation of his swing.

The hitting example in the previous paragraph suggests the third limitation and the focus of this chapter: Errors are not always the result of poor technique. Many errors can be attributed to deficits in the area of motor learning. Since we see only the output of a learner's performance, however, practitioners tend to focus on the outcome of the movement and to provide feedback only about those technical aspects of the skill that can be observed (Rothstein, 1986). As a result, the underlying processes leading to the performance are often overlooked, as they are not directly observable. The purpose of this chapter is to identify potential errors that might manifest not because of poor technique but because of problems related to motor learning and control.

PLANNING AN OBSERVATION

Accurate skill analysis begins with good observational skills. After all, you cannot fix an error unless you first detect it and determine its cause. Observational and analytical skills do not come naturally to most human movement practitioners (Rink, 2014); with practice and the understanding of how to conduct a systematic observation, however, any practitioner can develop these skills. Test your observational skills in Exploration Activity 11.1.

Unlike the still pictures presented in the Exploration Activity, human movement occurs both dynamically and quickly, so the observer has only fractions of a second to assess a performance. Hence, good observations start with a plan (Hall, 2015).

Identify the Skill's Purpose and Key Elements

Prior to conducting an observation, the practitioner should identify both the purpose of the skill to be observed and its key elements. Key elements, also known as critical features, are specific body movements that are observable and affect the performance of the skill (Coaching Association of Canada, 1993) (see Figure 11.1 for an example). Their identification requires a thorough understanding of both the skill itself and biomechanics. Numerous textbooks, sport-specific books, web pages, and journals, as well as other movement practitioners, may be of assistance. Once the key elements of the skill have been identified, the practitioner can determine those that will be the focus of the observation.

Determine the Viewing Perspective

The second step in developing the observational plan is to determine the optimal viewing perspective from which to observe the skill and, more specifically, the key elements chosen as the focus. In order to see all of the skill's critical aspects, it might be necessary to watch the skill from several different positions. In addition, the distance from which the practitioner observes will vary depending on the focus of the observation. To focus on the entire movement, for example, the observer will need to be positioned farther away from the learner; if the practitioner needs to observe the performer's eye movements to determine where the athlete's visual focus is directed, a close-up view might be necessary. The observer should select a position that permits a good view without distractions.

exploration ACTIVITY   11.1

Diagnosing Errors

EQUIPMENT

- Stopwatch or digital watch
- Partner

PROCEDURE

After reading this paragraph, examine the figure below.

Three differences exist between the two pictures. Time how long it takes you to find them. Then, time someone executing a vertical jump. Be sure to note the time needed to complete each task.

QUESTIONS

1. What was the difference in time between how long it took you to find the three flaws in the diagram and the performance of the vertical jump?
2. List the differences in observing a static picture versus a dynamic movement for the detection of performance flaws.

Decide on the Number of Observations

How many trials should be observed prior to making a judgment as to the quality of the performance? No concrete number exists, but analysis based on a single performance attempt should be avoided. Practitioners with limited observational experience will need to view additional trials to determine the underlying cause of an error. Also, as the complexity of the task increases, so too will the number of observations needed to accurately assess performance. Finally, as noted previously, a characteristic of beginning learners is inconsistency in performance. Determining the consistent and/or critical error might, therefore, require repeated observations.

FIGURE **11.1** Key elements of fielding a ground ball

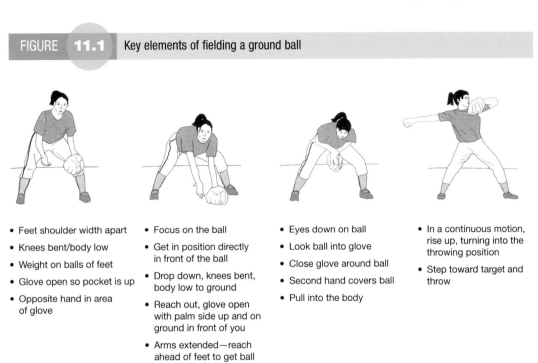

- Feet shoulder width apart
- Knees bent/body low
- Weight on balls of feet
- Glove open so pocket is up
- Opposite hand in area of glove

- Focus on the ball
- Get in position directly in front of the ball
- Drop down, knees bent, body low to ground
- Reach out, glove open with palm side up and on ground in front of you
- Arms extended—reach ahead of feet to get ball

- Eyes down on ball
- Look ball into glove
- Close glove around ball
- Second hand covers ball
- Pull into the body

- In a continuous motion, rise up, turning into the throwing position
- Step toward target and throw

CEREBRAL challenge 11.1

For a skill of your choice, list the key elements and determine the optimal viewing perspective from which to observe each.

KEY ELEMENTS	OBSERVATION PLAN

Consider Using Video

The final decision is whether or not to capture the performance on video. Video is useful because it permits repetitive viewing by both the practitioner and the learner; it can be slowed, paused, and advanced frame by frame; and it captures movements that occur too rapidly (less than a quarter of a second) for the human eye to see (Hall, 2015). Video does have a few disadvantages, though. Learners who are not used to being recorded might be intimidated or self-conscious and alter their performance. Also, playback is difficult to view on a digital video camera or even a smartphone because of the size of the screen.

DETERMINING THE CAUSE OF AN ERROR AND ITS RESOLUTION

Once the practitioner has observed the performance and detected the existence of one or more movement errors, he or she must determine their underlying cause. The practitioner should start by asking why a certain behavior is observed. Why is the backhand late? Why is the patient losing balance? Remember, as was noted earlier, the answer might not be related to technique. Fatigue, incorrect anticipation of a teammate's location, or a technique error could all be viable causes of an off-target pass in soccer, for example. Because the appropriate intervention strategy will be different for each possibility, correctly identifying the true cause of the error is critical to the performance enhancement process. Consequently, the practitioner must be aware of the variety of potential sources of error in order to ensure that the corrections being offered are both accurate and effective. Sources of error can be grouped into the five major categories, as depicted in Figure 11.2: (1) errors due to individual, task, or environmental constraints, (2) comprehension errors, (3) response selection errors, (4) execution errors, and (5) sensory errors.

FIGURE **11.2** Possible causes of error related to motor learning and control

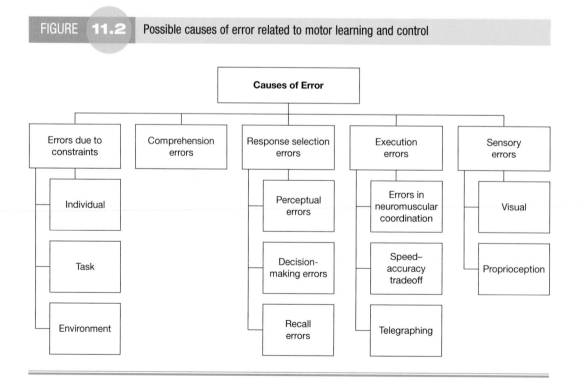

Errors Due to Individual, Task, or Environmental Constraints

Constraints shape behavior. Accordingly, errors might emerge as a result of the task or environment relative to the performer's personal developmental level. For example, a common error displayed by young learners executing a free throw is projecting the ball in a shot put-type manner. This unorthodox pattern emerges not because the learner doesn't understand the correct technique but because it is the only way he can generate enough force to get the ball to a basket that is positioned too high. When the practitioner lowers the basket to accommodate the learner's developmental level, the error will likely be corrected.

Equipment can also create unwanted movement errors. A bat that is too heavy will alter a learner's swing pattern, crutches that are not properly fitted will cause problems with a patient's locomotion, and the speed of a treadmill can dictate the user's stride length and frequency.

Errors can also result from the structure of a task or drill. For example, by 5 or 6 years of age, the visual system develops to the point that objects moving in the horizontal plane can be efficiently tracked (Payne & Isaacs, 2016). However, it is not until between the ages of 8 and 9 that a child can track a ball traveling in an arc (Morris, 1980). The common practice of tossing a ball with a high arc to give a youngster more time to get under it actually makes the task much more difficult and reduces the learner's chances of catching the ball successfully. Instead, the ball should be thrown straight toward the child in order to accommodate his or her visual development, until the learner is about 8 or 9.

Other errors will arise when the environment changes from one that is closed, such as hitting off a tee, to one that is more open, such as hitting a thrown pitch. Practitioners should expect to see a decline in performance as learners adapt to the new demands imposed on them. Prolonged recurrence of errors without signs of adaptation, however, could indicate that the demands of the new

FIGURE **11.3**

Unless properly fitted, crutches can cause errors in locomotion

COMMON MYTH

When teaching a youngster how to catch, you should toss the ball with a high arc to give the child enough time to follow it and get underneath it for a successful catch.

CEREBRALchallenge   11.2

List movement errors that could occur in sport or rehabilitation as a result of incorrect sizing of equipment, objects, or implements.

FIGURE **11.4**

The fear of falling can interfere with a rock climber's performance

task are exceeding the learner's current capacity. In such instances, the practitioner might have to revert to having the learner practice the skill in a more closed environment for a period of time.

Fear can also be a source of error. Beginning swimmers are often afraid of the water. Fear of the ball possibly hitting the learner plays a role in catching and striking. Fear of heights or fear of falling must be overcome before learners can correctly rappel, ski jump, or rock climb. Furthermore, performers might alter their technique if they are afraid of re-injuring a recently rehabilitated limb. Finally, a different type of fear, the fear of failure, may have a negative impact on performance. To counter this fear, practitioners should incorporate goal setting, provide opportunities for all learners to experience success in practice, and create an environment where learners are not afraid to make mistakes.

Comprehension Errors

A comprehension error occurs when the learner does not understand the requirements of the skill or what is expected. These errors develop when learners do not fully understand the instructions given, have a short attention span or limited attentional capacity, or lack motivation. In this instance, simply explain the skill again. Be sure to use terminology that is appropriate for the learner's age and skill level, and avoid overloading the learner with too much information. Finally, check for understanding.

Errors in comprehension can also occur when learners are trying to correct and refine their skills. Although the practitioner might have made the learner aware of the problem's existence, the learner might not fully understand what the error is or how it was created. A useful strategy in this situation is to film the performance and show the learner what he or she is doing wrong. In addition, learners must be taught to pay attention to the sensory consequences of their movements in order to develop their error detection and correction capabilities. Questioning strategies that encourage learners to evaluate their own performance prior to being given feedback are effective in accomplishing this and will be discussed in detail in the next chapter. On the other hand, the learner may understand the error but is uncertain how to implement a change to correct the behavior. In addition to continued demonstrations and feedback, manual guidance or a simulator might prove useful in this situation.

Response Selection Errors

The successful performance of many motor skills, such as a tennis backhand, depends not only on how the skill is executed but also on how quickly and accurately the performer assesses the situation and decides on a response. Any delays in the processes that lead to response selection influence the timing of the response as well as its quality. Practitioners must, therefore, be able to differentiate between slow movement execution and slow initiation of movement. Slow movement execution most often results from a problem with technique. On the other hand, if the movement is initiated slowly, the error can likely be attributed to a perceptual or decision-making problem. This distinction, had it been considered, would have assisted Sally's coach in diagnosing the cause of the backhand error. Since her technique was correct and speeding up the overall movement was ineffective, the next step would be to examine Sally's response selection strategies.

Perceptual Errors

Good decision making begins with good assessment. Unless the learner can quickly and accurately distinguish what is relevant to the task, from the abundance of stimuli present in the environment, response selection will be delayed or incorrect. Movement errors often result when a learner does not know what cues to look for in the environment, cannot distinguish between task-relevant and -irrelevant stimuli, or focuses attention on the wrong cues. For example, a basketball player who focuses attention on an opponent's head movements rather than the mid torso will likely be drawn into a fake. In some instances, the learner might understand what cues are relevant but fails to look at the information-rich areas in the environment where those relevant cues occur (Magill, 1998; Rothstein, 1986). This can equally hamper the learner's decision-making capabilities.

To determine whether any of these causes are the source of Sally's timing error, her coach must establish whether Sally can correctly read game situations. First, does Sally know what critical cues to look for? Second, is she able to detect that information during a game? If not, intervention strategies would focus on the following:

1. Teach the critical cues.
2. Prompt Sally to prepare her response sooner (e.g., beginning preparation as soon as the ball leaves the opponent's racket and getting the racket into the backswing position by the time the ball bounces).
3. Direct her attention to where in the environment cues occur.
4. Provide extensive practice opportunities in a variety of situations that contain common task-relevant cues.

Level of arousal can lead to a perceptual error, as it influences a learner's assessment proficiency. As we noted in Chapter 3, when arousal levels are too low, attentional focus becomes too broad; learners are then unable to focus solely on task-relevant cues. On the other hand, when arousal levels are elevated to the point where the learner becomes over-aroused, attentional focus becomes so narrow that the learner may no longer be capable of scanning the environment effectively, leaving potentially significant stimuli undetected. Both situations can lead to inaccurate responses, as the performer lacks the necessary information for appropriate decision making.

CEREBRALchallenge   11.3

You are teaching badminton to a seventh-grade physical education class. You have been working with the students on the long serve and have noticed that many of them are having difficulty hitting the shuttlecock after they release it. List possible reasons why the students are missing the shuttlecock and provide suggestions for correcting the problem.

Decision-Making Errors

Many errors result from problems in decision making. A learner who misjudges velocity, direction, height, weight, distance, trajectory of an object, or position of opponents or teammates could select the wrong response or could select the appropriate movement but apply erroneous control parameters for the situation. Paying attention to task-irrelevant stimuli, such as being tricked by a head fake, can also lead to momentary delays in responding. Furthermore, mispredicting the arrival of an object, person, or musical cue can cause learners to mistime the initiation of their movement and respond either too early or too late. Again, these decision-making errors can be resolved by increasing the performer's ability to identify and locate critical cues, and by helping the performer develop a stronger cause-and-effect relationship between a specific cue and the appropriate response.

Response delays can occur if the learner fails to reduce the number of response alternatives. According to Hick's Law, the higher the degree of uncertainty in a given situation, the longer it will take the learner to decide which response to make. Many decision-making problems can be resolved by reducing

CEREBRAL**challenge** 11.4

Throughout a rehearsal, one dancer is consistently out of sync with the rest of the dancers. Suggest possible reasons why this is occurring and provide suggestions to correct the problem.

CEREBRAL**challenge** 11.5

An athlete is constantly being beaten when playing person-to-person defense. What will you look at to determine why this learner is unable to stay with the assignment? What recommendations might you offer to correct the problem?

the number of possible response alternatives. Learners should be taught how to look systematically for key performance characteristics in a given situation, as a quarterback does during an option play. Increasing the learner's capability to identify potential predictors, such as opponent or situational tendencies, can also help reduce uncertainty. For example, if Sally knows that whenever her opponent gets into trouble during the game, she hits a shot to Sally's backhand, Sally can better prepare her upcoming shot.

Recall Errors

A common cause of movement errors is forgetting. Learners often have difficulty remembering movements and strategies because of the passage of time between practice sessions. Some learners will even forget what the instructor has just told them to try to incorporate into their next attempt.

At times, learners will be unable to recall what to do in a given situation. For example, in soccer, young learners are taught to play their positions, but in their excitement for the game many forget about positioning and follow the ball. Frequently, the learner is capable of performing the correct movement but simply forgets to do it at the appropriate time. Reminders and attention-focusing questioning strategies such as "What are you going to focus on this time?" are usually sufficient to correct errors due to forgetting.

Execution Errors

Sometimes the learner selects the appropriate response to a situation but cannot execute that response correctly. For example, a racquetball player might correctly choose a kill shot in a given situation but mis-hit the ball. Execution errors occur for a number of reasons, including insufficient practice and performing the movement too quickly.

Errors in Neuromuscular Coordination

Practitioners must be able to distinguish between what learners can do and what they know (Christina & Corcos, 1988). Often, movement errors occur not because of a lack of understanding but because the learner has not yet had enough practice time to establish the proper neuromuscular coordination (Wang & Griffin, 1998). In such cases, the error will likely resolve with additional opportunities to practice. However, in some cases, the learner does not possess the underlying abilities necessary to develop a high degree of skill proficiency or lacks the physical prerequisites to accomplish the task or a component of the task. If the problem stems from a physical deficit, such as inadequate strength levels or poor range of motion, the deficit must first be addressed. In other words, the learner will have to improve his or her strength levels or range of motion before the correct performance of the skill will be possible. If the problem stems from a physical quality that is genetically determined, then additional practice will not bring about a solution.

Problems in neuromuscular coordination will arise when a learner is trying to replace an established movement pattern with a new one. Throughout this process, negative transfer will occur, in that the previously learned pattern will interfere with the acquisition of the new movement. Errors will result not from a lack of understanding or ability but because negative transfer must be overcome. This, of course, takes time and practice. Negative transfer may also occur between two skills that are similar in nature, such as the golf swing and the baseball swing. Coordination errors will arise when an individual who has experience in one skill tries to resolve the similarities and differences with another.

Finally, neuromuscular coordination can be compromised when a learner consciously attends to the specifics of a skill normally performed automatically. Attending to movement components that are otherwise performed automatically causes the normal flow of the movement to be interrupted. This can be seen when first-time users of a treadmill are told to walk the way they normally would. Their gait pattern will exhibit changes until they become comfortable using the equipment and no longer think about how they normally walk.

Speed–Accuracy Tradeoff

Performance outcome may be influenced by the speed–accuracy tradeoff. For example, if the windmill pitch is executed too fast, the pitcher will lose accuracy and have difficulty getting the ball in the strike zone. Similarly, movement patterns will not be performed accurately if patients perform their rehabilitation exercises too quickly. By simply slowing down the execution of the movement, the learner can remedy the error.

In cases involving temporal accuracy, however, speeding up the movement can reduce errors. In the chapter-opening scenario, Sally's coach's suggestion to speed up her swing was a good one, but when increasing speed did not fix the error the coach should have continued to explore other potential causes.

CEREBRALchallenge   11.6

List situations in which a learner can gain an advantage by concealing an impending movement. Now, list ways a learner can inadvertently reveal intent, allowing the opponent to anticipate the upcoming movement.

Telegraphing

In competition, success can depend on the performer's ability to gain an advantage over an opponent. One method for gaining advantage is to increase an opponent's uncertainty in the situation, causing a delay in the opponent's response. This advantage can be lost if the opponent is able to guess correctly what event will occur and when. For example, the reason a learner's serve is always returned easily could be that the learner is somehow revealing his or her intent—or telegraphing it—thereby allowing the opponent to prepare for it in advance. The learner must be taught how to conceal his or her intentions.

RESEARCH NOTES

Several researchers have proposed that a relationship exists between the type of footwear worn and gait and balance for elders (Sudarsky, 1990; Wasson, Gall, McDonald, & Liang, 1990). According to Waked, Robbins, and McClaran (1997), this relationship results from the shoe's effect on proprioception. Thirteen elderly male volunteers walked along a balance beam (height 3.9 cm, width 7.8 cm, length 9 m) one time barefoot and then six times wearing shoes that were identical with the exception of midsole thickness and hardness. Measures included balance failure frequency, foot position error, and foot position awareness. Results showed that (1) stability and foot position awareness are related, (2) as midsole thickness increased, so did foot position error, and (3) harder midsoles resulted in lower foot position errors. Based on these results, the researchers concluded that footwear midsole thickness and hardness influence foot position awareness, which in turn affects stability. Interestingly, the elderly tend to prefer soft, thick running shoes. Consequently, stability problems in the elderly might be the result of their shoe preference.

Sensory Errors

Errors can result from limitations of the sensory mechanisms of motor performance. Given the importance of vision and proprioception in both perception and the response-produced feedback, interference with their contributions can hinder learning and performance.

Visual Errors

According to Knudson and Kluka (1997), movement errors can result from the visual demands of the sport exceeding what is physically possible. For example, a learner could fail to see important cues because she was in mid-blink or because the event occurred too quickly. Shadows can play havoc with the visual system and affect performance. An improper vantage point might obstruct a learner's field of view. Obstructions can also be intentionally set, such as in hockey when one teammate attempts to block the vision of the goalie as another teammate shoots the puck.

Proprioception Errors

Inaccurate sensory feedback stemming from musculoskeletal pain or injury to joint, muscle, or cutaneous receptors can lead to impaired coordination and control during voluntary movement, as well as faulty error detection and correction (Hodges, 2007). A patient with a proprioceptive deficit, for example, may lack control when performing everyday tasks. In this instance, equipment may be altered, such as enlarging the handles of kitchen utensils to enhance their "feel" and make them easier to control.

Proprioceptive deficits can also cause "delayed reflex responses as a result of increased time to reach the threshold for movement detection" (Hodges, 2007, p. 121). This delay will affect performance and might also increase the risk of injury or re-injury, as when a cross-country runner is unable to make the constant minor adjustments needed to maintain balance while running on an uneven surface.

SHOULD THE ERROR BE CORRECTED?

Christina and Corcos (1988) suggest that once the nature of the error has been identified, the practitioner should consider three questions before correcting it. These questions concern the learner's capability, time, and motivation (see Figure 11.5).

Is the Learner Capable?

The first question to ask is whether the learner is capable of making the correction. Successful performance of the corrected technique will depend on whether the learner possesses the necessary underlying abilities. In addition, if the learner does not have the physical prerequisites (strength level, range of motion, etc.) and intellectual capacity to perform the correction, changing the technique will be unsuccessful.

How Much Time Is Needed?

The second question to consider is how much time will be needed for the learner to make the correction. This will depend on the type of correction necessary.

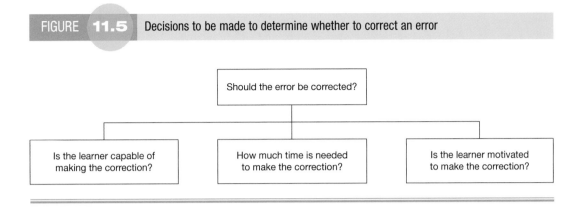

FIGURE **11.5** Decisions to be made to determine whether to correct an error

Corrections may be classified into three general categories, summarized in Table 11.1: (1) retry, (2) refine, or (3) rebuild (Coker, 2005).

In cases where the coordination pattern is correct and the change merely involves a modification in execution, the learner may simply need to *retry* the skill. Errors that occur because of forgetting, for example, can easily be rectified through reminders. Similarly, changes in the control of the movement, such as increasing the speed at which it is performed, are relatively easy to implement. A racquetball player might simply need to snap her wrist faster at contact to improve her kill shot's effectiveness, or a patient might have to adjust his cane placement during gait. Through attention cueing, these errors can be resolved relatively quickly and with little or no adverse effect on performance.

TABLE **11.1** Categories of corrections

RETRY	REFINE	REBUILD
Simple modification of established pattern	Improvement of established pattern	New pattern
Easy to correct	Moderate effort to correct	Difficult to correct
Little or no learning required	Reasonable amount of learning required	Extensive learning required
Can be changed quickly	Varying amounts of time	Substantial amount of time
Little or no adverse effect on performance	Initial performance decrement	Negative impact on performance initially
		Negative transfer
		Frustrating

Reprinted, with permission, from C.A. Coker, 2005. "Teaching tips for simplification," *Teaching Elementary Physical Education* 16(6): 8–9.

Other corrections involve *refining* a developing coordination pattern. For example, a common error in the freestyle swimming stroke is dropping the elbows during the recovery, which is often the result of overextending one's arms before they enter the water. To correct this error, the learner must further develop the existing movement pattern. Performance will be somewhat inconsistent initially as the swimmer learns to refine the timing and coordination of the skill. This type of correction can take weeks, months, or in some cases even longer (Melville, 1988).

Corrections involving fundamental changes to a well-learned technique are the most time consuming. Not only will the learner have to revert back to the cognitive stage of learning, but negative transfer will occur between the previously learned technique and the corrected technique. Consequently, the coordination pattern will have to be *rebuilt*, a process requiring substantial practice.

A cost/benefit analysis could reveal that the time spent relearning a fundamental skill is unwarranted. Instead, it might be more important and/or time effective to practice strategies, situations, and/or game skills. Furthermore, timing is everything. If such a correction is attempted two weeks prior to a major competition, the results could be disastrous.

CEREBRALchallenge 11.7

a. Identify and list five common errors associated with a skill of your choice. For each error listed, determine if the type of correction would be classified as (1) retry, (2) refine, or (3) rebuild.

b. While coaching a high school varsity soccer team, you notice that one of your athletes has a fundamental flaw in his technique. He is a senior and does not have a chance to obtain a college soccer scholarship. Will you fix the flaw? What considerations led to your decision?

Is the Learner Motivated to Make the Correction?

The final question that must be addressed is whether the learner is motivated to make the correction. In some instances, the learner will not be convinced that making the correction is the right decision. Also, if the correction involves the development of a new pattern of coordination, performance will deteriorate before it gets better, and the learner will have to invest a considerable amount of time and practice to see the change through. The practitioner must be certain that the learner is prepared and willing to accept this challenge.

PUTTING IT INTO PRACTICE

Learning Situation: Learning the Indirect Pass in Hockey

Passing is a two-way street. Receiving the puck is just as important as executing a good pass. Jennifer observes that one of the players is having difficulty receiving the pass as the puck is consistently rebounding off of his stick. He appears to be in position but is either not ready when the puck comes or is holding the wrists stiff, causing the puck to rebound off the blade.

Test Your Knowledge

Describe the nature of the two possible errors identified in terms of motor learning. How would you diagnose which of the two is the actual cause of the problem observed in order to select the appropriate intervention strategy for its correction? Compare your answer with the sample response provided at www.routledge.com/cw/coker.

A LOOK AHEAD

Once an error (or errors) has been detected, the cause identified, and the determination made to correct the error(s), the next step is to provide the learner with the necessary information to make the correction. The practitioner should structure feedback to convey information that will both assist the learner in improving skill proficiency and reinforce and motivate the learner. Principles and guidelines for accomplishing this will be explored in the next chapter.

FOCUS POINTS

After reading this chapter, you should know:

* When diagnosing errors, practitioners tend to focus on the outcome of the movement and provide feedback only about technical aspects of the skill that can be observed, but many errors can be attributed to deficits in motor learning.
* When conducting an observation, the practitioner should identify the purpose and key elements of the skill, determine the optimal viewing perspective, decide how many trials to observe prior to making a judgment regarding performance quality, and choose whether to record.
* Errors can occur as a result of individual, task, or environmental constraints.
* Comprehension errors occur when a learner does not understand the requirements of the skill or what is expected.

- Errors in selection can result from problems in assessing the environment for task-relevant cues, faulty decision making, or forgetting.
- Execution errors can occur when the learner has not had enough time to establish proper neuromuscular coordination, when movements are performed too quickly, or when the learner reveals intent, thereby allowing the opponent to anticipate the learner's movements.
- Errors in decision making and motor control might result from difficulties with vision and proprioception.
- Whether an error should be corrected depends on the learner's capability to make the correction, amount of time available, and level of motivation.

lab

To complete the lab for this chapter, visit www.routledge.com/cw/coker and select **Lab 11, Skill Analysis**.

REVIEW QUESTIONS

1. List and explain three possible limitations to using observations to assess performance.

2. What four decisions should be made when planning an observation?

3. When would you use a video camera to capture a learner's performance?

4. Once an error has been detected, what question should the practitioner always ask?

5. When working with children, why might it be useful to modify equipment size? Provide an example to support your answer.

6. What strategies might be useful in assisting a learner who is making a comprehension error? Fully explain your answer.

7. Errors related to response selection fall into three categories. List and explain each.

8. What should a practitioner consider in order to decide whether to correct a movement error?

9. What amount of time may be needed to incorporate a "rebuild" correction?

REFERENCES

Christina, R. W. & Corcos, D. M. (1988). *Coaches guide to teaching sport skills*. Champaign, IL: Human Kinetics.

Coaching Association of Canada (1993). *Coaching theory level I: National Coaching Certification Program*. Gloucester, ON: Author.

Coker, C. A. (2005). Correcting faulty mechanics: To fix or not to fix? *Strategies, 19*(1), 29–31.

Hall, S. J. (2015). *Basic biomechanics* (6th ed.). New York: McGraw-Hill.

Hodges, P. W. (2007). Motor control. In G. Kolt & L. Snyder-Mackler (Eds.), *Physical therapies in sport and exercise* (pp. 115–132). Edinburgh, UK: Churchill Livingstone.

Knudson, D. & Kluka, D. (1997). The impact of vision training on sport performance. *Journal of Physical Education, Recreation and Dance, 68*(4), 17–24.

Magill, R. A. (1998). Knowledge is more than we can talk about: Implicit learning in motor skill acquisition. *Research Quarterly for Exercise and Sport, 69*(2), 104–110.

Melville, D. S. (1988). When to teach new techniques. In J. K. Groppel, J. E. Loehr, D. S. Melville, & A. M. Quinn (Eds.), *Science of coaching tennis* (pp. 73–81). Champaign, IL: Leisure.

Morris, G. S. (1980). *Elementary physical education: Toward inclusion*. Salt Lake City, UT: Brighton.

Payne, V. G. & Isaacs, L. D. (2016). *Human motor development: A lifespan approach* (9th ed.). Scottsdale, AZ: Holcomb Hathaway.

Rink, J. E. (2014). *Teaching physical education for learning*. New York: McGraw-Hill.

Rothstein, A. L. (1986). The perceptual process, vision and motor skills. In L. D. Zaichkowsky & C. Z. Fuchs (Eds.), *The psychology of motor behavior: Development, control, learning and performance* (pp. 191–214). Ithaca, NY: Mouvement.

Sudarsky, L. (1990). Geriatrics: Gait disorders in the elderly. *New England Journal of Medicine, 322,* 1055–1059.

Waked, E., Robbins, S., & McClaran, J. (1997). The effect of footwear midsole hardness and thickness on proprioception and stability in older men. *Journal of Testing and Evaluation, 25*(1), 143–148.

Wang, J. & Griffin, M. (1998). Early correction of movement errors can help student performance. *Journal of Physical Education, Recreation and Dance, 69*(4), 50–52.

Wasson, J. H., Gall, V., McDonald, R., & Liang, M. H. (1990). The prescription of assistive devices for the elderly: Practical considerations. *Journal of General Internal Medicine, 5*(1), 46–54.

"How did that look?" asked the dancer. "I think I was able to keep my pelvis in line that time." Such inquiries are commonplace, as learners often turn to practitioners for feedback. That feedback, according to Chen (2001), is the most critical form of guidance that a practitioner can provide a learner. But feedback is not the only intervention strategy that can be employed to correct errors. Performance improvements can also be realized through the strategic manipulation of task and/or practice variables.

This chapter will discuss the various intervention strategies available to the practitioner for skill refinement. Remember from the integrated model presented in Chapter 1 that the learner, task, and environment should be considered when selecting which strategy to implement in a given situation.

TYPES OF FEEDBACK

Feedback is a general term used to describe the information a learner receives about his or her own performance of a movement or skill. That information can be available from both internal (intrinsic) and external (augmented) sources (see Figure 12.1). Intrinsic feedback is response-produced information that is available to learners through their sensory systems both during and as a consequence of performance; this includes vision, hearing, proprioception, and touch. Examples include a pitcher watching the flight of the ball after releasing it and a gymnast on a balance beam sensing that she is losing her balance. Augmented feedback is information received from an external source that supplements the learner's own sensory information. Examples of augmented feedback include a practitioner's comments; a video replay of the learner executing a skill; and the distance, time, or score resulting from one's performance as posted by an official.

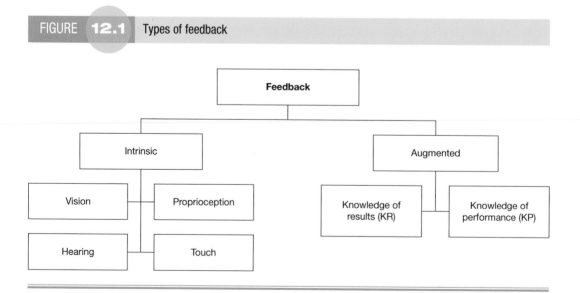

FIGURE **12.1**   Types of feedback

Generally, augmented information is presented to the learner after the movement is completed and is therefore labeled terminal feedback. On occasion, however, augmented feedback is provided during the execution of a skill. It is then termed concurrent feedback. When a coach yells out split times for a runner during a race, or a therapist reminds a patient to keep a good pelvic tilt during an exercise, this feedback is augmented and concurrent.

Augmented feedback can be further classified as either knowledge of results or knowledge of performance. Knowledge of results (KR) is augmented feedback that provides the learner with information about the outcome of a response and is concerned with the success of the intended action with respect to its goal. For example, a coach might tell a long jumper that his plant foot was 4 cm over the takeoff board, a therapist could tell a patient that his functional reach has improved by 20 percent, or a personal trainer might acknowledge the client's correct execution of an exercise.

Information regarding the specific characteristics of the performance that led to the outcome is known as knowledge of performance (KP). Informing a patient that she needs to shift her weight forward more before attempting to stand, telling a student that his elbow recovery in the freestyle should be higher, and showing an athlete a video replay of a performance attempt are all examples of providing knowledge of performance.

CEREBRALchallenge 12.1

Determine whether the following augmented feedback statements are examples of knowledge of results (KR) or knowledge of performance (KP).

a. Your foot placement on the beam should be more angled.
b. You have to keep your head down and your eye on the ball.
c. That was great! You stayed on the wobble board for 28 seconds.
d. According to the radar gun, that pitch was 92 miles per hour.
e. When you swing your leg through, try to pull your toes up.
f. You need to let the weight down more slowly.
g. Looking at the pattern of hits, you are shooting high and to the right.

FUNCTIONS OF AUGMENTED FEEDBACK

Augmented feedback serves three major functions: error correction, motivation, and reinforcement.

1. Error Correction

One role of augmented feedback is to provide information for the correction of performance errors. This information might include a description of the correct

exploration ACTIVITY   12.1

Knowledge of Results (KR) Guidance Properties

EQUIPMENT

- 5 paper clips
- Pencil
- Partner
- Enlarged reproduction of the figure (on right)
- Blindfold

PROCEDURE

Position the donkey target diagram on a desk or table. Blindfold one person. This person should attempt to "pin the tail" (place a paper clip) on the donkey. After each attempt, the other partner removes the paper clip and makes a pencil mark where the tip of the paper clip had been placed. This process continues for five trials. For the next five trials, the blindfolded individual is given KR specifying which ring the paper clip had been placed on and whether the paper clip was on the left or right half of the vertical line drawn through the target. (If the target is completely missed, indicate to which direction.) Using a different symbol, the partner will place a pencil mark where the tip of the paper clip had been placed. After all 10 trials have been completed, the blindfolded partner may remove the blindfold and look at the results.

QUESTIONS

1. How do the results of the two KR conditions (no-KR versus KR) compare?
2. Reflect on your thoughts during the two conditions. Were there any differences?
3. In general, under what conditions do you think it would be important to provide the learner with KR? Do any conditions exist where the provision of KR may not be necessary?

and/or incorrect aspects of the performance, an explanation as to why an error occurred, the prescription for how to fix the error, or specifics of the outcome of the performance (Christina & Corcos, 1988). This information guides the learner to modify subsequent movement attempts in order to enhance skill acquisition and performance. This outcome is demonstrated in Exploration Activity 12.1.

2. Motivation

Augmented feedback can play a motivational role in the learning process. When learners receive information regarding their performance, they can compare it

RESEARCH NOTES

Injuries from repetitive stress may result from impact forces such as those that occur in the jump–landing sequence in spiking. Cronin, Bressel, and Finn (2008) investigated whether a single session of augmented feedback regarding landing technique would reduce the impact forces of the volleyball spike. After five practice jumps to help them become familiar with protocol, 15 female Division I intercollegiate volleyball players performed five baseline spikes from a four-step approach, landing on both feet, with one foot landing on a force platform. After the performance of the baseline jumps, the researchers conducted a two-minute intervention session, where participants observed the coach demonstrating the correct landing technique—emphasizing toe–heel action, an even landing on both legs, and knee flexion close to 90 degrees to absorb landing forces. The participants were then given five practice jumps with feedback about limb kinematics from the coach. After the intervention, participants performed five additional test jumps without instruction or feedback. Augmented feedback was found to reduce vertical ground reaction force by 23.6 percent, a significant reduction. Consequently, this study demonstrated that a single session of augmented feedback had an immediate effect in reducing landing impact forces.

QUESTION

In this study, a post-test was used to examine the effects of augmented feedback on reducing impact forces in landing. What suggestions do you have for determining whether these results are persistent? In other words, how could you see whether the intervention had a long-term effect?

with pre-established goals to determine their progress. If that comparison indicates improvement, learners will be encouraged to continue trying to achieve their goals. Statements such as "You can do it!" and "Hang in there, you're on the right track" can also help learners work through tough practices, difficult challenges, and performance plateaus.

3. Reinforcement

The third function that augmented feedback can serve is to reinforce the learner's efforts. When used in this manner, augmented feedback increases the likelihood of a response recurring on future attempts under similar circumstances. Statements of praise, such as "Great effort" and "Way to get after the ball," or a celebratory gesture like a high-five, can positively reinforce and, therefore, strengthen a behavior. Similarly, the satisfaction that learners derive from an acknowledgment that they have successfully executed a response might instill the desire to repeat the successful action. Eliminating a negative consequence can also reinforce behaviors. If you have learned how to drive a car with a manual transmission, you probably experienced what is known as *negative reinforcement.* Until new drivers learn to coordinate their movements when shifting gears, the car will jump or stall. Because the learner wants to avoid this embarrassing result, negative reinforcement serves to strengthen the desired coordinated movement.

SOURCES OF AUGMENTED FEEDBACK

Perhaps the most common sources of augmented feedback are verbal descriptions and demonstrations. However, feedback can be delivered in a number of other ways.

Auditory Sources

In many instances, augmented feedback takes an auditory form. For instance, sounds that result from skill execution can assist learners in evaluating their performance. Information about rhythm can be conveyed through clapping or a metronome. Auditory feedback also exists in the form of buzzers and warning signals.

Auditory feedback devices have been shown to have positive effects in correcting foot position in a bar exercise in dance (Clarkson, James, Watkins, & Foley, 1986); assisting swimmers in maintaining a desired stroke cadence and

exploration ACTIVITY   12.2

Functions of Augmented Feedback

Download the Dartfish EasyTag app onto your phone or tablet. Create a panel similar to that shown in the graphic and familiarize yourself with how the app works (view www.youtube.com/watch?v= Hc3GAdFu97I). Observe a teacher, coach, or therapist, or videorecord yourself teaching a skill. For each feedback statement offered, identify and record which function it served (see figure on right).

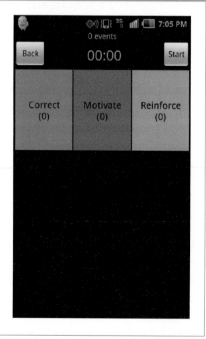

QUESTIONS

1. Which category received the most tally marks? The fewest?
2. Speculate as to why you obtained these results.
3. Speculate as to how effective the pattern revealed will be for the learner's skill acquisition.
4. What other observations are noteworthy?

In high-performance rowing, visually based feedback is often provided for technique refinement. Given that this strategy is only accessible to sighted athletes, Schaffert and Mattes (2015) examined the influence of auditory feedback on mean boat speed during on-water training of visually impaired rowers. Participants were six athletes in the mixed coxed four of the German National Para-Rowing team. The protocol was conducted over the course of seven feedback sessions during a two-week period. The feedback system, Sofirow, measured and stored the boat's acceleration and distance travelled, which was then converted into acoustic feedback that was presented to the athletes via speakers of the existing Cox Box® over a 500 m distance. Each 500 m performance block was divided into five sections with auditory feedback and without in an alternating order. Acoustic feedback was shown to significantly increase boat speed and improve the time structure of the rowing cycle. Further, subjective reports indicated that the athletes believed it to be a supportive training aid.

overall swimming velocity (Chollet, Micallef, & Rabischong, 1988); aiding gymnasts in maintaining desired body alignment while performing a circle movement on the pommel horse (Baudry, Leroy, Thouvarecq, & Choller, 2006); increasing stroke rates and mean boat velocity and improving synchronization in rowing (Schaffert, Mattes, & Effenberg, 2011); improving the functional base of support in gait rehabilitation (Aruin, Hanke, & Sharma, 2003); modifying running gait (Agresta & Brown, 2015); and restoring gait speed and standing and walking symmetry and balance in stroke patients (Sungkarat, Fisher, & Kovindha, 2011).

Biofeedback

When physiological measures are concurrently fed back to a learner through some form of instrumentation, the augmented sensory information provided is known as biofeedback. Shown to be effective in shaping behavior, biofeedback permits the constant monitoring of physiological conditions during a response. Some of the auditory devices used in the studies listed in the previous section are examples of biofeedback. Other examples are marathon runners taking their own pulse during a workout or using a heart rate monitor to determine their level of intensity.

Using information from biofeedback, performers learn to alter and control their movements. For example, using a portable electrodermal response (EDR) feedback device with the members of the U.S. Rhythmic Gymnastics Team, Peper and Schmid (1983/84) illustrated how the athletes' thoughts and feelings affected their physiological state. The researchers used this information to help each athlete not only identify and stop negative thoughts and feelings but also restructure their self-talk, making it more positive.

Biofeedback is particularly useful for teaching rehabilitation patients to regulate their movements. Using a computer-assisted feedback system that provided instantaneous feedback on muscle activity and joint angular excursions, Colborne, Olney, and Griffin (1993) examined the use of biofeedback for retraining gait in stroke patients. Muscle activity and joint motion targets, along with cues regarding their specific timing during the gait cycle, were provided throughout the training period. Based on their findings, the authors concluded that computer-assisted feedback is an effective tool for gait retraining in stroke patients. Other examples of the beneficial effects of biofeedback in rehabilitation include minimizing body sway during quiet standing (e.g., Jehu, Thibault, & Lajoie, 2016), improving scapulothoracic control (e.g., Antunes, Carnide, & Matias, 2016), improving neuromuscular coordination and control after meniscal repair (Oravitan & Avram, 2013), and gait retraining (e.g., Willy et al., 2016). For a review of developments in biofeedback concepts, technologies, and applications for neurorehabilitation, see Huang, Wolf, and He (2006). To see an example of biofeedback for posture improvement, go to www.youtube.com/watch?v=p8qJT3RKhFE.

Visual Displays and Observational Interventions

Performance feedback can be displayed visually in a number of ways. Game statistics can be charted on graphs, and shot patterns can be revealed by inspection of targets. Frame-by-frame pictorial sequences can display important information about the execution of numerous skill components and can be combined with graphical representations of kinematic variables including time, displacement, velocity, and angles (see Figure 12.2). Those same variables can be measured and displayed on video recordings captured using a variety of skill analysis apps such as Dartfish, Hudl Technique, Coach My Video, and Coach's Eye, which also permit the user to toggle through the performance frame by frame. Wearable technology like heart rate monitors and fitness trackers provides instant feedback and, when combined with health tracking systems like the IHT Spirit System™ allow physical education students to track their performance and progress. Also, check out Tekscan's Balance Compass™, which provides real-time balance information to aide in rehabilitation at www.tekscan.com/balance-tests-made-simple.

Video Replay

Video recordings have found widespread use among movement practitioners, especially given the ease of recording, viewing, and sharing through smartphones and tablets. However, when utilizing observation as an intervention strategy, Ste-Marie and colleagues (2012) recommend that practitioners first consider observer and task characteristics then take into account the context and desired outcomes of the learner. For example, because younger children process modeled information differently than adults (see Chapter 8), Ste-Marie et al. (2012)

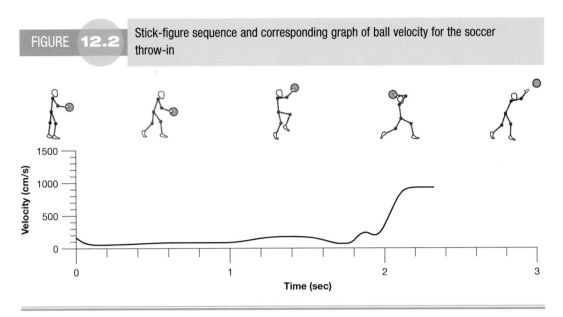

FIGURE **12.2**   Stick-figure sequence and corresponding graph of ball velocity for the soccer throw-in

suggest that a 6-year-old novice learning a dance sequence would benefit more from a skillful teacher (live or videoed) modeling in real time while metaphorically cuing task components rather than viewing their own performance via video replay. For an athlete working on skill refinement however, self-observation using video replay would be a viable strategy. Guadagnoli, Holcomb, and Davis (2002) for example, demonstrated that video feedback, coupled with verbal feedback during practice was superior for improving the shot distance and accuracy of moderately skilled golfers than verbal feedback alone or practicing without augmented feedback.

Clearly, one of the reasons for video replay is to improve technique. This was confirmed by Hars and Calmels (2007), who examined the use of self-observation by elite gymnasts. According to self-reports, the gymnasts mainly paid attention to spatial information and used video replay not only for performance improvement but to also increase imagery and visual perceptions as well as to improve self-assessment. But in order for this observational intervention to be effective, learners have to understand what to look for and how to interpret what they are seeing, which is dependent on both skill level and whether the replay is accompanied by cueing. In an extensive review of studies exploring the effectiveness of using video as a delivery mechanism of feedback, Rothstein and Arnold (1976) found that, when provided with cues to help direct their attention to the most important aspects of the performance replay, learners were better able to use video as a source of information to facilitate skill acquisition, especially in the case of beginning learners. Without the benefit of attention-directing cues, the novice likely becomes overwhelmed by the magnitude of information presented (Newell & Walter, 1981). A study of highly skilled gymnasts, however, also illustrated the value of augmented cues with video feedback, extending previous findings into the realm of skilled performers (Menickelli, Landin, Grisham, & Hebert, 2000).

Providing cues that direct the learner's attention to specific technical aspects of the movement before the learner watches the video replay has been shown to be effective; so, too, have cues that present information about the nature of the correction to be made. Kernodle and Carlton (1992) found that attention-focusing cues (e.g., "Focus on the left arm at the point of ball release") and cues that suggested what correction should be made (e.g., "Extend the left arm at ball release") were superior to the provision of KR (verbal information regarding outcome) and KP (video replay only) for learning the overhand throw. In addition, participants who received information about the nature of the correction to be made displayed more advanced throwing technique compared to participants in the three other conditions.

Interestingly, when participants learning the basketball set shot were given the choice as to when to watch a video replay of their performance (self-control video KP), Aiken, Fairbrother, and Post (2012) found an improvement in technique in the absence of individualized attentional cueing by an instructor. Although attention-directing cues were not provided, a poster listing seven instructional cues for proper set shot form was available throughout the acquisition period. The self-control group viewed the poster more than twice as much as the other group whose video replay viewing scheduled was imposed on them. The researchers hypothesized that the self-control group was likely more engaged in the learning process as they used more sources of information to assist with their skill development. It should be noted, however, that since there was no direct comparison to a group that did receive attention directing cues with video replay, additional studies are needed to fully understand the potential of this instructional strategy.

RESEARCH NOTES

One of the functions of augmented feedback is to motivate the learner to strive for goals. To examine how visual feedback aids in goal achievement, Hopper, Berg, Andersen, and Madan (2003) investigated the influence of video feedback on power during the performance of a leg press. Sixteen elite female field hockey players were randomly assigned to two groups, both of which were tested with and without visual feedback but in reverse order. All participants were required to complete a standardized warm-up prior to testing. Two trials of three repetitions at an absolute load of 50 kg were then conducted for both conditions (with visual feedback and without visual feedback). Visual feedback was provided in the form of a computer monitor positioned to the left of the leg press machine displaying power output on a bar graph. Results revealed that the provision of visual feedback had a positive effect on performance, as power output was significantly higher than when visual feedback was not provided. The authors suggest that the provision of visual feedback in both resistance and rehabilitation training could enhance performance.

Video Feedback Learning Stages

Hebert, Landin, and Menickelli (1998) identified four distinct stages through which athletes progress when introduced to video. Darden (1999) described these stages as shock, error detection, error correction, and independence; he suggested a number of practical tips based on the characteristics of each stage.

1. **Shock stage.** When learners are initially introduced to watching themselves on video, they go through a period of preoccupation with their appearance. Before they can begin to use video feedback as an instructional tool, they first have to get used to seeing themselves on screen. Until then, pointing out technical aspects of their performance will be futile.
2. **Error detection stage.** In the error detection stage, learners begin to observe their practice attempts critically and identify specific performance errors. The provision of attention-focusing cues regarding the environment or aspects of the movement itself is important in this stage to facilitate the development of error detection capabilities. As indicated earlier, learners are not always able to distinguish between task-relevant and task-irrelevant information. For example, if a projectile is involved in the performance, learners have a natural tendency to track it to see where it goes rather than looking at their technique. Learners should be reminded to attend to the movement pattern in addition to the performance outcome (Darden, 1999).
3. **Error correction stage.** With practice and guidance, learners will begin to make associations between specific technical elements and outcome and will progress to the third stage. Here, learners not only identify their own errors but begin to understand why an error occurred. This understanding, in turn, forms the basis for decision making with respect to the development of error correction strategies. Enhancing a learner's problem-solving skills should, therefore, be emphasized during this stage.
4. **Independence stage.** In the final stage, little, if any, dependency on teacher feedback remains. Learners can consistently identify and correct their own errors and should be encouraged to continue doing so. Self-guidance is, therefore, the focus of this final stage.

Equipment and Drills

Drills and equipment can provide performance feedback. For example, the extended club drill is designed to provide the learner with feedback as to whether the hands were too active during a chip shot (Owens & Bunker, 1995; Figure 12.3). A second club is introduced to the learner's normal setup, creating an extension that projects above the waist. If the hands are too active during the swing, the shaft of the second club will touch the learner on the side.

Augmented feedback can also come from devices available to monitor performance, such as a radar gun, or from the equipment being used to perform the skill. For example, playing catch with a raw egg is a fun but potentially messy strategy to teach the concept of absorption. Whether the egg is broken or intact

CEREBRALchallenge 12.2

For a sport or movement of your choice, list drills or equipment that are designed to provide learners with feedback.

FIGURE **12.3**

The extended club drill is designed to provide learners with performance feedback

following an attempt provides augmented information to the learner regarding the performance. Many teaching aids in golf, such as the hinged golf club, are designed to provide feedback. If a flaw in swing mechanics occurs, the hinge of the club will break, folding the club. Much of the aerobic fitness equipment found in health clubs is designed to provide the learner with both concurrent and terminal feedback; this includes how many steps have been climbed, calories burned, or distance rowed, ridden, or run. Similarly, heart rate monitors, pedometers, and cycle computers are popular informational sources. For pilot training, sophisticated flight simulators can capture measurements such as heartbeat, respiration rate, blood pressure, EEG, eye point of gaze, pupil size, and blink rate. After completion of the flight, these physiological variables can be correlated with recordings such as stick input and aircraft response, providing detailed performance feedback.

CONTENT OF AUGMENTED FEEDBACK

To ensure that feedback is useful, regardless of its source or delivery method, the practitioner must consider its content. Telling a learner that she has missed a shot when the outcome is clearly visible, for example, would be unnecessary. We now turn to questions concerning what information should be depicted in a feedback statement to best assist the learner. Should practitioners tell learners what was done correctly, or should they focus on performance errors? Should performance errors be described, or would an explanation of how to modify the movement be more beneficial? How precise should information be?

Error versus Correct Feedback

One important decision to be made is whether to focus on the learner's performance errors or to highlight what was done correctly. Recall that augmented feedback can serve three major functions: to motivate, reinforce, or provide information regarding the correctness of a response in order to modify future attempts. When a learner is given information regarding a performance error, he or she will use that feedback to modify future performances. Consequently, if the goal of the feedback is to facilitate skill acquisition, the practitioner should provide error-based information. If, however, the goal is to confirm the learner's progress or encourage persistence, the practitioner should focus on the learner's achievements and highlight the correct features of the performance attempt. A combination of both would likely be optimal. Coker and Fischman (2010) and Wrisberg (2007) support this recommendation and advocate the use of a "sandwich" approach, in which error correction information is sandwiched between reinforcement and motivation. With this strategy, the practitioner first gives the learner information to reinforce correct performance, then provides the learner with information to facilitate error correction, and finally offers encouragement to motivate the learner to incorporate the error correction recommendations. An example of using the sandwich approach for the dancer in the opening story might be:

Reinforcement: "Good! Your pelvis was in line that time."

Error correction: "On this next trial, try to maintain your outward rotation while still concentrating on pelvic alignment. When you can combine both pelvic alignment and outward rotation, your stability will improve and it will be easier to turn."

Encouragement: "You almost have it."

Interestingly, a learning advantage has been found when KR was provided after relatively good trials (higher accuracy scores) versus relatively poor trials (lower accuracy scores) for a beanbag-throwing task (Chiviacowsky & Wulf, 2007). A number of studies have since demonstrated the same effect (Ahmadi, Sabzi, Heirani, & Hasanvand, 2011; Badami, Kohestani, & Taghian, 2011; Chiviacowsky, 2014; Chiviacowsky, Wulf, Wally, & Borges, 2009). Additionally, when learners were given the option to self-control their feedback, they showed a clear preference for requesting feedback after relatively successful trials (Chiviacowsky & Wulf, 2002; Chiviacowsky, 2014; McRae, Patterson, & Hansen, 2015; Patterson & Carter, 2010). These findings support the contention that feedback serves a motivational function that can facilitate skill acquisition. In fact, Badami, VaezMousavi, Wulf, and Namazizadeh (2011) examined this specific issue and did indeed find higher levels of intrinsic motivation as well as greater perceived competence when feedback was provided after good trials.

Error Amplification

An error-based strategy that has received some attention involves the deliberate exaggeration of an identified error. Milanese, Facci, Cesari, & Zancanaro (2008) compared error amplification (Method of Amplification of Errors) to direct verbal instruction and no instruction on the standing long jump performance of 13-year-old physical education students. After identifying the main performance error of each student, those in the error amplification group were instructed to exaggerate that error as much as possible followed by a trial where no instruction was provided and they jumped freely. These two steps were repeated three times in an alternating sequence. In contrast, the direct instruction group was provided with prescriptive feedback as to how to correct their principle error following the same intervention, free jump alternating sequence. The control group performed their six jumps without feedback or instruction. While performance improved for both interventions, error amplification resulted in significantly greater improvement than the direct instruction method. Other researchers have also found error amplification benefits for correcting a technical error in the golf swing (Milanese, Corte, Salvetti, Cavedon, & Agostini, 2016) and learning a timing-based motor task (Milot, Marchal-Crespo, Green, Cramer, & Reinkensmeyer, 2010), but additional research is needed to determine the method's potential for adoption.

CEREBRALchallenge   12.3

> Rewrite the following statement, using the sandwich technique: "No, no, no. You are doing it all wrong. When you hit the ball you have to be facing your target. How many times do I have to tell you?"

Descriptive versus Prescriptive Feedback

The practitioner can provide knowledge of performance to a learner in two formats. In the first, descriptive feedback, the practitioner simply describes the nature of the performance error. If a learner's outside-of-the-foot pass in soccer is inaccurate due to excessive spin, for example, the practitioner might state, "You are putting too much spin on the ball." In prescriptive feedback, the practitioner offers a suggestion as to how to correct the problem; for example, "You need to contact the ball just left or right of its midline to eliminate unwanted spin."

Whether to use descriptive or prescriptive feedback depends on the skill level of the learner. Descriptive statements can be effective only if the learner understands their implications. Recall that novice learners are trying to develop an understanding of the movement's requirements. In addition, they lack the capability to associate the cause of an error with the adjustments required to correct it. This implies that, while descriptive feedback might be adequate for learners who have obtained a degree of skill proficiency, beginners would benefit more from prescriptive statements. A combination of descriptive and prescriptive feedback—"You initiated your movement too soon. Wait until you see the pitcher's back heel lift off of the ground"—could assist learners in developing associations between errors and corrections.

CEREBRAL challenge   12.4

Determine whether the following augmented feedback statements are examples of descriptive (D) or prescriptive (P) feedback:

a.   Your plant foot is landing too far in front of you.
b.   When you release the ball, continue to flex your wrist so that your fingers are pointing to the ground.
c.   Pull your arms in faster.
d.   The ball is behind your head when you contact it.
e.   The heel-to-toe motion should be fluid.
f.   Your knee is not reaching full extension.
g.   Shift your weight forward before you take a step.
h.   The racquet head angle is too low at contact.

CEREBRAL challenge   12.5

Select and view two clips from the following:

> Free throw: www.youtube.com/watch?v=ZGustJB-caY&feature=plcp
> Cartwheel: www.youtube.com/watch?v=3RX-1svEWMI&feature=plcp
> Soccer pass: www.youtube.com/watch?v=IFs83cdHs9w&feature=plcp
> Volleyball serve: www.youtube.com/watch?v=x5SaTdAzqAE& feature=plcp
> Volleyball pass: www.youtube.com/watch?v=rB77aHgsk7w& feature=plcp
> Walkover: www.youtube.com/watch?v=8F3gGwzFrlY&feature=plcp

1.   For each clip, identify one performance error.
2.   For each error that you have identified, develop one feedback statement.
3.   Would your statement be categorized as knowledge of results or knowledge of performance?
4.   Is the content of your statement descriptive, prescriptive, or both?
5.   Rewrite your statement using the "sandwich" approach.

Precision of Augmented Feedback

The practitioner can use varying degrees of precision to convey information to a learner. "Your angle of attack was only 30 degrees" and "The tip of the javelin was too low at release" are both legitimate feedback statements describing the same error. The question is how the degree of precision in feedback affects the learner's capability to use the information. Again, the practitioner must consider the skill level of the learner. During the early stages of learning, as the learner is trying to develop an understanding of the movement's requirements, feedback can be quite general and still be effective (Magill & Wood, 1986). When skills are being refined later in the learning process, more precise information becomes useful, provided that the learner understands its meaning.

FREQUENCY OF AUGMENTED FEEDBACK

Historically, it was thought that the more frequently augmented feedback was provided to a learner, the greater the gains in learning would be (Thorndike, 1931). According to this notion, an optimal learning environment was one where the practitioner provided the learner with augmented feedback after every performance attempt. Contemporary research disputing this claim has led to new ideas about how often practitioners should give augmented feedback.

The Guidance Hypothesis

According to the guidance hypothesis, augmented feedback can guide a learner in the correction of performance errors, but providing too much feedback can have a detrimental effect on skill acquisition (Salmoni, Schmidt, & Walter, 1984; Schmidt, Young, Swinnen, & Shapiro, 1989; Winstein & Schmidt, 1990; Winstein, Pohl, & Lewthwaite, 1994). This is believed to result from the learner's development of an overdependence on external feedback. A learner who receives augmented feedback at a high frequency, such as after every attempt, begins to rely on it and abandons the processing of other important sources of information, such as internal feedback. Rather than being actively engaged in the learning process, the learner instead might become a passive listener and fail to develop valuable problem-solving skills that will be needed on future occasions when augmented feedback is not available. In contrast, providing augmented feedback at a lower relative frequency encourages the learner to become a reflective thinker and enhances learning. The question that is yet to be resolved is exactly how much augmented feedback should be given to optimize learning.

> **COMMON MYTH**
>
> The more frequently augmented feedback is provided, the greater the gains in learning will be.

Another important question is whether reducing feedback frequency benefits motor learning in children in the same manner that it does adults. According to Sullivan, Kantak, and Burtner (2008), children use feedback differently than adults do and may require more practice trials with feedback as well as a more gradual frequency-reduction schedule. In their study, 20 young adults (mean age 25.6 years) and 20 children (mean age 10.7 years) performed a linear position-ing task and received feedback following each trial (100 percent) or on a progressively reduced schedule (100 percent in session one, 75 percent in session two, 50 percent in session three, and 25 percent in session four). While the retention test results of the young adults were consistent with previous literature, children demonstrated the opposite outcome; those who received feedback after every trial performed the task more accurately and consistently than their counterparts who received a reduced feedback schedule. The authors suggest that their findings are consistent with the challenge point framework (Guadagnoli & Lee, 2004). In other words, the reduced feedback schedule "exceeded the optimal challenge point in children and invoked a degree of cognitive effort that taxed their information-processing capability" (Sullivan et al., 2008, p. 729). Chiviacowsky, Wulf, de Medeiros, Kaefer, and Wally (2008) also demonstrated higher feedback frequency advantages for children; they found that self-regulated learners who requested more KR achieved higher accuracy scores on a bean-bag throwing task than the less-KR group. While additional research is needed in this area, Sullivan et al. (2008) suggest that practitioners who work with children need to be aware of cognitive effort during skill acquisition and adjust feedback frequency accordingly.

Feedback Frequency Reduction Strategies

Several strategies for systematically reducing feedback frequency are available. These include faded, bandwidth, summary, average, and self-controlled feedback approaches.

Faded Feedback

Faded feedback has been shown to be an effective frequency-reducing strategy (Winstein & Schmidt, 1990). In faded feedback, learners are provided with a high frequency of feedback in the initial stages of learning, in order to facilitate their understanding and acquisition of the basic movement pattern. Once learners achieve a basic proficiency level, augmented feedback is gradually withdrawn. The schedule for reducing feedback frequency will depend on each individual's progress.

Bandwidth Feedback

A technique that fosters important information-processing activities on the part of the learner is bandwidth feedback (Lai & Shea, 1999; Sherwood, 1988; Smith, Taylor, & Withers, 1997). It, too, is based on the concept of providing more information during the early stages of learning and gradually reducing feedback as the learner improves. In bandwidth feedback, a range of "correctness" is pre-determined, and augmented feedback is provided only on those trials where an error falls outside this range. For the volleyball serve, for example, a range of correctness for the toss might be defined as between the shoulder and one foot in front of the shoulder. If the learner's toss falls within this range, no feedback is provided, indicating that the toss was acceptable. If the toss falls outside the range, by being too far behind or in front, the practitioner gives the learner information for correction. The benefit of this approach is that feedback is systematically reduced according to the learner's level of proficiency. In addition, the learner receives positive reinforcement on those trials that do fall within the bandwidth, which will serve to strengthen the behavior that led to the outcome.

Vickers and colleagues (e.g., Vickers, Reeves, Chambers, & Martell, 2004) identified an interesting problem with the use of bandwidth feedback. A number of coaches who were using it reported that they had experienced communication problems with some of their athletes, parents, and even administrators. The coach's reduction of information was interpreted by some as a failure to assist the athletes, and some athletes felt neglected or ignored (Chambers & Vickers, 2006). In an attempt to resolve this dilemma, as well as other issues they had identified, Chambers and Vickers (2006) examined the effectiveness of asking athletes questions about their performance as feedback frequency was reduced. This combined use of bandwidth feedback and questioning was shown to be effective for improving swimming technique in competitive athletes. Questioning strategies will be discussed in more detail later in this chapter.

Summary Feedback

Summary feedback is another way to avert the potentially harmful effects of augmented feedback on learning. In summary feedback, the practitioner provides a summary of the performance after the learner has completed a certain number of trials. For example, in show jumping, a horse and rider have to negotiate numerous barriers. Augmented feedback would be withheld until the series of jumps is completed. The learner would then receive specific feedback about each jump in the series. Another example of summary feedback is showing the learner a video replay of his or her performance attempts after a certain number of trials.

Given the positive effect of summary feedback on learning (Schmidt et al., 1989), research has turned to defining the optimal number of performance trials that should be summarized. The answer may be a function of task complexity (Schmidt, Lange, & Young, 1990; Swinnen, 1996).

Average Feedback

Average feedback is another effective feedback-reduction strategy, similar to summary feedback. In average feedback, the learner receives augmented feedback after the completion of a certain number of attempts, as in summary feedback. This feedback, however, will be on the average performance error that occurred in the series. For example, to assist a patient learning how to rise from a chair using a walker, a therapist designs practice in which the patient receives feedback after every fifth attempt. Although the therapist notices several mistakes in the practice trials, the patient's most common tendency is to pull up on the walker while rising. Feedback would address only this error.

For the practitioner, average feedback offers several advantages over summary feedback. First, it eliminates the need to recount every error that is observed. Second, it forces the practitioner to focus the analysis to uncover true errors in performance and disregard occasional performance variability. Finally, it reduces the possibility of overwhelming the learner with too much information.

CEREBRALchallenge 12.6

Go back to Exploration Activity 12.1. When the performer was shown the pencil marks for each trial after the completion of all 10 trials, this was summary feedback. How would you redesign the experiment to provide bandwidth feedback? How would you redesign the experiment to provide average feedback?

Self-Controlled Feedback

In self-controlled feedback, rather than the practitioner determining when to offer feedback, the learner chooses when it is given and only then receives it. In addition to both reducing and individualizing feedback frequency (e.g., Aiken, Fairbrother, & Post, 2012; Laughlin et al., 2015; Post, Aiken, Laughlin, & Fairbrother, 2016; Janelle, Barba, Frehlich, Tennant, & Cauraugh, 1997), this strategy actively involves the learner in the learning process and is supported by numerous studies that have shown that giving learners the choice to select their feedback schedule results in better retention than traditional practitioner-controlled feedback (see Sanli, Patterson, Bray, & Lee, 2013 for a review).

Two explanations have been proposed to account for the beneficial effects of self-controlled feedback. First, a number of studies suggest that learners base requests for feedback on their performance and use the information to both confirm success and correct errors (Post et al., 2016). This perspective, known as the information processing explanation, is based on studies that have demonstrated that learners strategically choose when to receive feedback. In some instances, learners have demonstrated a preference for receiving feedback after perceived good trials (e.g. Chiviacowsky, 2014; Chiviacowsky & Wulf, 2002; McRae, Patterson, & Hansen, 2015; Patterson & Carter, 2010) while in others, requests for feedback have been made after both good and bad trials (Aiken, Fairbrother, & Post, 2012; Laughlin et al., 2015; Post et al., 2016). This discrepancy may be a function of the information provided by the feedback (e.g., KR vs KP) and its subsequent use (e.g., confirm success vs. correct errors) but additional studies are needed to examine this possibility. Regardless, Carter,

Carlsen, and Ste-Marie (2014), who extended the work of Chiviacowsky and Wulf (2005), contend that "the critical factor for increased learning appears to be the opportunity to decide *after* motor execution whether they want feedback," supporting the notion that the learning advantages of self-control feedback are performance-dependent (p.7).

According to Chiviacowsky, Wulf, and Lewthwaite (2012), the preference of self-control learners to receive feedback mostly after successful trials found in some of the above-mentioned studies may "reflect the expression of a basic psychological need for competence or participants' insights that their learning is better when success or a correlate such as self-efficacy is experienced" (p.6). This alternative explanation contends that autonomy has a motivational influence on learning—a notion also endorsed by the OPTIMAL theory proposed by Wulf and Lewthwaite (2016) and discussed in Chapter 7. Findings of greater perceived competence and self-efficacy in several studies support this perspective (Badami et al., 2011; Chiviacowsky, Wulf, & Lewthwaite, 2012; Chiviacowsky, 2014). Regardless of the explanation for the effect, during skill refinement, practitioners should consider giving learners control over their feedback schedule and providing information only when requested.

TIMING OF AUGMENTED FEEDBACK

The presentation of augmented feedback can be broken down into three temporal intervals, as illustrated in Figure 12.4. The time from the end of one performance attempt to the beginning of the next performance attempt is known as the inter-trial interval. That interval is further broken down into the feedback-delay interval, the time from the end of a performance attempt until augmented feedback is provided, and the post-feedback interval, the time from the provision of augmented feedback to the initiation of the next performance attempt. The following section examines these two sub-intervals, as their length and the nature of the activity that takes place within them both influence the effectiveness of performance-related feedback.

FIGURE 12.4 Temporal model of augmented feedback presentation

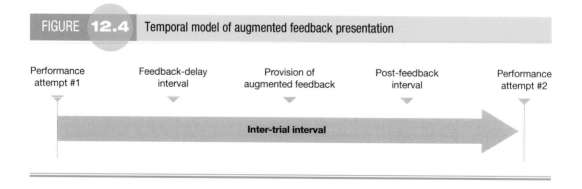

RESEARCH NOTES

In a study, Liu and Wrisberg (1997) manipulated KR delay and subjective estimation of movement form to examine their effects on throwing accuracy. Forty-eight participants were randomly assigned to one of four conditions: (1) immediate KR, (2) delayed KR, (3) immediate KR plus subjective estimation of movement form, and (4) delayed KR plus subjective estimation of movement form. The task was to throw a ball at a target placed on the floor as accurately as possible, using the non-dominant hand. Participants wore a visual shield on the target side of an eyeglass frame to impede their vision. After the release of the ball, participants in the immediate-KR conditions were permitted to turn their head, track the ball, and see it land. Those in the KR-delay conditions were shown where the ball had landed after a 13-second delay interval. Participants in the subjective estimation groups were asked to rate their form in terms of force, release angle, and trajectory either 2 seconds after the ball's landing (immediate KR plus subjective estimation) or during the 13-second delay interval (delayed KR plus subjective estimation). Results indicated that while the immediate-KR groups displayed higher accuracy scores during practice, those in the delayed-KR conditions were significantly more accurate during retention. Moreover, the performance accuracy of the subjective estimation groups was significantly higher during the retention tests, where no KR was given. These findings support both the recommendation to delay the provision of feedback and the use of subjective error estimation.

Feedback-Delay Interval

A misconception regarding the timing of augmented feedback is that it should be provided to the learner immediately after a performance attempt. On the contrary, research has demonstrated that the instantaneous provision of augmented feedback can have a negative impact on learning (Swinnen, Schmidt, Nicholson, & Shapiro, 1990). When augmented feedback is provided too soon, learners are prevented from evaluating response-produced intrinsic feedback, impeding their development of error detection and correction mechanisms. In research supporting this notion, Anderson, Magill, Sekiya, and Ryan (2005) found that learners who received delayed KR used a greater number and variety of intrinsic feedback sources than those who received KR immediately after each trial.

> **COMMON MYTH**
>
> Augmented feedback should be delivered to the learner immediately after the performance attempt.

How long should the practitioner wait before giving feedback? It appears that learners simply need sufficient time, generally a few seconds, to process their own movement-produced feedback. Delaying the provision of feedback for longer periods of time does not appear to affect learning adversely, although an extended delay could cause the learner to forget the details of the practice attempt.

Prompting learners to estimate their own performance errors before the practitioner provides augmented feedback has also led to superior learning (Swinnen et al., 1990; Liu & Wrisberg, 1997). Consequently, Chen (2001) recommends that practitioners assist learners in developing their self-evaluation skills by asking them questions during practice to provoke reflective thinking about their practice attempts. A practitioner might ask a learner, for example, "How was your follow-through that time?" or "Why do you think the ball went off to the left?" The dancer at the beginning of the chapter, who indicated that she thought her pelvis was in line, might be prompted to explain how she came to that conclusion. As stated earlier, Chambers and Vickers (2006) provide support for this strategy, finding a positive effect on performance when bandwidth feedback and questioning strategies are used. They contend that "questioning provides coaches with a method of encouraging active learning through problem solving, discovery and performance awareness" (p. 187).

Initially, learners might have difficulty responding to such questioning. Self-evaluation is a capability that must be developed. Practitioners can guide learners through the process by asking more specific follow-up questions that will lead learners to the answer. For example, a secondary question about a player's follow-through might be, "Do you think your arm came straight down, or did it cross your body?" Eventually, practitioner–learner interactions will become an exchange of ideas rather than the one-way transfer of information, and the learner will develop the problem-solving capabilities needed for further skill acquisition and performance enhancement.

CEREBRALchallenge   12.7

Make yourself a checklist for giving augmented feedback, based on the information provided in this chapter.

Post-Feedback Interval

During the post-feedback interval, the learner synthesizes the information received both internally and externally (via augmented feedback) and formulates a new movement plan. Again, sufficient time must be available to the learner to process and plan. Given that these operations depend on the complexity of the skill, the length of the post-feedback interval will vary accordingly.

In some instances, learners may need to be reminded to engage in processing activities. By asking the learner what he or she is thinking about with respect to the upcoming attempt, the practitioner can both encourage active processing for movement modification and check for understanding. The practitioner can further ensure the learner understands by observing the degree to which augmented feedback assisted the learner in modifying the subsequent response.

MANIPULATING TASK CONSTRAINTS

While there is a tendency to rely on the provision of feedback for error correction, recall from Chapter 8 that movement patterns can also be shaped by manipulating task and/or practice variables. To correct a poor entry in diving, for example, place a foam noodle at shin height and instruct the learner to dive over it without touching it. Learners will instinctively push harder as they leave the side of the pool, correcting the error. To improve stride length during gait retraining incorporate poly spots or targets positioned at desired distances. When the rhythm of the breaststroke is compromised due to a shortened glide phase, have learners exchange an object (like their goggles) from one hand to the other before they can initiate the next pull. This added action will prompt the desired behavior. A common error in executing a chip shot in golf is hitting up at the ball in an attempt to lift it into the air. An effective intervention strategy to correct this is to position a driver head cover approximately 12 inches in front of the ball and instruct the learner to accelerate the blade of the club toward it when executing the shot (Owens & Bunker, 1995). Running intervals while holding a potato chip in each hand without crushing it can correct a tense and inefficient running posture. Finally, go to www.youtube.com/watch?v=t0KKKIkDkYk to view an activity to improve wrist snap in squash using the hands-off approach.

PUTTING IT INTO PRACTICE

Learning Situation: Rehabilitation of an Ankle Sprain

The physical therapist has added a variety of step-down activities to Darren's rehab program (different heights, directions, landing surfaces, with and without a pack, etc.). While Darren is able to execute the movements, she notices that he is looking down, watching each step. This is a common error that occurs when proprioception is compromised.

Test Your Knowledge

Design an intervention activity that manipulates task constraints to help Darren take his eyes off of his feet and look straight ahead. Compare your answer with the sample response provided at www.routledge.com/cw/coker.

A LOOK AHEAD

Through augmented feedback, practitioners can guide, motivate, and reinforce learners in order to enhance skill acquisition and performance. The effectiveness of the feedback depends on a number of variables, including the feedback's type, source, content, frequency, and timing. But feedback is not the only intervention strategy that can be employed to correct performance errors. By manipulating task constraints, practitioners can also elicit technical and tactical corrections.

This book has introduced you to the processes that govern movement acquisition and control. By understanding the concepts and principles described here, as well as their applications, you can look ahead to future challenges with confidence that you will be able to make effective instructional decisions to maximize your clients', patients', students', or athletes' potential.

FOCUS POINTS

After reading this chapter, you should know:

- "Feedback" is a general term used to describe the information a learner receives about the performance of a movement or skill.
- Feedback can be intrinsic, coming from one's own sensory system, or augmented, supplied from an external source.
- Knowledge of results provides information regarding the outcome of a response and is concerned with the success of the intended action with respect to its goal.
- Knowledge of performance provides information regarding the specific characteristics of the performance that led to the outcome.
- Augmented feedback serves to provide information for error correction, to motivate, and to reinforce.
- In addition to verbal descriptions and demonstrations, sources of augmented feedback include auditory feedback, visual displays, video replay, equipment and drills, and biofeedback.
- In the sandwich approach, the practitioner first gives the learner information to reinforce correct performance, then provides information regarding error correction, and finally offers encouragement to motivate the learner to incorporate the recommendations.
- The provision of both descriptive and prescriptive information can assist learners in developing associations between errors and corrections.
- Learners need a high frequency of feedback in the initial stage of learning. However, unless that frequency is reduced as the learner becomes more proficient, the learner may develop an overdependence on augmented feedback.
- To reduce feedback frequency, the practitioner can use faded, bandwidth, summary, average, and learner-regulated feedback.
- Learners need time to process intrinsic feedback and formulate a new movement plan for the next attempt.
- Prompting learners to estimate their own performance errors before providing them with augmented feedback results in superior learning.
- The purposeful manipulation of key task and/or practice variables should be considered when correcting performance errors.

lab

To complete the lab for this chapter, visit www.routledge.com/cw/coker and select **Lab 12, Knowledge of Results**.

REVIEW QUESTIONS

1. Define the following terms:
   a. feedback
   b. intrinsic feedback
   c. augmented feedback
   d. knowledge of results
   e. knowledge of performance
2. Compare and contrast terminal and concurrent feedback.
3. Develop a flow chart to represent all of the categories and sub-categories of feedback.
4. Compare and contrast positive and negative reinforcement.
5. What three functions can feedback serve?
6. Name the four stages of video feedback learning and the characteristics of each.
7. Compare and contrast:
   a. error-based and corrective feedback
   b. descriptive and prescriptive feedback
8. What is the significance of the guidance hypothesis?
9. What strategies can a practitioner use to reduce the frequency of augmented feedback?
10. The inter-trial interval can be broken down into two additional intervals. Name and define them.

REFERENCES

Agresta, C. & Brown, A. (2015). Gait retraining for injured and healthy runners using augmented feedback: A systematic literature review. *Journal of Orthopaedic & Sports Physical Therapy*, 45(8), 576–584.

Ahmadi, P., Sabzi, A., Heirani, A., & Hasanvand, B. (2011). The effect of feedback after good, poor, good-poor and self-control conditions in an acquisi-

tion and learning of force production task. *Facta Universitatis: Series Physical Education & Sport*, 9(1), 35–43.

Aiken, C. A., Fairbrother, J. T., & Post, P. G. (2012). The effects of self-controlled video feedback on the learning of the basketball set shot. *Frontiers in Psychology*, 3.

Anderson, D. I., Magill, R. A., Sekiya, H., & Ryan, G.

(2005). Support for an explanation of the guidance effect in motor skill learning. *Journal of Motor Behavior, 37,* 231–238.

Antunes, A., Carnide, F., & Matias, R. (2016). Real-time kinematic biofeedback improves scapulothoracic control and performance during scapular-focused exercises: A single-blind randomized controlled laboratory study. *Human Movement Science,* 4844–4853.

Araújo, D., Davids, K., Bennett, S. J., Button, C., & Chapman, G. (2004). Emergence of sport skills under constraints. In A. M. Williams & N. J. Hodges (Eds.), *Skill acquisition in sport: Research, theory and practice* (pp. 409–433). London: Routledge, Taylor and Francis.

Aruin, A. S., Hanke, T. A., & Sharma, A. (2003). Base of support feedback in gait rehabilitation. *Journal of Rehabilitation Research, 26,* 309–312.

Badami, R., Kohestani, S., & Taghian, F. (2011). Feedback on more accurate trials enhances learning of sport skills. *World Applied Sciences Journal, 13*(3), 537–540.

Badami, R., VaezMousav, M., Wulf, G., & Namazizadeh, M. (2011). Feedback after good versus poor trials affects intrinsic motivation. *Research Quarterly for Exercise & Sport, 82*(2), 360–364.

Baudry, L., Leroy, D., Thouvarecq, R., & Choller, D. (2006). Auditory concurrent feedback benefits on the circle performed in gymnastics. *Journal of Sports Sciences, 24,* 149–156.

Carter, M. J., Carlsen, A. N., & Ste-Marie, D. M. (2014). Self-controlled feedback is effective if it is based on the learner's performance: a replication and extension of Chiviacowsky and Wulf (2005). *Frontiers in Psychology, 5,* 1325.

Chambers, K. L. & Vickers, J. N. (2006). Effects of bandwidth feedback and questioning on the performance of competitive swimmers. *The Sport Psychologist, 20,* 184–197.

Chen, D. D. (2001). Trends in augmented feedback research and tips for the practitioner. *Journal of Physical Education, Recreation and Dance, 72*(1), 32–36.

Chiviacowsky, S. (2014). Self-controlled practice: Autonomy protects perceptions of competence and enhances motor learning. *Psychology of Sport & Exercise, 15*(5), 505–510.

Chiviacowsky, S. & Wulf, G. (2002). Self-controlled feedback: Does it enhance learning because performers get feedback when they need it? *Research Quarterly for Exercise and Sport, 73,* 408–415.

Chiviacowsky, S. & Wulf, G. (2005). Self-controlled feedback is effective if it is based on the learner's performance. *Research Quarterly for Exercise and Sport, 76,* 42–48.

Chiviacowsky, S. & Wulf, G. (2007). Feedback after good trials enhances learning. *Research Quarterly for Exercise and Sport, 78,* 40–47.

Chiviacowsky, S., Wulf, G., de Medeiros, F., Kaefer, A., & Tani, G. (2008). Learning benefits of self-controlled knowledge of results in 10-year-old children. *Research Quarterly for Exercise & Sport, 79*(3), 405–410.

Chiviacowsky, S., Wulf, G., de Medeiros, F., Kaefer, A., & Wally, R. (2008). Self-controlled feedback in 10-year-old children: Higher feedback frequencies enhance learning. *Research Quarterly for Exercise and Sport, 79,* 122–127.

Chiviacowsky, S., Wulf, G., & Lewthwaite, R. (2012). Self-controlled learning: the importance of protecting perceptions of competence. *Frontiers in Psychology,* 3458. doi:10.3389/fpsyg.2012.00458

Chiviacowsky, S., Wulf, G., Wally, R., & Borges, T. (2009). Knowledge of results after good trials enhances learning in older adults. *Research Quarterly for Exercise & Sport, 80*(3), 663–668.

Chollet, D., Micallef, J. P., & Rabischong, P. (1988). Biomechanical signals for external biofeedback to improve swimming techniques. In B. E. Ungerechts, K. Wilke, & K. Reischle (Eds.), *Swimming V* (pp. 389–396). Champaign, IL: Human Kinetics.

Christina, R. W. & Corcos, D. M. (1988). *Coaches guide to teaching sport skills.* Champaign, IL: Human Kinetics.

Clarkson, P. M., James, R., Watkins, A., & Foley, P. (1986). The effect of augmented feedback on foot pronation during bar exercise in dance. *Research Quarterly for Exercise and Sport, 57,* 33–40.

Coker, C. A. & Fischman, M. G. (2010). Motor skill learning for effective coaching and performance. In J. M. Williams (Ed.), *Applied sport psychology: Personal growth to peak performance* (6th ed., pp. 21–41). New York: McGraw-Hill.

Colborne, G. R., Olney, S. J., & Griffin, M. P. (1993). Feedback of ankle joint angle and soleus electromyography in the rehabilitation of hemiplegic gait. *Archives of Physical Medicine and Rehabilitation, 74*(10), 1100–1106.

Cronin, J. B., Bressel, E., & Finn, L. (2008). Augmented feedback reduces ground reaction forces in the landing phase of the volleyball spike jump. *Journal of Sport Rehabilitation, 17,* 148–159.

Darden, G. F. (1999). Videotape feedback for student learning and performance: A learning stages approach. *Journal of Physical Education, Recreation and Dance, 70*(9), 40–45, 62.

Guadagnoli, M., Holcomb, W., & Davis, M. (2002). The efficacy of video feedback for learning the golf swing. *Journal of Sports Sciences, 20,* 615–622.

Guadagnoli, M. A. & Lee, T. D. (2004). Challenge point: A framework for conceptualizing the effects of various practice conditions in motor learning. *Journal of Motor Behavior, 36,* 212–224.

Hars, M. and Calmels, C. (2007). Observation of elite gymnastic performance: processes and perceived functions of observation. *Psychology of Sport and Exercise, 8,* 337–354.

Hawkins, D. (2000). A new instrumentation system for training rowers. *Journal of Biomechanics, 33*(2), 241–246.

Hebert, E., Landin, D., & Menickelli, J. (1998). Videotape feedback: What learners see and how they use it. *Journal of Sport Pedagogy, 4,* 12–28.

Hopper, D., Berg, M., Andersen, H., & Madan, R. (2003). The influence of visual feedback on power during leg press on elite women field hockey players. *Physical Therapy in Sport, 4,* 182–186.

Huang, H., Wolf, S. L., & He, J. (2006). Recent developments in biofeedback for neuromotor rehabilitation. *Journal of Neuroengineering and Rehabilitation,* 311.

Janelle, C. M., Barba, D. A., Frehlich, S. G., Tennant, L. K., & Cauraugh, J. H. (1997). Maximizing performance feedback effectiveness through videotape replay and a self-controlled learning environment. *Research Quarterly for Exercise and Sport, 68*(4), 269–279.

Jehu, D. A., Thibault, J., & Lajoie, Y. (2016). Magnifying the scale of visual biofeedback improves posture. *Applied Psychophysiology and Biofeedback, 41*(2), 151–155. doi:10.1007/s10484–015–9324–7

Kernodle, M. W. & Carlton, L. G. (1992). Information feedback and the learning of multiple-degree-of-freedom activities. *Journal of Motor Behavior, 24*(2), 187–196.

Lai, Q. & Shea, C. H. (1999). Bandwidth knowledge of results enhances generalized motor program learning. *Research Quarterly for Exercise and Sport, 70,* 79–83.

Laughlin, D. D., Fairbrother, J. T., Wrisberg, C. A., Alami, A., Fisher, L. A., & Huck, S. W. (2015). Self-control behaviors during the learning of a cascade juggling task. *Human Movement Science, 41,* 9–19.

Lewthwaite, R., Chiviacowsky, S., Drews, R., & Wulf, G. (2015). Choose to move: The motivational impact of autonomy support on motor learning. *Psychonomic Bulletin & Review, 22*(5), 1383–1388. doi:10.3758/s13423–015–0814–7

Lewthwaite, R. & Wulf, G. (2012). Motor learning through a motivational lens. In N. J. Hodges & A. M. Williams (Eds.), *Skill acquisition in sport: Research, theory & practice* (2nd ed., pp. 173–191). London: Routledge.

Liu, J. & Wrisberg, C. A. (1997). The effect of knowledge of results delay and the subjective estimation of movement form on the acquisition and retention of a motor skill. *Research Quarterly for Exercise and Sport, 68*(2), 145–151.

Magill, R. A. & Wood, C. A. (1986). Knowledge of results precision as a learning variable in motor skill acquisition. *Research Quarterly for Exercise and Sport, 57,* 170–173.

McRae, M., Patterson, J. T., & Hansen, S. (2015). Examining the preferred self-controlled KR schedules of learners and peers during motor skill learning. *Journal of Motor Behavior, 47*:6, 527–534. doi: 10.1080/00222895.2015.1020357

Menickelli, J., Landin, D., Grisham, W., & Hebert, E. P. (2000). The effects of videotape feedback with augmented cues on the performances and thought processes of skilled gymnasts. *Journal of Sport Pedagogy, 6*(1), 56–72.

Milanese, C., Corte, S., Salvetti, L., Cavedon, V., & Agostini, T. (2016). Correction of a technical error in the golf swing: Error amplification versus direct instruction. *Journal of Motor Behavior, 48*(4), 365–376.

Milanese, C., Facci, G., Cesari, P., & Zancanaro, C. (2008). "Amplification of Error": A rapidly effective method for motor performance improvement. *Sport Psychologist, 22*(2), 164–174.

Milot, M., Marchal-Crespo, L., Green, C. S., Cramer, S. C., & Reinkensmeyer, D. J. (2010). Comparison of error-amplification and haptic-guidance training techniques for learning of a timing-based motor task by healthy individuals. *Experimental Brain Research, 201*(2), 119–131. doi:10.1007/s00221–009–2014–z

Newell, K. M. & Walter, C. B. (1981). Kinematic and kinetic parameters as information feedback in motor skill acquisition. *Journal of Human Movement Studies, 7,* 235–254.

Oravitan, M. & Avram, C. (2013). The effectiveness of electromyographic biofeedback as part of a meniscal repair rehabilitation programme. *Journal of Sports Science & Medicine, 12*(3), 526–532.

Owens, D. & Bunker, L. K. (1995). *Golf: Steps to success.* Champaign, IL: Human Kinetics.

Patterson, J. T. & Carter, M. (2010). Learner regulated knowledge of results during the acquisition of multiple timing goals. *Human Movement Science, 29*(2), 214–227.

Peper, E. & Schmid, A. B. (1983/84). The use of electrodermal biofeedback for peak performance training. *Somatics IV, 3,* 16–18.

Post, P. G., Aiken, C. A., Laughlin, D. D., & Fairbrother, J. T. (2016). Self-control over combined video feedback and modeling facilitates motor learning. *Human Movement Science,* 4749–4759.

Rothstein, A. L. & Arnold, R. K. (1976). Bridging the gap: Application of research on videotape feedback and bowling. *Motor Skills: Theory into Practice, 1,* 36–61.

Salmoni, A. W., Schmidt, R. A., & Walter, C. B. (1984). Knowledge of results and motor learning: A review and critical appraisal. *Psychological Bulletin, 95,* 355–386.

Sanli, E. A., Patterson, J. T., Bray, S. R., & Lee, T. D. (2013). Understanding self-controlled motor learning protocols through the self-determination theory. *Frontiers in Psychology, 3611.* doi: 10.3389/fpsyg.2012.00611

Schaffert, N. & Mattes, K. (2015). Effects of acoustic feedback training in elite-standard para-rowing. *Journal of Sports Sciences, 33*(4), 411–418.

Schaffert, N., Mattes, K., & Effenberg, A. O. (2011). An investigation of online acoustic information for elite rowers in onwater training conditions. *Journal of Human Sport and Exercise, 6,* 392–405.

Schmidt, R. A., Lange, C. A., & Young, D. E. (1990). Optimizing summary knowledge of results for skill learning. *Human Movement Science, 9,* 325–348.

Schmidt, R. A., Young, D. E., Swinnen, S., & Shapiro, D. E. (1989). Summary knowledge of results for skill acquisition: Support for the guidance hypothesis. *Journal of Experimental Psychology: Learning, Memory and Cognition, 15,* 352–359.

Sherwood, D. E. (1988). Effect of bandwidth knowledge of results on movement consistency. *Perceptual and Motor Skills, 66,* 535–542.

Smith, P., Taylor, S., & Withers, K. (1997). Applying bandwidth feedback scheduling to a golf shot. *Research Quarterly for Exercise and Sport, 68,* 215–221.

Ste-Marie, D. M., Law, B., Rymal, A. M., Jenny, O., Hall, C., & Mccullagh, P. (2012). Observation interventions for motor skill learning and performance: an applied model for the use of observation. *International Review of Sport & Exercise Psychology, 5*(2), 145–176.

Sullivan, K. J., Kantak, S. S., & Burtner, P. A. (2008). Motor learning in children: Feedback effects on skill acquisition. *Physical Therapy, 88*(6), 720–732.

Sungkarat, S., Fisher, B., & Kovindha, A. (2011). Efficacy of an insole shoe wedge and augmented pressure sensor for gait training in individuals with stroke: A randomized controlled trial. *Clinical Rehabilitation, 25*(4), 360–369.

Swinnen, P. S. (1996). Information feedback for motor skill learning: A review. In H. N. Zelaznik (Ed.), *Advances in motor learning and control* (pp. 37–66). Champaign, IL: Human Kinetics.

Swinnen, P. S., Schmidt, R. A., Nicholson, D. E., & Shapiro, D. C. (1990). Information feedback for skill acquisition: Instantaneous knowledge of results degrades learning. *Journal of Experimental Psychology: Learning, Memory and Cognition, 16,* 706–716.

Swinnen, P. S., Walter, C. B., Lee, T. D., & Serrien, D. J. (1993). Acquiring bimanual skills: Contrasting forms of information feedback for inter-limb decoupling. *Journal of Experimental Psychology: Learning, Memory and Cognition, 19,* 1321–1344.

Thorndike, E. L. (1931). *Human learning.* New York: Century.

Vickers, J. N., Reeves, M., Chambers, K. L., & Martell, S. (2004). Decision training: Cognitive strategies for enhancing motor performance. In A. M. Williams & N. J. Hodges (Eds.), *Skill acquisition in sport: Research, theory and practice* (pp. 103–120). New York: Routledge.

Willy, R. W., Meardon, S. A., Schmidt, A., Blaylock, N. R., Hadding, S. A., & Willson, J. D. (2016). Changes in tibiofemoral contact forces during running in response to in-field gait retraining. *Journal of Sports Sciences, 34*(17), 1602–1611. doi:10.1080/02640414.2015.1125517

Winstein, C. J., Pohl, P. S., & Lewthwaite, R. (1994). Effects of physical guidance and knowledge of results on motor learning: Support for the guidance hypothesis. *Research Quarterly for Exercise and Sport, 65,* 316–323.

Winstein, C. J. & Schmidt, R. A. (1990). Reduced frequency of knowledge of results enhances motor skill learning. *Journal of Experimental Psychology: Learning, Memory and Cognition, 16,* 677–691.

Wood, C. A., Gallagher, J. D., Martino, P. V., & Ross, M. (1992). Alternate forms of knowledge of results: Interaction of augmented feedback on modality in learning. *Journal of Human Movement Studies*, 22, 213–230.

Wrisberg, C. A. (2007). *Sport skill instruction for coaches*. Champaign, IL: Human Kinetics.

Wulf, G. & Lewthwaite, R. (2016). Optimizing performance through intrinsic motivation and attention for learning: The optimal theory of motor learning. *Psychonomic Bulletin & Review*, doi: 10.3758/s13423–015–0999–9.

Epilogue:
Teaching Scenarios

Your effectiveness as a practitioner will depend on your ability to integrate multiple motor learning and motor control concepts and principles. Following are two scenarios and corresponding questions designed to provide you with the opportunity to apply what you have learned in this book. Remember to consider the learner, the task, and the environment in which the task is performed in all cases.

SCENARIOS

Physical Education

As part of your teacher preparation, you have to complete several observations of a physical education class at the local junior high school. You decide to observe an eighth-grade coeducational class that has just started a unit on soccer. There are 30 students in the class, including Chris and Morgan. Chris's movement experiences have been limited and were predominantly acquired through physical education. Morgan, on the other hand, is very active, and has played baseball, softball, and basketball and runs track.

Question 1.1

During your first observation, the teacher introduces dribbling. Following the *initial* description and demonstration, the students are paired up for a drill. In this drill, one student is to dribble the ball to the other side of the gym while the partner tries to take it away. The goal of the drill, the teacher emphasizes, is to dribble without looking at the ball. As the drill progresses, the teacher notices that all of the students are either losing the ball or totally focusing their vision on it.

a. Explain why this is not an effective drill.
b. Suggest an alternative drill that would be more effective for this group of learners, and provide a comprehensive rationale for your suggestion.

Question 1.2

When you arrive for your observation the following day, you notice that there are not enough soccer balls for everyone. Apparently the soccer coach borrowed some of the balls and has not yet returned them. In order for everyone to have a ball for the lesson on passing, the teacher has decided to replace the missing soccer balls with playground balls that are similar in size.

a. Assess the potential advantages and disadvantages of this strategy.
b. Based on your assessment, would you agree or disagree with using the playground balls in this situation? Justify your answer.

Question 1.3

The next skill to be introduced to the class is trapping.

a. Which method, part or whole, would you use if you were going to teach this skill?
b. What factors did you take into consideration when making your decision? Fully explain your answer.

Question 1.4

When teaching trapping, the teacher makes a reference to cushioning or absorbing the ball like you would when fielding a softball or baseball.

a. What strategy is the teacher using to try to facilitate learners' understanding of the concept?
b. Will this cue be equally effective for Chris and Morgan? Why or why not?

Question 1.5

a. Which method, segmentation or simplification, would you suggest using to teach learners the skill of heading a soccer ball? Defend your selection.
b. Outline how you would design the learning experience, using the method that you selected.

Question 1.6

a. Design a drill that incorporates both random practice and variable practice to assist your learners in refining their dribbling, trapping, and passing skills.
b. Would incorporating random and variable practice be equally effective for Chris and Morgan? Explain.

Question 1.7

Chris is having a tough time passing the ball, and the teacher goes over to help. Having analyzed Chris's attempts, the teacher provides the following extrinsic feedback: "No, that's not it. You are too tense. Why are you so uptight? Your head isn't straight and you aren't kicking through the center of the ball—no wonder it doesn't go straight! Can't you do better than that?"

a. Rewrite this statement to provide Chris with more effective feedback.
b. Explain why your version is more effective.

Question 1.8

Chris has come a long way in practice and has become quite proficient in shooting. However, every time the ball is passed near the goal, the defender steals it before Chris can get the shot off. The teacher decides that Chris's shooting technique is okay, but Chris is taking too long to react to the ball.

a. List potential reasons for Chris's inability to respond quickly in this situation.
b. Provide suggestions for each reason given to correct the problem.

Rehabilitation

You have just started working at a rehabilitation clinic. One of your first cases is a patient who has had a below-the-knee amputation (BKA) of the left leg. The patient has been fitted with a prosthetic and is ready to start balance training, transfers training (e.g., to the car), and gait training.

Question 2.1

The psychological effects that accompany the amputation of a limb are a significant factor to consider during the patient's rehabilitation. The patient's level of motivation, for example, will directly influence the learning process. When patients are not progressing as fast as they anticipated, frustration can lead to a loss of motivation. What strategies will you employ to motivate the patient during the rehabilitation process?

Question 2.2

A major concern for the patient, common for those learning to use a lower limb prosthesis, is the fear of falling.

a.   What arousal level might you expect to be associated with the fear of falling?
b.   How might that influence the patient's training? The performance of activities of daily living?
c.   What strategies will you incorporate into the patient's rehabilitation program to reduce the fear of falling?

Question 2.3

Describe how you could incorporate goal-setting into the rehabilitative process for this patient. Include an example of a goal that might be appropriate in this situation.

Question 2.4

Given the loss of proprioception, patients with BKA will have difficulty learning to equalize stride length. What alternative feedback mechanisms could you use to compensate for the patient's lost proprioception?

Question 2.5

In order to design effective variable practice experiences, the practitioner must assess the nature of the skill and the contexts in which it will be performed. List variations that should be incorporated into prosthetic training for

a.   learning to fall safely
b.   transfers (e.g., to the car)
c.   gait (both indoors and outdoors)

ANSWERS

Physical Education Scenario

Question 1.1

This is not an effective drill for several reasons. First, the learning goal expressed by the teacher, to dribble the ball without looking at it, is too advanced. Given that the students have received only an initial explanation and demonstration, most of them would be in the cognitive stage of learning. Consequently, they should be given the opportunity to practice the skill in order to develop a basic understanding of the movement. Once the learners have developed some proficiency in dribbling, the next step would be to learn to do so without looking at the ball.

Second, the drill does not target the learning goal. According to the teacher's instructions, the goal of the drill is to dribble to the opposite side of the gym without looking at the ball. With a defender in front of the dribbler, the goal of the drill for the learner becomes protecting the ball.

Third, with a defender in front of the learner whose task is to try to take away the ball, the context in which the skill is being performed becomes open and, as a result, more complex. Given that the learners are in the cognitive stage, the attentional demands of movement production are high. The additional demand imposed by the defender exceeds the learner's attentional capacity, causing interference to occur. The result is either a decline in the level of performance or a disregard for one of the tasks. This was evident in that the learners were either losing control of the ball or totally focusing their vision on it.

Question 1.2

Two factors should be considered here. The advantage to utilizing the playground balls is that it will increase the amount of time on task. The question the practitioner must ask prior to implementing this strategy is whether use of the playground balls will cause the learners to execute a pattern of movement that exceeds the boundaries of the generalized motor program being developed. Provided that distinct movement pattern changes would not manifest as a result of using the alternative equipment, this is a good strategy.

Question 1.3

Given that the skill is high in task organization and low in task complexity, whole practice would be recommended.

Question 1.4

The teacher's reference to cushioning the ball like you would when fielding a softball or baseball is an example of attempting to capitalize on positive transfer. Anytime you attempt to capitalize on transfer, it is important to be sure that the skill or concept you refer to has been well learned. Given Morgan's past experiences with baseball and softball, the reference will likely be effective. For Chris, who has limited movement experiences, the reference will not be meaningful and the idea the teacher is trying to convey will not be communicated effectively.

Question 1.5

Again, the practitioner must assess task organization and task complexity to determine which method, segmentation or simplification, should be used. First, the skill would be considered relatively high in task organization. Second, given that heading requires the learner to time his or her actions to an oncoming ball, the movement is somewhat complex. That complexity can easily be reduced, however. Practice could start with each learner placing a small piece of masking tape on the middle of his or her forehead. Then, using lighter balls, such as beach balls, learners could throw their balls up into the air and try to hit them with the masking-tape spot on their foreheads. As they become proficient at this, they could progress to slightly harder balls, such as volleyballs or playground balls, and finally to soccer balls. In addition, the practice could progress from self-toss to partner toss. Tosses should initially be predictable and from close range, progressing gradually to farther away and unpredictable.

Question 1.6

One partner would dribble the ball down the field and then pass it to the other partner, who would trap it and dribble it down the field before passing it back to the first partner. Variations in distance, speed, foot used, type of pass, type of trap, and so forth would be incorporated.

High levels of contextual interference can be overwhelming if the learner is still trying to develop an understanding of the movement. Given the past experiences of Morgan and Chris, it is possible that Morgan will progress through the learning process faster and be ready to handle a drill of this nature, while Chris may not. The answer depends on the learner's degree of proficiency when the drill is introduced.

Question 1.7

The sandwich approach would be more effective in this situation. Using this strategy, a more effective version would be: "Good! Your contact with the ball is much stronger. On this next trial, focus on kicking through the center of the ball. That will make the ball go straight. Let's try again. You almost have it."

This version is more effective because it confirms the learner's progress, encourages continued persistence, and offers prescriptive feedback, which is more beneficial for novice learners.

Question 1.8

The error in this situation is a delay in responding. Multiple reasons could be the cause of this delay. First, the practitioner must establish whether Chris can correctly read game situations. Does Chris know what critical cues to look for?

Can Chris detect that information during a game? If not, intervention strategies should focus on teaching Chris what the critical cues are, prompting Chris to prepare a response sooner, directing Chris's attention to where in the environment the cues occur, and providing extensive practice opportunities in a variety of situations that contain common task-relevant cues. Second, Chris's attentional focus may be either too broad or too narrow, depending on levels of arousal. Third, delay in responding may result from problems with decision-making. Reducing the number of response alternatives and increasing Chris's ability to identify potential predictors, such as opponent or situational tendencies, could resolve the problem.

Rehabilitation Scenario

Question 2.1

Throughout the learning process, the patient must have opportunities to experience some degree of success. This will lead to feelings of achievement that will further motivate the learner to practice. The patient must also be taught that challenges are an integral part of the learning process. Positive feedback and the provision of encouragement and reinforcement are critical. The monotony of repeated training can be reduced if the therapist makes practice fun and introduces variety into the training protocol when possible. Another powerful motivational technique is goal-setting. It will be discussed in the answer to Question 2.3.

Question 2.2

One would expect the fear of falling to result in a high level of anxiety, leading to high levels of arousal. Fear of falling will obviously influence the patient's motivation to perform various activities. Furthermore, the patient is likely to demonstrate an overdependence on the uninvolved limb. As the patient progresses, high arousal will influence her attentional focus, and the performance of activities in more open environments will likely be compromised (e.g., walking through a crowd). To reduce the patient's fear and subsequent anxiety, the practitioner must not only teach her how to fall safely (in a way to minimize the risk of injury) but also what to do in the event of a fall. Balance and coordination exercises that reinforce good posture should be incorporated in the initial stages of the rehabilitation protocol.

Question 2.3

The practitioner should take several steps to incorporate goal-setting into the rehabilitative process. First, the practitioner and patient should set a combination of short-term, long-term, performance, and process goals. Those goals should be SMART: specific, measurable, action-oriented, realistic, and timely. The patient should be included in the goal-setting process and encouraged to evaluate progress frequently. Finally, the practitioner must be supportive and provide positive reinforcement throughout the rehabilitative process.

An example of a goal that might be appropriate in this situation is: "Perform an independent and safe transfer to a bed, while being spotted by the therapist, eight out of 10 times, by the end of week two."

Question 2.4

To assist the patient in developing a frame of reference for various activities, the practitioner should provide the opportunity to experience a variety of positions and movements across a broad assortment of environments. The practitioner should focus the patient's attention on the feelings associated with a movement to help the patient recognize and interpret the proprioceptive cues received from other sources. In addition, the practitioner should assist the patient in developing self-evaluation skills by asking questions during practice to provoke the patient's reflective thinking regarding practice attempts. Information regarding movement and body position is also available through visual feedback. Other alternative feedback mechanisms might include the use of biofeedback (e.g., a load-monitoring device), mirrors, and video replay.

Question 2.5

a. Manipulate height and position. (*Note*: Safety is a priority.)
b. Manipulate the location to which the transfer occurs. Examples include bed, wheelchair, toilet, tub, shower, floor, car, and a variety of furniture.
c. Manipulate the surface (smooth, rough, carpeted, uneven); train on stairs, ramps, curbs, elevators, and escalators; ambulate and maneuver in narrow places and in crowds; practice managing doors, stepping over obstacles, and so forth.

Glossary

Ability   A genetic trait that is prerequisite to the development of skill proficiency

Abstract targeting task   A task with a target that is fixed in space but with an optimal aiming location that is more difficult to detect

Afferent   Literally, carrying to; describes the part of the PNS that detects changes in the environment and conducts nerve impulses from the sensory receptors to the CNS

Affordances   Action possibilities of the environment and task in relation to the perceiver's own capabilities

Ambient system   Visual system that functions at a subconscious level and is thought to be responsible for spatial localization and orientation

Analytical learner   Learner who prefers to have new information presented in a sequential manner building toward the main concept

Anticipation   Prediction of what event will occur or when an event will occur

Anxiety   An emotion resulting from an individual's perception of a situation as threatening

Arousal   "A general physiological and psychological activation of the organism that varies on a continuum from deep sleep to intense excitement" (Gould & Krane, 1992)

Associative stage   The intermediate stage of learning in Fitts and Posner's model

Attention cueing   A practice technique in which the learner directs attention to a specific aspect of the skill during its performance as a whole

Attentional focus   The process of selectively attending to specific environmental information

Attractor state   Preferred state of stability or pattern toward which a system spontaneously shifts

Augmented feedback   Information received from an external source that supplements the learner's own sensory information

Automaticity   A capacity to perform a skill with little or no conscious control

Autonomous stage   The advanced or final stage of learning in Fitts and Posner's model

Average feedback   Augmented feedback, provided after a certain number of attempts are completed, regarding the average performance error

Backward chaining   Part practice technique in which the parts of a skill are presented and practiced in a sequence that progresses from the final skill component to the initial one

Bandwidth feedback   Augmented feedback in which feedback is provided only on trials where an error falls outside a predetermined range of correctness

Bilateral transfer   Practice with one limb enhances the rate of skill acquisition with the opposite limb on the same task

Biofeedback   A form of augmented feedback in which physiological information is concurrently available to the learner

Blocked practice   Practice schedule in which the learner practices one variation of a skill repeatedly and then moves on to another variation

Central executive   Component of working memory that controls the flow of information between the phonological loop and visuospatial sketchpad, regulates information processing, and governs attentional activities

Cerebral cortex   The outermost layer of the cerebrum

Choice RT   Reaction time resulting from a situation that involves a choice as to how to respond

Closed skill   Skills performed within a stable and predictable environment, allowing the performer to control the performance situation

Closed-loop control   Mode of control in which feedback aids error detection and correction

Cognitive stage   The initial or beginning stage of learning in Fitts and Posner's model

Concurrent feedback   Augmented feedback provided during the execution of a skill

Constraint   A boundary that has a bearing on the movement capabilities of an individual

Constraint-led approach   Model of skill learning in which the instructor is a facilitator who identifies and manipulates constraints in order to facilitate skill acquisition

Contextual interference   Interference that results from switching from one skill to another or changing the context in which a task is practiced from trial to trial

Contextual interference effect Low contextual interference often produces superior short-term performance during practice, but high contextual interference leads to greater long-term learning gains

Continuous skill A skill whose beginning and ending points are either arbitrary or determined by some environmental factor rather than by the task itself

Control The manipulation of variables within a movement to meet the demands of a given situation

Control parameters Variables that move a system into new attractor states

Coordination The process of organizing a system's available degrees of freedom into an efficient movement pattern that will effectively achieve a goal

Cortical re-mapping Reorganization of an area(s) in the cortex of the brain resulting in a new cortical map

Critical features Specific body movements that are observable and that affect the performance of a skill

Cue utilization hypothesis A paradigm in which changes in attentional focus occur according to arousal levels

Deafferentation the loss of sensory input as a result of the interruption or destruction of the sensory nerves of a limb(s). Condition is surgically induced in animal experiments so that response-produced feedback cannot reach the central nervous system

Deception The deliberate presentation of false precues in order to prompt an incorrect response

Declarative knowledge Information used to decide what to do in a given situation

Declarative memory That portion of our memory used for facts or events; commonly broken down into two types: episodic memory and semantic memory

Degrees of freedom Independent elements of movement that must be organized to produce a controlled movement pattern

Degrees of freedom problem Problem of how we coordinate and control the available degrees of freedom to produce a particular movement

Descriptive feedback Augmented feedback in which the practitioner describes the nature of the performance error

Discrete skill A skill whose beginning and end points are clearly defined

Disguise An attempt by a player to hide or delay the onset of precues about the intended action in order to prolong an opponent's decision making

Distributed practice Practice schedule in which the rest component between sessions or practice attempts is equal to or greater than the practice component

Ecological approach   Model of perception in which the perceiver interprets the environment and tasks directly in terms of affordances

Efferent   Literally, carrying away from; describes the part of the PNS that transmits impulses away from the CNS to the effectors

Episodic memory   The memory of personal experiences and events that are associated with a specific time and context

Event anticipation   Prediction of what event will occur

Explicit learning   Knowledge acquired through explicit verbal explanations

External focus   Focusing attention on the effects of one's actions

Exteroceptors   Receptors located at or near the body's surface that detect stimuli outside the body and provide information about the environment

Faded feedback   Feedback technique in which learners are provided with a high frequency of feedback initially and then the feedback is gradually withdrawn

Feedback-delay interval   Time from the end of one performance attempt until augmented feedback is provided

Feedforward   Describes the sending of information ahead of a movement, for advance preparation or adjustments of the movement

Fine motor skill   A motor skill involving very precise movements normally accomplished using smaller musculature

Fixation   Focusing visual attention on a specific object

Fixation/diversification   The second and final stage of learning in Gentile's model

Fixed target   A target that is stable and predictable in position and requires a performer to fixate on a specific location prior to executing a response

Focal system   Visual system that functions to identify objects primarily located in the central region of the visual field

Foreperiod   Time interval between the presentation of a warning signal and the stimulus it warns of

Forward chaining   Part practice technique in which the parts of a skill are presented and practiced in a sequence that progresses from the initial skill component to the final one

Fractionization   Part practice technique in which skill components that are normally performed simultaneously are partitioned and practiced independently

Freezing the degrees of freedom   Strategy in which a learner freezes or fixes the movement possibilities of a joint, causing the limb(s) to function as a single unit or segment, in order to accomplish the goal of a task

Functional movement pattern   A movement pattern that will accomplish a specific task goal

Generalized motor program   An abstract representation of a class of actions or pattern of movement that can be modified to yield various response outcomes

Getting the idea of the movement stage   The first stage of learning in Gentile's model, characterized by the learner trying to develop an understanding of the movement's requirements

Global learner   Learner who learns more easily when first presented with the big picture and then asked to concentrate on details

Golgi tendon organs   Proprioceptors located at the junction of a tendon with a muscle that indicate the level of tension development in a tendon

Gross motor skill   A motor skill that places less emphasis on precision and is typically the result of multi-limb movements

Guided discovery   Learning technique where the practitioner asks a sequence of questions, each of which elicits a single correct response discovered by the learner

Hands-off practitioner   Redefined role of the practitioner as a facilitator who identifies and manipulates key constraints to guide the learner's search for optimal movement solutions

Hick's Law   The higher the degree of uncertainty in a given situation, the longer the time needed to decide which response to make; choice RT is logarithmically related to the number of response choice alternatives

Imagery   The visualization or cognitive rehearsal of a movement in the absence of any physical execution

Implicit learning   Knowledge acquired without conscious awareness

Individual differences   Relatively stable and enduring characteristics that make each of us unique

Information processing   Model of perception in which a performer receives an abundance of information, focuses on pertinent stimuli, selects a response, and receives intrinsic feedback about the results of the response

Internal focus   Focusing attention on one's own body movements

Interneuron   Nerve cell that lies between a sensory and a motor neuron in a reflex arc

Interoceptors   Receptors that detect stimuli from the internal viscera and provide information about the internal environment

Inter-trial interval   The time from the end of one performance attempt to the beginning of the next performance attempt

Intrinsic feedback Response-produced information that is available to learners from their sensory system both during and as a consequence of performance

Invariant features Relatively fixed underlying features that define a motor program

Inverted-U principle Relationship between arousal and performance in which there exists an optimal level of arousal for peak performance

Ironic Effects The phenomenon where the action an individual was trying to avoid is actually carried out

Joint kinesthetic receptors Receptors located in and around synovial joints that respond to pressure, acceleration and deceleration, and excessive strain on a joint

Key elements Specific body movements that are observable and that affect the performance of a skill

Knowledge of performance Augmented feedback that provides information about the specific characteristics of the performance that led to the outcome

Knowledge of results Augmented feedback that provides the learner with information about the outcome of a response and is concerned with the success of the intended action with respect to its goal

Learning A relatively permanent change in a person's ability to execute a motor skill as a result of practice or experience

Learning style Individual preference for receiving and processing new information

Limited attentional capacity A limitation in the amount of information one can process or attend to

Long-term memory Memory characterized as having a seemingly limitless capacity and duration

Manual aiming The act of reaching or transporting the hand to a target location

Manual guidance Physically moving a learner through a goal movement

Massed practice Practice schedule in which the amount of time allocated to rest between sessions or practice attempts is comparatively less than the time a learner is engaged in practice

Memory The ability to store and recall information

Mirror neurons Nerve cells that fire both when we perform an action and when we watch someone else perform the same action

Mixed observation The observation of both a novice and an expert model versus a skilled or unskilled model alone

Modal strength The preferred perceptual mode through which a learner takes in and processes information

Motivation   An internal condition that incites and directs action or behavior

Motor control   The study of the neural, physical, and behavioral aspects that underlie human movement

Motor learning   The study of the processes involved in acquiring and refining motor skills and of variables that promote or inhibit that acquisition

Motor program   An abstract representation of a movement plan, stored in memory, that contains all of the motor commands required for carrying out the intended action

Motor skill   A goal-oriented act or task that requires voluntary body and or limb movement and must be learned

Movement concepts   Describe how a skill is to be performed

Movement time   Interval of time between the initiation of a movement and its completion

Moving target task   Task that requires the performer to anticipate the target's impending location

Muscle spindles   Proprioceptors located between the skeletal muscle fibers in the muscle belly that indicate how much and how fast the muscle's length is changing

Negative transfer   The learning of a new skill or its performance under novel conditions is negatively influenced by past experience with another skill or skills

Neural plasticity   The ability of the brain to change its organization and ultimately its function throughout the lifespan

Non-linear pedagogy   A theoretical approach to practice based on the interacting role of constraints in shaping movement behaviors

Open-loop control   A mode of control whereby an action plan is generated that contains all of the information necessary to complete a response

Open skill   A motor skill that is performed in an unpredictable, ever-changing environment

Optic chiasm   Point at which some fibers from each of the optic nerves cross, allowing visual signals to be processed by the opposite side of the brain

Optic flow   The perceived visual motion of objects as the observer moves relative to them

Outcome goals   Goals that are concerned with the final result of a competition relative to one's opponent

Parameters   Flexible features that define how to execute a generalized motor program

Part practice method   Teaching strategy in which the instructor breaks the skill down into natural parts or segments and learners practice those parts separately until they are learned and then integrate them to perform the skill in its entirety

Perception   Process by which meaning is attached to information

Perceptual-motor workspace   The individual's perceptual information sources and range of movement possibilities for a particular task

Perceptual narrowing   The narrowing of attentional focus with increasing levels of arousal

Performance   The act of executing a skill

Performance goals   Goals that are concerned with self-improvement

Performance plateau   A period of time during the learning process in which no overt changes in performance occur

Phase shift   Change in the state of stability of a system causing a spontaneous reorganization into a new form

Phonological loop   Memory system responsible for short-term storage of spoken and written material

Photoreceptors   Light-sensitive cells located in the eyes

Positive transfer   The learning of a new skill or its performance under novel conditions is positively influenced by past experience with another skill or skills

Post-feedback interval   Time from the provision of augmented feedback to the initiation of the next performance attempt

Post-test   Skill performance test administered directly following a practice period, used to determine what the learner can do after practicing a skill

Power law of practice   When learning a new skill, there tends to be a large initial improvement in performance, which slows later in practice (Newell & Rosenbloom, 1981)

Precue   Clues in the environment that can assist a performer in anticipating

Prehension   The action of reaching and grasping

Prescriptive feedback   Augmented feedback in which the practitioner offers a suggestion as to how to correct a performance problem

Proactive interference   The interference of old memories with the retention of new ones

Procedural knowledge   Information regarding skills, operations, and actions

Procedural memory   The memory of how to perform various skills and actions

Process goals   Goals that direct the performer's focus to achieving some technical element during skill execution

Process Assessment   Specific aspects of the skill's execution

Product Assessment   The outcome of the performance

Proprioception   The continuous flow of sensory information that is received from receptors located in the muscles, tendons, joints, and inner ear regarding movement and body position

Proprioceptors   Receptors that provide information regarding body position and movement by detecting changes in muscle tension, joint position, and equilibrium

Psychological refractory period (PRP)   Delay in responding to a second stimulus in a situation where two stimuli, each of which requires a different response, are presented in succession within a short period of time

Quiet eye   The final fixation located on a specific target or object before the initiation of movement

Random practice   Practice schedule in which the learner performs multiple task variations in a random order

Rate limiters   Constraints that hinder or restrict the ability of a system to change

Reaction time   Interval of time between the moment when a stimulus is presented and when a response is initiated

Reflex   An automatic, involuntary response to stimuli

Reflex arc   The simplest pathway by which a reflex occurs

Regulatory conditions   Environmental factors that specify the movement characteristics necessary to perform a skill successfully

Relative force   The concept that when the overall force used to execute a movement changes, the actual force characteristic of each component should change proportionately

Repeated blocked practice   A form of serial practice where a set sequence of practice trial blocks is repeated

Response time   Time interval from the moment when a stimulus is presented to when the response is completed (combination of RT and MT)

Retention test   Skill performance test given following a period of no practice that measures the persistence of improved skill performance

Retroactive interference   Interference of new learning with the retention of older memories

Schema   A rule or relationship that directs decision making when a learner is faced with a movement problem

Segmentation   Part practice technique in which the skill is separated into parts according to spatial or temporal elements

Selective attention   The ability to attend to or focus on one specific item amid countless stimuli

Self-control   Giving the learner control to choose some characteristics of the learning situation

Self-controlled feedback   Augmented feedback provided to a learner only when he or she requests it

Self-organization   Spontaneous emergence of a movement pattern as a result of the interaction of ever-changing organismic, environmental, and task constraints placed on the learner

Self-talk   Cues used by learners to guide themselves through an action or a movement sequence

Semantic memory   The memory of general knowledge that is developed through experiences but is not associated with time

Sensory memory   Memory system that retains a brief impression of a sensory stimulus after the original stimulus has ended, allowing the determination of whether or not it demands further attention

Serial practice   The repetition of a set sequence of practice trials

Serial skill   A motor skill that is composed of a number of discrete skills whose integrated performance is crucial for goal achievement

Simplification   Part practice technique in which the level of difficulty of the task or some aspect of the task is reduced

Specificity hypothesis   The hypothesis that individuals inherit a large number of motor abilities and the inheritance of each ability is independent of the others

Speed–accuracy tradeoff   The fact that an emphasis on speed in performance negatively affects accuracy and vice versa

Spotting   Fixating one's visual attention on a specific spot during rotation of the body in order to reduce dizziness and remain oriented

Stimulus   A change in the environment that evokes a response

Stimulus–response compatibility   The extent to which a stimulus and its required response are naturally related

Summary feedback   Augmented feedback in which the practitioner provides the learner with a summary of the performance after a certain number of trials are completed

Task analysis   The breaking down of a skill into its component parts and corresponding underlying abilities

Tau   Optic variable that provides time-to-contact information by taking the size of the retina image at any position of an object's approach and dividing it by the rate of change of the image

Taxonomy   Model into which skills are classified

Temporal anticipation   Prediction of when an event will occur

Terminal feedback   Augmented feedback that is presented after the movement is completed

Trait anxiety   An individual's propensity to perceive situations as threatening or non-threatening

Transfer   Phenomenon in which the learning of a new skill or its performance under novel conditions is influenced by past experience with another skill or skills

Transfer appropriate processing theory   Theory that we should expect positive transfer when practice conditions require learners to engage in problem-solving processes similar to those that the criterion task requires

Transfer test   Test that measures the adaptability of a response, determined by testing the learner's ability to use a skill in a novel context or manner

Variable practice   Practice schedule in which multiple variations of a given task are practiced

Verbal cue   A word or concise phrase that focuses the learner's attention or prompts a movement or movement sequence

Vestibular apparatus   A collective group of receptor organs in the inner ear that respond to changes in posture and balance

Visual search   The process of directing visual attention while trying to locate critical regulatory cues in the environment

Visuospatial sketchpad   Memory system responsible for the temporary storage and manipulation of spatial and visual information

Working memory   A set of interacting information processing components that actively stores and manages information required to carry out complex cognitive tasks

Zero transfer   Past experience with another skill or skills has no influence on the learning of a new skill or its performance under novel conditions

Zone of optimal functioning   Range of arousal levels that leads to optimal performance

REFERENCES

Gould, D. & Krane, V. (1992). The arousal-performance relationship: Current status and future directions. In T. S. Horn (Ed.), *Advances in sport psychology* (pp. 119–42). Champaign, IL: Human Kinetics.

Newell, A. & Rosenbloom, P. S. (1981). Mechanisms of skill acquisition and the law of practice. In J. R. Anderson (Ed.), *Cognitive skills and their acquisition* (pp. 1–51). Hillsdale, NJ: Lawrence Erlbaum.

Index